THE ARCHITECTURAL HERITAGE

of

NEWPORT, RHODE ISLAND

THE ARCHITECTURAL HERITAGE

of

NEWPORT, RHODE ISLAND

1640–1915

By

ANTOINETTE F. DOWNING
and
VINCENT J. SCULLY, Jr.

SECOND EDITION—REVISED

American Legacy Press • New York

This edition is published by American Legacy Press,
distributed by Crown Publishers, Inc.,
225 Park Avenue South, New York, New York 10003,
by arrangement with the Harvard University Press.

Manufactured in the United States of America

Library of Congress Cataloging in Publication Data

Downing, Antoinette Forrester.
  The architectural heritage of Newport, Rhode Island,
1640–1915.

  Originally published: 2nd ed., rev. New York:
C. N. Potter, 1967.
  Includes bibliographical references and index.
  1. Architecture—Rhode Island—Newport. I. Scully,
Vincent Joseph, 1920–   II. Title.
NA735.N54D6   1982   720′.9745′7   82-6836
                                             AACR2

ISBN 0-517-09719-2

h g f e

CONTENTS

ILLUSTRATIONS

KEY TO ILLUSTRATIONS AND PLATES

The following abbreviations are used (in the list of illustrations and plates) and on the captions:

Adv.	Advertisement in *American Architect and Building News*
C.C.	W. King Covell Collection
C.D.	National Society of Colonial Dames in Rhode Island
H.A.B.S.	Historic American Building Survey
M.M.A.	Metropolitan Museum of Art
N.H.S.	Newport Historical Society
P.S.N.C.	Preservation Society of Newport County
R.I.H.S.	Rhode Island Historical Society
R.I.S.D.	Rhode Island School of Design
R.L.	Redwood Library
S.P.N.E.A.	Society for the Preservation of New England Antiquities

Bergner drawings and photographs are in the Newport Historical Society.

Meservey photographs and Warren Oakley drawings belong to the Preservation Society of Newport County

PUBLISHER'S NOTE: All footnotes newly added in the Second Edition are indicated by marginal letters in the text. The footnotes themselves are positioned at the end of each chapter in which they appear.

FOREWORD TO THE FIRST EDITION

It is known that those who have the inner eye to observe people and their activities, those who are constantly fascinated by man's behavior, have the capacity to face life in all its phases and tribulations. It is this type of person who is able to recognize what are the eminent and lasting values in life. Knowing what happened to our world in the first half of this century, it is easy for such people to see that the results of the economic and political débâcle which the world is now witnessing are only underlining where these lasting values lie.

Europe alone is now clearly proving to us that these values lie not in the accomplishments of her so-called great statesmen, kings, emperors, kaisers, tsars, and dictators, with their symbolic coloured shirts, but in the creative work of her men of letters, of the arts and crafts, music, architecture, and the sciences. In fact, it is only the creative work of these men that keeps Europe alive today and still prominent. The last two world wars have shown that the so-called glorious accomplishments in Europe's political, economic, and military life, even when built, as they thought, on a "Rock of Gibraltar," have only a fluctuating value. Time has proved that.

Europe's tragic experiences, no doubt, are having a great influence on us here. Observing the interest of the people in this country during the past generation in what is going on in the arts and music alone, and seeing their urge to preserve things of national and cultural value are really amazing. It seems that more and more people are aware that material welfare alone cannot play the dominant rôle in the life of a nation — as if they meant to say: to have money now is not enough. The problem is how to use it.

Newport, in my opinion, is a striking example of this problem. As we know, this city has the glamorous reputation of being the fashionable resort for millionaires. We all know what has happened here since 1929. We are actually witnessing an era passing before our own eyes. The fortunate thing for this city is that a few thoughtful citizens realize that Newport has something that represents lasting values. It has a cultural background and an architectural inheritance of true importance, extending from the mid-seventeenth century to the present. Thanks to these few enlightened persons, the Preservation Society of Newport County was organized not only to save the architectural heritage, but also to prove that even the future economic existence of the city itself may depend on that heritage.

The Preservation Society is only six years old. It is not for me to give an account here of its accomplishments. The way it started — as the saying goes, "on a shoestring" — and the struggle it had to survive those first years are healthy signs for its continued life.

ix

To me it is a fascinating experience to witness what a few people with real enthusiasm and belief in a cause can accomplish in such a short time. It also shows that good deeds are as contagious as bad ones, if not more so. One by one, people joined to help the Preservation Society save houses of architectural importance. From the very beginning and at nearly every subsequent meeting of the Society, the vital need for a Survey of Newport's architectural treasures was stressed. The problem was where to find a person who was willing to help make such a survey and publish it — to let the people see how rich Newport is in that field. And here, fortunately, stepped in Mrs. Michael M. van Beuren.

When the aims of the Preservation Society were described and a slight suggestion was made to her to help publish the book on Newport's architecture, she answered: "I will do something to help you. Let me think about it for a while."

After talking it over with her husband and her son Archbold, she decided to do the whole thing — to sponsor the Survey and publish the book, saying: "This will be my contribution to Newport." Realizing what the Preservation Society stood for, she helped further the project under its auspices and for its benefit.

As Mrs. van Beuren asked me to supervise the arrangements for the publication, I take the opportunity to tell the story of how it happened. This was not merely a generous gesture of a woman who could afford to be generous, but it stemmed from her belief in the cultural significance of the book and in the meaning it would have for all scholars, students, and architects.

I believe that the reason she so readily responded to the need of the Preservation Society was that she was one of the few who could differentiate between the lasting and the passing values. I may quote her own phrase: "Perhaps a little late, but I finally realized its importance." With that remark of hers, we can appreciate the meaning and the value of Mrs. van Beuren's contribution to Newport. It will last, I am sure.

MAXIM KAROLIK

PREFACE TO THE SECOND EDITION

Soon after its formation twenty years ago the Preservation Society of Newport County commissioned the publication of the Architectural Heritage of Newport Rhode Island *as part of a broad program to record and protect the extraordinarily fine body of historic architecture of all periods that has made Newport a city without equal in the nation.*

The publication of this second edition affords an opportunity to assess the success of the Society's efforts to preserve historic Newport and to comment on current threats to the colonial part of the city.

The Preservation Society has been responsible for saving and brilliantly restoring the Hunter House, one of the most important Colonial mansions in the country and for restoring the seventeenth-century Whitehorse Tavern and the late-eighteenth-century Joseph Rogers House, now Society Headquarters. The Vernon House, where Rochambeau was quartered, and Matthew Calbraith Perry's childhood home on Second Street will soon be restored. Through the generosity of the late Countess Laszlo Szechenyi, "The Breakers" has been opened to visitors since 1948, and the Society has miraculously raised money to acquire "The Elms"; the Newport home of Edwin Berwind, and "Marble House," William K. Vanderbilt's Newport mansion. These buildings and the important roster of colonial buildings open to the public on a plan coordinated by the Society now attracts nearly 125,000 visitors a year. The Society has also been instrumental in launching Historic Newport Reproductions, a business enterprise which has received national recognition for fine reproductions of Newport furniture, silver, pewter, fabrics, wallpaper, and other Newport crafts.

All these programs and others have helped bring to the nation an increasing awareness that Newport must be preserved as a living document of America's past and, as Carl Weinhardt has written, as "perhaps one of the most poignantly beautiful places remaining on the Atlantic coastline." (1)

In the meantime, the problem of finding ways to protect and renew the hundreds of smaller early houses, that even in dilapidated state give to Newport much of its unique quality as a visible and tangible eighteenth-century seacoast town, remained largely unsolved until Operation Clapboard *was formed in 1963. Through its efforts and inspiration and the efforts of the recently organized* Oldport Association *nearly sixty early houses, most*

(1) Carl J. Weinhardt, Jr., "Newport Preserved," *Art in America*, June, 1965.

xi

of them in the Point section east of Washington Street, have been restored. Upper Thames Street, where nine of the restored houses make a fine row, has become a showpiece.

For Newport, time has been running out. For years many citizens and visitors alike, captivated by the streets of little early houses, have been wondering, as Henry James did, "at the indifference and neglect" though "breathing thanks for the absence of positive ravage." On the eve of a potential full-scale restoration program the time of positive ravage has come, and plans that will cut up parts, and totally destroy anther part of the eighteenth-century town are taking final form

Already, over the past fourteen years, more than fifty of the approximately four hundred houses built before 1830 ana listed in The Architectual Heritage *in 1952 have been torn down. Important later-nineteenth-century houses have also been razed, and two shopping centers, which, in the words of Carl V. Weinhardt, although "no worse than their endless counterparts across the country" have shattered "the quiet elegant homogeneous quality of middle Bellevue Avenue where in this context they become vulgar symbols of all that is wrong with mid-twentieth-century America."*

Disintegration of the eighteenth-century closely knit town has also unfortunately clearly begun, and the State and Federal governments, to whom Historic Newport should be able to turn for positive support, are now financing road and renewal programs requiring further destruction. The Jamestown-Newport Bridge, soon to be built, brings with it a state-financed road ninety-eight feet wide, that as now designed will cut a divisive north-south swath through the oldest part of Newport, and a federally financed urban renewal project will sweep away all the old buildings on the west side of Thames Street, south of the Brick Market, together with the eighteenth century wharves and wharf buildings.

Therefore this foreword not only serves as a tribute to the Preservation Society of Newport County for its role in calling attention to Newport's importance as a living document of the past and for its share in saving and magnificently restoring some of her most important buildings; it must also serve as an obituary for the eighteenth-century city now under attack. The erosion of a heritage uniquely Newport's has serious import for future growth, since it implies indifference to a dazzling undeveloped potential for historic restoration; and the citizens, the city, the state and the federal government must share the responsibility for the choice. Impoverishment of Newport's architectural and social history is a loss not only to the city but also to the nation. The loss is double and unredeemable.

ANTOINETTE F. DOWNING

PREFACE

The Preservation Society of Newport County hopes that the publication of this book will bring fresh attention to Newport's ancient architecture and thereby help to stem the tide of neglect that has been steadily submerging many of the town's colonial buildings.

The book itself has been designed to give a brief insight into the life of the seaport town and to present a chronological history of the city's architectural growth from its foundation to the first years of the twentieth century. An attempt has also been made to indicate the extent and condition of the remaining colonial buildings and to suggest a method by which the restoration of the historic sections of the city may be accomplished.

Many people have had a share in the production of this book. I have been assisted throughout by Mr. Philip D. Creer, A.I.A., of the firm of Creer, Kent, Mather, Cruise and Aldrich, and a member of the Department of Architecture of the Rhode Island School of Design. He was responsible for the section on the restoration of Clarke Street. Mrs. Peter Bolhouse has been in charge of the exacting task of looking up the deed records for the houses and Mrs. Joseph Goulart has assembled the notebooks containing the information for the survey records. Mr. Robert Meservey took most of the photographs. Mr. Wayne Andrews, Mr. W. King Covell, and Mr. Samuel Kerschner supplied others, while Mr. Covell has allowed me to draw freely upon his excellent collection of negatives of old photographs. Mr.
a Ralph Kinnicutt has kindly let me use his measured drawings of Trinity Church, the Wanton-Lyman-Hazard House, and the Brick Market. Mr. Warren Oakley made most of the floor plans. Mr. Robert Hill and Miss Marian Stickney drew the large map showing the
b remaining old buildings in Newport.

Mr. Wilmarth S. Lewis, in his capacity as a member of the Board of the Preservation Society, has read the manuscript and given invaluable help and advice, as have Miss Alice Brayton and Mrs. William W. Covell, members of the Committee for the Survey. Mr.
c Henry-Russell Hitchcock of Smith College and Mr. Bruce Bigelow of Brown University have both kindly taken time to go over the text and make suggestions. The whole work has been benefited by Mrs. Ruth Whitman's able editing.

The Newport Historical Society, the City of Newport, and the Rhode Island Foundation have given their financial support to the research necessary for the survey. Mr. Herbert
d B. Brigham, Librarian of the Historical Society, has given me continuous access to the Society's materials for study and for reproduction. The Redwood Library, The Providence

Public Library, The Rhode Island School of Design, the John Hay Library at Brown University, the Rhode Island Historical Society, Widener, Houghton, and the Architectural libraries at Harvard University, Yale University Library, the Society for the Preservation of New England Antiquities, the Boston Public Library, the Newport National Bank, Miss Pauline Weaver, Mrs. E. Maitland Armstrong, Mr. George Piltz, and Mr. Maxim Karolik have all kindly allowed me to use rare material for reproduction. The *Architectural Record* has permitted us to republish drawings from the *American Architect and Buildings News* and from George Rotch Ware's *The Georgian Period*.

Mr. Lawrence Wroth of the John Carter Brown Library and Mr. Clifford Monahon and Mr. Clarkson Collins of the Rhode Island Historical Society have helped with research and advice.

Mr. Elton Manuel has given me help and information drawn from his full files on Newport history. Mr. Lloyd Robson has allowed me to read his unpublished *History of Newport*. Mr. John H. Greene and Miss Susan B. Franklin have helped me many times. Miss Ruth Davenport and Mrs. Robert C. Davis have supplied original material concerning Whitehall.

I would like also to pay tribute to Jonas Bergner, who worked for years before his death in 1936 to bring together the materials for a history of Newport architecture. His notes on the construction of the houses and his measured drawings have been an invaluable aid to this work, as have the studies of Newport made by Miss Maud Lyman Stevens and Miss M. E. Powel, and the unpublished and published works of the nineteenth-century local historians, George H. Richardson, C. H. Hammett, Jr., Benjamin Howland, and Dr. Henry Turner.

Mr. and Mrs. John Howard Benson, Mr. and Mrs. Henry A. Wood, Jr., Mrs. E. Maitland Armstrong, and the many other owners of the houses visited have patiently allowed us to ask questions, study and measure, photograph and sometimes rephotograph in the interest of this survey.

The generous patronage of the late Mrs. Michael van Beuren and of Mr. Archbold van Beuren has made the publication of the book possible. Mr. Maxim Karolik has maintained a steadfast interest in the progress of the survey from its inception to its completion.

For illustrations not specifically credited in the plate section, acknowledgment is due the following: Rhode Island Historical Society: Plate 1; Plate 71, top; Plate 73, bottom. Newport Historical Society: Plate 7, bottom; Plate 17, right; Plate 21, top; Plate 26, top; Plate 29, bottom; Plate 47; Plate 52, Plate 53, Plate 54; Plate 55, bottom; Plate 56, top; Plate 61; Plate 64; Plate 67; Plate 68, bottom; Plate 69; Plate 70; Plate 71; Plate 72, bottom left; Plate 75; Plate 76, top; Plate 79, top; Plate 96, bottom right; Plate 116; Plate 132, bottom right; Plate 135, right; Plate 155, bottom; Plate 156. Lewis G. Morris: Plate 21, bottom (photograph by Covell). Society for the Preservation of New England Antiquities: Plate

22, top; Plate 38, top; Plate 182, bottom right; Plate 208, bottom; Plate 209, top. Art Department, Brown University: Plate 31. Redwood Library: Plate 50; Plate 155, top. Plate 196, top. Miss S. B. Franklin: Plate 62, top. Miss Pauline Weaver: Plate 72, bottom right. Society of Colonial Dames of Rhode Island: Plate 85. Metropolitan Museum of Art: Plate 103, bottom; Plate 162, drawing from the Office Book of A. J. Davis; Philadelphia Library Company: Plate 104, bottom. Newport National Bank: Plate 128, top. Courtesy of the Architectural Book Publishing Company: Plate 198; Plate 214, center right. Mrs. E. M. Armstrong: Plate 160. Houghton Library, Harvard University: Plate 186, top. New York Historical Society: Plate 227. John Howard Benson: Plate 14, top; Plate 17, left. George Piltz: Plate 125, right.

Sources not indicated in the plate section include the following: Palfrey's *History of New England*: Plate 23, top. Whitefield's *Homes of our Forefathers*: Plate 25, top. Historic American Buildings Survey: Plate 39; Plate 40; Plate 41, top; Plate 42; Plate 57; Plate 60; Plate 89, bottom; Plate 90, bottom; Plate 91, top; Plate 92, bottom; Plate 93, bottom. *Seventh Day Baptist Memorial*, 1852: Plate 56, bottom. *American Architect and Building News*, 1895: Plate 65; Plate 118; Plate 119, bottom; 1896: Plate 68, top; Plate 69; Plate 77, top; Plate 78; 1897: Plate 97; Plate 135, bottom, and top left. Photograph by Meservey: Plate 94. Photographs by Kerschner: Plate 74, bottom left and right. Drawing by Ralph Kinnicutt: Plate 23, bottom. Drawing by Mrs. William Greenough: Plate 131, bottom. Ware's *The Georgian Period*: Plate 130, bottom; Plate 140; Plate 142, bottom; Plate 143, bottom; Plate 144, bottom. Hitchcock's *H. H. Richardson and his Times*: Plate 186, center and bottom. We are further indebted to the Redwood Library for permission to publish Ezra Stiles' map, to Mr. Maxim Karolik for de Barres' map and to the Newport Historical Society for Blascowitz' map and the drawings of small Newport houses by Jonas Bergner.

The ornamental cuts used throughout the pages of the text in Part One are drawn from sources relating to early Rhode Island books and Newport printing. The vignette on the title page is taken from *A Looking Glass for Elder Clarke and Elder Whitman* by William Claggett of Newport. It was printed in Boston in 1721 before Newport had a press of its own and was sold by "John Rhodes, shopkeeper in Newport on Rhode Island." The heading for the Introduction is taken from a cut of the old Rhode Island Colony seal. It was owned and probably designed by James Franklin and was used as early as 1730 and for many years thereafter for official papers. The heading appearing in Chapter One is taken from a letter ornament in *A Speech made before the House of Lords* by Francis Rous, published in London in 1641. This work has been attributed to Gregory Dexter, the printer who published most of Roger Williams' writings. The heading for Chapter Two was taken from a cut used as a chapter heading in *A Key into the Language of America* by Roger Williams, printed by Gregory Dexter, London, 1643.

The Royal Arms used as a heading for Chapter Three is taken from a cut owned by the Franklin Press when it was run by Ann Franklin. It was used as a heading for the *Newport*

Mercury and for official papers in 1762 and somewhat earlier. The tailpiece for this chapter is a vignette, reduced in scale, which appeared as a tailpiece on *An Act of the Assembly*, printed in 1763 by S. Hall, Newport.

The heading used for Chapter Four is taken from the little drawing of the First King's Chapel in Boston, which was used as the endpiece in *The History of King's Chapel*, by F. W. P. Greenwood, published in 1833. The crown used as a tailpiece for Chapter Four belonged to the Franklin Press. It appeared in 1730 on the title page of *Part of a Sermon Preached at Newport by Benjamin Bass, Rhode Island September twenty-eight, 1729*, printed in 1730 by James Franklin, and was used for many years afterward.

The Royal Arms used as the heading for Chapter Five appeared on official papers and after 1772 as the heading for the *Newport Mercury*, printed by Solomon Southwick. The tailpiece for this chapter is another version of the Royal Arms. This one appeared on *An Act of the Assembly* dated 1763 and printed by S. Hall. Solomon Southwick used it later.

The Arms of Rhode Island, the headpiece for Chapter Six, appeared after 1783 in the *Newport Mercury*, printed by Henry Barber. The headpiece for Chapter Seven is taken from a little cut appearing in the *Newport Mercury* of September 1, 1801, printed by Ann Barber, and the tailpiece for this chapter is from a cut appearing in the *Newport Mercury* of 1821, printed by William and H. J. Barber.

The headpiece for Chapter Eight, the Arms of Rhode Island surmounted by an American eagle, is taken from the heading for the *Newport Mercury* of the same year, 1821. The tailpiece, an American eagle, is taken from a cut appearing in the *Newport Mercury*, March 28, 1835.

The ornamental cuts in Part Two are taken from contemporary publications. The headpiece for Chapter Nine shows "A Villa in the Italian Style, Bracketted," from Andrew Jackson Downing's *Cottage Residences*, published in 1844. The tailpiece for this chapter is a cut showing the carriage house for the Daniel Parrish House illustrated in Calvert Vaux's *Villas and Cottages*, published in 1857.

The headpiece for Chapter Ten is taken from a drawing of the H. A. C. Taylor House which appeared in the *Century Magazine* of May 1886.

A. F. D.

March 1, 1952

---

a   Read "Richard" for "Ralph."
b   Now redrawn and brought up to date, and printed as endpapers.
c   Read "Dr." for "Mr."
d   Read "O" for "B"

e   Now also credited on the plates.
f   Add "Left."
g   Now also credited on the plates.
h   Read "Richard" for "Ralph."

INTRODUCTION
TO THE FIRST EDITION

NEWPORT'S ARCHITECTURAL HERITAGE, now spanning nearly three centuries, was evolved chiefly during its first years of settlement, its pre-Revolutionary period of maritime growth, and, a half century after the disaster of the Revolution, its many years as a popular resort. The purpose of the following survey has been to set forth the nature and extent of this long tradition.

Although the eighteenth century was Newport's most brilliant early period of building, there are still, along the old streets, some important seventeenth-century houses, as well as many buildings of post-colonial and Greek Revival times. It is Newport's almost unique distinction that nine early public buildings have survived. The earliest, the Quaker Meeting House, belongs to the seventeenth century. In the eighteenth century, six extraordinarily fine buildings were put up in the short span of thirty-seven years between 1726 and 1763. Three of them, Trinity Church, the Sabbatarian Meeting House, and the Colony House are connected with the name of Richard Munday, who styled himself "housewright" and who worked before 1740. The other three, Redwood Library, the Brick Market, and the Jewish Synagogue (now a national shrine), were built some ten to twenty years later by Newport's gifted amateur architect, Peter Harrison. St. Paul's Methodist Church on Marlborough Street represents the style of the early nineteenth century, and the latest, the Rhode Island Union Bank, was built in 1818 by the American carpenter-architect, Asher Benjamin. These buildings alone are enough to insure Newport's permanent distinction as an early New England town. Their merit has long been recognized, as has the worth of the great private homes of the eighteenth-century merchant princes, the "Quaker Grandees of Rhode Island." [1]

Pls. 1, 4, 5, 47–60, 63–70

Pls. 6, 104–110

Pl. 129

Pl. 145

But Newport's unique character as a colonial town lies not only in its fine public buildings, but in the row on row of small dwellings, spread throughout the old part of the city. They are the substance of eighteenth-century Newport, the physical evidence of a coherent architectural style, where the homes of small farmers, dock workers, merchants, and shop keepers were constructed as sturdily, and ornamented not as lavishly but as suitably as the mansions of the great merchants.

Sketches of typical small Newport houses by Jonas Bergner.
Courtesy Newport Historical Society.

The building of the summer colony in the second half of the nineteenth century has made Newport rich also in nineteenth-century domestic architecture. The vigorous stream of domestic building which developed in America at that time appears in all its phases from the early Gothic Revival houses and Italian villas of the thirties and forties to the indigenous shingled buildings of the eighties. The later eclectic palaces of the summer colony are to be seen nowhere else on such a scale and in such number.

During the nineteenth century, colonial architecture was considered old-fashioned. At first disliked, and then ignored or modernized, the buildings later ran the risk of being "colonialized." Articles like those published on the "Queen Anne Style' in 1881 by George Champlin Mason, Jr., of Newport showed an awakening interest in our colonial past.[2] Mason's own work as an architect, however, exemplified the current feeling that the buildings themselves needed elaborating. The men who first worked in the "colonial style" seized upon particular features and from them developed a period style of their own. While often interesting in its own right, the style unfortunately added confusing elements in connection with the restoration of old buildings. This tendency to "colonialize the colonial" was at its height during the same years that the then fashionable "Queen Anne" cottages (1880–1890) were being built on Bellevue Avenue. In the meantime, enthusiasm for colonial building showed itself in a mania for collecting and installing elsewhere stairways, mantels, paneling, and doorways from old houses in run-down areas. Museums and individuals, students and architects alike have been responsible for these depredations.

As knowledge of the character of colonial building has increased, however, so has the realization that this architecture was an expression of a way of life. To illumine that way of life, all its aspects must be seen as a whole, each part of which is dependent on the others. The house, with its yard buildings, and gardens; its furnishings within, and the street on which it stands, forms a coherent index not only of the family who lived there, but the times as well. All these can be and have been studied separately; put together they explain each other, and help to evoke for us an understanding of our colonial past.

As a basis for the survey reported in these pages, the Preservation Society has made a study of the land records, the history, and the construction of most of the remaining old houses in the central part of town. The full reports on the individual houses are now available in the files of the Newport Historical Society. A map, based on two maps of Newport made in 1850, has been drawn to show the locations and indicate the dates of these buildings. It is included here at the end of the book.

There were about eleven hundred dwellings standing in Newport at the beginning of the Revolutionary War.[3] According to records, about three hundred houses were destroyed by the British during their occupation. The current survey shows that over four hundred houses built before 1840 are still standing, at least three hundred of which are of pre-Revolutionary date.

Pls. 88–94,
98

Pls. 123, 124

Pls. 98, 102

Some one hundred old houses have survived in the Point section alone. The Jonathan Nichols (Hunter) house at 54 Washington Street, the Thomas Robinson house at 64, the Captain John Warren (known as the Henry Collins) house at 62, as well as the Finch, Rivera, and Dennis houses were all built during the days when Washington Street, then *c* called the Water Street, was the scene of much of Newport's shipping. Here some of Newport's merchant princes lived with their wharves and shops close at hand, near to the gardens where they grew their own tobacco and raised exotic imported plants.

Pl. 8

Pl. 7

The first free school established in 1814 by the Proprietors of the Long Wharf met in the Simeon Potter house,[4] a broad gambrel-roofed building built before 1749 by Jacob Dehane on the corner of Washington and Marsh Streets.[5] The house and shop of the cabinet maker, John Goddard, originally stood on Washington Street at Willow. Both still stand, but they have both been moved from their original location, the house to 81 Second Street, the shop to Smith's Court. Matthew Calbraith Perry, who was to be instrumental in opening Japan *d* to western trade, was born in the gambrel-roofed house on the northeast corner of Walnut *e* and Second Street.[6]

Pls. 8, 9

Historic houses line the crooked old Shipwright's street, now called Bridge. First named for the ship carpenters who lived or worked there, its second title came from the bridge built across the northern part of the former cove in the early eighteenth century.[7] In 1800, twenty-one sea captains lived on Bridge Street, and long before that, Townsends and Goddards built their homes and shops along the cove side, where they could load their newly finished furniture directly into the ships for export to Charleston and the West Indies. Christopher and

Pls. 95, 96

Job Townsend's houses are both still standing, one at No. 72 and one at 19, and John Townsend's grandson, also a cabinet maker, once owned the tiny house at No. 78. Captain Peter *f* Simon's handsome house, some of it built before 1738, stands at 25 Bridge Street.[8] Here the *g* young dancing master, Peter Simon, Jr. brought beautiful Hannah Robinson, his young

Pls. 9, 46

Pl. 9

South County bride, whom he later abandoned.[9] Caleb Claggett's brick-end and gambrel-roofed house built between 1725 and 1750 is still at 22 Bridge Street. The house of his son, William Claggett, who made the clock in the Sabbatarian Meeting House, stands, much altered, next east at 16 Bridge Street.[10]

Pl. 10

Pl. 11

On upper Thames Street above North Baptist stands an uninterrupted row of eight or nine small pre-Revolutionary houses and shops. The Dr. James Keith mentioned by Dr. Alexander Hamilton in his *Itinerarium*, lived in the square one at No. 44.[11] Across the street, *h* at No. 29, John Stevens' stone-cutting shop, run since 1705 by members of the Stevens family, father and son, is now owned by John Howard Benson, sculptor. It is still operated under its original name.[12]

Public and religious buildings are clustered in the central part of Newport, from Farewell Street on the north to Church Street on the south. This section also encompasses many fine mansions and many more small houses. At 17 Broadway stands the seventeenth-century

Sketches of typical small Newport houses by Jonas Bergner.
Courtesy Newport Historical Society.

Pls. 29–37, 101

Wanton-Lyman-Hazard house. Once owned by Governor Richard Ward, it was later to be the scene of Newport's bitterest Stamp Act riot. Nearby Marlborough Street, leading off Broadway to Thames and the old Marlborough Dock, was one of the first centers of building in Newport. Here at the corner of Farewell Street stands Whitehorse Tavern, at least

Pl. 37

part of which was built by 1673. Originally the home of the pirate, William Mayes, it served as a tavern by the beginning of the eighteenth century and, while the Colony House was being built, a Criminal Court was held there. On Coddington Street, a block north, laid out through William Coddington's original grant of land, stands the Reverend Daniel Wightman's house, built in 1694. Wightman probably also built the story-and-a-half cottage at 6 Coddington Street, where his grandson William Hookey, the goldsmith, lived for many years. Jonathan Otis, the silversmith, lived at 87 Spring Street. *i*

pp. 464–467
Pls. 113–115

Just south of Washington Square runs Clarke Street with eleven historic buildings on its block length, the most famous of which is the Vernon house, noted as Rochambeau's headquarters in 1780–1781. Several important buildings stand on Washington Square, while others, once there, have been moved away to allow for later structures. The old Peter Buliod *j* house, now the Salvation Army Headquarters, was built about 1760 on the Touro Street side

Pl. 116

of Washington Square and bought by Moses Seixas in 1794. It became the home of the Rhode Island Bank, the first bank in Newport, in 1795, and in 1818 was bought by Oliver Hazard Perry, the hero of Lake Erie and Matthew's brother.

Across the square, the Newport Bank, the third bank in Newport, opened its doors in 1803. The gambrel-roofed mid-eighteenth-century house, once the home of Abraham

Pl. 87

Rodrigues Rivera, which served as its first place of business, is still in use today. It has recently *k* been restored, although partially cased in brick. Pitt's Head Tavern, moved to 5 Charles

Pls. 1, 43–45, 122, 128

Street from Washington Square in 1878, was once owned by Henry Collins, Newport's *l* eighteenth-century patron of the arts. After 1742 it was the home of his niece and nephew, Mary and Ebenezer Flagg, and after 1765 became a popular coffee house run by Robert Lillibridge.

Up the hill, Division Street, formerly called High Street, has sixteen old houses along its three blocks. Dr. Hopkins, pastor of the First Congregational Church and hero of Harriet

Pl. 99

Beecher Stowe's *The Minister's Wooing*; Christopher Ellery; and Isaac Touro, the Rabbi for whom the synagogue was named, all lived in houses still standing on this street. The house at No. 40, home of the French Huguenot, Augustus Lucas, was, like the Wanton-

Pl. 45

Lyman-Hazard house, to become the scene of rioting in 1765, when it was the home of the Stamp Master Augustus Johnston, grandson of Lucas.[13]

Down Thames Street, Dr. Cotton's house on Cotton's Court is the only house left of the many which once stood set back on the old wide line of the street. Further south and across

Pl. 126

the street on Bowen's Wharf stands Robert Stevens' Ship Chandler's Shop, the only one left in Newport. Now owned by George Piltz, it serves as the office of George Bowen's Coal *m* Company. The Robert Stevens mansion house at the corner of Bowen's Wharf and Thames Street is a double house of unique plan. Peter and Elizabeth Harrison owned this property before the Revolutionary War and the shop Peter and his brother operated may have been located here. Plans of the wharf with all its buildings were drawn by Arn Hildreth, who worked in his blockmaker's shop from 1840 to 1900. His sketch shows the sailmaker's shop, the sail-drying lofts, and the whole array of wharf buildings essential to a busy maritime life.

Even further south on Thames Street, in the part of the city known years ago as the "court end of town," the Francis Malbone house (now St. Clare's Home) is an early survivor of a former favorite residential spot. Here the rich merchants liked to build on the east side of the street, planting their gardens on the water side where their wharves were built. The Gidley, Redwood, and Ayrault houses are gone; so too is the great brick house that Godfrey Malbone was building in 1728, as are all the gardens and wharves. But the Samuel White-horne house at the corner of Dennison and Thames Street, built of brick about 1804, is a fine early Republican mansion; properly cared for, it would rival the post-Revolutionary houses of Providence and Salem. At the corner of John and Spring Streets, still in the court end of town and set a little back from the street, which is rare in Newport, is the house Governor Benedict Arnold's daughter, Godsgift, and her husband, Jireh Bull, probably built in 1680. Captain John Mawdsley acquired it from descendants of the Bulls sometime in the mid-eighteenth century. Mawdsley was married in 1747 and built soon afterward the fine house which stands in front of and completely conceals the old seventeenth-century structure. William Ellery Channing lived in the house at the southeast corner of School and Mary Streets.

n On Corné Street at Pelham is the late eighteenth-century barn which Michel Felice Corné, the Italian mural painter, bought in 1822 and converted into his dwelling house. The wall paintings on canvas that he executed to decorate the southwest chamber have been taken off and dispersed. The town's annals still record stories of his longevity and how he introduced the tomato to Newporters. He arrived in America in 1799 on the "Mount Vernon," a ship owned by General Derby of Salem, who became his friend and patron. He painted many views of the "Mount Vernon," decorated the Derbys' Salem house, the Hancock house in Boston, and painted the scenes of Naples which still adorn the Sullivan Dorr house of 1809 in Providence. His large paintings of the Great Lakes battle scenes were among his most notable works. The only known examples of his work in Newport are some drawings in the Newport Historical Society and several small paintings of the "Mount Vernon," some of them cut from the decoration of his own house.[14]

Further up the hill at 142 Mill Street stands the square gable-on-hip-roofed house that John Tillinghast built in 1760. Here General Nathaniel Greene had his Newport headquarters, where he was visited by Baron von Steuben and Kosciusko. Governor George Gibbs owned the house in the early nineteenth century, and it remained in the Gibbs family for many years. Old photographs show that its original front door was finished with a seg-

Pl. 127

Pl. 125

Pl. 111

Pls. 80, 72, 82
Pl. 74
Pl. 133

Pls. 38, 117–120, 142

Pl. 16

Pl. 17

mental pediment, but this has long since been replaced by the present porch. The house has also been almost doubled in size across the back, and most of the interior detail has been altered. The stairway, however, with its ramped rail and beautiful twisted balusters has survived unchanged.[15]

Pl. 131
Of the surrounding country estates many have been lost. Vaucluse, Samuel Elam's country house in Portsmouth, known later as the home of Shepherd Tom Hazard, is entirely gone. So also is Metcalf Bowler's country house with its gates surmounted by great carved eagles and its fine gardens. The handsome Georgian mansion house which was almost cer-
Pl. 111
tainly designed by Peter Harrison for Matthew Cozzens, the king's customs collector, was
Pl. 112
torn down only a few years ago. But John Banister's beautiful country seat, built, like Redwood Library, of wood rusticated to resemble stone, stands just beyond the One Mile Corner.
Pl. 97
His town house, where General Prescott of the British Army had his headquarters, is still located at Spring and Pelham Streets. The house where David Buffum, the Quaker preacher, lived is at the Two Mile Corner. This great gable-on-hip-roofed house, once the summer
Pl. 81
home of William Redwood, was probably built about 1745 by Governor Joseph Whipple.

The "House of Four Chimneys," built by William Brenton in 1641 at Hammersmith Farm on the neck near Fort Adams, had already fallen into disrepair by the Revolutionary War, when it was used as a hospital for British troops.[16] It was demolished soon afterward,
Pl. 46
but the farm house, which was probably built about 1720, when Jahleel Brenton owned the property, still remains, one of the small yard buildings once so common to the early great estates.

This brief resumé of some of Newport's more important houses omits the many little houses that Henry James likened to "little old gray ladies," which stand in nameless rows on the old streets. They are built exactly on the sidewalk's edge, sometimes side to the street, or end to the street; some covered with gable, some with gambrel or gable-on-hip roofs, but each serving to give Newport the quaint eighteenth-century air for which it is famous.

The even better known nineteenth-century architecture along Bellevue Avenue and eastward to the ocean shore is an equally significant part of the composite picture of a town whose development must be told in terms of widely divergent elements. The opulence of the nineteenth-century resort architecture, still largely intact and clearly evident, may be interpreted as a nineteenth-century parallel to the now submerged opulence of the old colonial port town; with the great difference, however, that the luxury of the more modern architecture represents the wealth of national mercantilism distilled into one small summer resort.

In summary, the maps show that the building of the old part of Newport extends from Equality Park to Warner Street on the north to Pope Street on the south. It is sandwiched between the water front on the west to Bellevue Avenue on the east, where the great estates pick up the thread of nineteenth-century building and carry it around the drive. Much of old Newport lies in outgrown or blighted sections. As the residential and business portions of *p* the city have extended gradually outward, they have left parts of the historic town in jeopardy. The real character of many of its buildings has become obscured, and it is doomed to disappear unless an effort is made to save the old houses. If they are cared for and restored, they will immeasurably enrich the life of modern Newport, for then only will the old part of town become, in the words of Kenneth Chorley, President of colonial Williamsburg, "a fitting memorial to the days when a forest of tall masts grew in the harbor and to those men of the sea who first made the name of Newport great." The old town, freed from its shabbiness and disrepair, will then take its rightful place in the modern city, and colonial Newport, with its irreplaceable heritage, will still remain a tangible part of Newport today.

---

a Demolished after 1952.

b Now as endpapers.

c Read "Riviera" for "Rivera."

d The shop has been demolished.

e His childhood home. See Supplement 31 Walnut Street.

f For "72 and 19" read "74 and 59." #59, Job Townsend's house, has been demolished since 1952.

g Read "70" for "78."

h Dr. Keith owned two houses, numbered 42 and 36, just north of 44 (the square house, which was built by Job Bennett about 1721). All are shown on Plate 10.

i Read "109" for "87."

j Read "Buliod" for "Buloid."

k Read "Riviera" for "Rivera."

l Moved to Bridge Street west of Second in 1965.

m Now George Bowen Fuel Company, Pinnegar and Manchester.

n Read "Mill" for "Pelham."

o Demolished after 1952. Stair hall and parlors now installed in the Henry Francis du Pont Winterthur Museum.

p Read "Colonial."

PART ONE

SEVENTEENTH-CENTURY COLONIAL ARCHITECTURE

CHAPTER ONE

Early Settlement

N THE BEGINNING OF MAY THIS YEAR," young Peter Easton wrote opposite the year 1639 in his copy of Morton's *Memorial*, "The Eastons came to [Newport] Road Island and builded the first English building and then planted there."[1] The first English house so recorded was burned to the ground by the Indians some three year later,[2] but the building and planting of the farmlands of Newport was the first germinal of a future thriving maritime town.

From the first, both the unique nature of Newport's colonists and its superb geographic location inevitably provoked the colony's rapid growth. In 1638 some two hundred supporters of Ann Hutchinson's Antinomian heresy, considered politically as well as religiously dangerous, had left Boston to found their own colony in Portsmouth. In the following year William Coddington, William Brenton, John Clarke, the Eastons, and some thirty others broke away from the Portsmouth colony and founded Newport.

Many of these settlers were men of broad culture and outlook, outstanding both politically and socially. William Coddington had not only been accounted the richest man in Boston, but, like William Brenton, John Clarke, and others, he had been eminent in England before his departure for the new world.[3]

The settlers brought with them a natural ability for commercial enterprise and a capacity for orderly and conservative government, based on the then novel concept of separation of church and state, still untenable in Massachusetts. This concept had already been expressed in the words "only in civill things," written in Roger Williams' Providence compact of 1637, and was clearly set forth by 1656 when President Benedict Arnold replied to the Bay Colony's sharp demand that Quakers be excluded from Rhode Island, saying, "We have no law among us whereby to punish any for only declaring by words their minds and understandings concerning the things and ways of God."[4] Newport's John Clarke is credited with the words written into the liberal Rhode Island Colony charter of 1663 that they wished: "to hold forth a lively experiment, that a flourishing civil state may stand and best be maintained, and that among our English subjects, with a full liberty in religious concernments; . . . ." [5]

With such a policy, all the "muster of opinionists" were admitted citizens. So many Quaker merchants — Walter Newberry, Walter Clarke, the Goulds, Coggeshalls, Eastons, and the Wantons — settled in Newport that in time almost half the town's population belonged to the Society of Friends.[6] It was Sir Edmund Andros who called them "The Quaker Grandees of Rhode Island," and indeed their solid worth contributed to the community's commercial success: their characteristic sobriety influenced civic affairs for a century and a half to come.

Jews emigrating from Lisbon, Holland, and the West Indies during these years found in Newport an enduring welcome.[7] Their very choice of a new home attested to the commercial possibilities of the not yet twenty-year-old town; and their enterprise and mercantile genius were to help forge Newport's maritime greatness in the years to come.[8]

The physical elements which contributed to the town's prosperity lay in its fine natural harbor and in its inland resources. Newport citizens soon capitalized upon the fact that, in the words of the King's Commissioner, the "Nanhygonsett Bay is the largest and safest port in New England, nearest the sea, and fittest for trade." [9] William Brenton and Nicholas Easton had built wharves into the cove as early as 1639. By 1680, Newport merchants had banded themselves together as "The Proprietors of the Long Wharf" to promote the town's rapidly growing volume of shipping.[10] Newport and Boston already led the colonies in shipbuilding.

In that same year of 1680 Governor Peleg Sanford cautiously reported to the Lords of the Committee of Colonies that "the Principal town in our Colloney for Trade is the Towne of Newport, that the generality of our buildings is of timber and generally small." [11] He said little about the increasing amount of shipping and commerce, for he hoped to avoid further taxation by the Crown. His own *Letter Book* gives a clear picture of the lively coastwise traffic and the trade with the Barbados at the end of the seventeenth century.[12]

Coffers were also occasionally filled by the spoils of illegal but profitable pirating which extended, as records show, as far away as the Red Sea.[13] The Rhode Island pirate, Captain Thomas Paine, retired to build a house on Jamestown. Captain Kidd visited him and is supposed to have buried treasure there. Thomas Tew, John Bankes, Thomas Jones, and William Mays, Jr. were all pirating in Madagascar and the East Indies in 1699 when Richard Coote, Earl of Bellomont, unleashed his attack, "The Irregularities of Rhode Island." [14] Newporters showed a tendency at this time to side-step English efforts to mete out justice which might interfere with profit, even though in 1694 John and William Wanton captured a pirate ship off Block Island almost single handed and won British acclaim in 1702 for the capture of a French privateer.[15]

By 1680, then, Newport had become a thriving seaport town, with grist and sawmills, tanneries, cooperages, breweries, and bakeries. It supported shipwrights and housewrights, blacksmiths, masons, cordwainers, mechanics, and shopkeepers, as well as silversmiths and artisans.[16] By this time there were over four hundred houses in the town and although "the generality of building" was, and continued to be "of timber and generally small," a few were of stone, and some were spacious according to the standards of the day.[17] William Brenton's seat, built at Hammersmith farm in 1640, was imposing enough to be known as the "House of Four Chimneys." Moreover, if the houses were small, New England winters were partly responsible for keeping them so, and the estates they belonged to often were not. In time, Brenton's holdings in Newport, on the Neck, in Connecticut, New Bedford, Gay Head, and across the bay in Narragansett amounted to well above fifteen thousand acres.[18] Benedict Arnold owned extensive tracts in Newport, much of Jamestown, Coasters Harbour Island, which he gave to Newport, and more lands in South County.[19] William Coddington, who was proud of his fine sheep, aggregated farms amounting to nearly a thousand acres.[20] The Dyres, Eastons, Cranstons, all owned land and farmed it, though their eyes were also turned seaward.

Healthy trade, a fine natural harbor, inland resources to draw upon, and a population composed of men of means, daring, and broad liberal outlook had now set the scene for the town's expansive growth.

THE TOWN PLAN. Massachusetts towns were Congregational towns, with church and state still all but synonymous. They were laid out according to plan around the village green, and were set with church, school, and town house all built, if not first, at least simultaneously with the dwelling houses.

Rhode Island towns were settled not by a single church, but by often contumacious individualists. As a result, the towns grew casually along the lines of the land grants. In Newport, this growth was conditioned by the shape of shore and cove and by common water lots and upland meadows. From the first, the main street stretched along the marshy shores of Narragansett Bay.

Henry Bull, the historian, drew up a rough sketch of Newport in 1641, preserved in a copy on the melange map now in the Newport Historical Society made by the Reverend Henry Jackson in 1853. It shows the high swampy shore line, the spring, the river, and the "Great Common" laid out along the river's course. According to this map, the old Broad Street, known at first as "the big highway," included all the land between Broadway and West Broadway. Here the river ran from what is now Pond Avenue down Tanner Street (West Broadway) to Marlborough and into the cove. Peleg Sanford's orchard and three houses were drawn in — Nicholas Easton's on what is now Farewell Street, William Coddington's on the north side of the river near the cove, and Henry Bull's hard by the spring which gave Spring Street its name. A water mill was marked by the river in the middle of the Great Common.

Of these structures, the mill has long since gone. Nicholas Easton's house was the one burned by the Indians in 1641. Henry Bull's house survived until 1912 when it, too, succumbed to fire. William Coddington's house was taken down by Clarke Burdick, its owner in 1835, to his later regret.[21]

In 1654, when William Dyre wrote a report "conserning High Wayes Lay'd out by Mr. Nicholas Easton, Mr. John Clarke and myself," [22] the lines of the town's first settlement "by the spring and to the seaside southward" [23] had become clearly crystallized into several little centers of building. A settlement had developed by the tan pits along the river on Tanner Street and down Marlborough Street to Marlborough Dock, the first dock of the town. Houses clustered around the spring back of the Colony House and followed the shore southward on Thames Street. A separate village with mill and meeting house had grown up by Bailey's Brook about a mile northeast of Newport proper in the "End or Endship of Green End," as it was called in the early records.[24]

The first structures in such a town naturally were located according to need. Wharves, water mills, and tan pits were built along the cove and riverside and early town records show that choice lots were set aside almost at once in the heart of town (the present Mall) to attract tradesmen to Newport. But the town had no colony house until 1687 and no meeting houses were built in the central part of town until the latter years of the century.[25] As late as 1690 in a pamphlet entitled, *A Short Account of the Present State of New England*, the anonymous author, known only as N.N., wrote "Here is a medley of most Perswasians butt neither church nor meeting house, except one built for the use of Quakers, who are very numerous." [26] When the churches and public buildings were built, they went up too late to affect the town plan.

It was by fortunate chance rather than early design that the eighteenth-century buildings of the Colony House and the Brick Market form today the opposite sides of what amounts to a town square. The map of Newport drawn up by the Reverend Ezra Stiles in 1758 shows a short street in the middle of the present Mall. Here the town school house and the printing office, housed in the school basement, a market house, and several shops and dwellings had already been standing a long time. In 1770 three of these buildings burned down.[27] The others, including the town school house, were torn down during the Revolution. Their cellars were left exposed until 1800, when the present Mall was laid out.[28]

p. 34
Pl. 47

In 1712, seventy-three years after the Eastons "builded the first English building," the town council authorized John Mumford, surveyor, to make the first survey of the streets, since, in the words of the meeting, "the town had grown to the admiration of all and was the Metropolitan." [29] This map, long misplaced, has recently come to light and has been placed in the Newport Historical Society. The town's long roads by the shore land grants had

a

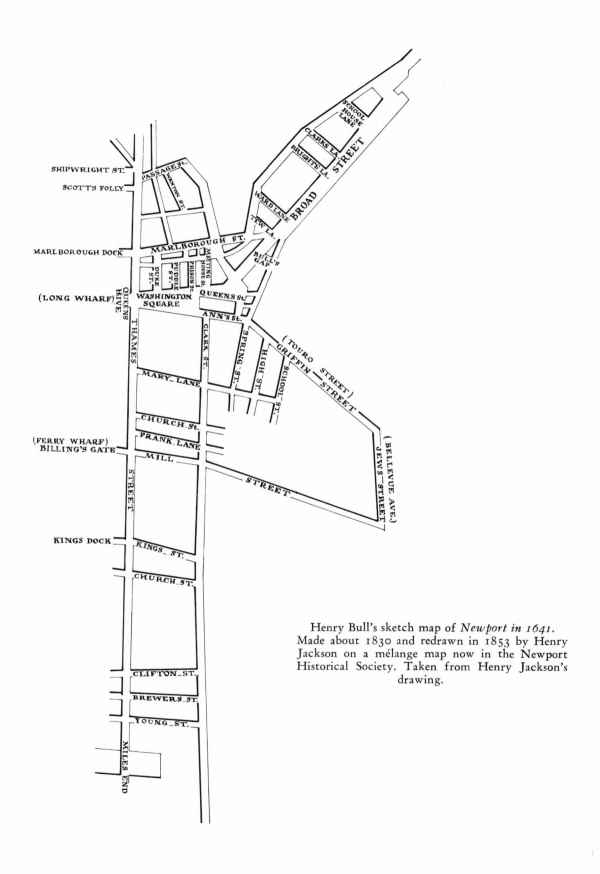

Henry Bull's sketch map of *Newport in 1641*.
Made about 1830 and redrawn in 1853 by Henry
Jackson on a mélange map now in the Newport
Historical Society. Taken from Henry Jackson's
drawing.

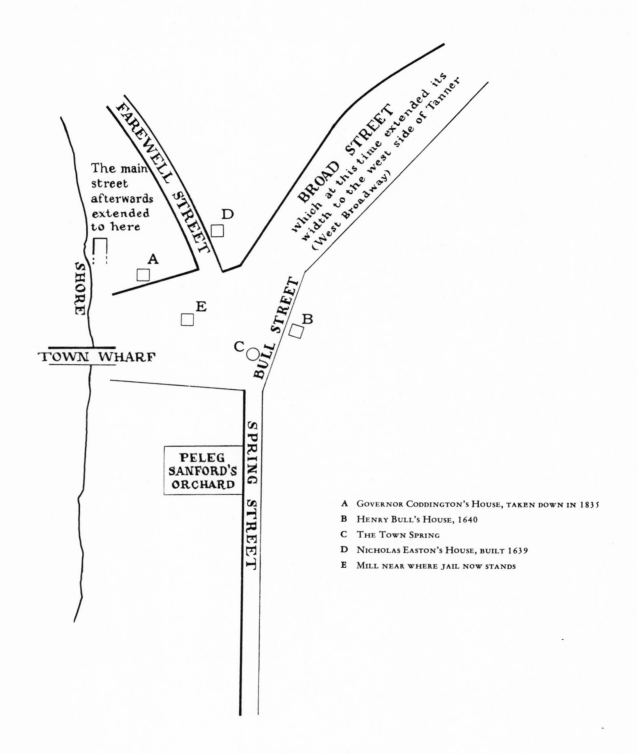

FAREWELL STREET

The main
street
afterwards
extended
to here

BROAD STREET
which at this time extended its
width to the west side of Tanner
(West Broadway)

SHORE

D

A

E

BULL STREET

B

C

TOWN WHARF

SPRING STREET

PELEG
SANFORD'S
ORCHARD

A GOVERNOR CODDINGTON'S HOUSE, TAKEN DOWN IN 1835
B HENRY BULL'S HOUSE, 1640
C THE TOWN SPRING
D NICHOLAS EASTON'S HOUSE, BUILT 1639
E MILL NEAR WHERE JAIL NOW STANDS

John Mumford's *Map of Newport* made in
1712. The original is in the Newport Historical
Society. Redrawn by Marian Stickney, 1951.

developed until Newport was essentially a town of two parallel streets, Spring and Thames, with a pair of short cross streets, Touro and Mill, running up the hill to Jew Street, the later Bellevue Avenue.

According to an act of the Town Council in 1707 "concerning the paving of streets," the compact part of town extended from the town pound in Broad Street down Marlborough Street and along Thames to Stephen Hookey's land, located, as proven by early deeds, on Thames at Cannon Street.[30] James Birket wrote in 1750 that the Main Street was "called a Mile Long"[31] while the southern part of Thames Street was generally known as "Mile's End." "The town of Newport" wrote Alexander Hamilton, a Scottish physician traveling for his health in 1744, "is about a mile long, lying pretty near north and south. It stands upon a very level spot and consists of one street, narrow but so straight that standing att one end of it you may see the other."[32]

———————————

a   See page 108.

CHAPTER TWO

Early Building

THE GOTHIC TOWN. When John Mumford made his map in 1712, Newport was still almost entirely a Gothic town. The "fayre, English houses" which clustered in numbers well above four hundred along Tanner, Marlborough, Broad, the Back Street, and Thames were medieval in concept and construction, a late afterglow of Gothic tradition on colonial soil. They were massive and small, with great exposed hewn beams, huge space-consuming chimneys and fireplaces, steeply pitched roofs, small leaded casement windows.

In 1620, twenty years before Easton, Coddington, and Bull built their Newport houses, Inigo Jones had returned to London from his grand tour of Italy. In that year he made designs for the royal Banqueting Hall at Whitehall Palace, in the Italian sixteenth-century style. Nearly fifty years later, when the great fire of 1666 laid waste the heart of London, Sir Christopher Wren was entrusted with the rebuilding of many of the city churches. Most of these buildings went up in the last years of the seventeenth century, and they left their baroque stamp on England's capital. Their later influence in the colonies was profound.

But the houses and meeting houses of seventeenth-century Newport were built by carpenters who knew little of Inigo Jones' trip to Italy or Christopher Wren's London churches. These men followed medieval building methods handed down to them by generations of English yeomen slow to change their ways. The tools they used (axes, froes, augers, and adzes) and the materials they selected (oak was the choice for framing) belong to late English Gothic tradition.[1] The character of the boxlike houses they built lay in the typical framed and braced medieval construction. After they had hewn, squared, and dressed the heavy oaken timbers to a smooth face, usually with the axe alone, they chamfered them along the edge for a decorative finish. Then they framed them together with interlocking joints of mortise and tenon, dovetail and half dovetail, as expert and self-sufficient as the stone vaulting system of a Gothic church. As in all Gothic building, this structural framework was left

22

frankly revealed, especially on the interior, and treated as part of the decorative scheme. It has been rightly said that to know the seventeenth-century colonial house, one must know the structure, for the structure is the house.[2]

Steeply pitched gable, gambrel, or high-hipped roofs covered the frames; boarded or studded, and sometime brick-filled walls closed them. They were warmed by huge fireplaces set in wall-like chimneys of stone, or later, of brick finished with pilastered tops. Framed overhangs, hewn drops, peaked gables, jutting, irregularly placed ells, plain doorways, and batten doors carried out the medieval look. Casement windows were closed by wood shutters or filled with oiled paper or with diamond-shaped or rectangular panes of leaded glass. The panes were small because householders could afford neither the price of much glass nor the loss of warmth in winter.

The exterior walls, perhaps half timbered and plastered at first, were, after the experience of a few New England winters, clapboarded or finished with wide weatherboards. Inside they were plastered, or sheathed with wide boards, tongued and grooved together. If the wood was painted at all, it was colored either an Indian red (sometimes made of red earth, lamp black, and a binder such as sour milk) or decorated with some form of marbling. The colonists sanded their floors and furnished the rooms with trestle tables, benches, or forms, and an occasional Jacobean banister-work or paneled and carved court cupboard or chest brought from England or made at home.

Such were the buildings that filled Newport streets at the end of the seventeenth century. Some ten have survived, the largest number in any Rhode Island town. Four more on Jamestown help keep alive the remnant of seventeenth-century Newport. Most of the very first houses, like William Brenton's, William Coddington's, Benedict Arnold's, John Coggeshall's, John Cranston's, and Nicholas Easton's are known now only by drawing or description, but Jeremy Clarke's house stood until 1898, and Henry Bull's house of 1639 survived until 1912. Part of Governor Peleg Sanford's house, built about 1655, is standing, concealed in the nineteenth-century monitor-roofed building at 2, 4, 6 Broadway. The Wanton-Lyman-Hazard house at 17 Broadway, built before 1700, the back part of the Mawdsley house at 228 Spring Street, Whitehorse Tavern, standing in 1673, and the John Bliss house, built at the end of the seventeenth century, are the best known of Newport's extant seventeenth-century houses. The present survey has brought to light three more, the Daniel Wightman house, built around 1694, the Perry Weaver house on Coddington Street, and the Weston Clarke house at 18 Marlborough.

a

Pl. 27

Pl. 23

Pls. 25, 26

Pl. 24

Pls. 29–37

Pls. 38, 37, 28

PUBLIC BUILDING. As we have seen, few public buildings went up in Newport until the last two decades of the seventeenth century. The first Colony House was built in 1687[3] and doubled in size in 1711.[4] When the new Colony House of 1739 was built, the old one was divided in two parts and moved; the 1711 part to West Broadway and the original half to

Prison Lane.[5] Both halves have been torn down, but a photograph of the Prison Lane part shows that it looked like a plain one-story clapboarded building covered with a steeply pitched roof.

The Quaker Meeting House. Of the eight or nine earliest churches, only the Quaker Meeting House built on the site of the first one in Farewell Street has survived. According to Friends' records, it was erected in 1700,[6] and as if to verify this date, the legend "John Jones, the King's Own, in Ye Year of our Lord 1700" was inscribed on one of the garret timbers. The original building, which had a hipped roof, dormer windows, and a turret, resembled the Bristol Congregational Church of 1680, the First Meeting House in West Springfield, Massachusetts, as well as other meeting houses put up between 1680 and 1700. It is probably the sole remaining Rhode Island example of the hip-roofed turreted meeting houses being built in New England during these years. These houses had supplanted an earlier type of building covered with a pitched roof and were in turn supplanted by the long churches of Wren's day.

Pl. 22

Enlargements made in 1808 and 1818 to accommodate the throngs who then came to Newport Yearly Meeting "beginning on the ninth hour of the second sixth day of the sixth month of the year," almost conceal this first house, but the massive chamfered frame, the framing for the turret, part of the original hipped roof, and the north wall with its old clapboards and two small casement window frames are still to be seen under these later additions.

Fortunately an over-mantel painting taken from the old Phillips House on Mill Street (now demolished) which depicts a view of Newport in 1740 shows the little Meeting House before any changes were made. In addition, several eighteenth-century visitors considered the building unusual enough to describe. In 1706, George Keith, a Quaker turned Episcopalian who traveled between 1702 and 1704 as a Missionary for the Propagation of the Gospel in Foreign Parts, published his *Journal of Travels from New Hampshire to Caratuck*. He wrote:

Pl. 21

> The Quaker Had Built a new Meeting-House at Newport, large enough to hold Five Hundred Persons or more, with fair and large Galleries, and Forms or Benches below. But one thing very singular I observed, that on the *top of the turret* of their Meeting-House, they have a *perfect Iron Cross, two large Iron Bars crossing one the other at right Angles*, a more perfect Cross I never saw on any Church. I mention this the rather, because George Fox in some of his Printed Pamphlets makes a great outcry and noise against the Steeple Houses in England, as he calls them for having Crosses on the tops of them, and that it is Popery; what can the Quakers say to this? Are their Brethren of Rhode Island guilty of Popery for having the Cross on the top of their Meeting-House, which I suppose remains there to this day?

The iron cross so perfidiously accepted by the Quakers which Keith described is actually the braces of the turret. When James Birket, a Quaker, visited Newport in 1750, he viewed both Friends and their meeting house with some disapproval. "This day I was twice at Meeting which is very large," he recorded in his Diary, "the Meeting house is also large and has two tier of Gallerys and a Cupola on the top; but the Friends in my opinion are as Topping as their house." [7]

Henry Bull's *Memoir of Rhode Island*, written in 1832–1838, in the form of a chronological history, gives an accurate account of the building:

> 1701. The Friend's Meeting-House in Newport was commenced in 1699 and finished this year. It consisted of what is now the middle part — its dimensions were 45 by 46 feet, the roof hipped and surmounted by a tower about 10 feet square and about 10 feet high, the roof of which tower, was hipped with concave rafters, and from the peak about 6 feet up was a small, square wooden shaft. This house had two rows of galleries one above the other. The cost as taken from the records of Friends was £ 261:18:9.

The upper part of the ell at the north of the building is interesting in its own right. It has long been known as the old Ship Room because of its curved and cased ceiling timbers. The history of this ell is not entirely clear, but it was supposedly built in 1705. Henry Bull concludes his account of the church with the following:

> There was a Friends' Meeting House built before the one described probably about the first coming of Friends to this country — it stood on the East side of Farewell Street, opposite the Coddington burying place — which house was taken down in the year 1705 — and some of the materials worked into that which is now the north room of the present Meeting House, which extends 30 feet north of the Main building.

Records say that originally the ell was only one story high, and that later it was raised up to give added room. The structural evidence bears this out. This ell never had a south wall of its own, and as a result part of the finished clapboarded north wall of the main building is still left exposed to view. The interested visitor may see this seventeenth-century wall with its riven shingles and two old casement windows, as he climbs to the garret to study the turret braces, the second story girts, and the shingled hipped roof of the seventeenth-century building, now covered by the nineteenth-century roof.

The Quaker Meeting House is one of Newport's most important colonial buildings, and ought rightfully to stand someday revealed in its original form.

The Stone Mill. The Stone Mill and the Quaker Meeting House are probably the only surviving nondomestic buildings of the seventeenth century. Of recent years, after the publication of Philip Ainsworth Means' *Newport Tower*, the stone ruin in Touro Park has been accepted by many people as the remains of a Norse church, built some seven centuries ago. The theory of Norse origin, which was first propounded as a joke in 1839, has had a fluctuating but sometimes vigorous support since that time.

In the summers of 1948 and 1949 careful excavations under and around the base of the structure were made by William S. Godfrey, Jr., of the Society for American Archaeology

Pls. 3, 22,

61

of the R. S. Peabody Foundation. His investigation showed that the building was erected on a stratum of soil in which colonial artifacts were found, proof that it was built no earlier than the colonial period.[8] Since this evidence reinforces the available and long known historic and local information, there is no longer reason to doubt tradition's claim that Benedict Arnold, who arrived in Newport and bought the land in 1654, as deeds of that year show, built the round, arcaded stone structure. Although of unusual form, it was probably built to serve as a windmill, perhaps soon after 1673 to replace the Eastons' wooden mill. The latter was blown down, as Peter Easton's diary records, in a gale in that year.[9] In further support, the existing early seventeenth-century deeds called the lanes leading past the mill site "Carr's Lane" and "the way past Robert Griffin's house," without mention of a mill. The first known specific reference to the mill occurs in the deed for the land for the Jewish Cemetery dated in June 1677. In his will of that same year, Benedict Arnold refers to "my stone built wind milne."[10] The mill superstructure was burned in the eighteenth century (probably about 1740) and the remains have been used both as a powder magazine and as a hay mow.

The form of the building, set on its arcade of eight circular piers, is medieval in character, and resembles the central part of eleventh- and twelfth-century Norse churches. As Kenneth Conant, in a review of Hjalmar Holand's *America* has pointed out, the closest English parallel is to be found in the so-called Treasury of the Cathedral of Canterbury.[11] A round tower set on an arcade and constructed of dressed stone was built in 1632 by Inigo Jones as an observatory on the estate of Sir Edward Peyto at Chesterton, Warwick County, England,[12] about one hundred and forty miles from Limmington, near Ilchester, Benedict Arnold's English home.[13] The observatory was later converted into a windmill, which, coupled with the fact that there is evidence that the Newport building was once finished with stucco, makes the resemblance of the two buildings even more striking. Without doubt, the ultimate source of the form itself lies in the Middle Ages, and as the Treasury of the Cathedral of Canterbury proves, it was common in England, as well as on the continent. But built of dressed stone, and finished with classic detail, the English observatory reflects also the spirit of the Renaissance. Henry-Russell Hitchcock has suggested, in his volume, *Rhode Island Architecture*, that the Newport mill, with its arcade and its smooth stuccoed surface, may possibly be considered the first structure in Rhode Island to presage the coming academic approach to architecture.[14]

According to information Miss Joan Marion has offered to the Newport Historical Society, William Arnold, who was almost certainly a relative of Benedict Arnold, owned a circular stone sugar mill in Barbados, where he arrived in 1626. This mill is not set on an open arcade, but it has a fireplace with a flue built into the wall itself, one of the outstanding features of the Newport mill.[15]

The masonry of the mill belongs to a strong and early tradition of stone building in Rhode Island. There are frequent records of stone houses. Chimneys and end walls of early houses were almost invariably built of stone. Chimneys were also sometimes sprung from stone foundations built of square piers tied together by stone arches. The Sueton Grant house, built on Thames Street before 1675, probably by Jeremy Clarke, an original settler, had such a foundation, the arches of which were constructed like those of the mill. Long after chimneys were built of brick, their foundations were built of stone in the form of an arched vault. Pls. 25–26

Like most local seventeenth-century masonry, the stone, local gneiss split along the lines of cleavage, was laid up in shell lime mortar. According to chemical analysis made by Norman Isham, mortar samples taken from the Stone Mill, the Sueton Grant house, and the back wall of Benedict Arnold's house, which stood at Thames and Pelham Streets, were all of identical composition.[16]

George Champlin Mason's "The Old Stone Mill at Newport,"[17] Rex Wailes' "Notes on Some Windmills in New England,"[18] and F. H. Sheldon's "More Light on the Old Mill at Newport,"[19] give some of the best information about the mill and its construction. Perhaps when someone has studied more fully the mills and round buildings of England, questions concerning the origin of Benedict Arnold's structure may be satisfactorily answered. In the meantime, Sir Edward Peyto's Observatory is too close in form and geographically too near to Arnold's English home to be ignored as an inspiration for Newport's mill.

The history of the Norse controversy may be followed in Charles T. Brooks' *The Old Stone Mill at Newport* (1851) and in Philip A. Means' *Newport Tower* (1942), which includes an excellent bibliography arranged chronologically. Kenneth Conant's review of Holand's *America* gives a valuable analysis of the medieval character of the building as well as a reconstruction of the mill itself.

Even in its ruined condition, the Stone Mill is one of Newport's important buildings. Unique in form, but with its roots deep in Rhode Island stone building tradition, it is perhaps the earliest, and certainly the most imposing example of seventeenth-century masonry left in the state today.

DOMESTIC BUILDING.

Use of Stone. Most of Newport's houses were built of wood, as were most Rhode Island houses, but enough were built of stone to verify the tradition of building in stone, and to prove, as does the Stone Mill, that at least some of the town's first settlers were skilled masons.

Two stone houses went up in the first years of the settlement. Sergeant Henry Bull's house, built in 1639, stood on Spring Street at Bull's Gap, now Stone Street, until it was burned in 1912. It was enlarged several times, but Isham believed that, like many other Rhode Island houses, it was originally a one-room house with an end chimney, covered by a gambrel roof of very steep pitch.[20] All the original part was of stone. According to Henry Bull's account of Samuel Cranston, his father, Governor John Cranston, one of the town's Pl. 24

original settlers, built a house which was always called the "Stone Castle." It stood on the old wide line of the east side of Thames, near Mary, until it was torn down by Charles Feke after the Revolutionary war.[21] Jacob Chace in his manuscript, "Recollections of Newport," written in 1882 (now deposited in the Newport Historical Society) mentions five or six other early stone houses. Governor Caleb Carr, whose Newport house stood on Mill Street above Thames, built a house on Jamestown Island about 1686.[22] It was half of stone, and some of its masonry, which changed character on the end wall, is like that of the Stone Mill. The mortar in this part is also of the same kind as the mortar employed in the mill. A great stone chimney set at the side of the house was unusual in its location as well as in the fact that it was almost free-standing.[23] It fell down in 1885, but an old photograph shows its former appearance. The house itself may be seen standing in Carr's Lane on the northern part of the Island. It is one of the few remaining monuments to the work of the early Newport and Jamestown stone masons.

Many of the seventeenth-century wooden houses had massive end chimneys built of stone, once so common in Rhode Island that they came to be called Rhode Island stone-enders. Such houses have been found in Wales and elsewhere. Mr. John Hutchins Cady of Providence has recently been sent photographs of Miss Dorothy Boykett's cottage, "Mercer's" in Twineham, twelve miles north of the Sussex County town, Lewes. It is built on a plan known as a bay (sixteen feet square) and a half in size, and like Rhode Island houses, it is a story and a half in height. Its stone-end chimney, which is very old, forms one end of the house, and its walls, which have been brick filled, are half-timbered. The main room, with its system of exposed framing and great fireplace is also like most keeping rooms of seventeenth-century Rhode Island houses.[24]

Other ancient Sussex cottages, long unnoticed because of their insignificant size, have similar characteristics. The source of the Rhode Island stone-ender, a type also found in Salem, from whence Roger Williams was banished in 1636, is established by such surviving Sussex cottages, some of which have a history dating back to Roman times. Since Pardon Tillinghast,[25] Providence Baptist minister, came from this area, as did other Newport and Providence settlers, the English derivation is a direct one.

Governor William Coddington's Newport house, built in 1641, was a stone-ender. Benedict Arnold built a house with an end chimney of stone which stood on the old Thames Street at Mill, until it was torn down in 1780. George Mason records in his *Reminiscences of Newport* that an eyewitness of its demolition said:

> the chimney and the whole south end were built of rough stone and coarse morter, and plastered outside with the same. The stone and morter were so strongly cemented together that they could not take it down by commencing at the top, without great labor; for that reason the house was first pulled down, then guys were made fast to the chimney, — it was undermined, and it fell in one mass, and was afterwards broken up with sledges.[26]

Pl. 27

b

Pl. 23

In 1641, Colony President John Coggeshall built his farm house on Coggeshall Avenue near Ruggles, on his land laid out, as an old deed says, along a "way for fishing without offence." [27] This house, with its end chimney of stone, was, like most of its kind, of a one-room plan in which the keeping room served as the parlor and kitchen too. According to a description left by Benjamin Anthony, who lived there until it was pulled down in 1845, the timbers were very large, with two summer beams that were "crossed" in each of the upper and lower rooms.[28]

The sole surviving "stone-ender" in Newport today is perhaps the Elder John Bliss house on Bliss Road at Anthony Place. It was probably built in the last years of the seventeenth century by Elder John Bliss who deeded house and farm to his son Josiah in 1715. It remained in the Bliss family until 1807, when Clarke and Abigail Bliss sold the property to Anthony Wilbur. A hundred years later, in 1906, after standing deserted and in ruinous condition for many years, it was sold by the Wilbur estate to Henry C. Anthony. Recently purchased by Restoration Inc., it is now being restored.[29]

The house is built on the Rhode Island two-room plan. In this scheme, two fireplaces, one for each room, are set side by side in the stone-end wall. This way of increasing the size of the

Pl. 28

DEVELOPMENT·
OF THE RHODE·ISLAND·PLAN·
·1636—1800·

house from one to two rooms as opposed to that of enlarging to a central chimney plan, is especially characteristic of early northern Rhode Island building. Both schemes are found in Newport.[30] In the Bliss house, the side walls of both fireplaces are splayed as usual for stone, but the stonework above the chimney in the front room is crudely corbeled out in a way which suggests that there once was a huge cove (perhaps plastered) between the chimney tree and the chimney girt. This coved form was often found in the earliest brick fireplaces but was not common to stone. Its appearance here suggests that the construction of the chimney had been modified by a knowledge of brick-building practice.

Two rooms added on the side opposite the chimney made the ground plan one of four rooms. This same scheme for enlarging the house was employed for the Eleazer Arnold and Valentine Whitman houses in Lincoln in the northern part of the state. The ceiling beams and corner posts are still exposed and chamfered in the seventeenth-century manner, but the stone chimney has since been finished at the top with brick. The house was brought up to date in the eighteenth century, and its early character has been somewhat concealed.

Other Newport houses were built on this plan, but almost all have been destroyed. When the Ebenezer Voax house, which stood until 1923 at the corner of Duke and Marlborough Streets, was torn down, the original part of the house proved to be of the same two-room plan with two big fireplaces, one for each of the main rooms set side by side in the end chimney of stone.[31]

The use of stone for chimneys went out of fashion toward the end of the seventeenth century, but cellar walls were built of stone, generally laid up dry, and the chimneys themselves, though of brick, were often sprung from a vaulted stone foundation. The Wanton-Lyman-Hazard house chimney is so constructed. The old farmer's cottage (not the mansion house) which was built around 1720 on William Brenton's estate at Hammersmith Farm has two brick chimneys, one at either end of the two-room house. Each of these is sprung from stone piers tied together by a carefully laid brick vault. Such vaults are mentioned in old inventories as storage places and are common at least until after 1750.[32]

Use of Brick. In Newport brick was seldom used, except for wall filling and, after 1675, for chimneys. William Brenton built his "House of Four Chimneys" of brick, which records say he brought from Boston soon after he bought Hammersmith Farm in 1640.[33] His is the only brick house recorded in early Newport annals, and, as late as 1750, James Birket reported that there were but two brick buildings in Newport when he visited there (probably Godfrey Malbone's town house and the Colony House).[34]

The foundation of Nicholas Easton's house, burned by the Indians in 1641, was uncovered in 1922 when the cellar for the new Quaker Meeting House was built. According to Miss Maud Lyman Stevens, who saw them, the walls of this foundation were made of light, pinkish, soft, and almost unfired brick. Like early English brick, it was somewhat larger in size than the brick in common use today. Some Indian pestles, a pig of lead, and oyster shells almost a foot long were also found in the cellar in further confirmation of the building's early date. There are other records of the use of this soft large brick in Newport as a wall filling between studs.

The Rodman house, which was moved from Thames Street and Washington Square to Bridge Street and later torn down, also had such brick-filled walls. The gambrel-roofed old Newport Bank at Duke Street and Washington Square also has brick-filled, stud-constructed walls. Abraham Rodrigues Rivera, by whose name the house is known, owned it from 1793 to 1803. When John Gardner bought this property in 1722, a house was stand-

Pl. 46

ing on it,[35] but the architectural style of the present building belongs to the years of 1730 or 1740, and other buildings as late as this had brick-filled walls. The walls of the Jonathan Nichols house at 54 Washington Street are studded, filled with large (4½ x 9 x 3) brick and then plastered over and sheathed with oak. This method is like Elizabethan half-timbering and reveals the continuing medieval tradition.

Brick chimneys built before 1720 generally followed stone tradition in that they were finished with pilasters at the top. Lawrence Clarke was granted the liberty to dig clay and make brick in 1691,[36] but evidence seems to point to the fact that most of Newport's brick came from elsewhere.

The Framed Overhang. The framed overhanging second story appeared in Newport more than once. As mentioned above, Governor William Coddington raised his Marlborough Street mansion house of wood in 1641. It was torn down in 1835 by Clarke Burdick, but a drawing in Palfrey's *History of New England*, published in 1860, shows that it had a medieval overhanging second story, a great stone-end chimney and small leaded glass casement windows. The Sueton Grant house, razed in 1898, had a front overhang finished with hewn drops, while the house of Captain Thomas Paine, Captain Kidd's retired pirate friend, which stands on Jamestown, still retains its framed overhang, although it is much altered otherwise.

Pl. 23

Pl. 25

Pl. 27

The recent study of the land records confirms an old tradition that Captain Peleg Sanford, Governor from 1680 to 1683, whose report has already been quoted, built his house where the nineteenth-century monitor-roofed building at 2, 4, 6 Broadway stands today.[37] The later house is built around and over a very old hipped-roof building. The old roof, which was never removed when the building was enlarged, was simply enclosed and may be seen today by looking through a storage closet door. Although no rain can fall on it, it covers part of Peleg Sanford's house. The huge framing timbers of this old house are also concealed in the present thick walls, but the overhanging second story is visible, supported by nineteenth-century brackets. An old photograph of the house in the Newport Historical Society shows it when it still retained one hewn drop.

Bent-Tree Construction. The house known as the Lawton house, which stood until 1931 in the triangle of West Broadway, Branch, and Marlborough, had an end chimney built of brick, pilastered at the top.[38] It also had a very early type of roof, hipped back to a high peak at one end and gabled at the other. This roof was constructed with tree timbers chosen because they were shaped naturally to the hipped line of the roof. One of these has been saved. It may be seen today in the garret of the Wanton-Lyman-Hazard house as proof that the colonial builders occasionally used the "bent-tree principle" of building encountered in English medieval work. Mr. Carleton Lawton, the owner, reported that when the house was torn down in 1931, piles of oat and wheat chaff were discovered, perhaps indicating that a water mill had once coursed through the cellar way. The fact, when considered together with the central location of the house, gives rise to the speculation that here might have been the site of the first town mill, mentioned in early records and shown on Henry Bull's map.

The Two-Room Central-Chimney Plan. Two-story houses built with a room on either side of a central chimney, unusual in northern Rhode Island building, were as common in seventeenth-century Newport as they were in Massachusetts and Connecticut. Their size was evidence of an earlier prosperity than may be found elsewhere in Rhode Island.

Pl. 25

The house known as the Sueton Grant or Atkinson house, which stood on the old line of Thames Street until it was torn down in 1898, was one of the most interesting of these. Built before 1670 on Jeremy Clarke's original grant of land, it was probably Jeremy's own house.[39] It was remarkable not only for its size and its framed wide front overhang finished with hewn drops, but for its huge central chimney, made of stone and pilastered at the top. This chimney, set on a base sixteen feet square, was U-shaped in plan, and was composed of piers tied together by uncentered arches. The stairs to the basement and to the second story were built between the piers in the chimney wall.

Pl. 26

According to the restored drawing made by Isham and Brown in 1895, the original house had a room on either side of the chimney and was two stories high, a mansion house in size. It was covered with a steeply pitched gambrel roof. This same type of early steep gambrel roof may be seen today in the house at 4 Elm Street, where it was moved in 1850 by Isaac Gould.[40] It was built by Jeremy Clarke's son Walter and originally stood on Thames Street just south of Washington Square.[41] The roof of Jeremy's house was once broken by two peaked medieval gables. These were removed later, when rooms were added across the back and the old steep gambrel was changed for an eighteenth-century roof of a broader, flatter pitch.[42]

c

Most of Newport's remaining seventeenth-century houses, discussed in detail in the Appendix, were built on the central-chimney, two-room, two-story scheme.

-----

a Other seventeenth-century houses have been identified since 1952. The Weaver and Clarke houses have both been demolished.

b This is the Nicholas Carr House, built about 1700. Caleb Carr's house was burned in 1952.

c Demolished after 1952.

PART TWO

EIGHTEENTH-CENTURY COLONIAL ARCHITECTURE

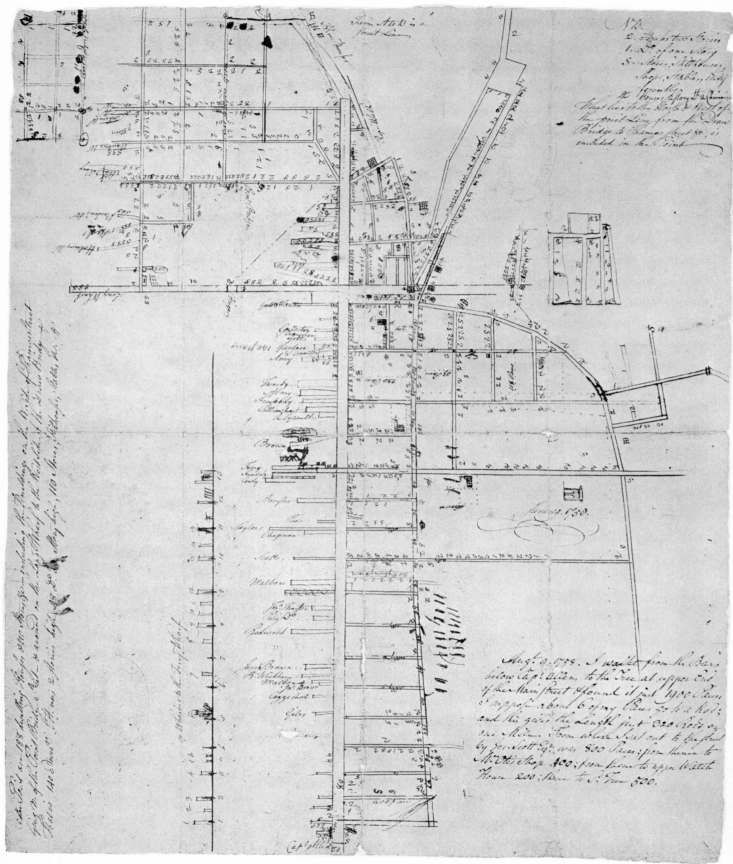

Map of Newport in 1758. Drawn by the Reverend Ezra Stiles.
Courtesy of Redwood Library.

CHAPTER THREE

Society and Commerce

 IN 1758, THE REVEREND EZRA STILES, pastor of the Second Congregational Church and later President of Yale College, painstakingly drew up a map of Newport for his own information. This map, now in the Redwood Library, shows how rapidly the town had grown in the forty-five years since Mumford had made his map.

"In the year 1759," as Samuel Ward had written on the front page of one of his Account Books (now in the Rhode Island Historical Society), "their was 953 houses in the Town of Newport and in the year 1766 the Grand and Magnificiant house of Col. Malbourn was consumed by fire." Stiles not only paced out the location of all these buildings, but marked out whether they were public buildings, houses, "shops, stills or stables." He also indicated which dwelling houses were one, two, or three stories high and which had one or two chimneys. He showed ropewalks and the full panoply of wharves ("17 wharves to the Ferry Wharf" alone), many of them designated by name. Easton's Point, only opened as Quaker land in 1711, had, by Ezra Stiles' count, "188 dwellings Houses and 110 Stores, that is 148 dwellings 2 stories high, 48 do. one story high, 110 stores, Stills, Shops, Stables, Etc." as well as wharves.[1] Many of these buildings are standing today, although the wharves and the ropewalks have long since gone.

When Stiles made this map, Newport was, in spite of war and the British trade restrictions, in the full pride of its prosperity. Since Governor Sanford's report of 1680, the little town had emerged as one of the principal places for trade not only in Rhode Island but in all the colonies. Its coastwise and West Indies traffic had expanded; trade with London and Lisbon flourished. Newport ships loaded with sugars, rum, and salt sailed from the West Indies. They brought salt from the Mediterranean, logwood from the Honduras; they shipped hemp, fish, lumber, flour, rice, and flaxseed and whale oil or spermaceti, either in crude form or in candles.[2]

Ropewalks to supply ships' needs were to be seen at the north of town, and shipbuilding was carried on at the water's edge so extensively that in 1741, according to the Governor's report, almost all the one hundred and twenty Newport-owned sail were Newport-made.[3] When in 1761 nine firms of spermaceti chandlers in Boston, Providence, and Newport formulated trade agreements which fixed prices and manufacture, the result was one of the first closed trusts in history.[4] Traffic in whale oil and in candlemaking, already important, became major industries.

During all these years Newport was called a free port, and Newport fortunes were made in free trade, or smuggling, as the British Admiralty bluntly termed it. The increasingly stringent British Navigation Acts, including the duties on French and Spanish sugars and molasses, particularly restrictive to New England trade, were primarily intended to protect British commerce. They met open defiance among Rhode Island merchants convinced that the laws favored the West Indies' colonial trade at the expense of the northern and that compliance to them spelled commercial disaster. Rhode Island's illegal traffic with the West Indies was sometimes extended to trade with England's enemies of the Spanish and French wars.[5] Newport merchants also engaged profitably in privateering against the same enemies, legalized by the same wars.[6] Such independence of action helped pave the way for the coming break between colony and parent nation.

The chief foundations of Newport wealth were laid in the African trade, with its auxiliary enterprises of barrelmaking and rum, the one to be used for the shipment of molasses from the West Indies to New England, the other made from the molasses and used as the purchase price for slaves needed on the West Indies sugar plantations.[7] In 1715 the General Assembly voted that half the revenue derived from the profit on the slave trade for seven years to come, be used to pave the streets "from the Ferry House to the Colony House." [8] In that same year, the Treaty of Utrecht put slave trading on a profitable basis and in time Newport came to be known as the slave market of New England. In other words, Newport consistently followed the commercial pursuits open to a typical port town in the eighteenth century.

From the banding together of the Proprietors of the Long Wharf in 1680 to the trade agreements made by the spermaceti chandlers in 1761 had spanned just eighty-one years. The bold enterprise that had characterized these early Newport affairs stamped its later undertakings with an audacious success. As wealth increased, Newport society took on a cosmopolitan and more stratified aspect. The important merchants built, fitted out, and owned the ships; their energy engaged them in ever broadening pursuits. But they in turn were dependent on the skills of seamen, shipwrights, and dockworkers, ironmongers and tanners, artisans and craftsmen, laborers to make rope and candles, rum and casks, and on their wharfside and Thames Street shops to sell wares brought from ports throughout the world.[9]

The sea paved the way for contacts with Boston, Charlestown, New York, and other colonial towns, as well as with foreign centers, and this contributed to a broadened social life made even more attractive by Newport's pleasant summer climate. After 1729 West Indies visitors often summered in Newport. So many families of the Charleston merchants came to escape the southern heat that the cool island town was known as the Carolina Hospital and Newport soon took on the aspect of a resort town almost unique among the colonies. Mr. Carl Bridenbaugh's illuminating article, "Colonial Newport as a Summer Resort," [10] suggests how much and how early the town's social life was tempered by its annual tide of summer visitors.

In the meantime opportunities created by the expanding world allowed merchants like the Quaker Redwoods to develop a colorful network of business associations in far-flung port cities. Dr. Bruce Bigelow's study of Newport commerce in the eighteenth century gives a vivid account of the city's growing trade with the West Indies, Europe, and Africa.[11]

Abraham Redwood, whose forbears had lived in Bristol, England, arrived in Newport in the 1720's via Antigua, Salem, and Philadelphia. He died in 1729, but his son maintained the important Casada Garden sugar plantations in Antigua, while other members of the family established themselves in Salem, Charleston, and Philadelphia.[12] They were thus in a position to push forward their affairs from the key cities of the new world. Such men were typical of an increasing number of colonial merchants who contributed much to a broadened civic outlook and to the advancement of arts and letters. They lived patrician lives, building their town houses near the harbor where their wharves and shipping lay and building their country seats where they could retire to live like country squires.

Abraham Redwood, Jr. married Martha Coggeshall in 1727 and began soon afterwards to build his square hip-roofed town house on the water side of Thames Street just south of the Perry Mill. Back of the house on the water front stood his warehouses and the private wharf at which cargo-laden Redwood-owned vessels docked and set sail. He had the whole estate, including his town gardens, enclosed by a brick wall with wrought iron gates, which we know were imported from London, because Rowland Frye, his London agent, wrote in April 1728 concerning "certain Lead and Stone work":

Pl. 72

> I shall be glad to hear the Iron Gates and Stone work are as you directed, the Workmen inform me that your directions were not so perfect as could be desired, however everything was performed in the best manner, and the Stone Work fitted to the Gates, that there cannot be a mistake in putting them up.

Frye went on to say:

> Flower potts are not now in Fashion; so that I have now sent you two pineapples of a new sort of stuff which wears as well as stone, and comes very cheap; for in stone they would cost above £12. If you do not like them they will probably serve for some other place about your house, and I will

then send you any sort you please to order. There are 1 M [1000] of Bricks more than you ordered but as you did not mention what sort they were to be I first shipped Grey Stocks. I was afterwards informed that the Coins [quoins] should be Red Bricks, and have therefore sent 1M. of them.[13]

Fifteen years later, in 1743, Redwood bought a country estate in Portsmouth from his father-in-law, Daniel Coggeshall. The house, which is a plain and sturdy gambrel-roofed building with a plaster-coved cornice, still stands on the West Road behind a grove of im-   *b* ported linden trees. His gardens were his pride and he soon set to work to lay them out. Mrs. E. Maitland Armstrong has in her possession an undated letter written about 1745 to his Antigua agents, Wm. Mackinen and Stephen Blissard, requesting shipment of various West Indies plants.

I desire that you speak to ye overseer, Mr. Atteson to put up in Durt, one dozen of small china orange trees that has boren one or two years, with the young fruit upon them if to be had, one douzen roots of pineapple with the young fruit upon them, if to be had, that has boren two or three years, three roots of Sappadilla trees, four young figg trees, and some guava roots, to put in my greenhouse. For I have made a garden of 1½ acres of land and I have built a greenhouse twenty-two feet long, twelve feet wide and twelve high, and a Hot House sixteen feet long, twelve wide and twelve feet high, and I have growing in my Green House fifty young fruit trees from six inches to four feet high, and my gardner says ye largest will not bear these two years, and I have in my Hot House strawberries, Bush Beans, and crownations in blossom. *Pray* don't forget to send the above and you will greatly oblige.

In 1767 Solomon Drowne, later to be the first Botany Professor of Brown University, but then just fourteen, visited Newport with his father. He described Mr. Redwood's garden as

one of the finest gardens I ever saw in my life. In it grows all sorts of West Indian fruit, viz Oranges, Lemons, Limes, Pine-Apples and Tamarinds, and other sorts. It also has West India flowers — very pretty ones — and a fine Summer House. It was told my father that his Garden was worth 40,000 Pounds, and that the man that took care of the Garden had above One Hundred Dollars per annum. It has Hot Houses where things that are tender are put in the winter, and Hot Beds for the West India Fruit. I saw one or two of these gardens in coming from the beach.[14]

Redwood's gardener, who received this fabulous "One Hundred Dollars per annum" was Charles Dunham, perhaps the town's first professional gardener. As *Mercury* advertise-   *c* ments of the 1760's and 1770's show, he set up a business on Thames Street for himself, where he sold seed and garden supplies.

Newport soon boasted at least one other professional gardener.[15] Johann Casper Ohlman arrived in 1754, highly recommended in letters from King Frederick of Poland, and from the Dresden horticulturalist for the Royal gardens, Johann Alnger. Ohlman, whose name was later anglicized to Ailman, is supposed to have served as gardener of Vaucluse in Portsmouth. It is more likely that he cared for Charles and Metcalf Bowler's beautiful country gardens nearby, which were laid out soon after 1760, and were described in detail by the Reverend Manasseh Cutler after a visit in 1778. The Vaucluse gardens were

established by Samuel Elam in the early nineteenth century on property he had inherited   Pl. 131
from his uncle Gervais after 1777. By this date Ailman was no longer living, according to
the Newport census made at the time of the Revolutionary War which lists his wife as head
of the household.

Redwood's town gardens were supposed to have been botanical gardens.[16] Little is actually known of them, but a plan of the Portsmouth garden has come down to us, and traces
of the garden itself may still be seen. The great hedges of arbor vitae, stone walls, and terraces
faced with stone remain in their early condition; old fruit trees, indications of a formal
garden, and a fish pond help us picture what this country seat once was.[17] Fiske Kimball
attributes the delightful rusticated summer house mentioned by Solomon Drowne to Peter   Pl. 105
Harrison.[18] It may be seen today on the grounds of the Redwood Library, where the wrought
iron gates and their fashionable "pineapples" instead of "flower potts" have been transferred   Pl. 73
from the town house.

Some of Abraham Redwood's fine furniture made by Thomas Goddard is also on display there and his portrait, painted by Robert Feke, hangs on the wall. His handsome coach,
which was celebrated in its day and perhaps the first to be maintained in Newport, has long
since disappeared.[19]

The manner of life led by Redwood and his family may be considered typical of the life
led in varying degrees by other important merchant aristocrats. Godfrey Malbone, a rough
and ready merchant who came from Princess Anne County in Virginia about 1700 and
amassed a fortune in the slave trade, lived on a perhaps even more lavish scale.[20] His town
house, built of brick, formerly stood on the northeast corner of Thames and Cannon Streets.
It may have been designed by Richard Munday[21] and was certainly being finished in 1728
because in that year John Fletcher, painter, sent Malbone his bill for £ 50 for 2500 leaves of
gold for "gilding the Great Room and the spout heads." He charged £ 5 more for the trip
to Boston to buy the gold. The same bill listed "1552 yards of painting at the brick house"
and included painting two bedsteads green.[22] John Stevens cut and set a marble chimney-
piece in 1749.[23]

Malbone's grounds, like Redwood's, were enclosed by a wall pierced by wrought iron
gates. The two wealthy merchants whose Thames Street town houses were almost opposite
each other were evidently vying with one another. At any rate, Malbone's gate posts were
surmounted by pineapples, just as Redwood's were. The Reverend Edward Peterson, writing
in 1853, reported then that the "ancient brick building still had an imposing appearance with
its portico, double flight of lofty steps and its . . . iron gate and railings." He reported
further that the "iron railings around the portico bore the initials G.M. in the center," that
"a splendid hall, with a noble flight of circular stairs rose to the top of the house," and that the
walls were paneled, the mantels were of rich marble, and the cornices retained traces of
gilding.[24] A single ornate carved capital from the front doorway and a richly ornamented

Pl. 74

marble mantelpiece now in the Newport Historical Society are all that is left of all this splendor, but the 1740 View of Newport shows the house as a gambrel-roofed building with a balcony, dormers, roof balustrade, and cupola which confirms reports that it resembled the Colony House in style, and means that it stemmed from the same tradition that produced the Hancock house in Boston.[25]

In 1741 Malbone was building near Miantonomi Hill his fabulous and now legendary country seat, "Malbone Hall," of pink sandstone he had brought from his own stone quarry on his property in Brooklyn, Connecticut.[26] Although Richard Munday died about this time, *d* he was supposed to have made designs for this building, too,[27] and like the town house and the Colony House, it had, according to Peterson, a double pitched roof, dormer windows, and a cupola. "The fifteen steps leading to the hall," he added, "were spacious, and standing as the building did, on elevated ground, gave to it an imposing appearance." [28]

Inside, it was magnificently finished, with mahogany doors and a circular staircase to the attic. The whole was reputed to have cost the then fabulous sum of £20,000. Several pieces from a large chest of armorial silver Godfrey Malbone had made for the house in London in 1742 are still in existence. Mr. Richard Le Baron Bowen, in his recently published "Godfrey Malbone's Armorial Silver," gives an account of Malbone himself, his Newport palaces, as well as a history and description of this handsome silver.[29]

Every visitor to Newport walked or drove out to Malbone Hall. Dr. Alexander Hamilton, in Newport in 1744, gives an excellent description of it in his *Itinerarium*.

> I went with Dr. Moffatt att 10 a'clock to see a house about half a mile out of town, built lately by one Captain Malbone, a substantiall trader here. It is the largest and most magnificent dwelling house I have seen in America. It is built intirely with hewn stone of a reddish color; the sides of the windows and the corner stones of the house being painted like white marble. It is three storys high, and the rooms are spacious and magnificent. There is a large lanthorn or cupola on the roof, which is covered with sheet lead. The whole staircase which is very spacious and large, is done with mahogany wood. This house makes a grand show att a distance, but is not extraordinary for the architecture, being a clumsy Dutch modell. Round it are pritty gardens and terrases with canals and basons for water, from whence you have a delightfull view of the town and harbour of Newport with the shipping lying there.[30]

When James Birket was in Newport in 1750 he too visited Malbone and left an illuminating description of the house.

> I dined at John Jepsons and in the Afternoon I went with my fellow travellers to See Captain Malbons Country house It Stands upon a tolerable Advantageous Scituation About a Mile out of the Town And makes a good Appearance at a distance, but when you come to Survay it nearer it does not answer your Expectation. It is Built of Hewn Stone and all the Corners and Sides of the Windows are all painted to represent Marble, you Enter from a large flight of Steps into the first Story which is very Grand the Rooms being to Appearance 16 or 17 foot high but the upper Story is Neither of the proportionable in the height of the rooms nor Size of the Windows the Cellars

Kitchens &c are below Stairs, 'tho Only upon the Surface of the Earth before the house is a Handsome Garden with variety of wall fruits And flowers &c: this house and Garden is reckoned the wonder of that part of the country not being Such another in this Government.[31]

Malbone Hall burnt down in one of the most dramatic fires of the town's history, on June 7, 1766, just twenty-two years after its completion. In the words of Henry Bull, writing some seventy-five years later,[32]

It caught in the roof, from the sparks out of the kitchen chimney, just before dinner, and such was the rapid progress of the flames, that before assistance could be had from the town, it was past the power of the firemen to extinguish it. The Colonel had a family party there to dine, and when he found the house must be lost, he ordered the dinner to be carried to an adjacent building and the table set there for the company, saying that "if I have lost my house that is no reason why we should lose our dinners."

Bull, of the same opinion as other narrators and visitors, added:

This was the most splendid country seat in Rhode Island, and probably in New England at that time. The ruins, like that of Palmyria still give evidence of its former grandeur.

In 1784, Francis Miranda, the inspired Venezuelan patriot who hoped to form a federal republic of all the South American countries, arrived in Newport during a year-long visit to the United States. He visited the grounds of ruined Malbone Hall as one of the town's show places. "I went to see a garden a mile distant from the town belonging to Mr. John Malbone," he wrote in his diary:

Its situation is extremely agreeable and the house commands a fine prospect, the Bay, Islands, and neighboring Continent. It has been entirely destroyed by a fire which accidently ignited it, and as can be seen by its ruins and the natives have informed me it seems that it was the most elegant building in the whole of the State. The garden is very large and well arranged, with a pretty bathing pool and many and excellent fruit trees, but it is entirely neglected. For 9 pennies or half a real one can go into it to walk where one pleases and take all the fruit one wants.[33]

Perhaps all that is left of this garden and house is a pineapple from one of the gate posts now set up at Fort Adams. But nearly ninety years later, the pink sandstone was reused when Prescott Hall bought the property in 1848 and commissioned Alexander Davis to design a new and Gothic "Malbone" to rise Phoenix-like out of the ruins of the old.

The influence of Henry Collins, Newport born and bred, the son of Arnold Collins, the silversmith, was of particular significance in the group of wealthy merchants who nurtured Newport's civic growth, and his name has become a symbol of the best type of citizen the age produced.[34] As an ardent patron of art and public affairs, he was a leader in every cause for community welfare.

Not only was he on the committee responsible for extending Long Wharf, but he made an outstanding collection of paintings which included portraits by Smibert, Feke, and Stuart.[35] On his death at least part of this collection came into the possession of his relatives,

the Ebenezer Flagg family, who lived in the house now at 5 Charles Street before it became
Pitt's Head Tavern.[36] With Peter Bours, Abraham Redwood, and others, he was a founding
member of the important Philosophical Club, which later grew into the Redwood Library
company and he gave the land for the new library building. He also helped (as did Redwood) various young men, including the painter Robert Feke and the printer Solomon
Southwick, later editor of the *Newport Mercury*, to establish themselves in their chosen
fields.[37]

Of the several houses he owned in Newport only Pitt's Head Tavern is standing. Town
records indicate that his mansion on the Water Street was taken down for fuel in 1780, and
there seems to be no existing description of it.[38] Like other merchants of the day, he had a
country seat in Narragansett, a farm consisting of over seven hundred acres along the shore
of Narragansett Bay. "My little country villa," as George Rome, agent for the interests of the
British firm of Hayley and Hopkins, called it during his occupancy, was famous both for its
gardens and for such elaborate features of interior arrangement as concealed beds which
appeared from the wainscotting "as if by magic" at the touch of a spring.[39] Wilkins Updike
reported, however, that when the house was examined in about 1870 the only unusual feature
to be noted was the vast fireplace in the kitchen, large enough for a tall man to walk into.

The firm of Collins, Flagg, and Engs went into bankruptcy in 1765, ruined partly because of trade difficulties during the Seven Years' War and partly because of the stricter enforcement of the British Navigation Acts which curtailed free trade and temporarily crip-
pled Newport commerce. All Collins' property was taken over by George Rome, but he had
justly merited the title of "the Lorenzo di Medici of Rhode Island," later bestowed upon him
by Dr. Benjamin Waterhouse, Newport physician and scholar.

The role of other merchants, equally wealthy, was sometimes less public spirited.
Charles Bowler's town and country estates were laid out on the same scale as Collins'. An
Englishman of substance, Bowler had arrived in Boston in 1740. In 1753, when he received
the appointment of Collector of Revenue in Newport, he sold his Boston holdings and
bought the house now famous as Rochambeau's headquarters on the corner of Clarke and
Mary Streets. He also bought an estate of seventy acres in Portsmouth, built his country
house and dwelt there the year round after 1759, when he sold the town house to his son
Metcalf. Here he laid out the elaborate gardens that were to come into Metcalf's possession
later.[40]

The Reverend Manasseh Cutler, L.L.D., Pastor of the Congregational Church in
Hamilton, Massachusetts, a volunteer chaplain in General Titcomb's brigade, saw Bowler's
gardens while he was stationed in Newport and described them in his diary. Under the date
of August 16, 1778,[41] he wrote:

> Went in the afternoon with a number of officers to view a garden near our quarters, belonging to
> one Mr. Bowler, — the finest by far I ever saw. It is laid out in the form of my own, contains four

acres, has a grand aisle in the middle and is adorned in the front with beautiful carvings. Near the middle is an oval, surrounded with espaliers of fruit trees, in the center of which is a pedestal, on which is an armillary sphere, with an equatorial dial. On one side of the front is a hot-house, containing orange trees, some ripe, some green, some blooms, and various other fruit trees of the exotic kind, curious flowers etc. . . . There are espaliers of fruit trees at each end of the garden.

Johann Casper Ohlman, the gardener who came so well recommended in 1754 may have had a share in the laying out and care of these fine gardens. Of the house itself, Cutler wrote,

> At the lower end of the aisle is a large summer-house, a long square containing three rooms — the middle paved with marble — hung with landscapes and other pictures. On the right is a very large private library, adorned with very curious carvings. The collection of French and English authors, maps etc. is valuable. The room is furnished with a table, chairs, etc. . . . The room on the left in the summer house, beautifully papered and designed for music, contains a spinet. But the whole garden discovered the desolations of war, and the want of a gardener to dress it. The Marquis de la Fayette took quarters at this house.

A square gable-on-hip roofed building with a doorway topped by a segmental pediment, the house stood on Wapping road until some twenty-five years ago. When it was torn down, the parlor paneling was given to the Metropolitan Museum, where it is now installed in the American wing.

Pl. 81

Pl. 103

Tradition says that the entrance gate posts were surmounted by two fine carved gilded eagles, long since removed. In the mid-nineteenth century, these eagles both served for many years as Thames Street shop signs. One of them may be seen today in the collection of the Historical Society.[42]

Jane Clarke's article, "Metcalf Bowler as a British Spy" published in 1930, proves that Metcalf, though made Chief Justice of the Supreme Court in 1776, never broke his English ties, but used his eminent position to give information against the struggling colonists in the Revolutionary War. Few others engaged in such duplicity, but the loyalist point of view was upheld by many important merchants.[43]

Jewish merchants also came to play an outstanding role in Newport's commercial life. In 1684, when their rights of citizenship were questioned, the General Assembly declared that they might "expect as good protection here as any stranger residing among us in His Majesty's Colony, ought to have, being obedient to His Majesty's law."[44] In return, their mercantile ability proved profitable to the town that afforded them such haven. The traffic in whale oil and candlemaking was largely pushed forward by Jewish merchants, but they entered into other commerce as well.[45] The career of Aaron Lopez may be cited particularly to indicate the degree of success achieved by Newport's Jews.[46]

Lopez, who was to Newport just before the Revolutionary War what Abraham Redwood and Henry Collins had been earlier, arrived with his younger brother David from Portugal in 1752. The history of his mercantile ventures shows uncommon flexibility and an ability to surmount seeming disaster and turn it to advantage. Like some other merchants of his race, he first began business in candlemaking. Within a few years he entered the Bristol trade in which he so overextended his credit that he nearly failed. In time he turned to the West Indian trade. With the aid of Benjamin Wright, his canny Scotch Presbyterian friend and ship's captain, he recovered his losses and evolved a successful trade based on the so-called factor system, whereby after Wright had established himself in the West Indies, he sent itemized orders for saleable wares. Such personally superintended sale and purchase of goods was a marked advance over the older method of hawking cargoes from port to port, and Lopez made his fortune because of his adherence to the factor system.

His vision, adventurous spirit, and personal integrity made his name respected wherever his vessels touched port. The period of his most successful ventures came in the few years of comparative calm after the turbulence of the Stamp Act riots had subsided and before the open hostilities of the Revolutionary War. Together with the Vernon and Champlin families, he was largely responsible for Newport's last golden era of prosperity. Like other patriots he left Newport when the British occupation choked off commercial life. It was on his return journey in 1782 to take up residence in Newport once more that he was accidentally drowned. His death was a heavy blow for a town that had suffered the permanent loss of most of its important citizens: both the patriots, who wanted to avoid life in a British occupied town, and the loyalists, who retired to His Majesty's colonies in Canada or the West Indies.

One of the finest tributes to any Newport citizen was written by Ezra Stiles on the occasion of Aaron Lopez' death.

> On 28th of May died that amiable, benevolent, most hospitable and very respectable Gentleman, Mr. Aaron Lopez Merchant. . . . He was a Jew by Nation, came from Spain or Portugal about 1754 and settled at Rhode Island. He was a merchant of the first Eminence; for Honor and Extent of Commerce probably surpassed by no Merchant in America. He did Business with the greatest Ease and Clearness — always carried about him a Sweetness of Behaviour, a calm Urbanity and an agreeable and unaffected Politeness of Manners. Without a single Enemy and the most universally beloved by an extensive Acquaintance of any man I ever knew. His Beneficence to his Family Connecxions, to his Nation, and to all the World is almost without Parallel. He was my intimate Friend and Acquaintance.[47]

Undoubtedly the character of such men as Aaron Lopez helped not only to push forward mercantile prosperity, but to anneal the peaceful relationship of Quaker, Congregationalist, Anglican, and Jew, which marked Newport society throughout the colonial era.

The lavish aspect of pre-Revolutionary life in Newport was maintained especially by the loyalists and the Church of England families, but Henry Collins belonged to the Sabbatarian faith and even the Quakers went far beyond the tenets of simplicity held out for them. James Birket, as already noted, had complained that he found "the Friends in my opinion . . . as topping as their House."[48] Dean George Berkeley's daughter-in-law reported in her commentary on the Dean's New World visit that

In one thing the various sectaries at Newport, both men and women are all agreed — in a rage for finery, to the great amusement of Berkeley . . . the men in flaming scarlet coats and waistcoats, laced and fringed with brightest glaring yellow. The sly Quakers, not venturing on these charming coats and waistcoats, yet loving finery, figured a way with plate on their sideboards. One . . . sent to England had made on purpose a noble large tea-pot of solid gold, and inquired of the Dean, when drinking tea with him whether Friend Berkeley had ever seen such a curious thing. On being told that silver ones were much in use in England but that he had never seen a gold one, Ebenezer replied "Aye that was the thing — I was resolved to have something finer than anybody else. They say that the Queen has not got one." [49]

In spite of George Berkeley's amusement at the tendency toward display, the list of eminent and gifted men drawn to Newport during these years was an imposing one. When Berkeley himself, then Dean of Derry and later Bishop of Cloyne, arrived in Newport on a January Thursday in 1729 to await funds promised by Parliament with which to establish a college for the training of ministers in Bermuda, he came into an established and aristocratic society. His own serene tolerance and literary capacity left a lasting imprint on the intellectual life of the town. [50] Here, as he wrote to his friend Thomas Prior, he found

four sorts of Anabaptists, besides Presbyterians, Quakers, Independents, and many of no profession at all. Notwithstanding so many differences, here are fewer quarrels about religion than elsewhere, the people living peaceably with their neighbors of whatever persuasion. They all are agreed in one point, that the Church of England is second best. [51]

During his three-year stay in Newport he composed his Plato-like *Alciphron* and the poem *On the Prospect of Planting Arts and Learning in America* which contains the famous line "westward the course of empire takes its way." Berkeley sailed for England in 1732, his hopes for the college dashed when the promised funds were not forthcoming. But his charm and erudition have become legendary in town annals.

Trinity Church had been organized in 1698, by which time Quakers and Jews had been settled in the town for over forty years. Baptists, Sabbatarians, and Congregationalists were all established in their churches, and Rhode Island's heterodox way of life was firmly entrenched. But the new church gathered strength rapidly, and the Scottish Reverend James Honeyman, who had come as clergyman in 1704, was able to report proudly in 1732, that "Betwixt New York and Boston, there is not a congregation in the way of the Church of England, that can compare with mine or equal it in any respect." [52] In time, the church's aristocratic connotations lured many nonmembers like Peter Harrison and William Wanton to its ranks. Its conservative tendencies also helped to sharpen the growing political cleavage between loyalist and patriot.

Because of the town's liberal religious principles, scholarship and theology were understandably marked by a temperateness rare elsewhere in New England. [53] After 1731, the Baptist pulpit was filled by John Callender, whose *Historical Discourse*, written in 1739 for the Centenary of the Founding of the Colony, stands today as an able and important account.

Isaac Touro came to Newport in about 1758 to assume the duties of minister for the Jewish Congregation, and Samuel Hopkins, who had the courage to thunder against slavery while slave ships docked in the harbor below, came in 1770 as a minister for the First Congregational Church.[54] They were both to become life-long friends of the Reverend Dr. Ezra Stiles, who had accepted the call to the Second Congregational Church in 1755, "partly," as he wrote, "because of my friends, especially my father's inclination, partly an agreeable town, and the Redwood Library." [55]

This scholarly theologian, one of the most learned men in the colonies, made a profound contribution to Newport's spiritual and intellectual life. His interests included such diverse matters as the study of Abyssinian geography, raising silkworms, and making astronomical calculations. Besides caring for his own flock and attending many services in the Synagogue and at Dr. Hopkins', he concerned himself with the spiritual welfare of the negroes and found time to write his *Ecclesiastical History of New England and North America*. He fulfilled the duties of Librarian of the Redwood Library for nearly thirty years. He made maps of Newport and New Haven, and visited Dighton Rock to see the inscriptions. He described the Synagogue in detail and his diary is a storehouse of information and commentary. It reflects a mature and considered approach to theology and the ways of other creeds and races, as well as a lively interest in science, history, and the passing events of the day.

"It has been a principle with me for thirty-five years past," he wrote,

> to walk and live in a decent, civil, and respectful communication with all, although in some of our sentiments, in philosophy, religion and politics of diametrically opposite opinion, hence I can freely live and converse in civil friendship with Jews, Romanists, and all the sects of Protestants and even with Deists. I am all along blamed by bigots for this liberality, though I think none impeach me of hypocrisy. I have my own judgment and do not conceal it.[56]

Newport had its share of doctors, lawyers, and men of letters, as well as theologians. Dr. Thomas Moffatt,[57] Peter Harrison's good friend, and the nephew of John Smibert, came soon after Berkeley arrived. An able physician, he was politically one of the Newport loyalists, and his part in publishing the pro-Royalist O.Z. letters in the *Newport Mercury* of the early 1760's helped precipitate the storm provoked by the passage of the Stamp Act in 1765. Dr. William Hunter,[58] also a loyalist, and the father of the three Misses Hunter who were belles in Revolutionary war days, delivered some of the first lectures in anatomy given in the colonies. Dr. Benjamin Waterhouse,[59] mentioned above, born in Newport in 1754, was a physician, naturalist, author, and a professor at Harvard College for thirty years. His letters and writing contain some excellent contemporary information about early Newport citizens. William Ellery,[60] ardent Son of Liberty, practiced law. In 1776 he was elected to the Continental Congress where he later signed the Declaration of Independence.

James Franklin, Benjamin's older brother, came to Newport in 1725. He published the first newspaper in Rhode Island, the *Rhode Island Gazette*, which appeared for a short time after 1732. Mr. Lawrence Wroth, Librarian of the John Carter Brown Library, has established the fact that he was an engraver as well as a printer, and that he probably designed and engraved the beautiful old state seal owned by the press.[61] It appeared on official documents as early as 1733.

After Franklin's death in 1734, his widow Ann ran the printing press, housed in the basement of the town school which stood in the middle of the Mall until about 1780. She thus became the first woman printer in the colonies.[62] Benjamin Franklin continued to visit Newport in his capacity of Postal Official long after his brother's death, while in 1758 James, Jr. established the *Newport Mercury*, which has continued without break (except for three years during the Revolution) until the present day.

William Claggett,[63] Newport clockmaker, who, as mentioned above, lived in the house now numbered 16 Bridge Street and who made the clock which has ticked on the walls of the Sabbatarian Meeting House since 1731, also conducted early experiments in electrical phenomena. He staged several well advertised demonstrations in Boston in the year of 1746.[64]

The list of painters associated with Newport is an important one.[65] Gilbert Stuart, born the son of a snuff grinder in South Country, spent his youthful years in Newport, where he received his early training in art and at the age of thirteen painted "Dr. Hunter's dogs," his first known commission.[66] He painted two portraits of Abraham Touro, and his portrait of Abraham Redwood hangs in the Redwood Library. His self portrait was done in his Newport days.[67]

John Smibert arrived in Newport in 1729 on the ship which brought Dean Berkeley. He painted a number of Newport and Narragansett notables, including Dean Berkeley and his entourage, and Dr. McSparren, the Rector of the Narragansett Church and his wife.[68] Nathaniel Smibert painted portraits of Peter Harrison and his wife, Elizabeth Pelham Harrison.[69] Robert Feke, described by Dr. Alexander Hamilton as having "the perfect phizz of a painter," painted under the patronage of Henry Collins and produced portraits of the Reverend Mr. Callender, the Reverend Mr. Hiscox, Ebenezer Flagg, and Mary Ward Flagg, as well as of Henry Collins himself.[70] Ezra Stiles and his wife "sat" to Samuel King.[71] Cosmo Alexander, who painted the portrait of Dr. Manning, first President of Brown University, now hanging in Sayles Hall, lived in Newport a number of years.[72] Washington Allston was a pupil of King's when he lived on Clarke street while attending Clarke Street's Academy.[73] The miniaturist, Edward Green Malbone, was born and brought up in Newport.[74]

Newport craftsmen were also justly celebrated. The cabinet makers of the eighteenth century not only furnished the homes of the wealthy merchants with mahogany desks, chests of drawers, teaboards, chairs, and made maple desks for Newport's vessels, but exported furniture to Charleston and the West Indies as well.[75] At least fourteen members of the Townsend family engaged in fine cabinet making. Christopher, Job, Edmund, Thomas, and John Townsend all had houses and shops on Easton's Point.[76] John Goddard, who learned

f

Pl. 9

Pl. 7

his craft from Job Townsend and who perfected the "block front" design,[77] had a house and shop at Washington and Willow street. In later years his son, Thomas Goddard, carried on the same business there. In the early nineteenth century Holmes Weaver also lived and worked in this "furniture maker's center," as the Point section came to be known. These craftsmen take their place beside the best cabinet makers of New York and Philadelphia.

The work of the silversmiths of Newport, Arnold Collins, Samuel Vernon, Jonathan Clarke, Jonathan Otis, Benjamin Brenton, Thomas Arnold, William Hookey (whose house still stands at No. 6 Coddington Street), and Nicholas Geoffroy attest the perfection which local artisans achieved in this craft.[78] During all these years, the taste and appreciation of the employer, whether private individual or public committee, was consistently comparable to the taste and training of the skilled craftsman and artist. The resulting universal standard of craftsmanship and style was partly responsible for the synthesis and integration which characterized the eighteenth-century achievement in the arts: painting, the crafts, and architecture. Newport now emerged, not only as an important center of commerce, but also as an intellectual, artistic, and aristocratic colonial center.

---

a Newport's commercial enterprises were extraordinarily varied. It is more exact to say "Part of Newport's wealth was garnered in the African trade," etc.

b Demolished after 1952.

c Dunham (called Dunbar by Redwood) was also laying out Redwood Gardens in 1765. A letter in the Redwood Papers in the Newport Historical Society indicates that he came to Redwood through the good offices of Richard and Thomas Oliver, merchants. Redwood, in writing to his "Esteemed Friends" on June 9, 1765, reports: "And now I must say something in praise of my Gardner Charles *Dunbar* who you sent me. I think he understands his business and he is very well contented and satisfied, (And I think I shall have as handsome a garden of two acres as any in Rhode Island when it is finished)."

The summer house was built in 1766, evidently part of this same garden plan because Abraham Redwood, Jr., writing to his father from London on November 19, 1766, says: "I hope you will finish the summer house soon. I flatter myself that I shall spend many agreeable hours with my Father in that pleasant and happy situation." He adds a postcript, "I hope your espalier trees grow well, suppose they will bare this summer."

N. H. S. Abraham Redwood Letters 1756-1773 Vault A #647 page 58.)

d Godfrey Malbone also furnished the sandstone for the trim of the Colony House.

e Recently moved to Bridge Street west of Second.

f Used as the headpiece for the Introduction, page 3.

CHAPTER FOUR

Richard Munday's Era

THE TRANSITION FROM GOTHIC TO BAROQUE. When John Mumford made his map in 1712, a few of the new houses in the Newport that had "grown to the admiration of all and was the Metropolitan" had begun to reflect a consciousness of the seventeenth-century baroque architecture of Wren's day. Newport builders now, as elsewhere in the colonies, showed a tendency to eschew their native English Gothic traditions and to turn to the more formal and classic models which had in turn been imported to England from Italy nearly a hundred years earlier.

The new point of view had little in common with Gothic building. Henceforward structural elements were to be minimized and concealed; buildings were to be conceived in terms of simple rectangular symmetrical masses, with flat roofs and level cornices, designed to have a center of interest and decorated at focal points with detail drawn from a classic repertoire of ever increasing correctness. This is the basic concept of our eighteenth-century style, and this concept not only remained constant throughout the colonial period, but continued into the nineteenth century. The resulting long and unified tradition explains the integrity and consistency of our colonial and early republican building.

The buildings put up in the first two decades of the eighteenth century formed in a real sense a bridge between the Gothic and the classic points of view. The massive framed construction typical of the seventeenth century still survived, and houses were built with small cramped stairways, great fireplaces, and steeply pitched roofs, whether gable, gambrel, or hipped. But grafted on to the medieval structure were ornamented doorways, a few sash windows, and cornices of classic profile. Inside, the big structural beams, still too large to be enclosed in the walls, were cased with thin boards, beaded at the corners. Paneled work of huge scale decorated walls once sheathed or left plain. Drawn from the repertoire used by seventeenth-century English builders, and scaled not for small colonial dwellings but for English baronial halls, this paneling and molding possessed the same massive quality that

49

the houses had. In common with Jacobean and late Stuart work, the ornamentation tended to be broken up into small sections of complicated shape and outline. When classic details were used, they were somewhat awkwardly handled. In time, however, the structural elements became reduced in size, the scale of the paneled work was made correspondingly lighter, and the archaic character disappeared.

Most of the outstanding buildings of these years, like the first Trinity Church, have been lost, but records and pictures give the character of the style, and a number of small houses retain some of the old and transitional features.

The congregation of Trinity Church had been organized in 1698 by Francis Nicholson, Lieutenant Governor of New York, and later Governor of Virginia and Maryland.[1] In 1702 the Reverend Lockyer wrote to the Society for the Propagation of the Gospel in Foreign Parts that "the place wherein we meet to worship is finished on the outside, all but the steeple, which we will get up as soon as we are able; the inside is pew'd well altho' not beautified." This building was removed when the second Trinity Church was built and little is known of its appearance except, as the Reverend Lockyer reported, it was designed to have a steeple. Mr. Norman Isham has reconstructed it in the more current English manner as a pitched roofed building with a square tower and spire at the front, like the first King's Chapel in Boston shown in the headpiece for this chapter.[2] So built, it would contrast sharply with the still Gothic and turreted Quaker Meeting House of just two years earlier.

Pl. 21 Little is known of the other public buildings or meeting houses other than where they stood, occasional records of dimensions, and the fact that the first Barney Street Sabbatarian Meeting House of 1706, a plain pitched roof building 17 x 20 feet, was built with casement windows, which were in common use until about 1720.[3] When Job Bennett bought the adjoining land in 1711, he agreed that "the window lights and casements of the said meeting house shall not forever after be disturbed, annoyed, fastened up, shaded or darkened." [4]

As has been said above, the dwelling houses that went up in these two or three decades were characterized by their seventeenth-century construction and archaic classic detail. Chimneys, now almost universally built of brick, were massive and, until after 1720, often finished at the top with pilasters. Although end-chimney houses were very common, it had become less usual to construct the chimney so that it was exposed on the exterior as part of the finished house wall. The gable, gambrel, or high hipped roofs, the three most typical forms, were still steeply pitched. They were often further distinguished by their wide overhangs carried across the front of the house in projections of as much as three feet. When the roof was hipped, the overhang was carried around all four sides. These wide overhangs were boxed back to the house wall with flat boards and were finished by bed moldings of classic profile which also formed the upper window caps.

Most of the Newport houses with wide overhanging cornices can be dated before 1730, some before 1720. There are many of them and they are in part responsible for the antique appearance of Newport's streets. Division Street has four, two of which are very wide, while there are several on Broadway and more on Thames. The Phillips House at 42 Elm and the David Huntington house at 43 Elm, the latter probably standing in 1719, both have very wide ones, as does the little house at 78 Burnside Avenue.

The use of plaster-coved cornices, to be more fully discussed in connection with the Wanton-Lyman-Hazard house (built, probably, by Stephen Mumford between 1690 and 1700), showed a desire to fill in the sharp angle produced by the wide overhang above the vertical wall and to give the effect of a classic cornice. Abraham Redwood's great gambrel-roofed summer home in Portsmouth, which was not built until 1743,[5] also had a coved cornice, but most of them were earlier.[6]

Pls. 29, 31

Some doorways were now ornamented with classic detail, but many of them were still plain, topped with moldings similar to but heavier than the ones used for the window caps. Sometimes a row of small transom lights set in leaded glass were inserted above the door to let in a little hall light. When a classic order was used to decorate the doorway, the flanking pilasters were apt to be set on high pedestals, a treatment customary until about 1750. Doors were finished either with or without pediments, but the pediment with a high and flat segmental curve was a favorite form.

Sash windows began to supplant the earlier casement windows about 1720.[7] The first ones were narrow and high, framed together, and capped with the same moldings used for the interior ceiling cornices. Windows in Newport took on squarer proportions earlier than they did elsewhere in Rhode Island. The upper windows were invariably set directly under the eaves and were capped by the eaves' cornice which broke out around them. In the same way, the heavy square blocks of the first modillion cornices were broken out around the upper windows. The sashes themselves were filled with small 4″ x 6″ or 5″ x 7″ panes of glass set in heavy muntins.

Walls were shingled or clapboarded (sometimes both were used in the same house) and then they were finished at the corners with vertical corner boards. The early shingles were hand-split and were applied to the wall with a very long lap. Early clapboards were hand-riven out of the quarter log of wood. They were feathered off and lapped over at the end joins, fastened with large-headed wrought iron clapboard nails and often applied to the house wall closer together at the bottom than at the top. The irregularities of hand-worked shingles and clapboards catch the light. The resulting charm of surface, together with the strong pattern produced by the small-paned heavily framed windows, the big chimneys, and the high overhanging roof lines, gives these early houses much of their characteristic appeal.

The gambrel-roofed house at 56 Farewell Street, known as the Shaw house, partly built about 1710 and once owned by the Walter Challoner who gave the town records to the British when they evacuated the city in 1779, has such exposed cased beams. There are many others, but after 1720, the summer beams were generally framed into the top part of the

Pl. 30

girts, and the ceilings dropped below them. The kitchen fireplaces where the cooking went on were still very large, but the brick side walls were no longer always rounded, as in the Wanton-Lyman-Hazard house. They were more apt to be splayed or even almost rectangular; the upper part of the back wall was frequently recessed three or four inches to form a ledge about two feet above the hearth level. The parlor fireplaces were also large and often finished with enormous bolection moldings.[8]

The dome-shaped ovens seemed to keep their old inconvenient location on the backwall of the kitchen fireplace until near the middle of the century. There are still a great many of them in the old houses of Newport, and a few, like the ones in the George Gibbs house at 9 Chestnut Street, have their original iron doors. This house was probably built soon after the lot was purchased in 1729 by Abraham Borden. George Gibbs, who owned the property later, willed the house to his wife in 1755.

The house that Thomas Richardson built in 1715 on Thames Street near Marlborough [9] soon after he married Sarah Robinson illustrated better than any other house in Newport the combination of the old heavy seventeenth-century construction, the heavy scaled archaic paneling and the large run moldings used to decorate the mantels and stairway. Unfortu-

Pls. 39–42

nately for the study of the style of these few transitional years, the house was torn down in 1940, but it had been measured by the Historic American Buildings Survey, and old photographs help tell the story of its appearance. Built on a five-room, central-chimney plan, the structural evidence indicated that it originally had a steeply pitched gable roof. This had been changed long ago for one of slightly lowered gambrel form. The enormous brick chimney was pilastered at the top, just as were the chimneys of an earlier day. The two remaining fireplaces were mammoth and were constructed with rounded side walls like those commonly found in early brick chimney construction.

Pl. 42

One of the most interesting features of the house was the treatment of the fireplace walls. These were finished with raised paneling framed by the huge bolection moldings much in use in England during the last years of the seventeenth century. The fireplace surrounds, made up of this molding mitred at the corners, were almost twelve inches across. As we have seen, moldings made on such a large scale appeared only for a few years and were used for the very earliest paneled work produced in the colonies. Thomas Richardson's house was one of the few known in Rhode Island to have had such paneling.

The stairs were set in the accepted position in a cramped central entry in front of the chimney. They were built in three short turns fitted with the wedge-shaped steps commonly used to make them swing around the two intermediate posts, and they were finished with

Pl. 41

flat balusters sawn out to an S-shape. This S-shape was a popular design for balusters until about 1725, and six or seven houses in Newport as well as Adam Mott's house in Portsmouth all have stairs with sawn S-shaped balusters. The closed string course which took the balusters was decorated with a very large cove molding.

As in the Hazard house, half balusters butted against the plain square posts, and the straight hand rail, which was framed directly into the posts, was molded in the early fashion only on the outer face. The newel caps and the drops had been removed, but typical newel caps were ball shaped, simply turned and slightly flattened. The early drops were heavy, plain, and shaped like acorns. All these features were common, with slight variations, to the stairs of the first twenty-five years of the century.[10]

The back stairway of the Augustus Lucas house at 40 Division Street has sawn S-shaped balusters and a molded boxed string course. Because such staircases were considered more suitable for the front of the house, it is probable that this one may belong to a house built soon after Lucas bought the land in 1713,[11] and that it was converted into the rear staircase when extensive additions were made in about 1740. Old wall painting in an Indian red diamond design on a dark ground is still visible on the garret stair wall. It resembles the painting in the ell of the Wanton-Lyman-Hazard house.

Recently studied deeds prove that at least part of the old Pitt's Head tavern, now located at 5 Charles Street, was standing in 1726 when John Clarke, mariner, sold his land and a dwelling house to Captain Jonathan Chace. The stairway, which has been carefully returned to its original appearance by John Perkins Brown, has sawn S-shaped balusters, but the string course is finished with paneling instead of the heavy run moldings noted above.

The stairway of the Wanton-Lyman-Hazard house, with its squat turned balusters set in a string course finished with a large cyma molding and the stairs of the old Taggart house built circa 1708, part of which was moved in the early nineteenth century to Green End Avenue, are discussed in the Appendix. They show that early eighteenth-century builders used turned balusters as well as sawn.

The houses of these few years, then, are marked with certain characteristics found at no other time. Soon after 1720, their wide overhanging cornices, the pilastered brick chimneys, the heavy cased structural timbers, and the colossal scale and archaic detail of the molded and paneled work all tended to disappear.

By 1758, when Ezra Stiles was pacing out his map, the transformation was nearly completed and Newport had changed from a medieval-looking colony of steep pitched roofs, turrets, and overhanging cornices to an urban center with spired churches and balconied public buildings. Broad gambrel or gable-on-hip roofed mansions with pedimented doorways, dormer windows, and cupolas, stood in state behind fine brick walls pierced by wrought iron gates in gardens filled with rare trees and plants imported from France, the Indies, or England.

Richard Munday's Trinity Church, inspired by Sir Christopher Wren, had been standing for thirty-two years; his red brick and freestone trimmed Colony House, for nineteen. The new town school house with its cupola had taken its place in the center of the Mall since

Pl. 45

Pl. 44

Pls. 34–35

Pl. 47

Pls. 4, 48–56

Pls. 5, 63–70

1733, and the Second Baptist church had already been enlarged once. The "proper and proportionate" spires of Cotton Palmer's Mill Street and his Clarke Street Congregational Churches had made, together with Trinity's spire, three tall landmarks to greet Newport-bound ships for a quarter of a century past. Harrison's Redwood Library, a correctly classic Roman Doric temple, presaging the severely academic architectural concepts yet to come, had been standing at the head of Mill Street since 1748, nearly forty years ahead of its time.

Each new building that had gone up had been fresh proof of the desire on the part of the citizens to improve the appearance of the prospering town, as well as to meet its immediate physical needs. To accomplish this aim, the architects and the committees, still impressed by Wren's London buildings after the fire of 1666, adapted in wood and on a somewhat smaller scale the designs of Wren and the later work of Queen Anne's time. But the tastes of a wealthy seafaring merchant society stamped these new buildings with a provincial and matter-of-fact, almost burgher lavishness. Newport building, like Newport furniture, now developed a quality of intrinsic richness wherein the ornament became an inseparable part of the whole.

ECCLESIASTICAL BUILDING. The most important single factor in the universal acceptance of the English baroque style in the colonies was the influence of the Society for the Propagation of the Gospel in Foreign Parts.[12] Dissenting churches had broken with the forms as well as the faith of the Episcopal Church. When the Church of England became established toward the end of the seventeenth century, it brought with it all its cherished formal religious traditions, both spiritual and physical. The New World Church of England buildings were almost invariably the first to reflect London's churches of Wren's time.

Trinity Church. By 1725, the first Trinity Church building of 1702 had been outgrown. The little church, which had "been pew'd well but not beautified" and was to have had a steeple, was given to a congregation in Warwick. Although it disappeared from Newport, it seems never to have arrived at its destination, and its fate is unknown.[13] In 1726, the Reverend James Honeyman wrote the Society that the new church "is well nigh finished and will be ready for the Society's present as soon as it can be sent." [14]

The second Trinity Church, one of the first Newport buildings to embrace fully the baroque forms which were to stamp Newport architecture for the next twenty-five years was without doubt built by Richard Munday. Constructed on a plain rectangular plan, covered with a pitched roof and lit by two tiers of circular-headed windows, its pedimented main entrance was set in the traditional place in the square tower at the west end of the church.

Its design was proof of the close liaison between the Anglican churches of the colonies and London. Munday and the committee clearly turned for inspiration to the recently completed Christ Church (Old North) in Boston, the plans for which have been ascribed to Wil-

Pl. 61

Pls. 104, 105

Pls. 48–56

liam Price, Boston print dealer and book seller. But Isham in his careful and authoritative monograph on Trinity Church has come to the conclusion that Price served in his capacity of print dealer to procure rather than to draw the plans. He suggests the possibility that Christ Church (and Trinity) may have been built from plans "in some way secured," drawn by Wren himself, perhaps for a church like St. Anne, Blackfriar's, which was designed but never rebuilt after the London fire of 1666.[15] Students today consider it unlikely that the plans were acquired in this fashion, but the fact remains that Christ Church and Trinity are closely allied to Wren's London churches, and that the Society for the Propagation of the Gospel in Foreign Parts was in a position to offer its colonial builders material aid in the selection of their new church plans.

The system of superimposed piers which forms the basis of the interior design of Christ Church was also employed in Trinity. It resembles such Wren churches as St. Stephens Holborn and St. Andrews Wardrobe and does not appear elsewhere in colonial building. The fine wooden steeple, composed of a square tower, arcaded belfry, a lantern, and a slender spire, was modeled after the original spire of Christ Church and both were derived from the spire of Wren's St. Lawrence Jewry. Trinity spire was designed in 1726, but it was not actually put up until 1741, and in 1768, when found to be defective, it was taken down, although it was rebuilt soon after along the old lines. In spite of such a history, it is now earlier in character than its Christ Church model, which was completely rebuilt by Charles Bulfinch in 1807. Newport thus possesses a fine colonial spire, one of the few left of the type being built before 1740.

In 1762 the church, originally of five bays, was cut apart and lengthened two bays. A study of the molding details, the paneling, and the orders used in Trinity makes clear the somewhat naive divergence from the established classic norm. Where Peter Harrison's use of the orders was to be correct and academic, as found in the pages of the architectural books he owned, there were as yet few books available when Trinity was built. This lack would help to explain the fact that the system of proportion and the combination of parts for the pilasters, pediments, piers, entablatures, and cornices found in Trinity Church varied enough from the forms of Sir Christopher Wren to make a system of their own, at once archaic and fresh, entirely suited to the wood of which they were built. In spite of this divergence, the raised paneling used for the gallery breasts, like a signature for Newport work of the second quarter of the century, harks back to English seventeenth-century work.[16] So also does the Jacobean "Union Jack" paneling under the warden's pew, which is repeated in the Sabbatarian Meeting House for the paneling under the sounding board, and appears again under the balcony of the Colony House.

Some of the interior furnishings are worthy of note. The triple deck wine-glass pulpit, composed of preaching desk, reading desk, and clerk's desk, is unique in colonial building. Its position in the center aisle is also most unusual, since the normal place for the pulpit is

Pl. 55

b

against a side wall of the church, with the east end and central aisle left clear for the communion service. Isham could find no evidence that the location of the pulpit, with its fine sounding board above, had been changed, however, and came to the conclusion that for some reason it had probably always stood in the center aisle. The pupit stairs, with their thin turned balusters and single flight seem weak in comparison with the beautiful stairs in the Sabbatarian Meeting House.[17] They may have been changed, since Mason, in his *Annals of Trinity Church*, speaks of the "twisted balusters" of the stairs leading to the pulpit,[18] and according to notes left by Miss Edith Powel, the original stairs to the organ loft had twisted balusters.[19]

The organ, signed by Robert Bridges, London, and dated 1733, was a present from Dean George Berkeley. He sent it to Trinity on his return to England in 1732, after his three-year stay in Middletown. It has been a traditional story that it was first sent as a present to the Congregational Church in Berkeley, Massachusetts, the town named in his honor, but that the selectmen there voted that "an organ is an instrument of the devil for the entrapping of men's souls" and refused the gift, whereupon it was offered to Trinity. Mr. W. King Covell, who has written an excellent account of the organs of Trinity Church,[20] has discounted this story. Trinity had a prior claim on Berkeley's affection, and the dates of the making of the organ and of its arrival in Newport are too close together to allow for an intermediate journey to Berkeley, Massachusetts. The original case is still almost unchanged, but the first organ has been enlarged and finally removed. The present organ was installed in 1929.

Historically, Trinity has played an important part in Newport annals. Here Dr. Brett, Dr. Moffatt, Martin Howard, the Bulls, Ellerys, Malbones, Cranstons, and Vernons came to worship. Here George Washington is supposed to have attended divine service in 1781, and Admiral DeTernay, Commander of the French Forces, who suffered his last illness in the Hunter house on the Point, lies buried in the churchyard. The Bishop's Mitre which served as its weathervane saved the building from vandalism during the British occupation of Newport in the Revolutionary war.[21] Isham's fine restoration of 1936 has brought the building back to its ancient appearance of a wooden colonial church with wine-glass pulpit, sounding board, and box pews all in place, built as Isham has said, by "a man who seemingly had first-hand knowledge of Wren's work."

It is fitting that Trinity, as Newport's first important eighteenth-century building, was the first to be erected by a man whose name is known. The increased importance of the designer was concomitant with the changing approach to architecture. The housewrights and carpenters of the seventeenth century had been anonymous workmen who did not design buildings, but put them up according to traditional usage. They were "joyners," and if we have learned the names of some of them, we have most often found them not in connection with the houses they built, but in the records of their court proceedings and their land transactions, where it was customary to designate a man's occupation.

Only in the eighteenth century, when the design of the building came to be considered apart from the building itself, did one man occasionally gain eminence over others as a drawer of plans or an architect. Even so, he kept his old status as a carpenter or a master builder. The architect *per se* did not begin to emerge as a man apart, with a professional standing, until the later years of the eighteenth century.[22]

Richard Munday called himself house carpenter and innkeeper. We know that he was responsible for the building of Trinity Church, not because he was heralded as its architect or even its master builder, but rather because of the frequent appearance of his name in the Church records.[23] For many years, the proof that he worked on the new Colony House at all was a claim put in by his widow for his unpaid fee. A mass of papers and bills pertaining to the building of the Colony House have recently been found in the State Archives by Miss Mary Quinn and studied by Mr. John H. Greene.[24] Among these papers, one allotted Richard Munday £ 25 for "draughting a plan." Thus, two hundred years later, and because of the survival of a slip of paper, Richard Munday is established beyond doubt as Newport's first named architect-builder.

What little is known of Munday's life has been published by Isham in his study of *Trinity Church*. He was living in Newport in 1713 when he married Martha Simons. In 1719 he renewed his license to keep a tavern and when he bought a house in 1721, he called himself "house carpenter" on the deed. A year later he was admitted as a freeman. He was a member of Trinity and was given pew 75, probably in payment for his architectural services.

In 1725, when he built Trinity, Munday had been living in Newport at least twelve years. Although his name has never been connected with an earlier building, it is safe to assume he must have established his reputation before receiving such an important commission. He may have built some of Newport's first fine houses, like the Jahleel Brenton house of 1720, or the John Gidley house of 1724. He is credited with building Godfrey Malbone's town house, and his name has been connected with the Sabbatarian Meeting House of 1729, although there is no documentary proof to verify the claim.

The Sabbatarian Meeting House.[25] The first meeting place of the Sabbatarians had been at Green End, about a mile north of Newport proper. In 1706 they built their Newport Meeting House east of Spring on Barney Street on the land given them by Arnold Collins. This first little house was only 17 x 20 feet, and by 1729 it had been outgrown, whereupon Jonathan Weeden and Henry Collins were selected to raise money and to see to the erection of a larger building.

The new church, a plain two-story clapboarded building still only 36 x 26 feet, was of meeting-house plan, with the door on the long side and the pulpit opposite. It was towerless

Pls. 56–60

and covered with a pitched roof, but its plain exterior belied the interior which, although small, compared with Trinity for richness of finish, and attested the completeness with which a dissenting congregation had adopted the style of the new Episcopal churches. The detail resembles that of Trinity closely. Galleries with fronts of raised paneling extend around three sides of the room, while the fourth side is given over to the wine-glass pulpit with its paneled sounding board above. The stairway leading to the pulpit is one of the earliest in Newport to have the twisted balusters which were to appear almost universally in the finest houses built in the next two decades.

Pl. 59

It has already been remarked that the "Union Jack" paneling under the sounding board is baroque in spirit and repeats that of the warden's pew in Trinity Church and the balcony of the Colony House. The round-headed panels on the pulpit front occur on Trinity pulpit and on the stair soffits of the Jonathan Nichols house. They are characteristic features of the late Stuart paneling used in the first half of the eighteenth century.

Pl. 58

Although the ceiling is slightly arched, this classic effect masks an archaic construction, since the curve is formed by ceiling timbers curved to shape and tenoned together in the center. This treatment caused the walls to spread so much that it has been necessary to insert tie rods to keep them in place.[26]

In the course of time, a few interior changes have been made. The walls were originally sheathed below the chair rail with three plain horizontal boards. When the old square pews were taken apart in the nineteenth century, they were used to make the present wainscotting. The piers which support the gallery were put in between 1864 and 1869, and, as first built, the gallery stairs rose from the corner in three runs instead of the present two flights.

Some of the furnishings are worthy of note. Besides the clock made by William Claggett in 1731 which still ticks in its place on the gallery front opposite the pulpit, a three-piece communion service was provided for by Hannah Martin in 1750. The silver chalice was made by Nicholas Geoffroy, Newport silversmith, and the flagon and plate of pewter were made by Calder. The scroll with the Ten Commandments was given by John Tanner in 1773.

The Sabbatarian Meeting House, like Trinity, has had important names linked with its history. As mentioned above, the land for the first church was given by Arnold Collins, silversmith, and his son Henry Collins was responsible for the second. The Reverend William Hiscox, whose portrait was painted by Robert Feke on commission of Henry Collins, was an early pastor, and Richard Ward, Governor of the Colony of 1740, belonged to the meeting. Ezra Stiles preached to his congregation there while his own meeting house was serving as a hospital for the French soldiers.

After the Sabbatarians disbanded in 1835, the little building was put to varied uses, and in 1884, when it was transferred to the Newport Historical Society, it was moved from Barney Street to Touro where it served as the Society rooms for eighteen years. In 1915 it was moved to its present position and cased in brick. When the new Historical Society building was put up, the Sabbatarian Meeting House was freed of its encumbering collections. Once again it stands, except for the lost square pews and the brick casing, as an early eighteenth-century dissenting meeting house, bearing the stamp of Richard Munday's style.[27]

Trinity Church, the Sabbatarian Meeting House, and Godfrey Malbone's town house were all built before Munday removed to Bristol in 1731, presumably to construct the galleries of St. Michael's.[28] Eight years passed before his name was mentioned in Newport again.

The First and Second Congregational Churches. In the meantime Cotton Palmer, listed in the church records as "of Taunton" was called to Newport in 1729 to design the new First Congregational Church on Mill Street which was to replace the original Tanner Street church of 1696. The frame of the new church was apparently made in Taunton because there is a record that the bill for its cartage was paid.[29]

Pl. 61

Six years later Palmer, this time recorded as living in Providence, was asked by the Second Congregational Society to build its meeting house on Clarke Street, "to be 62 feet long 42 broad 26 between joints with a proper and proportionate spire." [30] Both of these buildings are still standing, but so much altered that old photographs and the 1740 View of Newport give better information of their early appearance. The latter shows that, although handled simply, these churches, like Trinity, were built with towers and spires placed at the gable end, but like the Sabbatarian Meeting House, their main entrances adorned with pedimented doorways opened in the middle of the long side opposite the pulpit. The handsome doorway with its segmental pediment and carved foliage now on the balcony of the Mill Street church is probably the original western door. An 1816 plat of pews for the Clarke Street church shows the typical side entry arrangement. In other words, although they followed the current architectural trend, these churches retained the "preaching house" plan of the dissenting meeting houses.

Pl. 61

Pl. 62

The vicissitudes of time have wrought sorry change in both these buildings. The Mill Street church where Dr. Hopkins preached, was used as a barracks for the British 29th regiment during the British occupation of 1776–1779. Later it served as a hospital for the French forces. In the course of these years, the pulpit vanished and the interior was so badly damaged that it was never entirely put to rights. The spire itself was taken down in 1832, and in 1910, when the church was finally disbanded, the corner stone with its legend "For Christ and Peace" was removed to the Parish house of the United Congregational Church.[31]

The land for the Clarke Street church was purchased in 1733. Two years later Palmer was engaged to build the meeting house.[32] In 1755 Ezra Stiles accepted the Newport call where he preached for the following sixteen years, and from that day until long after the Revolutionary war the Clarke Street church was known as "Dr. Stiles meeting house." In 1776, the troubled events of the war depleted the congregation to the point where it had to be dismissed, and a few months later Dr. Stiles took sorrowful leave of his beloved Newport for

Dighton. Although he was elected President of Yale University in 1777, he could not bring himself to sever his Newport connection until 1786, nearly ten years later.

Like the First Congregational Church, Dr. Stiles' Meeting House fared badly during the war. It too served as a barracks for the three years of the British occupation, during which time the old square pews were burned for fuel, and the bell of 1740 was removed. It was used as a hospital by the French during the year they were in Newport, and it emerged from the ordeals of war so badly damaged that it could not be used for meetings without extensive repairs. These were undertaken and completed in 1785 at which time "the whole inside was entirely and elegantly rebuilt." The following year the Reverend Dr. Patten was called to the pastorate.

Pl. 62

When the Central Baptist Society bought the building in 1847, they made extensive changes which included lengthening the house to ninety-three feet and enclosing the tower in the body of the church. They also added Greek Revival exterior and interior detail, but Cotton Palmer's spire above the tower remained untouched, and a view of Clarke Street made by J. A. Williams before 1874 shows it still unchanged. In 1874–1875 wings were added and Victorian detail was encrusted on the façade and spire, although the basic lines of the original spire were kept until it was taken down in 1946, leaving the present ungainly stump. The building is now owned by the Catholic Church.

Cotton Palmer's two Newport churches have suffered a steady loss of dignity and character, but they nonetheless have a rightful place in the study of Newport's first expansive period of building. They are the only structures of this era known to have been built by an "outside" architect. Richard Munday, as a member of the Church of England, was evidently not in line for a commission from the Congregationalists, who turned to a member of their own flock, albeit from out of town, to build their new meeting houses for them.

Pls. 71, 82, 83

PUBLIC BUILDING. Richard Munday had returned to Newport by 1739. In that year he designed the Colony House, built Stephen Ayrault's house in partnership with Benjamin Wyatt, and according to tradition drew up plans for Godfrey Malbone's country seat near Miantonomi Hill.

Pls. 63–70

The new Colony House, the last of Newport's public buildings to reflect the work of Queen Anne's day, replaced (as we have said) the earlier wooden one of 1687. The council voted that it was to be built of brick "consisting of eighty feet in length and forty in breadth and thirty feet stud, the length thereof to stand near or quite north and south." The building committee consisted of Peter Bours, Ezbon Sanford, George Goulding, and George Wanton.[33]

Conceived as a plain rectangular building with rusticated freestone belt course, window frames and quoins set on a rusticated basement, it is designed with a strong central section accented by a cupola, segmental headed dormers, a truncated gable, and a balcony. The long line of the roof, cut off to make a flat deck, complements the almost brusque character of the flat topped gable. It imparts the same unacademic air to the building that the broad gambrel roofs give to the mid-eighteenth-century mansions along the waterside.

The focal point of the design, the balcony, finished with its balustrade of twisted balusters, resembles that of the Hancock house in Boston, built in 1737. The fine doorway, with its broken pediment enriched by the swirl of carved foliage repeats the form used by Cotton Palmer for the Mill Street church of 1729, and it exemplifies the strong baroque feeling for lavish detail evident in most Newport work of these years.

Like Malbone's town house, the Colony House was built of brick. Mrs. E. Maitland Armstrong has recently given the Newport Historical Society a letter written to Abraham Redwood by his agent Stephen Greenleaf dated Boston, July 3, 1740. It reports a "cask of ale just arrived from Bristol," and says further: "The sloop sails this day youl hear of her by Mr. Bours to whom have shipped Bricks for the Colony House." The Colony House bricks may have come as ballast from Bristol or have been made in Boston. They clearly did not come from Newport.

The very choice of the brick at once sets the building apart from its predecessors. Brick was never commonly used in Newport. In 1750, James Birket wrote, "Newport is . . . all of wood (except the Statehouse and one of Capt. Malbone's which are of brick)." [34] There were still only six brick buildings at the beginning of the Revolution, and generally speaking, colonial Newport was a town of wood. But Sir Christopher Wren often used brick trimmed with free stone, and its use here suggests the manor houses of Wren's time. This combination sometimes had a Dutch air which, in the case of the Colony House, was remarked upon by Henry James in his nostalgic description of an "edifice ample, majestic, of the finest proportions and full of a certain public Dutch dignity, having brave, broad high windows, in especial the distinctness of whose innumerable square white framed panes is the recall of some street view of Harlem or Leyden." [35] Some hundred and fifty years earlier, Dr. Alexander Hamilton, visiting Malbone Hall in 1744, the year it was finished, described that mansion in less mellow terms. "This house makes a grand show at a distance," he wrote, "but it is not extraordinary for architecture, being a clumsy Dutch model." [36]

Although it has been suggested that the scale of the Colony House is somewhat domestic, the design is fresh and original, a fitting one for the colony's imposing new civic building. The interior, which had been much altered, was partially restored by Norman M. Isham in 1917.[37] At this time the fine lower hall with its single row of square Doric columns, set on high pedestals and finished by entablatures, was cleared of the many cluttering partitions built in the nineteenth century. These central columns were originally finished from the natural tree trunks and were cased after the Revolutionary war, probably during repairs made in 1784. Upstairs, the three rooms of Munday's design, the Council Chamber, the Middle Room, and the Chamber of Deputies have not been restored to their original propor-

Pl. 67

Pl. 68

tions, but the old lines of the Council Chamber can easily be traced. This room is paneled from floor to ceiling with raised paneling "subdivided by pilasters of the Corinthian order set on high pedestals and doubled and mitred at the corners." The double curved tops of the panels have a Regency flavor, and the whole combines to make one of the finest colonial rooms still in existence.

Pl. 69

The building was used as a barracks during the British occupation and then as a hospital while the French were in Newport. It was so badly damaged that in 1781 the courts and assembly had to meet in the synagogue. In 1784, Joseph Nightingale, Esek Hopkins, and Daniel Mason, appointed to report repairs needed, recommended that the Council Chamber (south room) have the wainscot and wooden work repaired, and that it "would be proper to paint it of a light stone colour." [38] Since the wood had much darkened, this suggests that the paneling had been left unpainted until then. The committee also recommended that the north room be enlarged by "removing the Partition to the First Beam South of the Present Partition," and that it be filled with proper seats, and the "Wainscotting and wooden work be thoroughly repaired and painted as the Council Chamber." The exterior woodwork was to be painted. These repairs were made and the bill paid in 1785. Further bills indicate that the Great Hall wainscotting was painted, undoubtedly for the first time. Internal evidence shows that the first color applied over the wood was a grey green. The walls were ordered whitewashed.

Pl. 89

Gold leaf was purchased in quantity, probably for the decoration of the cupola dome, and for the gilded pineapple in the balcony pediment. It was in 1784, according to receipted bills, that Jim Moody was engaged to carve this famous naturalistic pineapple. He was probably also responsible for the several others to be found in Newport, notably the one on the pediment formerly part of the water side door of the Jonathan Nichols house at 54 Washington Street.

Some of the most stirring scenes in Rhode Island history have taken place in the Colony House. From the balcony, the death of King George II was announced, and the succession of King George III proclaimed. In 1766 the people gathered to rejoice over the repeal of the Stamp Act. In 1776, John Handy read the Declaration of Independence from the balcony, and in 1826, fifty years later, he was called upon to read the epoch-making words once more. As already noted, the building was used during the Revolutionary war, first as a barracks by the British and then as a hospital by the French troops. When Washington came to visit the French allies, he was entertained at dinner in its Great Hall. [39]

During the eighteenth century, the basement was let out for shops and for storage space for rum, ebony, and molasses. Later a weaving establishment was set up, and still later a manufactory for candles and an oil refinery. In 1882, when an excavation for a new vault was being prepared in the cellar, a well was discovered buried under planks, paving stones, and concrete. Public life and practical concern went hand in hand, here as elsewhere in Newport.

Richard Munday's career was cut short by death in 1740. But he had won the distinction of having built two of the most beautiful early eighteenth-century public buildings produced in the colonies, and his two Malbone houses were acclaimed the most elaborate of their day. In the fifteen years between 1725 when he built Trinity Church and 1739 when he drew the plans for the Colony House, the baroque style of Newport's early eighteenth-century building was crystallized.

But Munday was by no means alone in his ability to produce fine buildings. The same Colony House papers that establish him as Newport's first named architect supply the names and trades of the other men who worked on that building.[40] The other houses of Newport make clear the fact that he was one of a unified group, working in a tradition understood thoroughly by all the carpenters, master builders, joyners, masons, and ironmongers alike.

Benjamin Wyatt's name headed the list, set apart in such a manner as to indicate that he served in the capacity of contractor. Munday and Wyatt had already signed a contract together to build Daniel Ayrault's house in 1739. Although this house was torn down in the early years of the twentieth century, the specifications are still in existence, preserved in the enlarged edition of Mason's *Reminiscences of Newport*, now in the Newport Historical Society.[41] Wyatt alone had signed a contract in 1735 to build a house for Ninyon Challoner.

According to the Colony House papers, Thomas Melvil and Israel Chapman were engaged as carpenters. Eight years later they signed a contract with Wing Spooner and Samuel Greene to build Redwood Library under direction of Peter Harrison, and thus, in a sense, spanned two eras. John Bliss was listed as a housewright and mason, Christopher Townsend was signed on as a housejoiner, Kendall Nichols and Henry Wright as masons. The Langworthy listed was a shot maker, and Mr. Greene suggests he made the lead roof mentioned in papers dated 1757 as being removed to be used for making bullets. John Warkman, the blacksmith who made the hardware for the Second Congregational Church,[42] was responsible for all the Colony House iron work.

These people emerge as a group of expert craftsmen, able to work independently in the tradition they knew. Evidence lies in the buildings themselves. Measured drawings have shown that the same set of hand planes was used to make the moldings of the gallery breasts of Trinity Church, the Sabbatarian Meeting House, the paneling of the Colony House Council Chamber, the Cheeseborough house parlor and the paneling in the Nichols house. The floor plan Munday and Wyatt made for Daniel Ayrault's house, and the one Benjamin Wyatt made for Ninyon Challoner's house are still in existence, also included in the Newport Historical Society's enlarged copy of Mason's *Reminiscences*. In accordance with general

Pl. 71

eighteenth-century practice, these plans were very rudimentary sketches with dimensions and location of chimneys and stairs barely indicated.

Pl. 72

Half of the first floor plan for a "Dwelling House to be Built on James Gordon's Farm" has been accidentally preserved on the back of a page of the *Perpetual Almanack*, the brilliant *tour de force* in the art of printing published by James Franklin's Press in 1730. This plan is carefully drawn with measurements, wall and chimney thicknesses, and locations of openings all clearly and exactly indicated. But such precise draughtsmanship was almost unique, and the rougher sketches generally employed are proof that houses were built according to a common body of working knowledge. Later on this traditional knowledge was to be augmented by the builders' handbooks which gave the rules for proportioning the rooms and the parts and for the execution of decorative detail. Such books often included detailed drawings of doorways and mantelpieces scaled for exact reproduction.

Richard Munday brought to Newport variety of architectural conception and a broad grasp of late Stuart style. The workmen of Newport left their stamp on the town in skilled execution and forthright and matter-of-fact duplication of the baroque forms Munday helped establish.

DOMESTIC BUILDING.

Exteriors. While the new public buildings were going up, Thames Street began to take on an air of commercial solidity, as successful merchants erected their big houses in front of the cramped seventeenth-century dwellings of Benedict Arnold, John Cranston, Jeremy Clarke, and Caleb Carr. These original houses had been built on the old wide line of Thames Street, literally behind the new line which the eighteenth-century inhabitants now established, thereby creating the narrow lane we know today.

During these years the merchants also established themselves on Easton's Point, recently divided into lots by the Quaker proprietors, where they built houses, shops, and wharves on the old Water Street and Shipwright's Street (Washington and Bridge), around the cove and along the bay.

Pl. 74
Pl. 72

The new houses were mansions and, as we have seen, Godfrey Malbone and Abraham Redwood, who were building on opposite sides of Thames Street in 1728, set their houses in gardens enclosed by brick walls fitted with high wrought iron gates. Still far from academic, many of these houses were covered either with broad gambrel roofs, as were the Malbone

Pl. 75

houses, or with gable-on-hipped roofs like those of Jahleel Brenton, John Gidley, and Abraham Redwood. In both gable-on-hip and gambrel, the decorative detail was like that employed in the public buildings. Both forms were to be supplanted about 1760 by the more correct hipped-roofed houses topped with flat decks concealed by double balustrades.

Exterior embellishment was confined to dormer windows, a classic cornice, roof balustrades, and handsome pedimented doorways. The cupolas and balconies which were dramatic features of the Malbone houses and the Colony House belong to Munday's work and were not often repeated.

Unfortunately, some of the most important early houses have been torn down, making it necessary to have recourse to photographs and records. Jahleel Brenton's house, built in 1720 on the old wide line of Thames Street and torn down in the 1920's, was one of the first fully to reflect the new style. As Henry-Russell Hitchcock has pointed out, the high gable-on-hip roof, narrow sash windows, pedimented dormers, and pilastered doorway stemmed from English houses like those being built in Inigo Jones' time almost a hundred years earlier.[43] The scheme of the parlor paneling in Brenton's house to be discussed later, was the one most frequently repeated, with only minor variations, in the best houses until after 1750. The known dates of these gable-on-hip-roofed houses suggest that they were built frequently after the 1720's and were somewhat earlier than the big gambrel-roofed buildings.

Pls. 75–79

John Gidley's house, built on the corner of Gidley and Thames in 1724, as John Stevens' account books indicate, had a gable-on-hip roof and a plain pedimented doorway. Old pictures show that Abraham Redwood's Thames Street house of 1727, already mentioned in Chapter 3, also had a broad gable-on-hip roof, a modillion cornice, and pedimented dormers. It looked like the Brenton house of 1720.

The Wanton family were prominent shipbuilders, merchants, and loyalists.[44] John and William, as other members of the family, had each served the colony in the capacity of governor. Early in the eighteenth century, Governor John built his house, a pitch-roofed building, on the east side of Thames Street, where it stood between Touro and Mary until about 1900. His brother William's house stood on the west side of the street where the Lincoln Store now stands. The view of Newport of circa 1740 shows that, like the Redwood house, William's house was a square three-story mansion with classic cornice and gable-on-hip roof. Photographs taken of it before it was wholly swallowed up by stores confirm this appearance. According to tradition, it was begun in the first decade of the eighteenth century and John Stevens' account books show that he was digging the cellar, building three stacks of chimneys, plastering, and making "mantel trees" for Major William Wanton in 1705–1707.

Pl. 128

Pl. 47

William's son, Joseph Wanton, who was elected governor from 1769 until he was deposed for his loyalist leanings in 1775, inherited the house in 1733. He is supposed to have been responsible for its final appearance, both on the exterior and the interior, with its "beautiful staircase, spacious hall and rich panelling." Dr. Henry Turner, writing in 1891, said that when he first saw the house in 1827, it had two semicircular flights of brown stone steps which flanked the main entrance and led to subsidiary doorways.[45] There are other records of the use at about this time of semicircular steps for fine houses.

Jahleel Brenton's book, dated Boston, 1712, and now in the possession of the Rhode Island Historical Society, contains among the mathematical exercises and miscellaneous letters, sketchily executed ground plans for three houses. Internal evidence indicates that, although undated, they were all drawn early in the eighteenth century. Two of them have semicircular front steps. One, with a center hallway the width of the house, had four chimneys, two on each end of the building, set in thick masonry walls of the type found in Jahleel's Thames Street house of 1720. This plan seems to be drawn in Brenton's own hand, probably before 1730. The John Potter house built in Matunuck circa 1730 and now under process of restoration, originally had similar steps. They were found separately about the property and have recently been carefully reassembled. Once again they lead up to the main entry on the water side of the house as they did in the 1730's when the "Great House" of Captain John Potter, a proven counterfeiter, was one of Narragansett's show places.

Pl. 73

The Wanton house semicircular steps had disappeared by 1895 when George H. Richardson made his rough sketch, now preserved in the Newport Historical Society.[46] But he showed an entry on Thames Street and one on the north side, both of which had iron railings and double flights of stairs, as well as doorways with the high rounded pediments characteristic of the early part of the eighteenth century. These were all altered in the late nineteenth century when Victorian detail on the pilasters and the window caps was added. In this changed state, one doorway and two windows have been installed on the house, formerly owned by Arthur Leslie Greene, which stands on Training Station Road.

Pl. 117

One of the best gable-on-hip mansions in Newport today is the house at 228 Spring Street that Captain John Mawdsley built when he enlarged the seventeenth-century Jireh Bull house, probably some time after his marriage in 1747. This new part of the house has interior detail which belongs to the second phase of Newport's eighteenth-century building, but in spite of its mid-century date, its exterior retains the appearance of the merchant mansions of the 1730's. The fanlight doorway was installed about 1795.

Pl. 81

The old house at Mile Corner in Middletown where the Quaker preacher, David Buffum, lived is shown as William Redwood's country estate on the map Charles Blascowitz made for the British Admiralty in 1777. Its early history, recently traced, is given here for the first time. In 1745 Deputy Governor Joseph Whipple bought a house and sixty-one acres of land bounded west on "The King's Highway or the Great Road" from Elisha Card. When in 1753 Whipple's property was sold "by order of the King's Commissioners" to satisfy his creditors, it was purchased by Samuel Holmes, who was William Redwood's father-in-law. Two years later he gave house and land to his daughter Hannah and her husband for "five shillings." [47] He had already given the young Redwoods the gambrel-roofed house which formerly stood on Bridge Street.[48] The Redwoods' new country estate was a high and square gable-on-hip-roofed mansion with a handsome Chinese Chippendale roof balustrade. It was ample proof of the lavish scale of country living maintained by Newport's early merchant princes. The house remained in their possession until 1775, when they sold it to George Irish, by whose name it is referred to in all the Revolutionary war diaries.

Of the early gambrel-roofed mansions, Godfrey Malbone's two houses represented the most ornate domestic building produced during these years. As John Fletcher's painting bill affirms, the town house was being built in 1728. It was of brick, and the early descriptions as well as the drawing of it in the view of Newport in 1740 show that it had dormer windows, roof railings, a cupola, a portico, and a balcony fitted with a wrought iron balustrade. In short, it was characterized by the elements which were to distinguish the Colony House ten years later, and were to be seen in such buildings as the John Hancock house built in Boston in 1737. On a small scale, it was an English manor house of Queen Anne's time.

Malbone Hall, built at Miantonomi Hill in 1741 and described at length in Chapter 3, repeated the same formula more lavishly in pink sandstone. Its corner quoins, as both Hamilton and Birket recorded, were wooden but painted to look like marble. The David Cheeseborough house, built on Mary Street in 1737, the year the Hancock House was built, and the Jonathan Nichols house belong to the same gambrel-roofed tradition. The Cheeseborough house was torn down in 1908, but fortunately the richly paneled Nichols house still stands, almost a sole survivor of the many which once lined the Water Street and Thames Street or stood, like Christopher Fry's great gambrel-roofed mansion, in isolated splendor on the hill top by the Stone Mill.

Newport's old streets are filled with other gable-on-hip and gambrel-roofed houses of lesser scale and later date. The exteriors of these buildings are distinguished by the incorrect and unacademic handling of the detail in common usage during these years. The doorways, as the focal points of the façades, are the most obvious examples of this archaic treatment. In the more elaborate doors, where an order was employed, the pilasters were almost invariably set on high pedestals made too large in scale. The groups of moldings were broken out and mitred around each of the vertical members. Even the back band above the door was turned up into the frieze and broke out the members above it. All this resulted in a complicated effect, characteristic of buildings before 1750.

Segmental pediments, which had been popular from the early eighteenth century, were marked by the same flat and linear character seen in the tower and north doors of Trinity Church. The Benedict Arnold, Jr. house, built about 1720 and demolished in 1925, had a door with a plain segmental pediment supported by Doric pilasters set on high pedestals. The door of Joseph Wanton's house has already been mentioned. The fine doorway of Metcalf Bowler's country house formerly on Wapping Road in Portsmouth was of this same form, but its later (1760) date was betrayed by the delicate row of dentils included in the cornice. The best door with a segmental pediment still left in Newport today is the one on the Captain Phillips house at 42 Elm Street. This little gambrel-roofed half-a-house, with its widely overhanging cornice, was moved to Elm Street from the corner of Washington and Poplar in the 1880's. Although its history before 1770 has not been learned, its architectural type belongs to the years of about 1730.

Pl. 74

Pls. 49, 51

Pl. 81

Pl. 81

Pls. 5, 65

The balcony door of the Colony House, with its broken segmental pediment, carved foliage, and gilded pineapple, has always been one of the show pieces of Newport. Although, as we have seen, the receipted bills prove that Jim Moody carved the pineapple in 1784, the rest of the door, with its finely executed Corinthian pilasters set on high heavy pedestals is characteristic work of the first half of the century. As already mentioned, the balcony door of the Mill Street Congregational Church, built in 1729 by Cotton Palmer, has a pediment of the same form. Thomas R. Hazard, in his *Recollections of Olden Times*, written in 1879, reported that he remembered the Captain Simon house at 25 Bridge Street when it had a portico topped by a foliage and pineapple-crowned pediment. This door has now completely disappeared.

Pl. 61

But the most famous door of all belonged originally on the waterside entry of the Jonathan Nichols house at 54 Washington Street. The pediment is almost a replica of its Colony House model, even to the pineapple, which Moody may also have carved. When the front and rear entries of the house were widened in the 1870's, this fine door was discarded, but a stereoscopic view of the waterside façade of the Nichols house shows it in its original position. Benjamin Smith salvaged the pediment and had it nailed over the old west entry of the Dennis House, now St. John's Rectory on Poplar Street and Washington. In 1924, Mr. James Gibson, working under the direction of Norman Isham, built a new undersection for it and installed it as the front door of the Rectory.[49] The scrolls and the pineapple of this pediment have now been returned to the Nichols House, but they are installed as part of the main entrance on Washington Street.

Pls. 88, 89

The shell-hooded doorway, characteristic of Queen Anne's time and made by Richard Munday and Benjamin Wyatt for Daniel Ayrault's house in 1739, may be seen today on the rear door of the Newport Historical Society. Its construction was described in detail in the building specifications. An entry in one of John Stevens' account books, dated 1737, shows that he was building a new shell hood for John Coddington's mansion house built some years before his death in 1732. This house, shorn of its doorway, still stands at the corner of Thames and Marlborough Streets. The only other known in Rhode Island was on the house, now demolished, that Richard Munday or Benjamin Wyatt built for John Wickes in Warwick.[50]

Pls. 82, 83

According to notes that Jonas Bergner made before the David Cheeseborough house was torn down, its front door once had Corinthian pilasters set on high pedestals which supported an elaborate broken scroll pediment.[51] Such ogee pediments, generally characterized by moldings of bold and broad scale, continued to appear until sometime after 1750. An ogee pediment was put on Dr. David King's house at 32 Pelham Street in the mid-eighteenth century when the old 1710 house was remodeled. Although the house is standing, the door itself has disappeared and is known only in photographs. In 1754 Wing Spooner and Henry Peckham

Pls. 15, 84

signed a contract to build a house ninety-eight feet long for John Townsend. The location of this house is unknown, but the specifications called for "a large outside Door fronting the South to be made in the manner and form of Jonathan Bower's front door belonging to his House with an O'Gea head." [52]

At this point it might be well to set down what is known of the early practice of painting the exteriors of buildings in Newport. In 1780, Louis Jean Baptiste Sylvestre de Robertnier, Lieutenant in the Regiment Soissonais of Rochambeau's Army, wrote in his diary that "the exteriors of Newport houses were painted in divers colors," and added that "all this gives a variety pleasing to the eye." [53]

Fifteen years later Samuel King made an engraving of "a southwest view of the Town of Newport," which was published by subscription. According to the *Mercury* notices of 1795, the price of the engraving was 3s, if colored, 2 4/6, plain. The colored print in the Newport Historical Society shows five different house colors, which would confirm Lieutenant Robertnier's note, and would indicate that these hues were in current use by 1795, and had probably been common for many years. White, a venetian type of red, colonial yellow, gray (probably natural weathering), and a grey blue are repeated throughout the engraving.

The earliest houses, if painted at all, seem to have been almost invariably painted barn red or Spanish brown, as the color was then called, doors, windows, and all. The old, hand-riven, lapped, and long protected clapboards of the Wanton-Lyman-Hazard house, the Maxson Jeffers house, and the Voax house were all painted red,[54] as well as the shingles on the back wall of Pitt's Head Tavern.[55] Even the outside wall of the stone chimney of the Voax house had been so painted. Found on such early houses, this color may well have been used in the seventeenth century.

The following notices in the *Mercury* indicate that houses were being painted blue well before the Revolutionary war:

Newport Mercury, Dec. 12, 1758

To be Sold or Let by *Col. Job Almy* of Tiverton.
A large Commodius new dwelling House, well furnished, and painted Blue; situate at the Upper End of Thames Street, near Capt. Joseph Wantons.

Newport Mercury, Feb. 10, 1766

To be let, a blue House, opposite Mr. James Lucena's on the point, between the ferries, with 12 Rooms, 8 fireplaces, a Shop, a dry cellar and a good garden. Any person inclining to hire the same may inquire of Thomas Webber at Cowley's Wharf.

Job Almy's house, part of which was built before 1720, is still standing. It has already been mentioned earlier as the house of Walter Challoner. Now known as the Shaw or Taggart house, it is No. 56 Farewell Street.[56]

White was an outside color evidently also used early in Newport. The records for Trinity Church show that "oils and colors" for painting the exterior were bought in 1733, but the building has never been painted any color but white. The first coat, according to Mr. Isham, was probably put on soon after the colors were ordered, and consisted of white lead with litharge as a drier. Litharge, a yellow powder of lead, would tone the white to a deep creamy color.[57] The first color on the old clapboards on Pitt's Head Tavern, applied over clear yellow and unweathered pine, suggests that this building too was painted a light tone (perhaps the same creamy white) at an early date.[58] Old clapboards on the north wall of the Jonathan Nichols house at 54 Washington Street (1748) show signs of having been left to weather unpainted for a number of years, but the first coat of paint applied to the dark weathered wood was the same off-white color found on the clapboards of the north wall (before 1765) of Pitt's Head Tavern.[59] The widespread use of white was not common, however, until after the War of 1812.

A *Mercury* notice of 1769 advertised:

Just Imported from London, in the Snow Tristam, Capt. Shand, and to be sold by Nicholas P. Tillinghast at the Sign of the Mortar in Thames Street. Gold Leaf, Prussian Blue, Vermillion, Verdigrise, Spanish White, Spanish Brown, Spruce, yellow, Copperas, Logwood, ground Redwood, and red Saunders.

By 1771 Tillinghast was advertising "white and red lead, Venetian red," as well as the colors mentioned above.

The Redwood Library of 1748 has always been painted and (at first) sanded to imitate stone. When the Vernon house was repaired in 1782, Samuel Vernon gave directions for mixing the colors — white lead with a little red thrown in — to produce the effect of stone. He also indicated that the walls were to be sanded.[60]

Interiors. The second decade of the eighteenth century saw the development of spacious interiors laid out on a central-entry, four-room plan which was to be repeated with only minor variations for many years. In 1719 Nathaniel Sheffield gave his son James the half of a mansion house west of the "entry that goes through the house," including the "two pares of stares" from the main floor to the garret. At this early date, then, Nathaniel possessed a two-and-a-half-story house with two rooms on either side of the central hall.[61]

In this four-room central-entry plan, the hallways were generally divided front from back by a low carved arch set on brackets, and the stairways, no longer steep and cramped, came into their own as the center of interest, generally set against the back wall. The formula was derived from smaller English houses of Queen Anne's time.[62]

Pls. 76, 77   The stairway of the Jahleel Brenton house, built in 1720, is the earliest elaborate one we know. Built in three runs, it introduced an archaic handling of the risers, each one of which was finished with a separate alternating scroll and rectangular boxing, but this complicated

8

treatment was not repeated. The stairway of the Hancock house in Boston, erected in 1737, established in New England the fully developed formula for fine stairs, and because it is well known, its construction may be used as a key date. Built with three twisted balusters to each step, it rose in two flights broken by a broad landing. The rails were molded, they ramped steeply over the newel and intermediate posts, and their curve was repeated by the wall wainscotting. The paneled soffits, flame drops, carved scroll riser ends, and scroll bottom step with its elaborate double-twisted newel post completed the scheme.[63]

As early as 1729 in Newport, the pulpit stairs of the Sabbatarian Meeting House were built with a curved bottom step, a set of three differently twisted balusters to each step, the curved and ramped hand rail and the double-twisted newel post found in the Hancock house. Such stairs were almost invariably to be seen in the finest houses of the second quarter of the century, but the detail of the Sabbatarian stairs appears early. The little gouged-out flowers used to decorate the riser ends went out of fashion before 1740, and the round headed panels which finished the pulpit sides only appeared until about 1750. They were also used as stair soffit panels.

Pls. 58–60

Although the stairs of the David Cheeseborough house, built the same year as the Hancock house, rose in a single flight, they were just as richly and completely finished, complete with double-twisted newel. They have been dismantled, however, and the Jonathan Nichols house at 54 Washington Street has the finest hallway and stairs with twisted balusters now in existence in Newport. Here, as in the Cheeseborough house, the hall is divided front from back by the typical low carved arch set on scroll brackets. Round-headed raised panels finish the upper hall soffits, but they have been removed downstairs. At one time in the history of the house the stair landing was lit by two unique segmental headed windows. They have *b* been replaced by a bull's eye window, but the old framing is still in place.

Pl. 92

Pls. 91, 92

The taste for twisted balusters hung on into the next and more academic phase of Newport building, and some of the finest houses of the 1750's and the 1760's, like the Banister country house, the Vernon house, and the Francis Malbone house, all retained the earlier hall scheme including the carved dividing archway and the ramped stair rails, as well as the elaborately twisted balusters.

Pl. 114

Hallways were generally wainscotted only to the chair rail. This treatment allowed the plastered or papered walls above to serve as a foil for the twisted mahogany balusters. But it was customary to panel the best rooms from floor to ceiling. The most outstanding example of early paneling left is that for the northeast parlor of the house John Gidley built in 1724. This gable-on-hip-roofed house was bought by Edward Breese in 1825, by whose name it was long known. When the house was torn down in 1906, the paneling of the north parlor was removed and is now installed in the Hoyt house built by George C. Mason about *i* 1875 at 31 Old Beach Road. It is now owned by Mr. John Nicholas Brown.

Pl. 80

Gidley family tradition has affirmed that the paneling was made for the house in England, but when it was dismantled, Jonas Bergner, who saw it taken apart, reported that the wood was found to be American pine.[64] Another venerable tradition of English importation must therefore be abandoned. Composed of bolection moldings, its heavy scale, complicated cornice, and double-curved panel tops are reminiscent of the late Stuart period and are even more baroque in spirit than the paneling of the Colony House Council Chamber. The many vertical breaks are emphasized by heavy bracket-like tabs which appear in the cornice, and which are seen only in the earliest colonial wainscotting. The pilasters marking the room corners are doubled, mitred, and set on high pedestals, all evidence of early date. An extra row of horizontal panels has been added to give the old paneling the necessary height in its new location, but the mantel in the Greek Revival manner was put in by Mr. Breese when he remodeled the house in 1825.

Pl. 80

The corner cupboard in the dining room of the Thomas Robinson house at 72 Washington Street has the same complicated form, with its bolection molding, gouged flower, bracket-like tab, and roundheaded panel. It is part of the paneling of the old half of the house, built sometime between 1725, when Walter Chapman bought the land, and 1736, when he sold the lot with a house on it to Benjamin Hazard.[65]

Such paneling as Gidley's gives some conception of the rich and baroque character of decoration common to the houses of the Redwoods, Malbones, Wantons, and others built in the 1720's and 1730's. The complication of this paneling was modified somewhat in a scheme which also appeared as early as 1720 in the parlor paneling of the Jahleel Brenton house,

Pls. 77–79

which is now owned by the Rhode Island School of Design. This scheme was the one generally adopted and was repeated many times until about 1750. As in the Gidley house parlor, raised paneling sheathed all four walls, but the panel tops were flat and plain.

Windows, built with the window seats always popular in Rhode Island, were recessed and had inside shutters which folded into the jambs. Fireplaces were framed with heavy bolection moldings and were often fitted with Dutch, English, or French tiles. The panels over the fireplace were large and plain, but they were flanked by pilasters and by round-headed cupboards, sometimes finished with handsome shells. Pilasters, doubled and mitred, and set on high pedestals, marked the room corners, and the cornices were invariably broken out and mitred around all the various vertical members.

Paneling of this type is to be found in English work of Wren's time. The parlor paneling of the Brenton house introduced the chief elements of the scheme in all its richness. The use of a boldly scaled Doric order reflects an early date. The parlor of the John Potter house in Matunuck (1730) has similar Doric pilasters and paneling employed in conjunction with roundheaded doors and deep shuttered windows. Here a handsome shell cupboard still retains its original dark marbling and its carved detail is picked out in heavy leaf gold. The parlors of the Jonathan Nichols and David Cheeseborough houses follow the same lavish

Pls. 93, 94

scheme interpreted in the Corinthian order. The Jonathan Nichols house is further distinguished by the pair of beautiful shell cupboards which flank the fireplace wall and the four carved cherub heads set in the cupboard arch spandrels. The paneling in the northeast chamber of this fine house repeats that of the parlor below, even to the cherub heads.

The effect of opulence was further enhanced by the papered or painted decoration often applied to the interior walls. James Birket, who visited Newport in 1750, gives us some interesting information on this subject. "The houses in general make a good appearance," he wrote, "and also are as well furnished as in Most places you meet with, many of the rooms being hung with Printed Canvas and paper, etc. which looks very neat. Others are well wainscotted and painted as in other places." [66]

Some of this printed paper and canvas was without doubt of the "flock" type popular in the mid-years of the eighteenth century. This was made with bits of chopped wool or silk dusted over patterns traced in glue to imitate textiles of the time. Notices in the *Newport Mercury* advertise paper hangings for sale as early as 1769. Elizabeth Coddington's inventory, dated 1745, twenty-three years before the *Mercury* was established, listed packets of wallpaper even at that early date.[67] A piece of eighteenth-century paper in a pattern imitating an India print in blue and white is preserved in the Wanton-Lyman-Hazard house, while a beautiful fragment of paper in Chinese design hangs on the wall of the Pitt's Head Tavern. It came from one of Newport's rooms "hung with printed canvas or paper," in the mid-eighteenth century, in accordance with the then current taste for Chinoiserie.

Woodwork was sometimes left unpainted. As we have seen, the Council Chamber in the Colony House was not painted until 1784, when it was ordered painted a light stone color, and the Great Hall was given its first coat of paint, a gray green (wainscot color) at the same time.[68] Trinity Church interior went uncolored even longer. Miss Mary Edith Powel in her illuminating notes reported that when her grandmother left Newport in 1815, "all the old houses and Trinity Church had woodwork in its natural color and many were dingy." When she returned in 1832, "all the woodwork had been painted white." [69]

One of the first colors to be employed for painting woodwork was a dark red like the Spanish brown used for the exteriors. Green "wainscot color" appeared almost as early and continued in use after the red had, except for country houses, gone out of fashion. Paneled walls were also darkened and grained to resemble mahogany, rosewood, or other rare woods, or were treated to imitate marbles of various kinds. Thomas Wentworth Higginson wrote in *Old Port Days* that the few remaining planks in Aaron Lopez' counting room on the second floor of his house at Lopez Wharf and Thames Street at the foot of Cotton's Court, were "grained to resemble rosewood and mahogany" and that the fragments of wallpaper were of English make.[70]

Sometimes the over-mantel panels were decorated with a landscape or sea view. The view of Newport, already mentioned several times in this text, was executed about 1740 as an over-mantel painting for the Phillips house which originally stood on Mill Street. When

k

Pl. 21

the house was torn down, the painting was saved and is now owned by Mr. Lewis G. Morris. It hangs in Malbone Hall.[71]

Pl. 115

The unique decoration found on the two outside walls of the north parlor of the Vernon house was evidently painted directly on the flat plaster. It shows what a wealthy merchant who was building a fine house in the second quarter of the century wanted his parlor to look like. These frescoed walls, which, as we shall see later, were probably executed in about 1740, were painted to imitate the rooms paneled from floor to ceiling with raised paneling, like the Brenton house parlor. Stiles, rails, and moldings were all carefully simulated, and finished to look like marble in accordance with the dictates of current fashion for decorating wooden paneling. The panel faces were painted with little Chinese scenes which have baffled students, but which again reflect the predilection both for pictorial decoration and for Chinoiserie. It is possible that underneath many later coats of paint, other Newport rooms, paneled in wood, may still retain such scenic decoration.

The walls of the main parlor of the Jonathan Nichols house seem to have been painted or finished at first with a red tone. The pilasters, the baseboards, the cupboards, the cupboard shelves, and the molding below the window seats were first painted to resemble black marble veined in gold. The cupboards were colored a rather dark blue-green, and the cupboard pilasters were marbleized in a sand color with dark veinings. The four cherubs in the arch spandrels and the two in the cupboards had pink cheeks, rosy lips, brown eyes and hair. Their wings were painted in rose, green, and ultramarine tones. Sometime later, the paneling of this room was painted a yellow gray-green and the marbleizing was certainly part of the new color scheme. The effect of such painted paneling was sober, matter-of-fact, and rich, like the house itself. Later all the marbling and polychroming was painted over with the same light stone color employed for the Council Chamber in the Colony House in 1784.[72]

The paneling of the south parlor was painted red and grained to imitate mahogany. The southwest room (also paneled) was painted dark red and then was "spreckled," a finish produced by rubbing flour paste over the surface and then scraping it off in a grained design. As has already been noted, some of the details in Godfrey Malbone's "great room" were picked out with the "2500 leaves of gold" John Fletcher bought in Boston in 1729. The Reverend Edward Peterson, writing in 1853, reported that traces of gilding were then still visible on the cornice and the panels.

Evidently whitewashing was the most universal treatment employed for finishing plastered walls. John Stevens' account books are filled with items for whitewashing rooms and entry halls of the important houses, as well as the small ones. Dr. Vinal, minister of the First Congregational Church from 1746 to 1765, put in a request to have his rooms rewhitewashed, since they had been done in the cold weather and had "yellowed badly." His house formerly stood on the northeast corner of Division and Church Streets.[73]

Although the large mansions generally followed the eighteenth-century scheme of four rooms laid out in pairs on either side of a central hall, most of the smaller houses clung to the half-a-house plan with an end chimney or to the central-chimney, five-room plan with entry and stairway butted against the chimney. In this latter plan, the two main rooms opened on either side of the chimney while a large kitchen, flanked by smaller rooms, filled the back part of the house.

m The Wickham house at number 32 Fair Street is an example of the house built on the central-chimney five-room plan, covered by the typical Newport gable-on-hip roof. It has a heavy block modillion cornice of early form, while the unpedimented doorway has six small transom lights of early glass, at least one of them bull's-eye. The interior detail is somewhat later in character. The central stairway butting against the big chimney has plain turned balusters and an open string course. The east parlor has a flush paneled mantel wall, the over-mantel panel of which is finished with "ears," a detail suggestive of a date after 1750.

Dr. Cotton's house at 4 Cotton's Court also belongs to this five-room plan. It was shown as a two-story house on Ezra Stiles' map of 1758. Ruth Champlin inherited the house in 1764. She was the wife of George Champlin, who built two houses on Thames Street, just south of Cotton's Court.[74] The exterior is like that of the Wickham house and, except for a later porch and doorway, has not been changed, but the interior has been modernized.

Sometime after 1725, Newport builders evolved an unusual square floor plan based on three rooms swung around a central chimney. In this plan, the entry and stairway were located in a front corner and the parlor filled all the remaining front part of the house. A bedroom and the kitchen, laid out on opposite sides of the big fireplace, made up the back. Each of the three rooms was served by its own fireplace in the big central chimney.

In the careful study made from 1946 to 1948 of many of the deed histories of early Newport structures, five houses built by members of the Townsend family of cabinet makers have been identified. Four of these (two covered with gambrel and two with high gable-on-hip roofs) were built on this three-room plan, and three of them show structural evidence of having been built between the time when the land was bought in 1725 and 1750.

Christopher Townsend, called "Shipjoiner" in the deed,[75] took up lots No. 51 and 49 of the first division of the Quaker lands on Easton's Point in 1725 and built a square, two-story gable-on-hip house. It still stands at 74 Bridge Street, adjoined to the ship joiners shop he added on later. The construction of the house, with its heavy framing plainly showing, but cased with thin boards beaded at the corners, is like that of others being put up between *n* 1730 and 1750 and its plan is the one described above. The mantel paneling in the parlor is exceptionally fine, made up of small sections of raised paneling, with two roundheaded cupboard doors over the fireplace. These are glazed now, but doubtless originally had solid panels. The projecting tab which breaks out the cornice above the mantel is late Stuart in character, but the flower that adorns it was carved in the late nineteenth century.[76] The detail

Pl. 121

Pl. 121

Pls. 95, 125

Pls. 95, 96

of the stairs, with its turned balusters and ramped rail, is similar to that of the two Stevens houses to be discussed later, as well as to the Thomas Townsend house stairs at No. 14 Third Street. The old joiners' shop has recently been restored to serve as the headquarters of Restorations, Inc.

Job Townsend, the famous first cabinet maker of that name, Christopher's cousin, also took up Quaker lands on Easton's Point in 1725.[77] His lot, numbered 86 of the First Division, lies along Third Street on the northwest corner of Bridge, and his house, now badly run down, still stands, its block modillion cornice mute evidence of the care with which it was built. Proof that Job Townsend was building his house not too many years after he took up his lots lies in John Stevens' account books, which show that in 1729 he was building "46 perch of cellar walls and a stack of chimneys." He had two "harths" laid, and lathing and plastering amounting to £ 34.

The plan of the house is like that of his cousin Christopher's; the stairs are in the southwest corner of the house and the space in front of the central chimney which is freed by this arrangement is a single large living room. The floor of this room has been lowered and the whole given over to a now abandoned shop, but the plan is clear and several two-paneled doors and a paneled section above one of these remain to attest the early date. The three-run stairway, however, is the exceptional feature. It has a molded rail which ramps steeply over the posts, delicately fluted balusters, and an open string course decorated with scrolls and carefully carved rosettes. It is later in style than the house and it is tempting to connect Job Townsend, Jr., son of Job and also a cabinet maker, with the execution of the stairs in the home he inherited in 1764; all the more so when his father's account books show that in 1762 he made, along with much furniture, 112 balusters for a stairway for John Franklin.[78]

Solomon Townsend, Christopher's brother, took up lot 146 of the Easton Point lands in 1725.[79] The little house he built is still standing on the southeast corner of Walnut and Second Streets. It is constructed on the same three-room plan, although it is covered by a gambrel roof. Thomas Townsend's house at No. 14 Third Street has the date 1767 painted on one of the rafters.[80] Like the Solomon Townsend house, it has a gambrel roof and is laid out on the same three-room plan. Its heavy framing, showing especially in the corner where the stairs are set, is like that of all these houses, although its date of building is somewhat later. The stairs are like those in Christopher's house.

In 1725 William Claggett, the clockmaker, leased a lot of land on the cove to his father, Caleb, a baker, with the stipulation that within twenty-five years he was to build a house "36 ft. long and 18 ft. broad and one bake house 40 ft. long and 20 ft. broad," and furnish the materials "together with the locks, keys, Bolts, Staples, Latches, Hooks, Hinges, Windows, door and glass. . . ." William was to have the use of a newly built wharf for "landing goods and carrying them away within 3 days after their landing."

The cove has been filled in and the wharf and bake house have been gone long since, but the brick end house, known as the Caleb Tripp house because of a later owner, is the house William Claggett stipulated in 1725.[81] Its steeply pitched gambrel roof and heavy frame, cased but showing on the interior, confirm the early date. Unexpectedly, the house has a central chimney which belies the brick end wall construction. Its four-room, central-chimney plan is like no other yet found in Newport.

Pls. 9, 46

---

a See also Pl. 84, the Henry Taggart (Fowler) House, at 32 Second Street.

b Read "rare" for "unique."

c Read "Daniel" for "Stephen."

d See Chapter 3.

e Read "stone" for "wooden."

f A number of eighteenth century easel and overmantel scenes show that the trim was often painted white and the doors a bright color such as blue or red. Nina Fletcher Little's *American Decorative Wall Painting* (1952) contains documented information about exterior and interior color.

Contemporary eighteenth-century documents sometimes refer to "stone color" or "light stone color" for both exterior and interior use.

g See Appendix A, page 454, The Vernon House. In a letter to his father dated August 26, 1781, Samuel Vernon wrote: "The clay I mentioned to have mixed with the wht. lead is something like pipe clay, its brought from the vinyard." The gambrel-roofed house at 108 Prospect Hill Street, standing in 1758, has retained rusticated siding under later clapboards and shingles. Some of its original finish may be seen in a protected areaway. It is a thick paint of rather strong gray color well sanded with dark specked sand.

h See Plates 88, 88a. The bull's-eye window was removed in the restoration of 1952–1953. For further information see page 441, note and new illustration.

i Now in the Henry Francis du Pont Winterthur Museum.

j Now owned by the Preservation Society of Newport County.

k This paper now hangs in 33 Touro Street.

l Exact information about the painted wall finishes in the Hunter House has been established in the brilliant restoration carried out under the direction of Ralph Carpenter in 1952–1953. As may be seen today these two southeast and southwest rooms were originally painted to imitate walnut and rosewood (rose cedar) graining respectively. Rose cedar graining was also discovered painted directly on the old plaster walls forming part of the restored little office room that adjoins the rosewood-grained dining room.

m Demolished after 1952.

n See Pl. 95. The three rooms at the rear of the house were added, probably in the late eighteenth century.

o Now privately owned.

p Read "brother" for "cousin." The house has been demolished since 1952.

CHAPTER FIVE

Peter Harrison's Era

PUBLIC BUILDING. Newport's building during the years which followed 1750 was as closely associated with the name of Peter Harrison as the two decades following 1725 had been with Richard Munday's. But while Munday's work harked back to the baroque style of Sir Christopher

Wren, already out of fashion in England, Harrison's brought to Newport a specific knowledge of the then current English Palladian revival. His role was that of an innovator as well as a distinguished designer.

Like Munday before him, who had called himself house carpenter and had kept an inn, Harrison's life was filled with so many other pursuits that it is difficult to understand how he found time to perfect himself in the art of architecture. Born in 1716 the fourth and youngest child of Yorkshire Quakers, Thomas and Elizabeth Harrison, the young Peter went with his brother Joseph, who was a draughtsman in his own right, to the port town of Hull, where he learned the art of shipbuilding. He evidently acquired other skills because when he arrived in Newport he was already proficient, as Carl Bridenbaugh has pointed out in his recently published *Peter Harrison, First American Architect*, in cartography, navigation, wood carving, draughting, surveying, and farming. It is not known how he acquired his architectural knowledge, but he was beginning then to buy books and to assemble an excellent architectural library which had a profound influence on all his work.

In 1738, when Peter Harrison was about twenty-two, he arrived in Newport, having shipped as cabin boy on "The Sheffield" with his brother Joseph, Captain. John Banister, the rich Newport merchant, placed him in command of the ship "The Leathley," which he had ordered built especially for Peter. Henceforward Harrison engaged in commerce continuously. He married John Banister's youngest sister-in-law, Elizabeth Pelham, but by 1746 he had fallen out with his former patron. The two brothers, Peter and Joseph, set up their own shop and shipping center near John Brown's wharf in Thames Street (on or near the present Bowen's Wharf inherited by Elizabeth from her father, Edward Pelham), where, although they led the busy lives common to Newport merchants of those years, Harrison found the time to become one of the most distinguished architects the colonial era produced.

Mr. Fiske Kimball, in his "Colonial Amateurs and their Models: Peter Harrison," [1] has pointed out that Peter Harrison was essentially an amateur, the product of the general education available in his century. Mr. Bridenbaugh has concluded that he is America's first architect, professional in every sense except that he practiced only as an avocation. But there is no record of how or where he obtained his architectural training. As Mr. Kimball has emphasized, the architectural books of the day were in the process of codifying an accepted body of classic formulae to the point where gifted men were designing from their pages buildings of respectable academic proportions and detail. The resources of the eighteenth century were such that amateurs could and did derive the specific knowledge they needed from a general, not a professional education. Most eighteenth-century architects were amateurs in this sense and Peter Harrison is Newport's proof of the availability and success of such training.

To compare the Brick Market at one end of the Parade with the Colony House at the other is to realize that whether Harrison was professionally trained or a gifted amateur, he had access to academic information that the builders of Munday's day had not. Harrison's personal inventory, made in New Haven in 1775, and published for the first time by Mr. Bridenbaugh, lists by name the books in his library. These included works on fortification (he had drawn the plans for Fort George in 1745), navigation, farming, and all the important contemporary books on architecture, as well as rule-of-thumb handbooks for builders.

Mr. Kimball shows that all the buildings both in Newport and elsewhere connected with Harrison's name evidenced a profound knowledge and specific use of such books as Colin Campbell's *Vitruvius Britannicus*, Hoppus' *Palladio*, Ware's *Designs of Inigo and Others*, Kent's *Designs of Inigo Jones*, and Gibbs' two publications, *The Book of Architecture* and *Rules for Drawing*. Harrison owned them all, and except for the two by Gibbs, they reflect the academic return to Palladian sources sponsored by Lord Burlington's powerful group. From their pages Harrison selected his designs and the details to complete them, which he executed with academic precision. It was because of his ability to adapt and interpret these two-dimensional English drawings into three-dimensional colonial reality that Newport's public buildings of the years after 1748 rank among the most advanced and academic in style in the colonies. The three Newport buildings connected with his name serve as proof of his architectural capacity. They also stand as symbols of the town's then cognizant and integrated culture.

Pl. 104

The Redwood Library. A lively feeling for architectural style and a specific knowledge of the current trends of English building were prerequisites for the selection of the design of the Redwood Library, built in 1748. This wooden rusticated Roman Doric temple with wings had stood completed at the head of Mill Street nearly forty years before Thomas Jefferson turned to classic examples for the capitol of Virginia. It was built at a time when a classic building was rarely found in Europe except as an occasional decorative garden temple.

Probably the seventh oldest library in the country, the Redwood Library was an out-growth of the Philosophical Club which had been organized in 1730 under the imposing title of "The Society for the Promotion of Knowledge and Virtue by a Free Conversation." The original membership was composed of outstanding citizens such as Peter Bours, Dean George Berkeley, Henry Collins, Abraham Redwood, and some twenty-five others.[2]

In 1747, when Redwood gave £500 for the purchase of books and Collins gave the land, plans for a building were made at once. The following year the building committee, composed of Henry Collins, Samuel Wickham, and John Tillinghast, signed specifications with Joseph Harrison as the architect, which indicated that the design for the building had already been chosen.[3] Peter Harrison was in London at this time, and Mr. Bridenbaugh has suggested that he mailed the plans to Joseph, who signed for him.[4] But it is possible that Joseph, who was also a draughtsman and had drawn maps with Peter, may have had a real share in helping select the design for Redwood. Access to Peter's library would have made this possible. An appendix to the articles, dated 1748, which sets forth some interior changes, was signed by Peter Harrison, who clearly took charge from that date forward.

But whether Peter or Joseph or the committee selected the design, the model for it, a Roman Doric temple with portico and wings, was derived from one of Harrison's books and stemmed from a Palladian source. As Mr. Kimball has pointed out, it was probably immediately inspired by the headpiece of book IV of Edward Hoppus' *Palladio*, published in London in 1735, which shows a garden temple on Lord Burlington's estate at Chiswick. Isaac Ware's *Designs of Inigo Jones and Others* also shows a casino for Sir Charles Hotham designed by William Kent, which repeats the same scheme with the addition of a dome.[5] Harrison owned both books.

Pl. 105

The rear elevation, consisting of a Palladian window under a large arch, was introduced to England in Webb's Whitehall Palace designs. The scheme was illustrated in Kent's *Designs of Inigo Jones*, in the headpiece for book II of Hoppus' *Palladio*, and in Ware's *Designs of Inigo Jones and Others*. The combination of the Ionic order for the rear and the Doric for the façade reflects the use of separate architectural plates to help design a building planned out of books, façade by façade.

Built of wood in accordance with Newport building tradition, the library was rusticated, sanded, and painted to imitate stone, in accordance with the current English Palladian taste.

The interior consisted of a square room with walls lined by bookcases treated architecturally. The details for these bookcases are to be found in Batty Langley's *Treasury of Design*. Bridenbaugh notes that Harrison's inventory did not include this book, but he drew from it so frequently that he must once have owned it.

The specifications for Redwood Library are the only ones extant for any of Harrison's Newport buildings. They contain so much specific information about the building methods employed that they have been reprinted here. As we have seen, two of the carpenters who signed on, Israel Chapman and Thomas Melvil, worked with Richard Munday on the Colony House. The other two, Samuel Greene and Wing Spooner, are known to have helped build the Francis Malbone house, which probably, from land evidence and architectural style, was erected about 1760.

The large Room to be thirty-seven foot long, and twenty-six foot broad in the inside, and nineteen foot high. At the west End (which is the principal Front) is to be a Portico of four Columns according to the Doric Order, with a Pediment over it, with Pilasters to suit the Columns. The Projection of the Portico from the Outside of the Building to be about nine foot, and the Roof to be continued out so much as to form the Pediment: The length of the Columns to be about seventeen foot including Base and Capital, and the thickness of twenty-six inches just above the Base: The Building to be fram'd Brac'd and Studded the outside and Roof to be boarded with Feather edg'd Boards, the Shingles to be shav'd and joynted and to be laid: The outside to be covered with Pine Plank worked in Imitation of Rustick, and to have a Dorick Entablature with Triglipphs &c. continued from the Portico quite Round the Building and to have a Plain Pediment at the East End. At the West end next the Portico, to be two small Wings or Outshots for two Little Rooms or offices, one on each side and both alike in form and Bigness, each to be about twelve foot square and (with a small Break or Recess) to Range in a line Parallel to the West End of the Building or inner part of the Portico. The Roofs of these Outshots to be Slooping from the lower part of the Entablature so as to form a Kind of half Pediment on each Side of the Portico, with a Cornice only to be work'd round instead of the whole Entablature, the heights to them to be about eleven foot at the outermost Side and seventeen foot at the Inner side or where they joyn the Body of the Building, and to be plank'd as the other in Imitation of Rustick: in the Front of said Building to be four whole windows and two Attic windows, on each side four whole windows and three attic windows: In all twelve whole Windows and nine Attick Windows: The whole Windows to be six foot high and three foot wide, and the Attick Windows to be three foot square within the Frames, of which are to be red cedar and quite plain without any Architrave on the Outside. At the East end to have a Venetian Window only. To have three outside doors, Viz., One large One in the middle of the Portico, eight foot six Inches high and three foot nine inches wide, and two Small ones in the back part of the two Outshots, and to have four Inside Doors, to consist of eight Pannels each and cas'd with Double Architrave. The Sides and Ends of the Great Room within to be furr'd out even with the Posts, and the ceiling to be furr'd out with a small Cove next the Walls about two foot Downwards at the Bottom of which over the Attick Windows an Ionick Cornice to run quite round: To be wainscotted about five foot high from the floor quite round the great Room: The Jambs of the Windows to be wainscotted With Architraves round and Seats in the lower Windows: within Great Door which is the entrance from the Portico a small [obliterated] is to be partitioned off for a Porch with a door on the inside and therein to erect a small Plain Stair Case, to go up to the Roof of the Building. The Floors to be laid with Plank Rabbitted or with

Double Boards. About four foot from the Walls or Sides of the Great Room must be a sort of Partition erected about ten feet high, with openings over against each window, on both Sides of which must be placed Shelves for the Books; there must also be five or six Desks for laying the Books on in convenient Places, and the whole to be finished and compleated well and workman-like according to a Plan or Draught drawn by Mr. Joseph Harrison and agreed on for that Purpose, On or before the last Day of October, which will be in the year of our Lord One Thousand Seven Hundred and forty-nine. For and in CONSIDERATION whereof the said Samuel Wick-ham, Henry Collins and John Tillinghast Do hereby Covenant, Promise and Engage to pay or cause to be paid to the sd Wing Spooner, Samuel Green, Thomas Melvil and Israel Chapman for sd Work the Sum of two Thousand and two Hundred pounds in good and passable Bills of Publick Credit of sd Colony, old Tenor; Six Hundred pounds thereof when the Roof is shingled, and the Remainder when the Building is finished; and to find and provide for the carrying on and finishing said Building all the Stuff and materials needful and necessary as the same shall be wanted. And for the true performance of these Articles and every clause thereof, the said Parties Bind themselves each to the other joyntly and severally firmly by these presents in the penal sum of FOUR THOUSAND POUNDS; Current passable Bills of Public Credit of said Colony, old Tenor, to be forfeited and paid by the Party failing to the other Party.

ARTICLES
FOR BUILDING THE LIBRARY

MEMORANDUM: That the Parties to the within written Articles of Agreement, notwith-standing what is therein written, Do hereby agree to the following alterations in that building therein mentioned upon the same penalty as within, viz., that the four Pilasters in the front of the House, all the windows in the north and South West of said House: the stair case and Partitions within side, the Venetian Window in the East End, and the wainscott on the north and south Side within the House, as far as the Shelves extend, be all omitted, and that instead of the Venitian Win-dow in the East end, there be three small Windows, that the Shelves for the Books be placed against the Walls of the Building, that there be a stair case at the west end of sd House, the Ceiling of the Portico to have a cornice and that the Planshear and Entablature and all other Parts of said Build-ing be finished and compleated well and workmanlike agreeable to a plan or Draught drawn by Mr. Peter Harrison, and all Parts of the within mentioned Articles of agreement to stand good excepting such alterations as are made by this Additional agreement, And in Consideration of the Builders Conforming to ye sd Draught drawn by Mr. Peter Harrison, and following his directions as to all the Alterations herein mentioned and all other parts of said Building according to the true Intent and meaning of said Articles, The within named Saml Wickham, Henry Collins and John Tillinghast Do hereby Oblige themselves to pay to the within-named Wing Spooner, Samuel Green, Thomas Melvil and Israel Chapman, the Sum of One Hundred pounds, old Tenor, over and above the two Thousand two hundred pounds within mentioned.

In Witness whereof the Parties to these Presents have interchangeably set their hands and seals the Sixth Day of February in the twenty second year of his Majty's Reign Anno Dominie 1748.

SAMUEL WICKHAM,
HENRY COLLINS,
JOHN TILLINGHAST.

Sign'd Seal'd and Deliver'd
in the presence of
SAMUEL ENGS,
GIDEON SISSON.

The Redwood Library building has been enlarged three times. In 1858, the present reading room was built under the direction of the architect George Snell of Boston. The original rear elevation of Peter Harrison's building, removed to the south side of this addition, was duplicated on the north. The large addition now used as a delivery room was designed by George Champlin Mason of Newport in 1875. In 1913 the fourth building, a fireproof stack room, was built. In 1915, Norman Isham carefully restored Peter Harrison's building (the interior of which had been altered) to its original appearance. The measured drawings and plans he made at that time are now on file in the Newport Historical Society.

The year after Redwood Library was built, Harrison was asked to build the lighthouse at Beavertail on Jamestown.[6] This first structure was burned in 1753, but he rebuilt it almost immediately afterward and the second stood until 1854. A little sketch of it in Harrison's hand exists on the map he made of the Town and Harbour of Newport in 1755, now in the Public Records Office in London. It shows a round three-story tower with a cornice gallery and a lantern.[7] About this same time (1754) he was called upon by the town to rebuild the fortifications of Fort George on Goat Island. They were never completely finished and have since been demolished, but Harrison's original plans are still in existence, and a drawing of the part actually built is preserved on the Map of Newport that Charles Blascowitz made for the British Admiralty in 1777.[8]

P. 93

The Brick Market. In the meantime, Newport's need for an adequate granary and market had become increasingly apparent. In 1753 the Proprietors of Long Wharf had voted that "liberty be granted the applicants to erect a market house where the upper watch house now stands." The matter rested until 1760, when the Proprietors set aside land on Thames Street for a market, "the upper part to be divided into stores for dry goods," and "the lower part thereof for a Market House, and for no other use whatsoever forever: (unless it shall be found convenient to appropriate some part of it for a watch house). A handsome brick building, to be thirty-three feet in front or in width and about sixty-six feet in length." [9]

Pls. 6, 106, 107

By the tenth of July, 1760, a committee composed of Henry Collins, Joseph Bell, Augustus Johnston, and Joseph Lyndon had been appointed to confer with Peter Harrison, architect. By 1772, more than ten years later, when the Market had at last been completed, Harrison had once more proven himself an architect of extraordinary distinction, as he had already in the Redwood Library, King's Chapel in Boston, and Christ Church in Cambridge. Here again he had turned to his own architectural library for ideas.[10] The scheme he selected, a single order embracing two stories set over a high arcaded basement, was, as Mr. Kimball has pointed out, a favorite one in England at this time. This particular version was derived from Inigo Jones' design for Old Somerset House illustrated in Colin Campbell's *Vitruvius Britannicus* of 1716, one of the earliest and largest of the many important architectural works sponsored by Lord Burlington and his group. The original source for the scheme was older,

Pl. 107

however, and Kimball suggests that it went back not to Palladian sources but to Michelangelo's Palazzo del Senatore in Rome.[11]

The strong influence of Lord Burlington's puristic and academic taste is clear, but Harrison's adaptation, which varies from the engraved plate, proves once more his ability to meet specific needs. Changes in detail stamped the Newport building with a suitably less grandiose air than that of its model. Whereas the original design called for stone, Harrison used brick, in accordance with the specifications. He also substituted the Ionic for the Corinthian order and altered the window detail. Gibbs' *Rules for Drawing*, published in 1745, furnished the information necessary for these changes. The resulting building, with its satisfying proportions, is imbued with the ordered clarity characteristic of Harrison's work, and has been accounted one of his best achievements.

The interior, probably always comparatively plain, has been altered more than once. For a number of years the lower part was used as a market and watch house. The second and third stories were let out for shops and offices as originally planned. Just after the Revolutionary war the upper stories were used for a printing office. Later, from 1793 to 1799, Alexander Placide rented this part as a theater, where a fragment of one of the theatrical scenes, a seascape with ships, painted directly on the plaster of the east wall, may still be seen today.[12]

In 1842 the building was altered to serve as a town hall. The third floor was removed and the second converted into one large room with galleries on three sides. The arcades were fitted with windows and doors and the lower part used for stores. The old structure served as a city hall from 1853 to 1900. The exterior was restored in 1928, and two years later the interior was completely rebuilt through the generosity of Mr. John Nicholas Brown under the direction of Norman Isham.[13] At this time the yellow paint applied in the nineteenth century was removed from the bricks. Unfortunately, the basement story was constructed of such soft brick that, except for the west and south walls, it had to be replaced. The small *b* paned windows which close the once open arcades also dissipate somewhat the original broad simplicity of effect. Otherwise it is as Peter Harrison designed it, a handsome market in the current English academic taste.

The Touro Synagogue. Peter Harrison's third Newport building, the Touro Synagogue, is now the oldest synagogue standing in the United States. Perhaps his most successful building, the cool beauty of its interior has remained almost unchanged since the day of the dedication ceremony on December 2, 1763.

Pls. 108–110

Isaac de Touro, recorded as a "chuzzan (reader) from Amsterdam," had arrived five years earlier, some time in 1758. He was a liberal, cultivated, and distinguished man, and with his coming fresh impetus was given the spiritual life of the Jewish community. Soon plans were being made for the building of a synagogue after over a hundred years of worshipping in private homes.[14]

In August of 1759 the cornerstone was laid, and four years later the new building, still not quite completed, was dedicated. The ceremony began, according to the account in the *Newport Mercury*,[15] with

a handsome procession in which was carried the Book of the Law to be deposited in the Ark. Several portions of Scripture, and of their Service with a prayer for the Royal Family were read and finely sung by the Priest and People. There were present many Gentlemen and Ladies. The Order and Decorum, the Harmoney and Solemnity of the Music, together with a handsome Assembly of People, in the Edifice the most perfect of the Temple kind in America, and splendidly illuminated, could not but raise in the mind a faint Idea of the Majesty and grandeur of the ancient Jewish worship mentioned in Scripture. Dr. Isaac de Abraham Touro performed the Service.

Ezra Stiles, who attended the service, described the building at length in his diary under date of December 2, 1763.[16]

The Synagogue is about perhaps fourty foot long & 30 wide, of Brick on a Foundation of free Stone: it was begun about two years ago & is now finished except the Porch & the capitals of the Pillars. The Front representation of the holy of holies, or the Partition Veil, consists only of wainscotted Breast work on the east end, in the lower part of which four long Doors cover an upright Square Closet the depth of which is about a foot or the thickness of the wall, & in this Apartment (vulgarly called the Ark) were deposited three Copies & Rolls of the Pentateuch written on Vellum, or rather tanned Calf Skin: one of these Rolls I was told by Dr. Touro was presented from Amsterdam & is Two Hundred years old; the Letters have the Rabbinical flourishes.

A gallery for the Women runs round the whole Inside, except the east end, supported by Columns of Ionic order, over which are placed correspondent Columns of the Corinthian order supporting the Ceiling of the Roof. The depth of the Corinthian Pedestal is the height of the Balustrade which runs round the Gallery. The Pulpit for Reading the Law, is a raised Pew with an extended front table; this placed about the center of the Synagogue or nearer the West End, being a Square embalustraded Comporting with the Length of the intented Chancel before & at the Foot of the Ark.

On the middle of the North Side & affixed to the Wall is a raised Seat for the Parnas or Ruler, & for the Elders: the Breast and Back interlaid with Chinese Mosaic work. A Wainscotted Seat runs round three Sides of the Synagogue below, & another in the gallery. There are no other Seats or pews. There may be Eighty Souls of Jews or 15 families now in Town. The Synagogue has already cost Fifteen Hundred Pounds Sterling. There are to be five Lamps pendant from a lofty ceiling.

Most eighteenth-century visitors mentioned the Synagogue, and the Reverend Mr. Andrew Burnaby, writing while the building was still unfinished, recorded the architect's name, an unusual thing to do, even well into the nineteenth century.[17]

"This building," he wrote,

was designed, as indeed were several others, by a Mr. Harrison, an ingenious English gentleman who lives here. It will be extremely elegant within when completed; but the outside is totally spoilt by a school, which the Jews insisted on having annexed to it for the education of their children.

The Synagogue is fresh evidence of Harrison's capacity as a designer. Although he again had recourse to his architectural library for suggestions, there was no precedent in English building for the form required for a Synagogue, with its Ark of the Covenant, and its twelve columns, each representing one of the twelve tribes of Israel.

The plan followed closely the eighteenth-century Spanish and Portuguese Sephardic Synagogues of Amsterdam and London, and for this, Harrison chose as a model a two-storied galleried hall shown in the pages of Kent's *Designs of Inigo Jones and Others*. Details for the columns, the balustrades, and the Ark of the Covenant were drawn from James Gibbs' *Rules for Drawing* and Batty Langley's *Treasury of Designs*. These books, except for Gibbs', reflected the current English academic taste, which influenced all Harrison's work so profoundly. In using them as sources for this building, Peter Harrison proved himself equal not only to achieving fine effects with traditional forms, but capable of creating a new form out of traditional parts.[18]

Pl. 111

The interior was enclosed in a severe square hip-roofed brick building reminiscent of dwelling houses like Francis Malbone's on Thames Street. It was decorated only by a sandstone basement and belt course, a modillion cornice and an Ionic columnated portico, an almost unique feature in Newport building. The necessity of the Jewish ritual that the Ark of the Covenant be placed on a wall facing Jerusalem meant that the building was set at an angle to the street. This, together with the mid-nineteenth-century buff paint applied over the red brick, has combined to increase the already severe appearance of the exterior.

Except for the addition of the chairs, not called for in the old Sephardic ritual, the furniture belongs to the eighteenth century. The candelabra and the perpetual lamp were all gifts made before 1765. The Synagogue also possesses a number of ancient Scrolls of the Law, one of which, brought in 1658, is now over four hundred and fifty years old. The ornamental silver tops for these scrolls were made in about 1765 in New York by Myers and Hays, eminent eighteenth-century silversmiths.[19]

In 1780 the Synagogue, almost the only public building to survive the Revolution undamaged, served as the meeting place for the Rhode Island General Assembly and for sessions of the Supreme Court of Rhode Island. George Washington visited the building on two occasions, the first, in 1781; the second, when he came as President in August of 1790. At this time he sent a letter to the Hebrew Congregation in Newport in reply to an address by Moses Seixas, Reader. This letter contains the words, "For happily the government of the United States, which gives to bigotry no sanction, to persecution no assistance, requires only that they who live under its protection should demean themselves as good citizens in giving it on all occasions their effectual support."[20]

A trap door still to be seen in the floor of the central reading desk of the Synagogue once opened into a tunnel of escape out to Barney Street. This tunnel, dug as a safety measure by a people whose memories of past persecution were not yet dead, affords background to Washington's earnest words.[21]

When Thomas Jefferson, in Washington's company, visited Newport as Secretary of State in 1790, he may have attended services at the Synagogue.[22] One cannot help feeling that he looked upon Harrison's buildings with full appreciation. His own designs for Monticello

in 1771, for the Capitol of Virginia in 1785, and the University of Virginia still later, were
to have a profound effect in turning the attention of Americans to classical models.[23]

In the Redwood Library, the Brick Market, and the Jewish Synagogue, the pervading
influence of Lord Burlington's academic taste on Peter Harrison's work completely super-
sedes the lighter, more exuberant spirit of Wren's time. Harrison, a loyalist in sympathies
and long since turned Episcopalian, left Newport before the Synagogue was completed to
accept the post of Customs Collector in New Haven. Mr. Bridenbaugh has given an excellent
account of the troubled last years of his life, climaxed in 1777 by the destruction, at the hands
of a rioting American mob, of his personal property, including all his drawings and papers
and his fine library, an irreparable loss to the history of one of the most brilliant chapters in
colonial architecture.

DOMESTIC BUILDING. The tendencies exhibited in the public buildings were also apparent
in the houses. Level hipped roofs, classic balustrades, and academically correct doorways
began to replace the broken and scroll pediments, the balconies with twisted balusters and
the broad gambrel-roofed houses of Munday's time. The rusticated wood Peter Harrison
used for the Redwood Library was evidently much admired and was soon repeated in other
Newport work.

The Vernon house of about 1760 at the corner of Clarke and Mary, the Peter Buliod
house, circa 1760, now the Salvation Army headquarters on Touro Street, the Banister country house of 1756 just beyond the Mile Corner, and the house of the Royal Customs Collector
Charles Dudley, circa 1750, which has been demolished, were all built within fifteen years
after the completion of Redwood Library. All these houses were finished with wood imitating stone, painted stone color, and probably were sanded as well. This alone helped to give
a more academic flavor to the new building. In his Memoir of Rhode Island, Henry Bull says
that Harrison designed Dudley's house [24] and more than any other domestic building, it evidenced the variety of form which stamped his public structures. A square two-story house, it
was outstanding because of its central pavilion defined by pilasters of the Ionic order, which
rose a full two stories high. This particular feature introduced a new and sophisticated element into Newport's domestic architecture and would seem to verify Bull's assertion.
Harrison's name has also been linked with the Vernon house which took on its present
exterior form about 1758. With its rusticated walls, correct classical detail, and level hipped
roof finished by a double row of balustrades, its exterior has the most academic proportions
of any colonial house still standing in Newport.

Since Harrison was John Banister's brother-in-law, he may also have lent a helping hand
in planning Banister's country house at Mile Corner. Its wooden rusticated exterior, however,
is less academic in proportion than the exteriors of the Vernon and Dudley houses, and the

Pls. 113–115,
116, 112

Pl. 111

Pl. 112

Pl. 111

interior shows no stylistic advance over the other fine houses of the day. Francis Malbone's brick house built on Thames Street about 1760, now St. Clare's Home, is another Newport house which has been associated particularly with Harrison's name. It is built of brick and resembles the Synagogue in general appearance, while the Ionic capitals of the pedimented doorway are like those of the Synagogue portico,[25] and were evidently drawn from the same source, Gibbs' *Rules for Drawing.*

Harrison's own house, known as Harrison Farm, is still standing. He built it about a half a mile south of Newport on property his wife had inherited from her father, and entries in John Stevens' account books show that it was in process of construction in 1747. Evidently a somewhat plain farmhouse from the first, it was moved across Harrison Avenue to its present location in the late nineteenth century, where its new owner so rebuilt it that only the typical four-room central-hall plan and a few paneled doors remain to suggest an eighteenth-century beginning. It is now owned by Lawrence Phelps Tower.[26]

Pl. 105

The little summer house built on Abraham Redwood's country estate sometime after 1743, and now removed to the Redwood Library grounds, was almost certainly designed by Harrison.[27] *Mercury* notices of the sixties and seventies frequently mention a summer house as an adjunct to the gardens,[28] but Abraham Redwood's is the sole Newport survivor. The inspiration for this rusticated, octagonal building with its double curved roof is to be found on plate LXXX of Gibbs' *Book of Architecture* (1728). It is additional proof of the role architectural books played in Harrison's work.

All these buildings represent the second phase of eighteenth-century colonial building which was curtailed in Newport during the period of its natural development by the devastation of the Revolutionary war. Otherwise, Newport, as was Providence, would have been filled with the square two or three-story formal brick or wooden hip-roofed mansion houses characteristic of the late Georgian and early Republican style.

Pls. 43, 122

Similar changes were also in evidence in the smaller houses. Gambrel-roofed buildings, especially one-story cottages, were still being built in the early nineteenth century, but the type in general gave precedence to the plain pitched roof. Some of the doorways, like that of Pitt's Head Tavern, reminiscent of the front door of Redwood, reflected the detail seen in Harrison's work. The high pedestals and archaic off-scale detail seen in the doors of Trinity Church had now disappeared, and the complication of earlier molded woodwork with its many vertical breaks gave way to simpler outlines. This showed in such details as the eaves cornices which no longer invariably broke out around the windows. The cornice of Pitt's

Pl. 122

Head Tavern is typical, with its shaped modillion course running in an unbroken line across the front of the house.

Even in the most advanced houses, however, the interiors were apt to follow traditional usage. They were almost invariably laid out on the central-hall, four-room ground plan, although the pilasters and the round-headed cupboards flanking the shelfless mantelpieces, the raised paneling, and bolection framed fireplaces trimmed with Dutch tiles of the earlier houses now yielded to beveled paneling and pedimented two-story mantelpieces, as in the Vernon, Francis Malbone, and John Banister houses. Sometimes of elaborate design, the mantelpieces were frequently finished with broken or scroll pediments, mitred "ears," and modillion or dentil work cornices. A refinement and reduction of the bold scale of earlier molded work was also apparent and the use of wood paneling was apt to be restricted to the wainscotting and to the mantel wall or to the chimney breast only.

Pl. 115

Pl. 118

The stair halls repeated the earlier scheme, with its broad carved arches supported on carved brackets making a break between front and back hall. Twisted balusters, sometimes of more delicate outline, continued in favor, but the landing opening was now more commonly handled as a window of Palladian (or Venetian) form. Houses of this date also often had stairways with rather squat turned balusters and ramped rails, like those to be found in the John Warren and Thomas Robinson houses on Washington Street and the Captain John Mawdsley house on John Street. Their stair drops, now turned to a somewhat complicated profile, were an elaboration of the simple old acorn-shaped form. After the Revolutionary war, the rich earlier schemes tended to be replaced by curving stairways or stairways of one run, both with lightly turned or plain stick balusters.

Pl. 114

Pl. 120

Ground plans of the smaller houses generally followed the old five-room, central-chimney scheme, but sometimes they were laid out with a central hall and two interior chimneys. Sometimes, as already noted in Whitehall, and shown in Ninyon Challoner's house, a side hall was included.

Pl. 71

Newport deeds also contain frequent references to double houses. Some of these, like James Sheffield's house on the Point which was divided in his will in 1719, were originally built as single houses, and were divided later, usually from front to back down the middle of the central hall. Others were built to serve as double houses from the first. At least two outstanding examples, both owned by members of the same family, were probably built, one during the years just before, and the other just after the Revolution.

The William Stevens homestead, at 59 Farewell Street on the corner of Warner, is a big gambrel-roofed two and one-half story building with two interior chimneys.[29] It would look like a typical eighteenth-century house, but for the pair of front doors. Each of these two doors opens into a handsome and separate stair hall, identical but laid out in reverse. The scheme of the two parts, also identical and laid out in reverse, is built on the three-room plan described in Chapter 4. The building was in William Stevens' family for many years after the Revolution; in 1770 the house was owned jointly by William Cozzens, hatmaker, and his brother, Joseph. The brothers had bought the land from Timothy Balch, but the date of this transaction has not been discovered. The detail of the fireplace paneling and of the stair-

Pl. 125

ways, with their turned balusters and ramped rails, would indicate that the house was built about the time the Mawdsley house was, probably between 1750 and 1760. Most of the paneling of the downstairs rooms is still in place, but otherwise one of Newport's most interesting houses is in sorry condition.

Pl. 127

The Robert Stevens house stands, sadly altered, on the southwest corner of Thames and the old Robert Stevens, now called Bowens' wharf.[30] Land records show that Elizabeth Pelham Harrison inherited this wharf with buildings from her father in 1740, and Peter and Elizabeth Harrison owned it jointly. Although some of the decorative detail of the house, which is constructed on an unusual U-shaped plan, belongs to the period from 1750 to 1775, it was probably built just after the Revolution.

The Harrisons removed to New Haven soon after 1760, but the wharf remained in Elizabeth's possession until 1783, when she sold to Robert Stevens and Henry Stevenson jointly, together with all "edifices and buildings." These two merchants were probably responsible for the double U-shaped house. The middle section, which faces on Thames Street, is handled as a gable-roofed house with a single room on either side of a central chimney. This chimney divides the building into the northern and the southern halves and is finished on both faces with handsome paneling to form the parlor fireplace walls in each house. Each arm of the U is composed of a pair of ells of diminishing size, set at right angles to the main body of the house. This means that each half of the building consists of three rooms and a stair hall laid out in a line down the wharfside. The ells are so arranged that not only do both stair halls have their own landing windows, but the middle ells also have their own west windows in the space freed by the proportionately narrower westernmost ells. Such an arrangement to allow for good lighting and cross windows in an already atypical ground plan represents advanced planning for a colonial house.

Pl. 120

The lower floors have long since been converted into shops, and otherwise changed, but some of the good wainscoting remains, even here, and the paneling in the Bowen's Wharf half is still in place in all three of the second story rooms. The stairway, set against the back wall of the main section, has turned drops and balusters, ramped and molded hand railings, and scroll decorations carved on the riser ends. It resembles the stairways in the pre-Revolutionary Mawdsley, William Stevens, and Thomas Townsend houses, as well as the Aquidneck house (Collins house) on School Street. The parlors in each half of the house have wainscoting to the chair rails, identical double dentil cornices, and carved "eared" mantel panels finished with pediments, details which suggest a post-Revolutionary date.[31]

Pls. 125–127

Stevens' will was probated in 1831, at which time the house was divided among members of his family. Shops and wharves, some of which are still standing, were mentioned. The lower rooms of the house had evidently already long been in use as shops, while the northeast room served as the post office, and the southeast as the Commercial Bank. Soon afterwards, George Bowen bought the wharf with all its buildings. Arn Hildreth, block and pump maker, who worked there for sixty years, drew a plan of the double house and the buildings, including the ship chandler's shop now used for the office of the Bowen Coal Company, the blockmaker's shop, and the sailmaker's shop and loft. The exterior of the house has been so changed on the Thames Street side that its colonial date can be surmised only from the waterside. Only three of the wharf buildings still stand, but with Arn Hildreth's plan and description in hand, we are able imaginatively to reconstruct the activities of a once prosperous colonial shipping center.[32]

Pl. 125

---

a The place of Redwood Library in American architectural history has perhaps best been summed up in Fiske Kimball's words: "The Redwood Library was the forerunner of the Virginia Capitol; Harrison the forerunner, as Jefferson was the founder, of American classicism."

b The south wall was not cleaned. There is good reason to believe that Harrison finished the entire building with some kind of smooth coating (which would explain the use of different kinds of brick) to imitate the stone or stucco preferred by the English proponents of the academic style. See page 85. The synagogue may also have been painted in the eighteenth century.

c The ark as it exists today is not the ark Ezra Stiles described. When the Synagogue was restored in 1956–1957 Mrs. Samuel Schwartz, who worked on the documentation of the fabric, proved once more the value of going to original sources by examining the manuscript of Ezra Stiles' diary. She discovered that Stiles had made a marginal drawing to accompany his description of the Ark.

The little drawing, published in the Summer 1958 issue of the *Journal of the Society of Architectural Historians* (American Notes) and reprinted here on Plate 109, is not of the present Ark. The question then becomes when was this Ark installed? Mrs. Schwartz concludes from Synagogue records that the original Ark was replaced during the restoration of 1822. However, since the design for the present Ark is drawn from Gibbs' *Rules for Drawing* and Batty Langley's *Treasury of Designs* (see page 86 and Plate 109), it seems likely that for some reason the Ark was rebuilt while these sources were still in fashion, which would mean soon after the Synagogue was

completed. Architectural detail executed in the 1820's would normally reflect Adam influence through (in New England) the more attenuated and refined style of Charles Bulfinch and Asher Benjamin. Benjamin's Island Union Bank Building had been standing on Thames Street since 1817. (See Plate 145.) It is also of interest to note that while Harrison evidently had access to Langley's *Treasury of Designs* it was not listed in the inventory of his library.

d He also came in 1784. See Bridenbaugh, "Peter Harrison, Addendum," in the *Journal of the Society of Architectural Historians* December 1959.

e Read "1775" for "1777."

f They are one-story pilasters set over the porch between the second and third stories.

Demolished after 1952. The stair hall and parlors are now installed in the Henry Francis du Pont Winterthur Museum.

g Another rusticated house, standing at 108 Prospect Hill Street, is described in the note on page 70. As shown by Bridenbaugh, Banister and Harrison were on very bad personal terms. Any attribution to Harrison of the Banister houses should probably be discounted. On the other hand, Harrison maintained a close association with the Malbone family. Mr. Rupert B. Lillie has assembled information showing that the Malbones visited Harrison Farm and that the relationship continued after Harrison left Newport. This adds further weight to the local tradition that Harrison designed Francis Malbone's brick house on Thames Street which is markedly similar in style to the Synagogue.

h Now in the hands of a developer.

i Built in 1766. See note c on Page 48.

CHAPTER SIX

Newport in the Revolutionary War

THE YEARS JUST BEFORE THE REVOLUTION saw Newport at its height, with its commerce greater than that of New York, but the war completely undermined its social and economic pride. In December, 1776, the British under General Clinton took possession of Newport and retained it until November, 1779. It is estimated that the population dropped from nine thousand to four thousand between 1775 and 1780. In 1776 and 1777 Charles Blascowitz made maps of Newport and Newport County at the request of the British Admiralty, showing the colonial town complete with city streets and outlying estates developed to their full extent. But gradually the British laid waste the timber of the island, and under pressure of the American blockade, house after house went down to meet the common need for firewood, until some four hundred and eighty buildings of various kinds were destroyed.

On May 31, 1780, Ezra Stiles, by this time President of Yale College and four years away from his beloved Newport, wrote after a brief visit,

> I took a melancholy farewell and left Newport on Return for New Haven. About three hundred Dwelling houses I judge have been destroyed in Newport. The town is in Ruins. But with Nehemiah I could prefer the very dust of Zion to the Gardens of Persia, and the broken walls of Jerusalem to the Palaces of Sushan. I rode over the Isld and found the beautiful Rows of Trees which lined the Roads, with sundry Coppices or Groves & Orchards cut down and laid waste, but the natural Beauties of the Place still remain. And I doubt not the place will be rebuilt & excede its former splendour.[1]

Jonathan Easton wrote in 1781, estimating the damage to his property during the war "One acre of turf taken off, about 2 acres in a fort and cellars and heaps . . . 3 houses burned, one pulled down, a good orchard cut, and upwards of 800 trees cut, near 2000 rails burnt, the only house left, crowded with British troops for near 3 years." After the British evacuated, the French fleet arrived and camped in Easton's meadow "before it was mowed."[2]

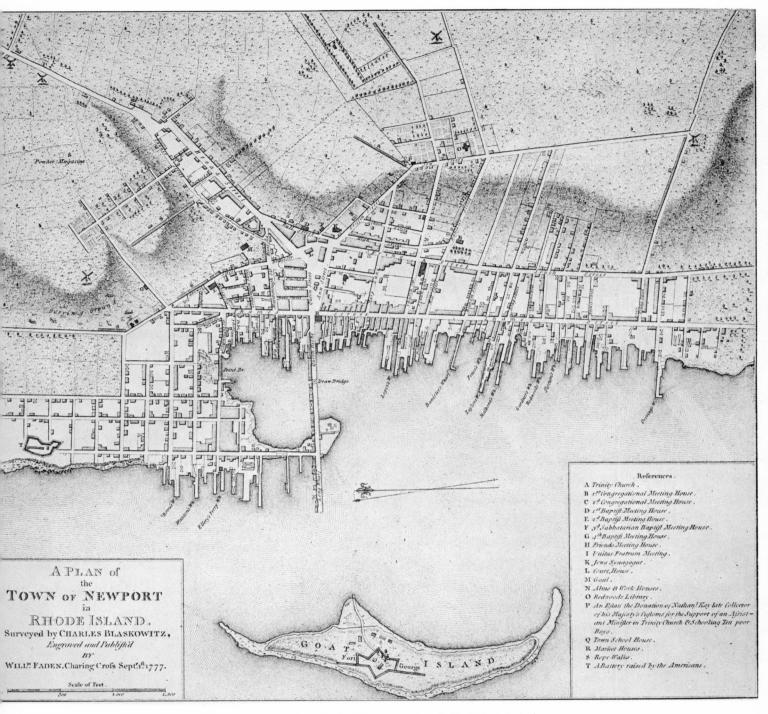

References.

A *Trinity Church.*
B *1st Congregational Meeting House.*
C *2d Congregational Meeting House.*
D *1st Baptist Meeting House.*
E *2d Baptist Meeting House.*
F *3d Sabbatarian Baptist Meeting House.*
G *4th Baptist Meeting House.*
H *Friends Meeting House.*
I *Unitas Fratrum Meeting.*
K *Jews Synagogue.*
L *Court House.*
M *Goal.*
N *Alms & Work Houses.*
O *Redwoods Library.*
P *An Estate the Donation of Nathanl. Kay late Collector of his Majesty's Customs for the Support of an Assistant Minister in Trinity Church & Schooling Ten poor Boys.*
Q *Town School House.*
R *Market Houses.*
S *Rope Walks.*
T *A Battery raised by the Americans.*

A PLAN of
the
TOWN of NEWPORT
in
RHODE ISLAND.
Surveyed by CHARLES BLASKOWITZ,
Engraved and Publish'd
BY
WILLm. FADEN, Charing Cross Septr. 1st 1777.

Scale of Feet.

Map of Newport, drawn by Charles Blascowitz for the British Admiralty, 1777.
Courtesy Newport Historical Society.

His "only house left" still stands, although not in its original location. It was moved to Cliff Avenue when DeLancy Kane bought the property in 1845. At present it is the home of Stephen B. Luce. *a*

In spite of camping in Easton's meadow "before it was mowed," the arrival of the French fleet and land forces, "the troops of Dr. Franklin," as Voltaire called them, gave welcome respite, as well as a fresh hope to the war-depleted town On July 10, 1880, after *b* the British had voluntarily evacuated the city and island they had virtually plundered, twelve French men of war and thirty-two transports, carrying five thousand troops in all, weighed anchor in Newport Harbor. The fleet was under command of Admiral de Ternay, the land forces under the command of Compte de Rochambeau, who retained Newport as their headquarters until June, 1781.[3]

Ezra Stiles wrote under date of July 12, 1780, that "the French are a very fine body of men & appear to be well officered . . . The arrival of the Fleet and Army hath given new Life to the Town. There is more Business transactg and money circulatg than formerly." [4] Certainly there was more gaiety. In spite of new common poverty, social life was resplendent this year, made so by the brilliant band of young officers in their uniforms turned back with green, red, or rose, according to their corps. The second evening after their arrival, the city was illuminated until ten o'clock, the Colony House decorated, and "13 grand Rockets were fired in front of the Statehouse." Those who were too poor to buy candles were furnished with them. "The Whigs put 13 lights in the windows, the Tories or doubtfuls 4 or 6, the Quakers did not chuse their Lights should shine before men, and their Windows were broken — a fine subject for Friends Meeting of Sufferings," Congregationalist Ezra Stiles acidly wrote.[5]

The city was illuminated once more on the sixth of March in 1781, three months before the French Army left Newport and on the occasion of Washington's visit with Rochambeau. The Honorable Daniel Updike wrote then "I never felt the solid earth tremble under me before. The firing from the French ships that lines the harbor was tremendous; it was one continuous roar, and looked as though the very bay was on fire." [6] That evening, as the *Mercury* reported,

> the town and fleet in the harbour were beautifully illuminated. The procession was led off by thirty boys, bearing candles fixed on staffs, followed by General Washington, Count Rochambeau and the other officers, their aides, and the procession of the citizens. The night was clear, and there was not a breath to fan the Torches. The brilliant procession marched through the principal streets and then returned to the headquarters.[7]

On the following evening Rochambeau gave a ball in Washington's honor, and it was on this occasion that Washington chose Miss Margaret Champlin as his partner for the dance opening the evening's festivities. It is recorded that the French officers took the instruments from the hands of the musicians and played Miss Champlin's selection, the popular "A Successful Campaign," while the couple went through the steps of the minuet.

Rochambeau's Newport headquarters was the Vernon house at the corner of Clarke and Mary streets and it was here that he conferred with Washington. De Ternay, who was seriously ill when he arrived in Newport, was quartered in the confiscated house of Lieutenant Governor Joseph Wanton, on Washington Street. He died in this house on the fifteenth of December in 1780 and lies buried in Trinity churchyard. His funeral procession, probably the most imposing the Newport of that day had ever seen, was headed by chanting priests and is said to have extended all the way from the old house in Washington Street through Thames to Trinity Church.[8]

p. 464

Pls. 113, 114

Pls. 88–94

A French billeting list records the houses, some of which are still standing, where other officers were quartered.[9] General Rochambeau's son, le Vicomte de Rochambeau, then Colonel *en second* of the Bourbonnais regiment, was quartered with his father in the Vernon house. Rochambeau's aides-de-camp, Axel de Ferson and the Marquis de Damas, were quartered at Robert Stevens' house, now numbered 31 Clarke Street, across the way. Axel de Ferson was a Swedish subject and a true soldier of fortune. He was a close personal friend of Marie Antoinette and there is ground for the belief that he joined the French forces because his feeling for the queen made it wise for him to leave the French capitol. Later he was to make more than one valiant but futile attempt to help her escape from France and her unhappy fate.[10] Many of his letters to his father show that he was lonely in Newport, and critical of the life there.[11] He did, however, become fond of the family of Mrs. Deborah Hunter, widow of Dr. William Hunter, the anatomist, and mother of William Hunter, who became the first ambassador to Brazil. Her three daughters were popular belles of the day, and feature in many of the descriptions left by the French officers. De Ferson particularly liked Eliza, the eldest, then just eighteen, of whom he wrote to his father that she was "pretty, sweet, gay and a very good musician."[12] He wrote in more detailed letters to his sisters that he often stayed at the Hunters' till midnight, that Eliza played the piano and he played his flute, that she was teaching him English and he in turn was teaching her French which "she already speaks charmingly." He added, "These evenings are very agreeable." A family story has it that de Ferson asked Eliza to marry him but that she refused. Her eyes, later to fail, were already troubling her, and the local doctors had told her that unless a famous London surgeon could help her, she was doomed to lose her sight.[13]

p. 465

The very gay Duc de Lauzan, de Ferson's close friend, was quartered at the Hunters' house, and like de Ferson, became much attached to the family. "Madame Hunter, a widow of some thirty-six years of age," he wrote, "had two [three] charming daughters . . . She received me into her friendship, and I was presently regarded as one of the family. I really lived there, and when I was taken seriously ill, she brought me to her house and lavished upon me the most touching attentions. I never fell in love with the Mesdemoiselles Hunter," he notes with an air of surprise, "but if they had been my sisters, I could not have been fonder of them, especially the eldest, who is one of the most charming persons I have ever met." [14]

A year later when the Prince de Broglie visited Newport, just before returning to Europe, he called on the Misses Hunter. "The eldest," he wrote, "without being regularly handsome, had what we might call a noble appearance and an air of aristocratic birth. Her physiognomy is intellectual and refined. There was grace in all her movements. Her toilette was quite as finished as that of Mademoiselle Champlin, but she is not altogether as fresh, in spite of what Ferson said. . . The younger sister, Nancy Hunter, is not quite so stylish looking but she is a perfect rosebud. Her character is gay, a smile always upon her countenance, with lovely teeth, a thing seldom met with in America." [15] The Hunters' house, which formerly stood on the north side of Mary Street at Thames, has long since been torn down.

De Laberdiere and Louis, Baron de Closen, who was also one of Rochambeau's aides and a Captain in the Royal Deux Ponts regiment, were both quartered with "Henri Potter" in the little house now numbered 39 Clarke Street. De Closen's invaluable journal has been drawn upon several times in this account for its descriptions of the Newport of those years. [16]

p. 468

Pls. 117–120

The Chevalier de Chastellux was quartered at Captain John Mawdsley's house, today numbered 199 Spring Street. Chastellux, who was an engineer, may have had a part in laying out the fortifications on Butts Hill in Portsmouth and the plans of the present Fort Adams. He built a large fortification on the crest of Halidon Hill, considered one of the most strategic forts on the Island. [17] Major Louis Toussard, who was in charge of the enlargements of Fort Adams, built the fort on the Dumpling and strengthened the North Battery, may also have been quartered in the Mawdsley house. [18] Chastellux was noted in Newport society for his "petits soupers." Even Ezra Stiles was impressed. He wrote in his diary under date of Oct. 9th, 1780, "Dined at Gen. de Chastelux in a splendid manner on 35 dishes. He is a capital Literary Character, a Member of the French Academy. He is the Glory of the Army."

Pls. 1, 43–45,
122
Pl. 116

Inspecteur Duval was quartered at Pitt's Head Tavern then located on the north side of Washington Square at the corner of Charles, and since removed to No. 5 Charles Street. *d* De Beville was stationed with Moses Levi in the square rusticated building on the south side of the Mall which now serves as headquarters for the Salvation Army.

Pls. 95, 96

Colonel de Buzelot, Chef de Brigade, with the rank of Major in the second battalion of the regiment of Auxonne, Corps of Royal Artillery, was placed with Joseph Tweedy, in the house now numbered 62 Spring Street; de Lombard was stationed in Christopher Townsend's house on the southwest corner of Bridge and Second Street. Townsend's old shop, attached to the house itself, has recently been restored and is now used for the showroom for Restorations Inc. Lieutenant Colonel Hogen was assigned to "Mad'e Harrison's, au neck." *e* This house, mentioned earlier, was formerly owned by Peter Harrison and was built by him.

Map of Newport, drawn by J. F. W. de Barres, 1776.
Courtesy of Maxim Karolik.

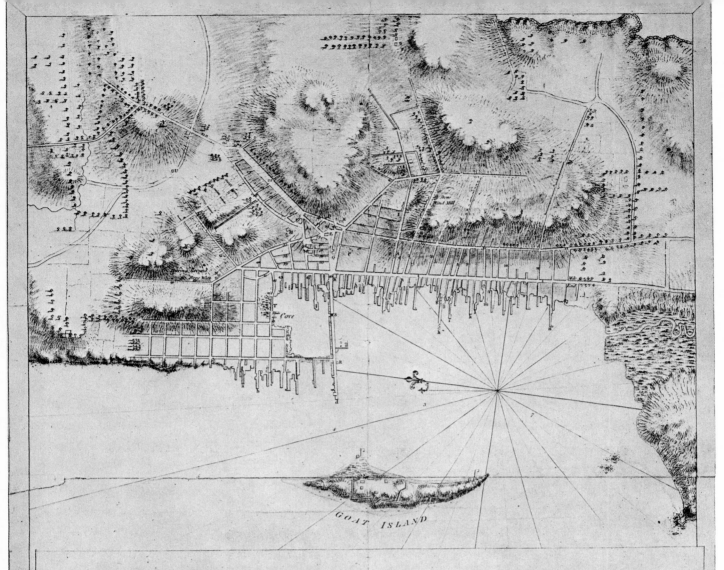

GOAT ISLAND

A PLAN
of the
TOWN OF NEWPORT.
in the
Province of Rhode Island

WHARFS		PUBLIC BUILDINGS.			STREETS.		
a	Homes	A	Trinity Church	Q	Town School House	9	Cannon	24	Clarkes Lane	39	Sweeting
b	Wantons	B	1st Congregational Meeting House	RRR	Market Houses	10	Brewers	25	Bright Do	40	Sanford
c	Ellerys Ferry	C	2d Congregational Do	S	Draw Bridge	11	Young	26	Wards Do	41	Triangle
d	Long Wharf	D	1st Baptist Do	T	Point Bridge	12	South	27	Fair Do	42	Shipwrights
e	Lopez's	E	Baptist Do	U	Powder Magazine	13	Spring	28	Tanners Do	43	Scots Folly
f	Banisters	F	3d or Sabattarian Do			14	High	29	Bridge	44	Clarke
g	Peases	G	4th Baptist Do		STREETS.	15	School	30	Meeting House Lane	45	Marlborough Dock
h	Saylors	H	Friends Do	1	Thames	16	Jews	31	Prison Lane	46	Queen Hithe
i	Malbones	I	Unitas Fratrum Do	2	Queens	17	Griffin	32	Puddle Do	47	Billingsgate
k	Gardners	K	Jews Synagogue	3	Ann	18	Spring Lane	33	Duke Do	48	Kings Dock
l	Redwoods	L	Court House	4	Mary	19	Harts Do	34	River Do	49	Passage
m	Slocums	M	Goal	5	Church	20	Bulls	35	Marlborough Do	50	Dudley
n	Overings	N	Alms & Work House	6	Frank Lane	21	Bulls Gap	36	Coddington	51	Pelham
		O	Redwood Library	7	Mill	22	Broad	37	Farwell	52	Banister
		P	Donation for Schooling Boys	8	King	23	School	38	Wanton		

Scale of Four Thousand Feet.

Baron Viomesnil, second in command of the French in America, and his handsome son, le Comte de Viomesnil, were quartered at Governor Joseph Wanton's house, while his other son, le Chevalier de Viomesnil, was assigned to Gould Marsh's house nearby. Both these houses stood on Thames Street just south of Washington Square.

Pl. 111

Viscount Desandrouins, one of the engineers at the seige of Yorktown, was quartered in the Francis Malbone house listed as "28 Thames, Col Malbournes." De Querenel stayed at Godfrey Malbone's numbered 83 Thames. De la Chez was stationed in Abraham Redwood's house, and de Palays at John Gidley's. All these mansions have long since succumbed to the demands of a business street.

Brigadier de Choisy, who commanded the detachment on the opposite side of the York River at the siege of Yorktown, was quartered on Bridge Street in the home of Jacob Rodriguez Rivera, which formerly stood at 50 Washington Street, just south of the Jonathan Nichols house. Captain de Lagrandeur lived at Francis Brinley's, also on Washington Street. Des Touches was with William Redwood on Bridge Street and de la Vicquette was assigned to John Townsend's, which stood across the street from Christopher's house. These houses are gone, as are the houses of George Scott and Nathaniel Mumford in Broad Street, occupied by the Deux Pont brothers. Le Baron d'Ezebeck, Lieutenant Colonel in the Regiment of the Royal Deux Ponts, was also stationed on Broad Street in the house of William Still. Other houses included in the French list may be located more exactly when the deed histories are completely compiled.

The diaries and letters written by the Frenchmen often give a vivid insight into the life of Newport of that year. Claude Blanchard, chief of the Commissary, Baron de Closen, Axel de Ferson, Prince Broglie, and Comte de Segur, among many others, have all left valuable information about the town. They brought fresh eyes to their new surroundings and described everything that attracted their attention. As we have already seen, the pretty girls, the belles of the day, came first in their scrutiny. De Broglie, whose descriptions of Eliza and Nancy Hunter have been quoted above, reported that Margaret Champlin was "dressed and coiffed with much taste, that is to say, in the French style," that "Newport possessed more than one rosebud," [19] while de Closen wrote that "the fair sex" were fond of dancing "which they do most unpretentiously." [20] The Count de Segur wrote that Newport "offered delightful circles composed of enlightened and modest men and of handsome women — all the French officers who knew them, recollect the names and beauty of Miss Champlin, the two Misses Hunter and several others." [21] He continued:

> Like the remainder of my companions I rendered them the homage to which they were justly entitled; but my longest visits were paid to an old man very silent, who very seldom bared his thoughts and never bared his head. His gravity and monosyllabic conversation announced, at first sight, that he was a Quaker. It must however be confessed that, in spite of all the veneration I felt for his virtue, our first interview would probably have been our last, had I not seen the door of the drawing room suddenly opened, and a being, which resembled a nymph rather than a woman,

enter the apartment. So much beauty, so much simplicity, so much elegance and so much modesty were perhaps never before combined in the same person. It was Polly Leiton [Lawton], the daughter of my grave Quaker. . . Her eyes seemed to reflect, as in a mirror, the meekness and purity of her mind and the goodness of her heart; she received us with an open ingenuity which delighted me, and the use of the familiar word "thou," which the rules of her sect prescribed, gave to our new acquaintance the appearance of an old friendship.

Her conversation also captivated him with its "candor full of originality." "Thou hast then," she said to him, "neither wife nor children in Europe, since thou leavest thy country and comest so far to engage in that cruel occupation war." She continued, "We ought never to interfere in other people's business unless it is to reconcile them together and prevent the effusion of blood," and "Thy King then, orders thee to do a thing which is unjust, inhuman, and contrary to what thy God orderth, thou shouldst obey thy God and disobey thy King, for he is a King to preserve and not to destroy. I am sure that thy wife, if she have a good heart, is of my opinion." "Certain it is," de Segur commented, having recorded her remonstrances, "that if I had not then been married and happy, I should, whilst coming to defend the liberty of the Americans, have lost my own at the feet of Polly Lawton."

The Prince de Broglie wrote of her, "when she spoke she used the 'thou,' but with a grace and simplicity only to be compared to that of her costume. This was a specie of English gown, pretty close to the figure, white as milk, an apron of the same whiteness, a fichu very full and firmly fastened. Her head dress was a simple little cap of very fine muslin, pleated and passed around the head, which allowed only half an inch of hair to be visible, but which had the effect of giving to Polly the air of a Holy Virgin. . . Whenever I recall her image," he continued, "I am tempted to write a great book against the dressing, the theatrical graces, and the coquetishness of certain rich ladies much admired in the world of fashion." [22]

The Viscomte de Noailles was quartered in the house of the Quaker Thomas Robinson, and the friendship he formed with Mrs. Robinson and her daughters, especially Mary, came to sustain him in the last years of his tragic life, broken not only because of despair over the disorders of France, but by the loss of his wife and family at the guillotine after the French Revolution.[23] In the summer of 1780 Madame de Noailles sent Mrs. Robinson a Sèvres tea set in appreciation of the kindness bestowed upon her husband.

"May I hope, Madame," she wrote, "that you will permit me to present some tea cups of a manufactory we have here, and that in drinking your tea with your charming daughters, you will sometimes think of me." [24] Molly Robinson's letters to the Viscomte de Noailles are still kept by the family at their château in Maintenon; because of them, present day members of the family made a special trip to Newport not many years ago to see the Robinson house, where they were pleased to find the Sèvres cups and saucers in the ancient corner cupboard.

American customs were a constant source of interest and comment. The habit of drinking toasts evoked the remark, "in spite of oneself one has to pretend to drink," [25] and of drinking tea, "I could vish zat servant into hell for bringing me so much hot water to drink"

Pl. 98

one young officer is reported to have said to his hostess.[26] The "little cakes of meal and water" which the natives ate were considered "not much for a Frenchman." [27]

Louis, Baron de Closen, wrote that "all the estates are enclosed by walls of stones piled one on top of the other, or wooden barriers called fences, which produce an attractive effect." He went on to say, "to one unfamiliar with the sight, it seems extraordinary that wooden houses built on stone foundations, when entirely finished are often moved from one quarter to another and even moved into the country. The frame as it is, is placed on little carts attached to one another. I have seen them drawn by 30 or 40 oxen or horses." [28] Louis Jean Baptiste Sylvestre de Robertnier, Lieutenant in the regiment of the Soissonais also commented in his unpublished diary now in the Rhode Island Historical Society on the practice of moving houses. "The houses are built of wood," he wrote. "Sometimes they are constructed outside the town and when finished are brought in on rollers (or carts) to their final location. This is for the most part true for the little houses, although it is not unusual to see the large ones so moved." He added that "it is customary to use diverse colors" in painting the houses, and that "all this gives a variety pleasing to the eye." [29]

The neatly kept houses also impressed the French. Robertnier wrote in his diary that "everything was scrupulously clean and airy," [30] although the houses were small and the furnishings utilitarian and plain. On the other hand, Claude Blanchard of the Commissary Department reported "They make use of wall papers which serve for tapestry; they have them very handsome. In many of the houses there are carpets, even upon the stairs." He went on to say, "They are very choice in cups and vases for holding tea and coffee, in glasses and decanters and other matters of this kind in habitual use." He commented, too, on the good housekeeping. "In general, the houses are very pleasant and kept with extreme neatness, with the mechanic and the country man, as well as the merchant and the general. In fact," he added, "their education is very nearly the same. So that a mechanic is often called in their assemblies, where there is no distinction; no separate order. The inhabitants of the entire country are proprietors. They till the earth and drive their own oxen themselves." [31]

The French forces withdrew from Newport in June of 1781 and Newport was faced with the problem of trying to recover from its impoverished condition and regain some vestige of its former commercial supremacy. In 1788, Brissot, the Girondist, visited Newport while in exile from France. His description of the sorry plight of the war-torn town gives a graphic account of its dissipated commerce:

> Since the peace everything is changed, the reign of solitude is only interrupted by groups of idle men standing with folded arms at the corners of the streets, houses falling to ruin, miserable shops which present nothing but a few coarse stuffs or baskets of apples, and other articles of little value; grass growing in the public square in front of the court of justice, rags stuffed in the windows.[32]

Ten years later the Duc de la Rochefoucauld-Liancourt wrote:

> Before the war there were many opulent inhabitants on Rhode Island, at present only the ruins of their houses, and traces of their former inclosures can be seen. The houses are either desolate or are inhabited by people who, on account of the smallness of their capitals, their dislike to labor, and many other reasons, are much inferior in condition to the people of other parts of New England.[33]

"Newport resembles an old battered shield," Benjamin Waterhouse wrote to Thomas Jefferson in 1822, " — Its scars & bruises are deep & indelible. Commerce and all the Jews are fled. The wharves are deserted and the lamp in the Synagogue is extinct; and the people are now so poor that there are not more than 10, or a dozen people who would have the courage to invite a stranger to his table." [34] As late as 1848, Lossing reported that "Rhode Island as viewed from the Providence steamer made a bald appearance, relieved only by orchards, which showed like dark tufts of verdure in the distance." [35]

---

a Now deceased.
b Read "1770" for "1880."
c Read "Lauzun" for "Lauzan."
d Now moved to Bridge Street west of Second.

e Now privately owned.
f Read "The last three" for "All these."
g Read "1781" for "1780."

PART THREE

EARLY REPUBLICAN ARCHITECTURE

CHAPTER SEVEN

Commerce and Building

TUESDAY, SEPTEMBER I, 1801.

IN SPITE OF THE LOSS OF HALF HER POPULATION and the sharp restriction of commerce in the two decades after 1775, Newport began to show some signs of recovery before the turn of the century.[1] Late in 1795 the first bank was established under title of the Rhode Island Bank. As the *Mercury* of October twentieth reported:

> The Facility with which the subscriptions were filled is a pleasing Proof of the Revival of this Town from the great and accumulated Losses it sustained in the late War. — And the general Confidence justly reposed in this Bank, will enable it to give a further spring to Commercial Enterprise.

The building which housed this bank is still standing on Touro Street. It was owned in the 1760's by Peter Buliod, and was purchased in 1794 by Moses Seixas, who became the first cashier of the new bank, an office he held until his death in 1806.[2]

Pl. 116

In 1803 two more banks were established. In September, the Rhode Island Union Bank opened its doors,[3] followed in less than two weeks by the Newport Bank, which still serves the public in its original place of business, the gambrel-roofed home of Abraham Rodriguez Rivera (perhaps built by John Gardner about 1740) on the north side of Washington Square.[4]

Pl. 87

The two most important business houses, the firms of Gibbs and Channing, and of Christopher Champlin, trading chiefly with Sweden and St. Petersburg in iron, with Java in coffee, and with Canton in nankeens, silks, and tea, almost equaled in their volume of trade Providence's now prospering commerce.[5] The Vernons, accounted among the richest merchants of pre-Revolutionary times, had also returned after the war to take up their business affairs.[6] The China trade was never to reach the sizeable proportions that it did in Providence, but the Champlins and the firm of Gibbs and Channing sent ships to the East Indies and China, and many Newport families have in their possession furniture, china, gameboards, silks, and jade brought back by their forebears who engaged in the export trade.[7]

Although the slave trade had been illegal in Rhode Island since 1787, Newport attempted, with success for a time, to revive her African traffic. Especially during the three years after 1804 when Charlestown repealed all slave laws, Newport vessels vying with Bristol carried 3500 negroes into Charlestown. Only the strict Federal law of 1807 succeeded in bringing this chapter of Newport history to a close.[8] Her shipping, and to a certain extent, her ship building continued, in spite of the fact that the American Embargo Acts of 1807 and 1809, the War of 1812, and the introduction of the railroad all had a damaging effect on her commerce.[9] But her population had continued to decline, and after the War of 1812 her ship building was curtailed, a state of affairs that remained unchanged for nearly twenty years.

Architecture between 1780 and 1830, those years when cities like Providence and Bristol were expanding under the stimulus of thriving commerce, was comparatively restricted. Newport's early republican buildings have always been overshadowed by her many pre-Revolutionary houses. But St. Paul's Methodist church and several fine three-story mansion houses stand in testimony, together with the three new banks, of the town's partial revival before the War of 1812.

In general, the building style of the early republican period was still colonial in character. But forces now at work were to accomplish essential although gradual changes in the basic concept of building. The trend toward the classic style which came to fruition in the Greek revival of the 1830's, was deeply rooted in the republican ideal. It was now felt that the limitations imposed by the colonial central-hall, four-room plan were no longer entirely acceptable to people who were consciously seeking comfort and convenience. Under French influence, curved bays, elliptical rooms, bow windows, and flying and spiral staircases began to appear, while stairways set in a small side hall, and such features as dressing rooms and service rooms, helped break down the inflexible four-room plan.[10]

The formal scheme of a central pavilion, flanked by wings and connecting passages, employed later for Greek Revival building, had been used by Thomas Jefferson in the 1780's.[11] That this scheme appeared in Newport in a domestic building as early as 1803 was due no doubt to its immediate English inspiration. Upon Samuel Elam's arrival from Leeds, England, he set to work at once to remodel the Portsmouth farmhouse he had inherited from his uncle, Gervais Elam.[12] He named his house Vaucluse and soon transformed it into a temple with a Doric portico flanked by a pair of subsidiary wings, the only edifice of its kind to be seen in Rhode Island for some years to come. Although this fine dwelling, known later as the home of Shepherd Tom Hazard of *Jonny Cake Papers* fame, has been demolished, it is still remembered not only because it was a beautiful house, but because of its equally beautiful garden and grounds.[13]

But such a marked departure from colonial tenets as displayed by Elam's temple house was rare at so early a date, and buildings of this type came rather as the product of a gradual

Pl. 129

Pl. 131

growth over a period of twenty or thirty years. The chief changes lay instead in slight variations in floor plan, an increasing lightness of scale, a fondness for elliptical arches, whether
for doorways or for alcoves, and a refinement of decorative detail. The severe and delicate
classic manner of the Adam brothers, who were inspired both by French building and by
the discoveries in Pompeii and Herculaneum, had a profound influence on English architects
after 1765 and on American builders of the late eighteenth and early nineteenth centuries.[14]

In 1785 Boston's Charles Bulfinch had gone to London for a year's stay. When he returned to Boston the following year to practice architecture on what amounted to a professional plane, he was completely under the spell of the Adam style, and his influence was
widespread throughout New England.[15] English handbooks of these years also consistently
reflected the work of the Adam brothers, and the ones written by James and William Pain
were popular enough in America to be republished and to run through several American edi-
tions. More than one doorway still standing in Newport has been drawn directly from the
pages of a Pain handbook.

By this time American builders were frankly adapting proportions originally designed
for stone or brick to the wood most commonly used in this country. They were also writing
their own books on architectural style. In New England, the works of Asher Benjamin,
carpenter-architect from Greenville, Massachusetts, were the most widely read of these
American publications. His first books, published in 1795, reflected the style of the Adams
and the Pains. The last ones reflected the Greek Revival style, but they clearly modified Greek
proportions to suit the needs of American building.[16]

The years of the early republican period also saw the development of a vernacular decorative detail which was distinctively American in character. Carpenters and carvers working with ordinary carpenter's tools approximated in wood the acanthus leaves, the lozenges,
ovals, swags, and the formulae for the classic orders in simplified, unorthodox, but delightful
form. Reeding, grooving, and gouged flowers decorated cornices, chair rails, and mantelpieces in endless combinations. This ornamentation varied enough from the correct classical
models to be regarded in large part as an original expression of American decorative skill,
which could enhance its charm while adapting its design to the wood with which it had
to work.[17]

PUBLIC BUILDING. In 1818, a German prisoner impounded for debt was allowed daily
freedom from the Newport jail for exercise. He used his liberty to paint three pictures of
Washington Square, one of which now hangs in the Newport Bank. It shows the new Mall,   Pl. 128
which had been financed by a lottery and laid out in 1800, one hundred and sixty years after
the first land grants were made. The town's new square, built after the ravages of fire and
war, now lent the first planned look to an unplanned town. The prisoner's painting shows it

as it was originally laid out in three circular walks with the largest at the top of the hill and all three enclosed by a white picket fence. The formal rows of Lombardy poplars which flanked the sides were given in 1800 by Major Toussard, who was in Newport at that time to direct the building of Fort Adams.[18] Four new three-story mansions, two on the north and two on the south stood in the lots between the old gambrel-roofed Lyndon, Decatur, Rodman, and Buttrick houses, Pitt's Head Tavern, and the Newport Bank. With their erection, the square took on a formal, well-built appearance.

The two maps of Newport, drawn in 1850, one by M. Dripps and the other by Walling, show, with all its houses, the plan of the square as it appeared for nearly fifty years. Only the paths in the Mall itself were changed. The central part of Walling's map is reproduced here.

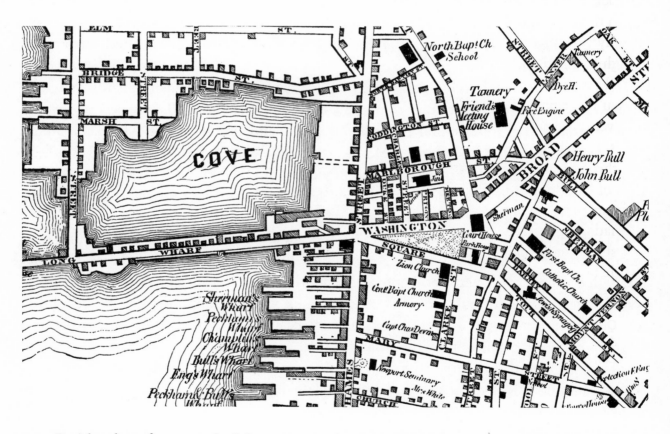

Pl. 129

Pls. 145, 133

Besides these four new buildings, St. Paul's Methodist Church on Marlborough Street, the Rhode Island Union Bank building on Thames Street, the Samuel Whitehorne house farther south, where the homes of the Malbones, Gidleys, and Ayraults had long since stood, and the many little new houses along Spring Street and up the hill were to constitute the chief changes in the town scene until after 1830.

Pl. 129

St. Paul's Methodist Church, built in 1806, is an excellent example of early nineteenth-century ecclesiastical building. In plan it followed the scheme of a parish church, with tower and belfry set at the main entrance, the style which had been introduced by the Church of England a century earlier. The window frames, however, were mitred at the corners and adorned with flat key blocks while the exterior and interior detail was attenuated in accordance with nineteenth-century taste. In the interior, the elliptical arch at the north end of the church, the dentil cornice, slender pilasters and columns, and the recessed paneling of the balcony front, were well and simply handled. Benjamin Pitman, who executed two of the mantels now installed in the Mawdsley house at 228 Spring Street, was entrusted with the decorative detail. The closed entry in front of the tower was added some years later and the building has been raised to allow for a basement story.[19]

The Rhode Island Union Bank building on Thames Street above Pelham is one of Newport's finest public buildings. Designed and built in 1817 by Asher Benjamin, for some reason the building has been almost forgotten and its red brick and marble facings have only recently been freed from coats of yellow paint put on in accordance with a later taste. Although handled with distinction, the concept of the design was a traditional one, based on a central pavilion with flanking wings. It had been employed for such college edifices as Old Nassau in Princeton and University Hall in Providence.[20] For the Newport Bank building, however, Benjamin used a full basement story and pushed the central section high above the wings. He also set the row of triple windows for the pavilion in a recessed arcade which carried through two stories. Such flat arcades were featured in Adam work, repeated in the work of Charles Bulfinch, and became one of Benjamin's favorite forms of surface treatment. They agreed with a growing taste for broad flat surfaces, relieved only by the shadows cast by unadorned recesses in the mass of the wall itself. The Bank's only other ornamentation consists of the modillion cornice, the lunette window in the pediment, and the handsome marble facings which frame the three main windows of the arcaded wall.

a

Pl. 145

Mercury notices of January 31, 1818, give an interesting account of the edifice.

On Monday last the President and Directors of the RHODE ISLAND UNION BANK removed their business into their New Banking-House in Thames Street, next north of Mr. Townsend's Coffee-House. This elegant building has been erected in the course of the last year; and for its correct proportions and chaste simplicity of design, reflects much credit on MR. ASHER BENJAMIN, of Boston, the Architect who furnished the plan; and its extraordinary strength and solidity as a place of deposit, will essentially promote the designs of the Institution; its appearance is highly ornamental to the town.

Now the home of the Newport Coöperative Association for Savings and Building, it has recently been somewhat elaborately restored, but its dignified brick and marble central pavilion remains intact to prove that the opinion of the *Mercury* that "its appearance is highly ornamental to the town," is a sound one. The Poor Asylum built of stone on Coasters Harbor Island in 1822 followed the same scheme of central pedimented pavilion flanked by wings.

Pl. 146

pp. 464-467

The only other building of consequence going on in Newport at this time was the 1824 portion of Fort Adams, designed by Colonel Joseph Totten of the United States Army.[21] The fine masonry walls which may be seen today were constructed by Alexander McGregor, Scotch stone mason who later built the Perry Mill, the Newport Artillery Armory on Clarke Street, Stone Villa, Swanhurst, and many other stone houses dating from the years between 1824 and 1860.[22]

Pl. 164

DOMESTIC BUILDING. The large houses built in Newport during these years were almost without exception square three-story hip-roofed structures. As in the years just preceding the Revolution, a few were built of brick, but more frequently they were of wood. While they were still laid out on the conventional four-room central-hall scheme, their lightness of scale and the use of delicate Adam detail helped differentiate them from their pre-Revolutionary predecessors of the same type.

Pl. 130

The Mumford or Hazard or Hertzog house, which stood on the north side of Washington Square until it was torn down in 1904, was, according to notes by Miss Mary E. Powel, built by the Misses Mumford about 1796.[23] It is probable that they were enlarging an earlier two-story building. The new house was a square three-story wooden mansion with a low hipped roof concealed by a balustrade of delicate Chinese Chippendale design. Roundheaded windows marked the stair landing and upper hallway, and the central doorway was pierced by the popular leaded glass fanlight. Measured drawings of some of the interior detail published in Ware's *The Georgian Period* and republished here, show that the parlor fireplace, with its reeding and Adam detail, was flanked by low elliptical arches and that the cornices and chair rails were decorated with carpenter detail.

Pl. 139

About 1795, Robert and Joseph Rogers built the wooden house now used as St. Joseph's School which stands on Touro near Clarke Street.[24] Like the Mumford house, it is square, three stories high, and laid out on the old four-room plan. The interior has been stripped of most of its trim, but the leaded fanlight doorway, straight out of the pages of Pain, is one of the most attractive in Newport. It resembles the beautiful one on the house originally owned

Pl. 140

by James Honeyman, Jr., at 27 Church Street.   *b*

Pls. 1, 128

In 1793, John Townsend, "joyner" and cabinetmaker, bought an unfinished mansion house together with "all the sashes for the same, the bords, lathes, stops and all the other materials in the said mansion house" from John Manchester for eight hundred thirty Spanish milled dollars. Two years later he sold the house, still unfinished, to Charles Feke, apothecary, and son of Robert Feke, the painter.[25] According to an old photograph, this building, which formerly stood on the northwest corner of Charles Street and Washington Square, where it served as Charles Feke's apothecary shop, was plain and square. It was torn down at the end of the nineteenth century, but its history takes on significance because it is

the house from which the apothecary's shop bow window, now in the Newport Historical   Pl. 132
Society, originally came.

Feke probably had his shop window installed soon after he bought the property from
Townsend. Its bowed outline and its delicately scaled reeding and dentil cornice suggest a
date of about 1795–1800. After Feke's business was sold, Dr. Johnson had the window put
on his Thames Street shop, where it served until this house was also demolished. An old
account of Newport streets signed by "Aquidneck" in 1884 lists five or six of these bow windows once to be seen along the length of Thames Street.[26] The shop owned by the Engs at
"The Sign of the Golden Eagle" boasted two, but Charles Feke's apothecary's window is
now the sole survivor.

Land records show that Joshua Wilbour, housewright, built the three-story wooden   pp. 464–467
house which stands on the east side of Clarke at Touro Street. He bought the land in 1800
and probably built the house between then and 1802, when he sold it to John Wood,
mariner.[27] The doorway, which was probably once like that of the Robert Rogers house,
further down Touro Street, has been widened and recessed, but much of the interior detail
remains. As in the Hazard house, which formerly stood across the Square, the fireplace
in the west parlor is flanked by alcoves framed by low elliptical arches and the cornices and
chair rails are finished with reeding alternating with gouged rosettes. This house served as
the summer home of the Powel family for some years before they built on Bowery Street.
It is described by Miss M. E. Powel in her notes on Newport.

In 1807, Samuel Gardner, merchant, bought the house on Mill Street (now No. 118)   Pl. 133
where, according to the British list, James Tanner had been living in 1777. In the following
year Gardner sold it to Robert Lawton, who is supposed to have built the handsome three-
story, hip-roofed brick building we see today.[28] It is now known as the Henderson or Paul
house. Of square central-hall plan, the flatness and refinement of detail, relieved only by a
third-story bull's eye window and a rather small modillion cornice, establishes its early republican character. The gouged and grooved carpenter work of the hall cornice and chair rail
and the applied scroll work on the stair riser ends are characteristic of the day. The interior
detail has been altered, and notes left by Miss Powel record that the first changes were made
by George Champlin Mason, Jr., to conform with the architectural theories propounded in
his *The Old House Altered*.[29] An advertisement in the *Mercury* announced that he remodeled the Mumford house at 104 Mill Street extensively in 1863, however, and she has
probably confused the two houses. The Lawton house has been remodeled at least once
since then. Charles Follen McKim had "colonialized" the kitchen of the Thomas Robinson   Pl. 192
house at 64 Washington Street and the back room of the Dennis house at 65 Poplar Street   Pl. 192
a few years earlier. These architects were both interested in the revival of the "Queen Anne"
phase of colonial building. But their first attempts to use colonial detail in their own work

showed that they felt a need for elaborating the originals, which, when they worked in colonial houses, resulted in a confusion of styles. The original square simplicity of the rooms in the Mill Street house, however, has not been lost.

Pl. 133

Although shabby now, the three-story, hip-roofed brick mansion that Samuel Whitehorne, successful merchant and distiller, built on the southeast corner of Thames and Dennison Streets in 1804, equals in charm of handling the best early nineteenth-century houses of Providence and Salem.[30] Like George Lawton's fine brick house on Mill Street, it is laid out on the old colonial four-room plan, and like the Lawton house, the flat detail and the basic delicacy of the scale contrast strongly with the boldly proportioned doorways and modillion cornices of the Vernon house or the Francis Malbone house, both built around 1760. The front door with its leaded glass sidelights and the elliptical leaded fanlight above, the roundheaded hall windows and the top story bull's eye windows combine to enhance the early republican character of the style. In the interior, a broad elliptical arch separates the front hall from the back, where the stairway rises in two runs to the second floor. In essence, this is the same scheme employed in the Hunter house of 1750, and again, the difference is one of detail and scale.

The interior decorative finish of the Whitehorne house is composed of reeded chair rails and dentil cornices. The wainscotting is made up of slender half-round moldings applied to the panels, and the quadrants taken from the corners of these point up an emphasis on dry geometric shapes which is repeated in the lozenges adorning the one story mantels. The play of light and shadow over wall surfaces, only slightly broken by the simplified Adam detail, gives an attenuated and precise refinement to rooms still essentially formal in spirit. The house has been abused and the lower floor has served as a store for years. Nevertheless, Samuel Whitehorne's mansion is one of Newport's finest nineteenth-century buildings.

Pl. 144

Although important houses were now almost invariably built with hipped roofs concealed by balustrades, a list of the smaller houses is, with only a few exceptions, a list of gable-roofed buildings. Occasionally a house like the Billy Smith house now standing at 7 Oak Street was covered with a hipped roof, but gambrel-roofed buildings, except for the ubiquitous one-story cottages and barns, were now generally out of fashion. With formal models the ideal, they suffered a temporary eclipse which was only to be dissipated in the 1880's by the late nineteenth-century revival of interest in the "Queen Anne" style.

Pl. 134

The two-story gable-roofed house at 29 Mary Street was built in 1800 by Christopher Fowler, merchant, who wrote in his diary under date of April 10 that he had "Purchased at auction a lot in Mary Street for $451. Made contract to frame, raise, cover and completely finish it outside for $280 — dimensions 40 x 30 and made another contract to finish it inside completely for $750." He made another entry in 1801 "Moved into my new House in Mary Street — it was finished in October. Lot & house & well pump cost $3900."[31] Of typical four-room central-hall plan, Fowler's house has a fanlight door and two very fine one-story mantelpieces distinguished by boldly carved Adam-inspired detail. The mantel in the west room is decorated with basket and fret work, reeding, carved flowers, and handsome carved foliage swags springing from either side of the Roman lamp motif prominent in Adam design.

According to the land records, the broad gable-roofed house with rusticated window caps which stands on the northwest corner of Church and School Streets, was built between 1798 and 1801 by Thomas Goddard, cabinet maker, and the son of John Goddard, the best known of the cabinet makers of that famous name. Ebenezer Shearman bought the house in 1801.[32] The door has been changed, but the house is an excellent example of the homes then built by Newport's craftsmen and tradesmen.

Several of the houses on upper John Street date from the years immediately following 1800, when William Handy began to sell this land in lots.[33] John Tompkins bought lots #3 and #4 in 1811, and built the house known as the Underwood house at what is now No. 66. The Swinburne house at No. 80 was built shortly after 1807, when Isaac Peckham, block-maker, bought lots #5 and #6. Both these buildings, with their gable roofs, fan doors, and interior carpentry detail, are typical small houses of the day. So also are such gable-roofed, fanlit houses as the Card house at 73 Division Street, the Durfee house at 399 Spring Street, the Sherman house on Sherman Street, built about 1810, the Hazard house at Sherman and Mt. Vernon Streets, built between 1809 and 1816 by Paul Bailey, housewright, and the Cremin house at 199 Spring Street, built by John Kerber in the late eighteenth century on land confiscated from Thomas Banister during the Revolutionary war. The simple wrought-iron railing and double sandstone steps of this last house lead to a handsome fanlight door.[34]

The house at 7 Oak Street known as the Billy Smith house was built soon after 1827 when Billy Smith, carpenter, bought the land from Timothy Peckham.[35] It originally stood on the northeast corner of Broadway and Oak streets, but was moved back some years ago to allow for a business building. Now in sadly rundown condition, this small hip-roofed house still has much character. The flat-headed doorway, which encloses a glazed fanlight and is decorated with gouged work, lozenges, and rosettes, is one of the most delightful early nineteenth-century doors in Newport. The interior, laid out on a four-room central plan, has kept its reeded chair rails and cornices, its wainscotting composed of applied half-round moldings used to frame the panels, and its lozenge-decorated one-story mantels. This refinement of proportion and detail is, on a smaller scale, the same which distinguished such large mansions as the Whitehorne house.

Most of the pedimented doorways with semicircular leaded glass fanlights date from 1790 to 1810 and can often be traced to their original models in English handbooks. These doorways were not only used for new houses, but were put on many older buildings in an attempt to bring them up to date. The door of the house that Captain John Warren, mariner, built before 1775 (now John Benson's house, No. 62 Washington Street), was doubtless

Pl. 136

Pl. 137

Pl. 136
Pl. 137

Pl. 138

Pl. 144

Pl. 123

added during repairs and changes made after the Revolutionary war, probably in 1800 when Walter Easton owned the house.[36]

Early nineteenth-century annalists say that no houses went up in Newport for over a decade after 1818. When a dwelling house was built in 1828, it was an event so exciting that the populace gathered round to watch.[37] As a result of this hiatus, Newport streets are marked by a dearth of the late republican and early Greek Revival buildings like the ones John Holden Greene was designing in Providence or Russell Warren was putting up in Bristol. By the time building was resumed, the Greek Revival style was in full swing.

---

a   Demolished after 1952.

b   James Honeyman, Jr., owned the land at an earlier date. The house was built by Joseph

Wood about 1810.

c   Demolished after 1952. The Preservation Society of Newport County owns the woodwork.

CHAPTER EIGHT

The Greek Revival

FOR ALMOST THREE DECADES after 1820, Americans built Greek temples for churches schools, town halls, and homes. They built them with full porticoes and pediments, prostyle and amphiprostyle, with flanking wings and with temple yard buildings.

Several factors were responsible for this flood of Greek building. From the first the young American nation had felt a natural kinship with the Greek ideals of democracy and when in 1821, Greece began its own struggle for independence, she roused the sympathy of the entire western world.[1] Beyond political affinity, however, the classic revival stemmed from an architectural tradition which had been evolving since the early days of the eighteenth century. Classic art and philosophy had been the dominating influence in the western world since the early Renaissance, and Palladio's preoccupation with Roman forms had been reflected in English building for nearly two centuries.[2] One of the earliest examples of this influence in the American colonies was in Newport, where Peter Harrison's Redwood Library clearly stated the classic ideal in Palladian terms as early as 1748. Later, Thomas Jefferson's feeling for architecture was to be steadfastly classic in intent and Roman in inspiration. His taste, although a forerunner, was a true index of the American ideal of the late eighteenth and the first quarter of the nineteenth centuries.[3]

New historical factors were also impinging on the consciousness of architects and students. The above-mentioned mid-century discoveries at Pompeii and Herculaneum served to draw attention to the archaeological past and supplied new classic motifs which were seized upon by the Adam brothers and others and repeated widely in America. When, in 1762, Stuart and Revett published their epoch-making *Antiquities of Ancient Greece*, the classic buildings of Athens and Corinth stood revealed for the first time to many people who had known Greek style only through its Roman derivations and its reflection in Italian renaissance and baroque architecture. The impact of Greek originals on eyes trained to Roman models palpably changed the classic image and brought it much more sharply into focus, touching off a period of American building where entire new cities took on classic proportions and older cities could claim at least one monument or public building reminiscent of Periclean Athens.

The new classic buildings satisfied a desire for a reserved and dignified effect, whether constructed expensively of stone, or economically and sometimes very simply of wood.[4] They were fashioned with smooth surfaces, broken only by the broad shadows of cornice and portico and their dramatic quality was meant to be enhanced by the setting, often of deep landscaped lawns, provided for them. Nonetheless, rooms built behind two-story narrow porticoes were apt to be dark, and the plan imposed by a classic temple was necessarily unyielding. Although scarcely less rigid, the colonial square house seemed flexible by comparison, and it continued in use now, refurbished with cornices of Greek proportions which concealed low hipped roofs, with classic porches or doorways, rows of engaged columns, or more simply, corner boards treated as pilasters. Small houses were often built with their gable ends, handled as pediments, set toward the street, like temples without porticoes. Often only the broadened scale of Greek proportions remained to distinguish these later buildings from the hipped and gable-roofed buildings of colonial days.

The restrictions imposed by the classic style extended to the building materials considered suitable. Stucco and stone lent themselves most readily to smooth walls.[5] In towns like Newport, where wood was the predominant material, flat surfaces were achieved by the use of siding instead of the common lapped clapboards. When brick was used, it received a covering coat of gray or white paint to give the illusion of pale unbroken walls. The critics of the day, led earlier by Jefferson, found the red brick and white trim of Georgian times unsatisfactory, just as they felt that the gambrel roofs and baroque detail of the earlier buildings were awkward and incorrect, a feeling that continued for many years.[6] In 1852, John Ross Dix wrote in his *Handbook of Newport* that the Colony House possessed "no claim to architectural correctness," although it was "rather an imposing looking structure." This was a representative opinion, and Newport's few brick buildings now received their first coats of paint, most of which have been painstakingly sandblasted off within the last three decades.

Everywhere the white painted buildings stood out in sharp contrast to the surrounding foliage meant to be their foil. "When I was little," wrote Miss M. E. Powel of Newport in the fifties, "all Newport was white painted or whitewashed or not painted at all. Blinds were Persian blue as they faded, green as they were painted. There was no colored paint anywhere, but there was a delightful predominating clean whitewashing of houses, yards, fences and even of tree trunks, where there were any trees."

Miss Powel carried the story further back to the years between 1815 and 1832, as mentioned above, when she wrote:

> My grandmother told me when she left Newport in 1815 all the old houses and Trinity Church had wood work in its natural color and many were dingy. She said when she returned in 1832, to her amazement all the interior wood work in Newport was painted white. A craze for clean white paint broke out after the War of 1812 — and she was quite unprepared for it, and much astonished at the change in Trinity as well as in the aspects of her friends' drawing rooms.[7]

Newport's revival in the 1830's after the depression of the twenties coincided with the later development of the Greek Revival, and was based on the rediscovery of the island town as a summer resort. Newport was never to become a whaling town as were Bristol, Warren, and New Bedford, and the attempts to establish textile mills were not successful. The Coddington Mill, the Perry Mill, and two others built in the 1830's had closed by the end of the nineteenth century.[8] Of these ventures, only the shell of the Perry Mill and a double row of mill workers' houses in the Greek Revival style built in 1837 at Thames and Richmond streets for the Coddington Mill remain today. But in these same years an increasing number of visitors came from the South, from Boston, and later from New York to build the houses they now invariably called their "villas." Streets long unchanged began to fill with imposing buildings of late Greek Revival character.

Pl. 147

b

The recent search for contemporary papers has brought to light the fact that Russell Warren of Bristol and Providence was responsible for at least seven of the important public and private buildings built in Newport in the decade and a half after 1834. Warren, the son of Gamaliel Warren and a Mayflower descendant, was born in Tiverton in 1783. He had arrived in Bristol in 1800 with an established reputation as an architect and engineer of skill. His own house in Bristol, which he built in that same year, was a two-story gable-roofed wooden building typically early republican in style. Already, however, he showed his flair for the imaginative use of detail by the way in which he slanted the corner quoins. The several houses for the de Wolfe family, built during the next ten years or so, were stamped with his fanciful interpretations of early republican forms.[9]

In 1825, when he and James Bucklin worked together on the Providence Arcade, they turned to the current Greek style, and some of Warren's later Bristol work is in this manner. Most of his first Newport buildings, described below, are also Greek Revival. He built the Bristol Court House and the conservatory for George de Wolfe's house, "The Lindens," however, in the Gothic manner.

In Newport, when he was asked in 1834 to design the new Second (or North Baptist) Church on Farewell Street, he again turned to Gothic Revival models.[10] This building was torn down in 1906, but old views of it show that it was built with double entries which flanked a central section lit by a large Gothic window. It was surmounted by a tower which did not project from, but was enclosed in, the body of the church, a feature which constituted the

Pl. 156

chief variation from the square-towered churches of colonial years. Otherwise, it was marked by the same symmetrical regularity of plan to be seen in the Gothic Revival buildings that Bulfinch and his contemporaries like John Holden Greene in Providence were putting up in the first decade of the century. An account in the 1846 *Herald and Rhode Islander* credits

Pl. 157

him with the drafting of the plans for the Second Ocean House of 1845.[11] This building was also Gothic. Four years later, according to the *Herald of the Times*, he was engaged in the construction of an addition to the Bellevue house which, as the account said, "was to be finished in the Elizabethan style."[12] He also, according to the newspaper notices, was responsible for the old Post Office and Customs House built in 1829 on Thames Street.[13] Unfortunately, none of these Newport buildings are standing today, but they serve to indicate Warren's place in the rapid transition that was taking place in American architectural ideals during the first half of the nineteenth century.

Zion Episcopal Church, one of Newport's first Greek Revival buildings, was also designed by Russell Warren,[14] and built in 1834 on Touro and Clarke Streets by William

Pl. 147

Weeden, carpenter-builder, who worked on other buildings of this period. Constructed of wood and designed in the form of an Ionic prostyle temple, it was complete with pediment and portico and embellished with a row of two-story roundheaded windows down the sides. It now serves as a motion picture theatre, its early character much changed, but an old photograph shows its original appearance.

Of Newport's few other true temple buildings, one of the most interesting is the Governor Van Zandt house on Pelham Street. In 1838 Captain Augustus Littlefield, mariner,

Pl. 150

bought land on Pelham Street from George Gibbs, and commissioned John Ladd to build an "authentic copy of an Italian Villa" he had seen on one of his voyages abroad.[15] Designed as a temple with pediment and portico, the late and lotus-like detail of the capitals suggests that the original model was a south Italian building reflecting in its use of Egyptian-inspired detail the influence of Napoleon's Egyptian campaigns. Ladd is reputed to have carved the capitals for Littlefield's house himself. The heavy bracketed cornice, at complete variance with Greek tradition, is Italian, evidently also a part of the detail copied from Littlefield's "Italian Villa." Captain Littlefield sold his house to Governor Charles Van Zandt by whose name it is still known. It serves now as the Headquarters of the Red Cross.

When Levi Gale came to Newport from New Orleans in 1834, he bought the old gambrel-roofed house at the head of the Mall where Stephen Decatur, the famous naval hero, had lived. He moved Decatur's house off to Charles Street where it still stands and on the cleared location facing the curving paths of the Mall, he instructed Russell Warren to design and build a handsome Greek Revival house. It too was constructed by William Weeden, who had built Zion Church.[16]

For Mr. Gale's house, Russell Warren departed from the strict temple form to build a square two-story house with a level cornice and a recessed attic story. He broke the flat façade with a single order of composite pilasters, and added a small one-story porch for the entry. The flat wood walls, finished with horizontally scored siding to imitate stone, contrasted well with the rich detail of the decoration. The interior, laid out on the old central-hall scheme, was severely simple, with the heavy cornices, door, and window casings characteristic of Warren's Greek Revival work.

Gale's house, also known for many years as the Sheffield house, stood on the Mall until 1915, when it in turn was moved away to make room for the City Court House. Now on Touro at Division Street, in far too cramped quarters for its massive size, it is used as the Jewish Community Center. But old photographs show that when the house stood in its original location at the top of the Mall, an imposing mansion set in seemingly spacious grounds, it achieved the grandiose effect already considered suitable in a Newport summer villa.

Pl. 148

Pl. 149

Elmhyrst, the once beautiful Greek Revival house standing at Mile Corner, was built about 1833 for William Vernon, a member of the Vernon family who had owned the famous house at Clarke and Mary streets before the Revolutionary war. According to notices for sale appearing in the *Mercury* in 1849, it, too, was designed by Russell Warren and built by Talman and Bucklin of Providence.[17] Like the Gale house, it was based on a square plan and designed without the temple portico and pediment. Its wide level cornices are supported by fine Ionic columns which form a shallow recessed porch, and an attic story originally completed and gave coherence to the façade. Unfortunately, this story has been recently removed, and the bald hipped roof which replaces it completely destroys the structure's former extraordinarily fine proportions. Two yard buildings, an office, and a porter's lodge were built as one-story Greek temples. They played their parts as staccato white spots in a planned scheme dramatizing the sober main theme of the house set deep in landscaped grounds. The estate has been broken up and all this is now lost, but Elmhyrst in the past, distinguished as it was by broad simplicity of form, warmth of detail, and finely conceived proportions, was one of Newport's great architectural achievements.

Pl. 151

The wooden house at 63 John Street was built for himself by Alexander McGregor, Newport's Scotch stonemason, soon after he bought the land in 1835. It is a severe square house, shorn of all columns and pilasters, but its Greek Revival character is revealed by the broad treatment of the cornice, the flat scored siding that covers the walls, and the correct Greek motifs used as ornament for the doorway.[18]

The Weaver house, built by Borden Wood in 1838 just beyond the Mile Corner on the west side of the West Main road, is plain, square, and hip-roofed.[19] Finished with flat siding, its chief embellishments consist of Ionic corner pilasters and a one-story Ionic porch. With these elements, it achieves a distinguished simplicity of effect.

The interiors of Greek Revival buildings generally followed a central or side-hall plan from which severe square rooms opened off in schemes which had been in use for many years.

Sometimes the main rooms were thrown together by the use of double doors. Sometimes classic columns or pilasters were used to emphasize the double openings, a deviation from the typical four-room plan. All the moldings were flattened and broadened. Curving stairs were popular and the earlier ones were delicately scaled, although they tended to become heavy toward the end of the Greek Revival period. Mantels, often of marble, were severe vertical and horizontal slabs either with or without pilasters and set up in harmony with Greek proportions. Carving, even of Greek character, was generally eschewed so that the general effect of the rooms, like the houses, was cool, self-contained, and sometimes somewhat severe.

Many smaller Newport buildings reflect the Greek Revival to a greater or less degree. The house at 122 Mill Street has, with its pediment end to the street and its walls finished with flat siding, an unpretentious reserve and dignity. The Royal Phelps Carroll house on Clay Street, built by William Spooner before 1850 and now owned by Mr. Francis X. A. Flannery, is also built with gable end to the street. This house is further finished with a pedimented entry, a common enrichment for many houses otherwise simply handled. In the interior, the curved stairway with its molded hand railing is typical of the period. The house that Mr. William Crandall built in 1833 at 63 Poplar Street, now St. John's Parish House, also has charming Greek detail. Tall windows opening onto a one-story porch across the front suggest the growing interest in a relationship between indoors and outdoors, which was to affect the concept of planning in the years immediately to come. This porch has recently been removed, with deleterious effect to the whole.

Alexander McGregor, who had built the new walls for Fort Adams and his own wooden house on John Street which has already been discussed, was responsible during the next decades for many conventional buildings in the Greek Revival spirit, most of them distinguished by fine random masonry walls. Records show that in 1835 McGregor designed and built the Clarke Street Artillery Armory. Originally a one-story gable-roofed building, it was raised another story in the early twentieth century.[20] He also built Dr. Thorn's house at Narragansett and Spring streets and Stone Villa on Bellevue Avenue. He is supposed to have built the latter, which has been much enlarged, for himself in 1845. Henry Middleton bought it later, but it is best known as the house of James Gordon Bennett, who was responsible for the enlargements of 1880, as well as for the installation of the gatepost owls, symbolic of the *New York Herald*. The Perry Mill, a long, high, and plain gable-roofed masonry building was also McGregor's work, built in 1835.

In the 1840's the building of several hotels, the most imposing of which were the first Ocean House, built in 1841 and burned in 1845, and the Atlantic House, built in 1844, reflected the then thriving state of Newport as a resort town. The first Ocean House was a four-story flat-roofed building with a little lantern, level cornices, and a two-storied pillared portico of simplest Greek suggestion. When it burned in 1845, it was replaced within the

Pl. 153

Pl. 154

pp. 464-467

Pl. 155

year by Russell Warren's Gothic Revival building — the second building on the same site to reflect consciously the forms of another style and era.

Pl. 155

The Atlantic House of 1844 survived until 1877, when it was broken up and moved away to be replaced by the private residence of Seth B. Stitt, now the Elks' Home. It was built on the familiar scheme of central pavilion flanked by hip-roofed wings. The pavilion was embellished with a high Ionic full portico. One-story porches continued across the length of the wings, but otherwise, except for the whiteness of the smooth-surfaced walls and the altered proportions of the ornament, the Atlantic house did not differ in concept from the first college edifices of the eighteenth century. As we have seen, Asher Benjamin used this same scheme, interpreted in brick with recessed arcades and Adam detail, for the Rhode Island Union Bank building of 1818, and it reappeared in stone in 1822 for the Poor Asylum, built on Coasters Harbor Island.

Such a building as the Atlantic House stands as a symbol of both past and future. It represents the end of the long eighteenth-century tradition, continued and unified in evolution. But it is also the product of a new point of view, born out of knowledge of the historic past. The Greek Revival is the first of the series of revivals in America in which the forms of other periods were duplicated with more or less archaeological accuracy. With this shifting point of view, the long eighteenth-century tradition was brought to a final close.

As we have seen, the Greek Revival also coincided with the early growth of the summer colony, the architecture of which was to have its roots, not in the town, but more broadly, in the nation itself. Building in Newport in the next decades was no longer an indigenous local growth. It was resort architecture, superimposed by chance on the island town. Both because of its changed character and its nonlocal derivation, its history belongs to another section.

---

a Peter Harrison's Brick Market and Touro Synagogue, inspired by academic Palladian models, may have had some kind of thickened or painted finish from the time they were built. See note b on page 91.
b Demolished after 1952.

c Demolished after 1952.
d Read "128" for "122." Owned by Charles Sherman in 1850.
e Demolished after 1952.
f No. 337 Thames Street.

PART FOUR

NINETEENTH-CENTURY RESORT ARCHITECTURE

By

VINCENT J. SCULLY, JR.

INTRODUCTION TO THE SECOND EDITION

THE FOLLOWING CHAPTERS WERE WRITTEN IN 1949 and have something of the character of a youthful effusion. I am therefore grateful to the publisher for this opportunity to make a few comments about them. It would hardly be fair to rewrite them, and indeed I have no desire to do so, since their perhaps rather single-minded focus, a product of youth, would only be dispersed thereby.

In the main, that focus, despite what seems to me now a certain naiveté in my treatment of it, still seems correct. The Stick Style and the Shingle Style, first published here, have become terms of common art-historical usage, and the architectural development they describe is now generally recognized as an important nineteenth-century phenomenon in its own right and as the fundamental tradition out of which the modern work of Frank Lloyd Wright and others grew.[*]

Another reason why these chapters should not be rewritten is that, like many reinterpretations of the art of the past, they have played their own part in the art of the present. They have had something to do with the architectural development of the past sixteen years: reflected it, influenced it, and changed with it. The identification of the Stick Style, for example, mirrored the desire of American architects in 1949 to develop an architectural expression out of skeleton construction, released from the closed wall planes of the balloon frame and exploiting the spatial possibilities of the post, beam, and spanning plank. At the same time, the Stick Style itself, once identified, certainly abetted that process.

The effect of the Shingle Style has been somewhat different. One of my major interests in it during the late forties derived from its eventual creation of continuous space and geometric order. Both these characteristics had been integral to the archi-

[*] The themes introduced here were developed further in my: "Romantic-rationalism and the expression of structure in wood: Downing, Wheeler, Gardner, and the 'stick style,' 1840–1876," *Art Bulletin 35* (June 1953), 121–142; "American Villas," *Architectural Review, 115* (March 1954), 168–179; *The Shingle Style: architectural theory and design from Richardson to the origins of Wright* (New Haven, 1955); *Frank Lloyd Wright* (New York, 1960).

tecture of Wright in the early twentieth century, and were also of considerable relevance to the architects of the early nineteen-fifties, who were becoming preoccupied at that time with large single spaces and abstract, strictly geometric shapes. Hence interest in the style tended to focus upon its later phases and in what it gave rise to, while active formal influence from its closed wall planes and complex window patterns was very rare. (An almost solitary exception was George Nelson's rather close adaptation of the Low House at Bristol, R.I., a lovely building since wantonly destroyed. Significantly enough, the Low House was the most continuous and abstract in form of any of the shingled houses.) Formal concern, as noted above, was generally directed elsewhere, especially toward the skeletal pavilion of simplified shape. My own house in wood, of 1950, is a representative example of the type.

But with the exhaustion, by the early sixties, of the impulse toward pure form and clarified frame, interest in the Shingle Style took a new turn: now not toward its spatial continuity or its final order but toward its complexity, toward the eloquent dialogue between interior and exterior functions which was developed in its irregular window placement, its bays and porches, and its gabled, shedded, and gambreled profiles. Advanced architectural thought and design is thus rejecting "purity" in favor of the complexity and contradiction integral to life, so avoiding simplification in favor of what the young architect Robert Venturi, who is developing this theme in a forthcoming book, calls "accommodation." Venturi has himself been critically influenced by the Shingle Style. Clearly enough, in any architecture based upon such principles, the richly varied, inventive, infinitely lively buildings of the nineteenth-century Newport achieve even greater relevance for the present than they had before.

In the larger sense, therefore, modern architecture has itself been moving from Stick Style to Shingle Style during the past generation. But it has moved further than that. In the late forties we in America were preoccupied with domestic architecture, and especially with the single-family suburban house and its nonmonumental values. Hence "monumentality" was treated very harshly in my chapters, and jargon words like "organic" and even, heaven forgive me, "stylistic" and "nonstylistic," appeared all too often in them. More seriously, sixteen years ago few of us ever really gave thought to the shape of the city as a whole or even to the more immediately graspable problems of group design. Here a persistently antiurban, rather Jeffersonian sub-theme in American mythology was joined by the late-Bauhaus sensibility which was so influential in the forties: by its tendency toward design at small scale, its suspicion of monumentality, its iconoclasm toward what it referred to as "styles," its blind lack of regard for the humanistic tradition or the traditional city.

It is perfectly obvious that most of these attitudes can be detected in my chapters. They had two effects. First, they caused me to undervalue the Greek revival and to write about the more academic and monumentally conceived houses of the Beaux Arts reaction of the eighties in an impatient and prejudiced manner that I now deplore. Secondly, they played a part in preventing me from dealing properly with the place as a whole, with, that is, the overall problem of urbanism which is the totality of architecture itself.

The two effects are interconnected, since the Beaux Arts designs were clearly founded upon a tradition which, even in country houses, valued urbanity and tended toward design at urban scale. Hence the finest late achievements of the academic tradition, and of the Beaux Arts which was its last historical phase, lay not merely in perhaps overscaled, suburban houses like those of Newport, but in true city building and in the coherent design of streets and squares. Most of the streets of New York, for instance, were excellent examples of that nineteenth- and early twentieth-century urban mode, and some of the finest of them, most conspicuously Park Avenue, have since been ruined by new buildings conceived within a later, impatient urban image which neither valued their quality nor perceived it. That newer image was derived in part from Le Corbusier's apocalyptic vision of the *Ville Radieuse* and in part from a simple inability among most architects to focus beyond single buildings upon the urbanistic relationships of buildings to each other and to the site. Thus my chapters too often deal with houses in a vacuum, as if built on the moon and related to others only in a historical sequence, not in physical fact.

True enough, those relationships were not overly planned or important in the resort architecture of nineteenth-century Newport, as it spread in a loose and uninterrupted grid pattern along Bellevue Avenue. It had none of the curvilinear, consciously picturesque, unified layout that was characteristic of the work of mid-century architects such as Olmsted and Vaux, as at Riverside, Illinois, or Central Park. Yet it did make its casual suburban grouping over the decades around its own "Main Street" at a generous new scale outside the old town, which was consequently not ruined by it. Such contrasts with events today throughout most of the world, where the new cities are bursting up through the old in a chaotic confusion of intentions and scales, while, in Newport as everywhere else, the automobile is taking over, first choking, then dissolving the urban fabric as a whole.

Yet precisely because of all this we can value Newport's heritage more intelligently now than we did before and can seek to preserve it in ways that make sense for any modern city, for New York no less than Newport. We can, first of all, open our eyes and free them from prejudice. All the buildings are better than we once thought they were. We can best protect them by understanding and sustaining their relationships to one another and to the whole. We can design against the automobile, for example, keeping it out of the old town, preventing the cancerous spread of parking lots, developing cheap public transportation, so bringing the buildings back into their intended scale, the old streets properly narrow, Munday's Colony House lifting free above its slope in the most Baroque urban climax to be found in America—the resort suburb Arcadian once more as it was meant to be.

VINCENT SCULLY

New Haven, 1965

CHAPTER NINE

The Stick Style

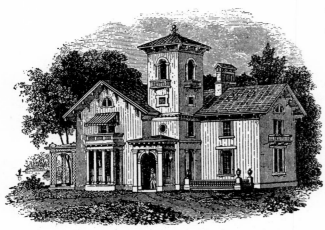

THE HISTORY OF NEWPORT ARCHITEC-
TURE from the eighteen-forties to the twentieth century can be told only in terms of
summer cottages and resort building. By
1840 the old town of Newport, partially cut
off from the streams of Jacksonian democracy which were introducing into the rest
of America a new industrialism and a new
political orientation, had become a social
and cultural backwater, existing upon the
residue of old memories and old activities
and only slightly touched by the vitality of the new.

The Newport of the eighteen-thirties was the wreck of an eighteenth-century town,
whose commerce and cultural force had never entirely recovered from the ravages of the
Revolutionary War, the War of 1812, and the hurricane of 1815. Attempts to remedy this
situation by the development of town industries met with only moderate success: the mills
founded in 1835 and 1837 were able to absorb only a small percentage of the available labor
supply and eventually failed. Similarly, the great whaling industry of the early nineteenth
century which vitalized New Bedford and other New England towns never became firmly
established here. Nor could Newport regain its status, irretrievably lost after the Revolution, as a major seaport. The Newport of the early forties, therefore, existed in a state of
arrested development, if not of partial decay, a condition made all the more poignant and
irrevocable by memories of the very brilliance of its eighteenth-century past.

Of Newport's major eighteenth-century assets, however, two still remained — its situation by the sea and its climate. The numbers of vacationists who had been coming to Newport since the eighteenth century began to swell in the eighteen-forties — inspired in part
by the new vision of nature which was being produced by the painters of the Hudson River
School — and their numbers grew steadily throughout the rest of the nineteenth century.

Lodged at first in rooming houses or in hotels, the summer colonists began by the forties to build their own cottages and villas. By 1900 the old town of Newport had become a comparatively small architectural island set in a sea of summer residences. For Newport as a town with a life of its own, this development, although it substituted a certain artificial prosperity for the poverty of the early nineteenth century, may well be regarded as deleterious. Instead of one unified culture as there had been in the eighteenth century, there were now two separate cultures, that of the town and that of the summer colony. In this artificial split of societies, it is with the summer colony that we must concern ourselves, since it was there that the most important architectural developments in nineteenth-century Newport took place. Yet, despite the cosmopolitan nature of Newport's summer colony and consequently of its architecture, the old town of Newport occasionally exerted its influence. It did so, for instance, for a few years in the early seventies, with important results; but on the whole the buildings with which we have to deal might have been built almost anywhere in the East in nineteenth-century America — anywhere, that is, where more or less elaborate cottages and mansions were erected. The roots of the nineteenth-century domestic architecture of Newport, therefore, are not specifically in Newport itself, but in the American domestic development as a whole.

The importance of Newport for the architectural historian is that, with certain exceptions, the most important developments in nineteenth-century American domestic architecture can be studied here as in a laboratory. If this process is somewhat artificial culturally, it nevertheless isolates one critically important phase of American nineteenth-century architectural creation, namely the cottage and the country house. The atmosphere which produced these cottages was typically American, for it was a suburban one, and it was the nineteenth-century suburb which continued to evoke, in a rapidly urbanizing society, that sense of the necessity for agrarian experience which had been so important in the political philosophy of Thomas Jefferson. Therefore, however inadequately the suburb may itself function as a social unit — being neither urban nor really agrarian — it nevertheless, in nineteenth-century America, assumed an importance as an area where deeply rooted cultural energies continued to operate. The domestic program of the single family house on its own land retained, therefore, the power to generate invention and growth.

This period in American architecture, examined through the microcosm of Newport, may serve to clear away certain critical misconceptions concerning the architecture of the middle and later nineteenth century and help us to arrive at a more meaningful evaluation of the period. Two generations of unfavorable criticism, based upon an academic point of view, have seen this period as "The Era of Bad Taste," as "The Battle of Styles," or as "A Confusion of Tongues." We shall see that these judgments are far from the truth and that the domestic architecture of these years was not only inventive, original, and full of life, but, through all its rich diversity, followed a course of development which was coherent and unified. In the larger historical sense this period brought to an end the long Renaissance complex of architectural development and laid the formal and philosophical foundation for the new architecture of the twentieth century.

THE PICTURESQUE REVIVAL. It was in the eighteen-forties, at the moment when Newport's summer colony began to grow, that a new phase of development gathered impetus in American domestic architecture, and the nature of this architectural shift can be seen in the hotels which were built at Newport during this period. The first Ocean House, built   Pl. 155 in 1840, was a typical Greek Revival cube, symmetrical and contained. It was a simple wooden box with applied classical detail, painted a uniform light color and expressive of the Greek Revival tendency toward the abstract elegance of geometrical shapes rather than the expression of space, structure, or materials.

The Atlantic House, built in 1844, belongs in the same category. More articulated than the first Ocean House, it made use of a large central portico with flanking wings, but its total effect was basically the same and was that of an abstract and implacable architectural enve-   Pl. 155 lope, gleaming white and negative in material, standing in sharp contrast to its natural setting and reflecting flatly rather than absorbing the natural light which fell upon it. These two hotels were almost the last Greek Revival buildings in Newport, and here, as in the rest of the country at this time, they represented the end of an era. The new development, already beginning, was to move in a different architectural direction. The Atlantic House remained standing until 1877, when it was broken up and moved away, but the first Ocean House burned with considerable melodrama in 1845, and the structure which was immediately built to succeed it was of a different type.

The inspiration behind the new building was that of the Gothic Revival, in the eighteen-forties entering, both here and in England, upon its most creative phase. Yet to call the second Ocean House "Gothic" in the sense that the first Ocean House could be called   Pl. 157 "Greek" is to state the case incorrectly, for the second building, for all its "Gothic" inspiration, can be seen to be less strictly stylistic than the first. Here the requirements of interior space push out through the architectural envelope, and the wooden structure erupts dormers from its high roof and thereby breaks up and articulates the mass in a way which expresses the lightness and flexibility of wood frame structure. Secondly, whereas the first Ocean House uncompromisingly rejected its site and the light which fell upon it, the second Ocean House pushes out porches laden with a fretwork of diagonal bracing which receives the light, breaks it up, recreates it in a pattern of shadows, and plays pictorially with the spatial volumes and tonal varieties.

The mixture of rationalism and romanticism which this building reveals is in a sense the key to the real nature of the new architectural development. It is more rational than the first Ocean House because, better verandaed and protected from the sun, it thereby fulfills more successfully its function as a summer hotel. It expresses more clearly the nature and possibilities of its wooden structure and by the same token allows thereby a greater freedom in its interior arrangement. With all this, it is also romantic, in the best nineteenth-century sense, in its movement toward the acceptance rather than the rejection of nature and in its creative manipulation of the pictorial possibilities of natural light, as well as in the related articulation of its mass. Its roots, as a structure based upon this mixture of romanticism and rationalism, are not only in that drive toward the picturesque which had been gathering force in England since the middle of the eighteenth century, but also in the new Gothic Revival amalgam of functionalism and structural morality — a rational concept based upon a romantic philosophy. In England, Pugin had already stated this new concept, and in America the writings of Andrew Jackson Downing, much more influential in their time than the more precisely stated functionalism of Horatio Greenough, were beginning to lead American architectural thought in a similar direction.

Pl. 158

The new functionalism and the new romanticism found a vital psychological soil for their growth in the Jacksonian America of the early eighteen-forties. The "Round House" at Southwick's Grove in Middletown is an example of this vitality. It was built about 1840 by Joseph Southwick, a shipwright, who had boasted at a dance that he could build a round house and, having been laughed at, built it. It is of the usual mortise and tenon framing system and supports a belled roof above which is a cupola. It was sheathed in very thin clapboards which took its curve easily, and has recently been shingled, a surface covering even more appropriate to its form. This house is, however, more than a *tour de force*. Its plan is an inspired interpenetration of ellipses in which the flow is continuous and smooth, and the interior spaces curve through and past each other with a rhythm of movement which for some startling moments recalls Borromini and the high baroque.

If the Round House is an isolated monument, it is at least an early example of that kind of architectural thinking about plan and basic shape which Orson Squire Fowler developed further in his book, *A Home for All*, published in 1848. In this publication Fowler advocated and described the building of octagon houses as space-saving and efficient. None of these, unfortunately, exist in Newport, but it can be said that the interior space developed in Southwick's Round House is considerably more coherent and powerfully organized than are the rather awkwardly worked out room shapes in Fowler's later octagons.

Pl. 159

This cultural urge toward experiment in the America of the early forties began to affect the design of even the smallest houses with a new sense of scale and proportion and a new feeling for structural expression. Much of the impetus for these developments came, as has already been indicated, from the Gothic Revival. The little cottage at the corner of School and Mary streets in Newport, built in 1840 by Benjamin Marsh, is an Americanization of that kind of semi-Gothic *cottage ornée* which had been a stock in trade of the English architectural books for the previous thirty years. Here the cross-shaped frame structure is capped by high, light planes of projecting gabled roof, which cut deeply into and articulate the mass and shadow the wall surfaces. The general proportions are vertical, but the sense of gentle and very human scale is the dominant element. Meant to slip naturally into surrounding foliage, houses of this type multiply dormers, trellises, and eave carving, for the purpose of varying the silhouette, breaking up the light, and enhancing rather than competing with their surroundings.

The major apostle of this movement in America was, as we have already noted, Andrew Jackson Downing, a landscape gardener, who stated in his *Landscape Gardening* of 1841 that, "Architectural beauty must be considered conjointly with the beauty of landscape." Downing in America was the heir of the great Regency landscape gardeners, such as Repton. His interest in domestic architecture in America was characterized by his concern with nature, his love of the land. Although he has been accused by hostile critics of thoughtless eclecticism, this is not quite true. He is anti-Greek Revival and in favor of picturesque variety because for him the Greek Revival house stood out cold and white in contrast to its natural setting, a glaring spot on the landscape rather than an artistic and tonal enhancement of it. We have observed this important distinction in the first and the second Ocean House.

In his *Cottage Residences* of 1842, Downing advocated a variety of pictorial forms. Some of these were of the so-called Italian villa type, such as the King house, which we shall discuss later. Others were "Gothic" piles such as Malbone Hall, by Alexander Jackson Davis, which we will also discuss further on. It is interesting to note that Davis collaborated with Downing on *Cottage Residences*, doing the renderings and contributing some of his own designs for publication. Others of the designs in *Cottage Residences* were for small *cottages ornées* such as the one at School and Mary streets, mentioned above. In presenting these types, Downing did not exhibit any particular originality, except in so far as the American development is concerned, since all of them had for some time been appearing in English publications.

With his feeling for natural process, however, Downing also took cognizance of an American development which was part of the new sense of the picturesque articulation of surfaces but which accomplished it more organically by an expression of the basic structure. In 1837, in his *Rural Residences*, a book which had very little circulation, Alexander Jackson Davis had already illustrated a type of small wooden cottage which was boarded vertically and which used battens over the joints between the boards. Davis built some cottages of this type himself, but on the whole was more interested in his larger, more Gothic structures. Downing, on the other hand, emphasized the wooden board and batten type as peculiarly American. By 1845, a very early date, a house of this kind had already been built by Thomas Galvin at 417 Spring Street in Newport. A simple gabled structure with one cross gable in front and a projecting veranda built of thin posts and exposed rafters, the Galvin house is most notable for its exploitation of creative techniques in wood. All its

Pl. 159
Pl. 162

Pl. 159

details are crisply wooden and nonstylistic, expressing in siding, window details, and porches the sense of milled lumber as board, plank, batten, and stick. Most important perhaps are its vertical battens, exterior indications of the vertical studs of the wooden frame beneath. The Galvin house is very similar to those published by Downing as the basis for an "American Cottage Style." In his *Country Houses* (1850), Downing said of this kind of building:

> We greatly prefer the vertical to the horizontal boarding, not only because it is more durable, but because it has an expression of strength and truthfulness which the other has not. The main timbers which enter into the frame of a wooden house and support the structure, are vertical, and hence the vertical boarding properly signifies to the eye a wooden house.

This is that rationalism, basically Gothic Revival in its genesis, which is an inherent part of the new development, for here in a sense the skin is stripped off the Greek Revival and the characteristically American wooden frame brought to light as an organic architectural expression.

In the larger villas at Newport the union of wooden framing technique and expression was not to play an important role until later, when a development of this expression of the structural skeleton was for a time to dominate architectural creation in the domestic field. Less advanced as structural expression, but also moving surely toward free, asymmetrical interior space and exterior massing are the new summer villas which began to be built in the forties. These already begin to divide themselves into two types, the first of which strives for informality, comparative gentleness of scale, and looseness of organization, the second of which tends toward monumental gravity, heaviness of scale, density of mass. Both types make use of irregularity and asymmetry and are freely developed architectural organisms which, whatever stylistic designations may have been used as literary labels in order to describe them, are in bondage to no style and to no precedent. This accounts for the wide range of expression of which they are capable.

Pls. 160, 161

Kingscote, designed by Richard Upjohn for Noble Jones, a summer resident from Savannah, is the first of the villas with which we must concern ourselves. According to the King family records, it was built in 1841 instead of in 1838, as it has usually been dated, but it is still the earliest of the new domestic types among the larger houses. It was bought by William H. King in 1864 and its present name dates from that time. It is another example of the *cottage ornée*. Asymmetrical in massing and gentle in scale, Kingscote, like the little house at School and Mary, sinks picturesquely into an embowered landscape and echoes with its jagged outlines and variety of shadows the changing forms of the foliage surrounding it.

It represents again that romantic yearning toward nature which has since been derided as a corrupt sentimentality but which, in its deeper sense, is rather part of that search for freer systems and more natural values which characterized some of the most creative aspects of nineteenth-century thought. Emerson and Thoreau especially reflect the influence of the same forces from which Kingscote springs, although in a sense their vision accords better

with the less elaborate expression of the smaller house discussed earlier, in particular that of
the Galvin house, which depended for its quality upon the organic nature of its indigenous
frame. Indeed, houses of this type must be considered not only as a conscious escape from
the growing, dehumanized industrialism of the mid-nineteenth century, but also as a creative
reflex of profound importance in the continuation of humanistic values.

All the aspects of Kingscote tend toward these ends. The entrance is canopied and
sheltered, the hall arcaded in dark wood and full of shadow. The interior details of molding
and mantels, remotely medieval in inspiration, are of a new mid-century originality, imbued
with a sense of their materials, wood, brick, and stone. While the interior space is only very
little freer than that of some Greek Revival houses, it opens more completely out again to
nature through the sliding full-length windows of the living room, which extend the interior
volumes of the house to the sheltered piazza. All the other windows of the house are casements which open out, giving a much more complete penetration of interior and exterior
than was possible with the rising sash which had been common since the eighteenth century
and which, unfortunately, was never entirely to disappear.

Structurally, Kingscote is much less expressive of its wooden frame than are the second
Ocean House and the Galvin house, both simpler and more straightforward buildings.
Kingscote's structural skeleton of the mortise and tenon system is sheathed horizontally
with wooden matched boarding, the joints scored in imitation of masonry courses (as were
those of the house at School and Mary streets), and the whole painted a stony gray. Kingscote
states, therefore, one premise only of the new architecture, namely the picturesque, based on
its pictorial union with nature. In terms of the new utility, it is only slightly advanced and in
structural expression not at all.

In these terms, Malbone Hall, by Alexander Jackson Davis, built on Tonomy Hill in
1848–1849, is even less advanced. As Kingscote is a *cottage ornée* out of the late Georgian   Pl. 162
books, so Malbone's roots are in the castellated ruins built in eighteenth-century English
gardens and in such early nineteenth-century Gothic houses as Wyatt's Belvoir. Its plan is
regular and academic, and only a few pictorial towers and bays break out of the basic cube.
Built of pink sandstone, it was meant from the very beginning to appear as dilapidated as
possible, and it remains a kind of stage set. Although it is a part of the new architectural
development in its attempt to slip into its picturesque setting, it is for 1848 already a back-
ward house, less important for new growth than the smaller cottages that Davis was draughting at this period as illustrations for Downing's publications.

More important than Malbone is the Edward King house, by Richard Upjohn, 1845–   Pl. 163
1847. It is characteristic of the new domestic "villa" mentality that more than one kind of
expression was felt to be possible. Consequently, where Upjohn in Kingscote strove for
lightness of scale and a breaking up of the mass, Upjohn in the Edward King house attempted massiveness, monumentality, and plastic weight.

To call the first house "Gothic" and the second "Italian" is to miss much of the point and to argue on the same superficial grounds which were used to discredit these houses by the academic critics of the early twentieth century. The King house, although designated as an "Italian villa," is actually a mid-century experiment in the composition of freely developed masses, asymmetrical, three-dimensional, plastic. Its smooth red brick walls with matching mortar joints form smooth hard planes which yet give a feeling of weight and density. Sharply cut masses are organized asymmetrically around the central entrance loggia and are capped by projecting roofs on heavy brackets, while a lower mass with a gabled roof projects at the side. The balconies with their flaccid canopies are massive, as is all the detail, in keeping with the brutal scale of the whole.

The interior volumes of the house are of the same character. The rooms are high, the moldings simple and heavy, and the space pushes sluggishly out of the academic cube into that freer and more irregular arrangement which is echoed by the massing of the exterior. There is a multiplication of spaces, shapes, and relationships. This greater freedom of interior space and exterior massing is the result on the one hand of a desire for a more useful, varied, and flexible living area, and on the other of a desire for general picturesque composition. In this the Edward King house relates to Kingscote, but differs from Kingscote in its weight and mass.

Two related but differing avenues of future development are thereby laid down in the forties. Both tend toward a more useful interior space; both are picturesque and three-dimensionally asymmetrical; both are basically nonstylistic, but one is light and best suited to wood structure and expression and the other is heavy and best suited to masonry. We shall see these two streams diverge, meet again, and interact in the mid-century development.

THE MOVEMENT TOWARD MASS. In the cottage villas built in increasing numbers at Newport in the fifties, it was the heavier, more plastic type which produced the greatest number of examples, and while work of very great quality was produced, nevertheless certain limitations in this method of design began to be apparent.

Pl. 164

From March to October of 1851, Alexander MacGregor, a Scotch stonemason and builder, built a house on Bellevue Avenue for Judge Swan, called Swanhurst, now the property of the Art Association. Swanhurst clearly shows the influence of such work as the King house but is slightly looser and more articulated, with a lighter gabled roof and more slender brackets. Its plan is the academic one of fairly narrow central hall with rooms arranged on either side. However — and this remains a common characteristic of mid-century houses — the rooms themselves are high and cool, with full-length windows which open out upon the piazzas. Their shapes also are varied, and one of them pushes out a well articulated polygonal bay on the west side of the house. This bay, sprouting heavy balconies above, is surrounded on the first floor by a piazza making use of some simple and effective wooden lattice detail.

The dry Doric porch on the east is a later addition, but the rest of the detail is original and recalls that of the King house. Except for the lattice work of the western piazza, most of it is not a very direct expression of wood, being heavy in section and flowing in profile, as if molded in clay or cut in soft stone. Nor do the walls express their construction, which is of the finest random masonry, beautifully laid as an expression of rough stone, but entirely stuccoed over so that its real nature is obscured.

It is characteristic of the domestic development of the mid-century that there was not that same desire for expression in masonry construction which was already developing in wood frame structure. The answer is probably obvious, namely that stone was more expensive, took longer to work, and was less easily procured than wood. Consequently, it always remained a luxury, while wooden structure formed a basic and daily developing tradition in every builder's hands. At any rate, the heavier, more monumental houses, leaning naturally toward masonry, give proof only rarely of any interest in their material as such, and we shall see that the most complete expression of plastic volumes was to come later, paradoxically, in wooden rather than in masonry construction.

One exception to this in the fifties was the Wetmore house, built in 1851–1852 by Seth Bradford, another local contractor, evidently assisted by William S. Wetmore himself. In 1872 this house was considerably enlarged by Richard Morris Hunt. The plan of the original house departed only slightly from the academic type of central hall on axis with symmetrically disposed rooms on either side. The structure was of rough Fall River granite, laid in a kind of ashlar and left unstuccoed, so that the very massiveness of the house was enhanced by the visual weight of its stone walls. Partially enclosed by a deep veranda, the exterior was a sculptural composition of advancing and receding masses, dominated by the entrance tower and topped by a roof of that mid-century semi-hipped type which was French in inspiration, although as yet by no means a full mansard. Curvilinear and deeply concave, roofs of this type represented in the fifties the first stage of that preoccupation with roof plasticity which in the early sixties was to develop into the higher and more solidly sculptured mansard.

More typical of the heavier, monumental style in the fifties, although by no means the most distinguished examples of it, are the Charles H. Russell house, by Richard Upjohn, 1852–1853, now gone, and the Daniel Parrish house, by Andrew Jackson Downing and Calvert Vaux, 1852–1853. The Parrish house burned in 1855 and was rebuilt by Vaux in precisely its original form, although at a point on its site farther away from Bellevue Avenue and closer to the sea.

Upjohn's Russell house was another of those asymmetrically massed, bracketed, and heavily detailed structures with which we have already become familiar. Yet here the actual structure of the house was wood frame sheathed by horizontal siding so carefully joined and painted as, in photograph at least, to force one to look carefully in order to make sure that

Pl. 165

Pl. 166

Pls. 167, 140

the surface is not really stucco. The details are molded and thick in section and, while less heavy than those of the King house, are still very unwooden. In the dense juxtaposition of the various elements in the Russell house there is a certain tension which is perhaps the greatest quality the house possesses, but which may also be considered a result of this kind of design in which the structural material and its possibilities for organic expression are ignored.

Another aspect of the more monumental trend may be seen in the Daniel Parrish house, built of brick covered with a warm tan stucco and coigned with stone. Here the free design is now drawn back into a block, articulated somewhat by the gabled projection of the façade over the porte-cochere and originally extended to the south by the heavy stone arcade of a pavilion. The service wing extends to the north. The house has been damaged by later academic alterations in which the side portions of the windows of the entrance façade were filled in with engaged columns and the southern pavilion torn down and rebuilt in a dryly academic manner on the sea side, ruining in the process the play between void and solid of that façade, originally the most distinguished feature of the house. The heavy entrance porch is also part of the original design, although it appears out of scale with the rest of the house.

This rigid plan, which multiplies spaces but holds them tightly within a cube, and the dry, contained block of the house — always excepting the original richly handled loggias and bays of the sea side — shows another result of the monumental manner. Whereas the Russell house multiplied an awkward series of complex relationships, the Parrish house tends to pull itself up and to become as abstract as the earlier Greek Revival houses had been. If, however, it is as abstract as they are, it is also considerably more dense, as if pushed in upon itself by massive forces and squeezing energy within its cube. Nevertheless, the line which it represents seems in a sense self-defeating. The really organic energies of architectural development and growth, of technical and spatial energy, are absent from it. It represents a preoccupation with monumental impressiveness at the expense of more vital qualities which was foreign to the most significant aspects of the nineteenth-century American genius. The little boarded and battened cottages like the Galvin house which Downing had advanced as an American cottage style were more important for later growth than the larger villas and mansions with which he, as here, also concerned himself.

Pl. 168

The end product of this monumental line before the Civil War is seen in such a house as Beaulieu, built in 1856–1859 for the Peruvian ambassador, de Barreda. This house, capped also by a concave French roof, high and almost a mansard, but curving out over heavy brackets to a greater extent than the true mansard, is built of hard red brick with narrow joints, producing a smooth dense wall surface. At some date this wall was stuccoed and painted over, and the present owner deserves credit for having had this covering sandblasted away. Beaulieu is a symmetrical block, set upon a terrace. The entrance front has a rectangular projecting bay and one asymmetrically placed porch, on the sea side, a polygonal center bay and a deep veranda. The plan, a collection of rooms around a central hall, recalls that of both the Parrish and Wetmore houses, and the interior space opens widely to the veranda on the sea side through full-length glass doors, while a large curved conservatory extends the volumes to the south.

The interiors have been redone by various firms of decorators and are of little importance here. Viewed from the sea, the real nature of Beaulieu becomes most apparent. Set behind its plot of lawn, which on that side is strictly geometrical, the house is an uncompromisingly monumental mass of brick, its solidity emphasized by its modeled roof and by the heavy, bracketed cornices over the windows. It is a contained shape of absolute density and weight. With more assurance and force than the eclectic architects of the end of the century were ever able to muster, this house achieves what they were later to attempt: monumentality, abstract dignity, and power. If Beaulieu is a monument, it is also no longer a cottage or really a villa, but a mansion, and as such it expresses in a way the final stage of this phase of the heavier monumental design. It stands, massive and complete, at a dead end, and — except for a short but powerful efflorescence of a similar attempt toward plastic monumentality in wood — the major forces of growth in the next decades were to move generally in a different direction.

THE MOVEMENT TOWARD ARTICULATION. If the seeds of organic growth lay in a development of wooden construction, nevertheless in the fifties only a very few distinctively wooden houses were built at Newport. A few vertically boarded and battened structures appeared, but most of these have been altered beyond recognition, most specifically the present Bozyan house on Indian Avenue in Middletown. This house would appear to have been an extraordinarily developed board and batten cottage with diagonally braced piazzas, but the remodelings of generations and the addition of an impressive number of bathrooms have now reduced it to an archaeological rather than an architectural problem. Dating from the fifties also, although not a cottage, was All Saints' Chapel, now destroyed. This was built in 1852 on Church Street and moved in the seventies to the corner of Cottage Street and Old Beach Road. A small, vertically boarded and battened structure, it was similar to the wooden churches of the same kind built by Richard Upjohn in the forties and fifties. Upjohn offered designs for these churches free to Anglican congregations in rural areas and published the type in his *Rural Architecture* (1852).

Pl. 169

One of the earliest results of the new American interest in the picturesque expression of wooden structure, by using it "boldly," as Downing had put it, had been a collateral interest in the Swiss chalet, the arch-manifestation in Europe of a similar preoccupation. Downing, in his anti-Greek Revival attacks upon the grand "styles" as unsuitable for domestic use, had seized upon the Swiss chalet as an example of a less stylistic substitute and an inspired exploitation of wood techniques. In this he was following the example of such English writers of the twenties and thirties as Robinson, Loudon and Brooks. Interest in Swiss wooden types at this time is therefore not simple eclecticism, but rather a kind of case study in materials and techniques. It represents the drawing together of parallel types for the support of creative experiment.

Pls. 169, 170

At any rate, a complete and elaborate example of the European chalet type appeared on Halidon Hill in 1854. Built for Hugh Willoughby, it was designed by Leopold Eidlitz of New York, who was a Bohemian by birth and had a sound German training. His own house overlooking the Hudson was also a chalet. The living areas of the Willoughby house ramble up and down the slope in several levels, the dining room and kitchen below, as often in the fifties, the drawing room and library on a cross axis above, organized around central fireplace masses. All rooms opened to terraces or verandas, a spatial penetration later somewhat obscured by the addition of more rooms. Equally important, and related to this freedom of plan and space, is the fact that this house is a boldly handled wooden structure, extended by wooden balconies and terraces and overhung by the widely sheltering planes of gabled roofs. These, like the balcony of the second story, are supported by diagonal braces under exposed rafters. As the planes of roof and piazza pass over and across each other, the shadowed voids which they create are punctuated by this diagonal stick work, and the light is further broken up by the jigsaw carving of the balconies and the shaggily cut ends of the vertical boarding of the upper zone. The house was painted in browns and tans, emphasizing its darkly wooden nature, and its jagged outlines pick up the shapes of the pines which were planted around it.

One is reminded of Henry William Cleaveland's comment concerning the chalet type in his book, *Village and Farm Cottages* (New York, 1856). Cleaveland, a disciple of Downing, has this to say of one of his own designs: "Circumstances similar to those which make this style proper on the Alpine slopes often exist among us, and it is for some such position that this design was intended. It would suit well the southern slope of some steep and rugged hill. . . ." As Cleaveland emphasizes the relation of his house to a natural setting, so Eidlitz at Halidon Hill exploits a similar position. The house belongs to its site and enhances it. It becomes a living architectural organism upon its slope and among its pines. A similar but less elaborate chalet was built at this same period on the hill slope above what was to become

Pl. 170

Bailey's Beach, and here the simple wooden qualities inherent in the type are again apparent — wide and light wooden balconies, the projecting planes of roof supported on brackets, a feeling of the lightness and extension possible with wooden structure. The European chalet type, consequently, soon merges with and enhances the basic qualities of the American development as a whole.

In the Eidlitz chalet on Halidon Hill much of the architectural character depends upon the bold expression of the diagonal braces necessary to support the balconies and the roof. We have already seen how the vertical battens advocated by Downing expressed upon the exterior the vertical members of stud construction. By the early fifties, Gervase Wheeler, an

Englishman who had come to America in the late forties and who was imbued with the point of view of Gothic Revival rationalism, had already built houses in which all the framing was exposed or expressed and who had stated of the stick work of his gable ends and his wall surfaces, "this being no sham, but the actual framing . . . within. . . ." Wheeler also said that in wood structure one should "Let timber, and timber only, be evident in every part of your design." The reason for this lay in the new Gothic Revival desire for what was called "reality." By the expression of your structure, said Wheeler, your design becomes "essentially real." For the concept of architecture as abstract design is substituted the concept of architecture as an organism. This point of view not only reinforces Downing's drive toward structural expression but relates also to Horatio Greenough's insistence, in the late forties and early fifties, upon what he called the "organic." By the early fifties, therefore, the philosophical basis for a new and organic development in domestic architecture was complete.

By the later fifties a house which had been affected by this drive toward the exterior expression of all the members of the interior framing had already appeared in the Newport area. This was the Hamilton Hoppin house, built at Middletown by Richard Upjohn between 1856 and 1857. While the plan of this house is symmetrical and academic, nevertheless the interior is of some interest, since it has never been remodeled and still retains its original dark and quiet atmosphere. More important than this, however, is the fact that Upjohn develops upon his exterior wall surfaces a series of vertical and horizontal members which schematically indicate the vertical posts and horizontal plates of the actual frame. His wall therefore breaks up into a series of panels, articulated by wooden stripping and further divided by a whole series of crossed diagonals indicative of the diagonal bracing of the frame. Vertical in proportion and rigidly contained, the main effect which the house produces is of the expressive articulation of its structural members, and this is further enhanced by the present painting scheme, probably close to that of the original, in which the wall plane itself is light gray with the skeletal stripping picked out in white. For the expressive and structural diagonal bracing of the balcony railing which Upjohn had indicated in his elevation drawing of this house, he unfortunately substituted in the finished version a smaller scale of the rather unwooden arcade of the main piazza.

Nevertheless, Upjohn's projected skeletonization of the surface is fairly early of its kind. The Van Rensselaer house, which was soon built beside the Hoppin house and imitated it, copied carefully the details of the piazza porch but retained of the skeletal articulation only a single rather meaningless frieze of diagonals under the roof. Before wood frame houses in large numbers were to take up and develop further this skeletal expression, they were for a time to follow quite different aims.

Pl. 171

Pl. 172

THE MANSARD REACTION. The fifties were, as we have seen, the period when the heavy, French-roofed houses built of brick, stone, or stucco attained their most powerful development in Newport. Although only occasionally expressive of their own masonry, these houses in the fifties had a profound effect upon wooden building and diverted it for a time from its own more organic expression. We have already noted that Upjohn's Russell house of 1852 had succumbed to such influences. The Charles Fearing house of 1853 is an example of an attempt toward a French-roofed sculptural effect in a wooden house. As in similar houses of masonry, the plan of the Fearing house is symmetrical, rigid, and not advanced, although, as in the masonry houses, it does make use of an ample piazza. The house itself is a simple block with symmetrically disposed wings and with an early French roof which gives an air of three-dimensional sculptural density to the main block.

Pl. 172

Fairbourne, built on Bellevue Avenue in 1853–1854 and now gone, is another example of a wooden house with monumental aspirations. Formal in plan and massing, the house exploits the possibilities of wooden articulation only in the diagonal braces of its porch railings and in the strip indication of its corner posts and second story plate. As in the Fearing house, it is a French roof which pulls the whole together into a plastic unity. The kind of reaction against wooden techniques which this trend represents can be seen in the entrance arcade of Fairbourne, where the heavy arches are obviously derived from masonry forms, containing no expression whatever of the wood in which they were executed.

Pl. 172

The attempt toward a monumental kind of building in wood, or what might be called a mannerist interlude in the organic wooden development, nevertheless produced in the sixties a few monuments of considerable power. The French roof of the fifties became by the early sixties the true mansard, and the added height not only provided additional headspace for the upper story, but also increased the sculptural effect.

J. Frederick Kernochan's villa, Edgewater, built at the end of the Civil War, but now destroyed, was an excellent example of the kind of power achieved in some of these houses. Edgewater had the virtues of a piece of primitive sculpture, an absolute density in its visual mass, a vitality of surface and detail which created a richly worked and polychromed effect. In this the mansard itself was the most important element, completing and drawing together the vertical, high-shouldered silhouette. It rounded off and made continuous the plasticity of the mass toward the sky, and upon it the polychromed shingles and the dormers with their bold detail crowded changes of plane and color together into a barbaric textual richness. Edgewater to our eyes would be a surrealist object, acting by power of shock to transform our vision. In plan and interior space it was undistinguished, and in structure no less so. The craze for the mansard seems temporarily to have atrophied all other architectural energies in its preoccupation with that single plastic hammerblow.

Pl. 172

Supreme in the perversity of this mannerism was Thomas Winan's first "Bleak House," built by the sea on Ocean Drive around 1865, and razed in 1894. Totally inappropriate upon its flat and windswept site, it gloried in that inappropriateness, even in its name. A great wooden barn with a high mansard, it was split in half by a mountainous cross volume thrust

Pl. 172

through the house above its entrance porch, and was without doubt one of the most awkward structures ever raised by man. Yet despite or because of all that, it had a quality. In a way it was the perfect acme and burlesque of a mansion by the sea, a child's dream of grandeur.

Perhaps the most distinguished of the mansarded houses of the sixties, because it is the most plastic, is the Ogden Mills house on Bellevue Avenue, by William R. Walker, 1866. Here the savage power of the Kernochan house and the surrealist arrogance of the Winans villa are transformed into a lucid expression of architectural volumes. The house is an irregular block with a polygonal bay, intersected by a deep and heavily detailed piazza, and facing the sea. The mansard roof spreads easily in a variety of planes over the irregular shape of the house and unifies it into one solid mass. Most significantly, the mansard itself is topped by a fairly high hipped roof, so that even from the ground very close to the house the impression of the continuous plastic modeling of the outline against the sky is quite apparent. The roof here is really three-dimensional and sculptural, a quality which is also characteristic of many of the smaller houses combining mansard and hip which were built in the town of Newport itself.

Pl. 172

Excellent examples of this type of house were some of the Sea-view Cottages built on the cliffs looking toward Middletown. These date from 1870 and were part of a large hotel complex of which the central element was a glassed-in dining pavilion, destroyed by fire in the nineties. Some of the cottages were of a late, symmetrical villa type, with a high central tower, while others were ballooning volumes with deep mansards. Even more plastic are the seven identical mansarded houses built by the Navy in 1871 on Goat Island, opposite the Newport ferry slip. These still stand, and are easily seen from the Jamestown ferry, seven contained pieces of sculpture in a neatly spaced row. In actuality, so full a treatment of the mansard seems somewhat more common in Newport than elsewhere, and in view of Newport's similar use of gable over hip and of deep gambrels in its colonial period, one might be allowed the supposition that a feeling for roof plasticity was a sensitivity indigenous to Newport. Significantly enough, Newport was to play an important part in the development of the great shingled houses of the early eighties, of which one of the most important architectural characteristics was to be an expression of continuous and bulging volumes.

Pl. 173

Pl. 173

Almost the equal of the Ogden Mills house as sculptural expression, and the last of the larger mansarded houses in Newport, is the Train villa, Showandasee, built in 1869 on Bellevue Avenue near what is now Bailey's Beach. Here a flat-roofed cross volume is inserted into the main block as at Bleak House, but the fewer stories sustain the density of the mass, and the whole is unified by the continuous porch. The arched windows, unsuitable to wood, should be noted. This house has since been stuccoed over, but it still retains that sense of the solid orchestration of masses which it possessed in its original material.

Pl. 174

With this house the practice of forcing light wooden structure into monumental effect came to an end in Newport and, at about the same time, in the rest of the country as well.

The mansard itself was to hold on for a while in the seventies, but its great period was over. The reaction of the sixties, having produced some powerful masterpieces and unforgettable images, had run its course, and the field was open for the resumption of a perhaps more organic development.

THE HIGH STICK STYLE. The next phase in wooden architectural expression cuts across, in a strange way, the history of the balloon frame. The use of the batten, as introduced in America by Davis and promulgated widely by Downing, paralleled but was apparently unconnected with the western technical shift to the continuous vertical stud of the balloon frame. Between the early forties and the later fifties it is difficult to tell how much the eastern builders knew of the new framing system. Most of the wooden houses with which we have been concerned appear to have made use of the old mortise and tenon system. In 1855 the balloon frame was discussed in the *New York Herald-Tribune* by Solon Robinson, who claimed to have been using it for twenty years. This article was quoted by Gervase Wheeler in his book, *Homes for the People*, which appeared in the same year. Not until 1858 did a technical manual describing the new frame appear. This was William E. Bell's book *Carpentry Made Easy* (Philadelphia, 1858).

The chief differences between the old mortise and tenon and the new balloon frame are twofold. The old frame is held together by the fitting of the tenon or dowel of one fairly good sized timber into the mortise or slot of another, while the balloon frame joins smaller pieces of timber by nailing. Secondly, the studs of the new frame rise uninterrupted from sill to rafter, and the plate of the second floor is nailed horizontally to their interior faces. The joists of the second floor are then placed upon the plate and against the side of the stud, into which they are nailed. This contrasts with the old frame where the studs rise only one story, and are tongued into the second floor girt. The members of the old frame were thick in section and, with the more or less rigid joint of the mortise and tenon capable of taking considerable lateral thrust, they achieved stability by the union of two members and required only a minimum of diagonal knee bracing. In the balloon frame the members are thin, by 1858 averaging 2″ by 6″ in section and by the later sixties shrinking to 2″ by 4″ and even 2″ by 3″. The whole system relies for stability not upon the rigid joining of any two heavy members, but upon the entirely organic union of a number of light sticks, nailed into each other in different directions. The balloon frame, consequently, thins down the framing sticks, multiplies their number, and emphasizes the multiplicity of their relationships to each other. The frame becomes a real skeleton, held together by its organic articulation.

In Bell's book the balloon frame had not reached full development. Bell still tenoned his studs to the sill and made no mention whatever of diagonal bracing, which, in the organically interrelated nature of balloon framing, was actually much more necessary for lateral stability than it was in the mortise and tenon system. It was not until George Woodward's

Country Homes appeared in 1865 that the fully developed balloon frame technique was described in an architectural pattern book. Woodward no longer tenoned his studs into the sill but nailed them in, and he advocated and illustrated a variety of diagonal bracing. By the mid-sixties, the balloon frame had become a real bundle of sticks, opposing to each other the tensions of each and including therein a full sense of the diagonal.

It would be absurd to say that in 1862–1863, when he built the J. N. A. Griswold house, now the Art Association, Richard Morris Hunt cared anything for the balloon frame. Pls. 174, 175 He never used it and, probably because it was an American invention, did not like it. In 1855, Hunt had returned from eight years at the Ecole des Beaux-Arts and related architectural activities abroad. He was the first American to attend the Ecole and, unlike Richardson and Sullivan who were to go there later, absorbed from it not only some of its sense of discipline, which was the best it had to give, but also its preoccupation with the grand manner, its academic historicity, and its real eclecticism. Returning to America where there was as yet little market for such overpowering grandeur, Hunt in domestic architecture embarked upon a series of wooden buildings which we today may well feel to have been his best work. He himself, late in life, claimed to prefer them to his later palazzi. Hunt's office was in New York, but he spent a great deal of time at Newport, as did his brother, William Morris Hunt, who had lately returned from the studios of Couture and Millet and was engaged, like Richard, in developing upon American soil a talent largely trained in Europe.

At any rate, in the J. N. A. Griswold house, Hunt picked up the kind of exterior structural articulation which had been used by Gervase Wheeler in the late forties, and of which Upjohn's Hoppin house of 1856–1857 had been an early Newport example and a more complete expression of all the elements of the frame, verticals, horizontals, and diagonals. It is probable that Hunt's inspiration for this kind of design in wood came mainly from European examples of "rustic" architecture, like the picturesque pavilions in the Bois de Boulogne and elsewhere, which were built by his colleagues at the Ecole in the early fifties. From the entrance side especially, the Griswold house seems to be a combination of similar gable-roofed pavilions, pictorial in their shades of dark and lighter gray. Moreover, it was undoubtedly a kind of half-timbered medieval expression which Hunt had in mind here. Nevertheless, his use in this house of a visual skeleton of sticks containing many diagonals, coinciding in time as it does with a similar development in the basic American wooden framing technique, can, in the long view, not be coincidental. It marks the beginning of that last phase of total skeletal articulation which was to displace the sculptural mansard and to dominate wooden domestic building in the early seventies.

If the Griswold house is an early example of this apotheosis of skeletal expression, it is also an excellent building in its own right and is perhaps Hunt's best. After the house was taken over by the Art Association, the service areas were altered, and the stable which originally stood on the side of the house was made into a large exhibition area. Enough of the original plan remains, however, to give an idea of its character, which is both articulated and open, flexible and ordered. One enters on the north under a stick-work porte-cochere, mounts a few steps, and stands in a central octagonal hall, the circulation core of the house. The stairs mount again to a large landing over the porte-cochere, which has a high and structurally expressive ceiling. From the octagonal hall a reception room and a study open left and right, while straight ahead, on a cross axis to the south, are the living and dining rooms. The room shapes take on vitality as they interlock with the central polygon, and, through the wide door openings, movement in the high-ceilinged interior space is rhythmical and varied. The light also is varied — muted in the hall, darker in the high landing, and brighter in the dining room, between which and the shadowed living room spills a bright pool of light from the central bay on the south. Glass doors open from the living room to the surrounding piazza, where the diagonal stick-work casts a further pattern of shadows. Less turgid than his later work, the Griswold house is also Hunt's most American creation. In its sense of open interior space expanded by piazzas, it looks forward to the spatial achievements of the cottages of the eighties, while in the skeletal explosion of its sticks it sets the stage for a similar development in the cottages of the late sixties and early seventies.

The houses of this period, whether built in the balloon frame or not — and many of them were not — are distinguished by a preoccupation with skeletal articulation. Some retain certain characteristics of the mansarded houses. Ednavilla, the N. H. Sanford (now King Covell) house on Washington Street, 1870, is an example of such a house. Built on a fairly academic central-hall plan, it is distinguished, nevertheless, by a stair hall which is open three stories to the roof, overhung by projecting balconies, and its walls decorated with flat, hard, and elegantly abstracted flower patterns in warm colors. The vertical volume of this hall is not expressed upon the exterior of the house, which is almost as dense in mass as the mansarded type, which its roof also recalls. Its clapboarded walls, however, are stripped skeletally, although without diagonals, and in this concern with its skeleton structure, with the organic nature of its frame, it differs from the real mansarded type, which was not at all interested in its skeleton.

This can be seen also in the Thayer Cottage on Bellevue Avenue, built about 1870, where a more or less mansarded roof weighs sculpturally over a structure which is not sculptural in the same sense, but skeletal, bringing to the surface an insistent sense of the opposing sticks which form its frame. The basic difference between the developed mansard and this stick style can be seen in the old Stanhope photograph dating from the eighties which shows both the Ogden Mills house of 1866 and the Thomas Cushing house of 1870. Where the Mills house is a contained plastic mass, the Cushing house breaks up into a series of articulated planes. Where in the Mills house the wall is an enigmatic support for the sculptural roof, in the Cushing house it is a stripping of sticks, which emphasizes its own interior nature. In the Mills house the windows are cut abstractly into the wall surface, but in the Cushing house the

Pl. 176

Pl. 177

Pl. 177
Pl. 177

windows slip between stripping which expresses the actual vertical studs between which the windows are structurally set. The esthetic drive behind the Cushing house is the sense of wooden framing as an articulated skeleton and of flat sticks multiplied and totally reactive.

This apotheosis of the skeleton in the early seventies has several aspects. On one hand it becomes an exacerbated baroque of the picturesque. This can be seen in such a building as the Mrs. Loring Andrews house of 1872. Here the stick really goes wild. The mass leaps up as if impelled by the vertical energy of its studs. Truss work proliferates elaborately in the gables, and the whole building gives the impression of exploding into a loose bundle of sticks. Many of the buildings at the important Philadelphia Centennial of 1876 were of this type, the full-bloom stick baroque. This represents in a way the first phase of the cottage style tending to blow itself to pieces with a kind of mechanistic fury in the new, urban, and harsher post-Civil War world. Expressive of this also was the Nathan Matthews house of 1871–1872, designed by the rising firm of Peabody and Stearns of Boston. This differs from most of these houses in its brick first story, a forerunner of future developments. But above this the frame structure again seems to separate itself into its component elements. Verticals and horizontals cross each other, and the windows slide between indications of the interior studs. Diagonals develop and are picked up by the criss-crossing planes of the gabled roofs, impelled by the picturesque energy of the conception to intersect repeatedly in a constantly changing system of relationships.

While this stick style reaches a kind of baroque in the early seventies, it has also certain other important aspects. It is undeniable that among its practitioners at Newport, if not among its contemporary theoreticians, such as E. C. Gardner, it was rather loosely conceived of as expressing some reminiscence of medieval half-timber construction. The external stripping, for instance, is heavier in section here than in most of the less pretentious building elsewhere and is usually chamfered in the late medieval fashion. George Champlin Mason, who since his return to Newport from Florence and Paris in 1846 had been exhibiting those antiquarian tendencies which were to become of importance later, consistently referred to the late stick houses as being "in the style of the old half-timbered houses." In his book, *Newport and Its Cottages* (1875), he so designated, among others, the Thomas Cushing and Nathan Matthews houses. Mason's own house of this period, built in 1873–1874, while it has the stock virtues of free mid-century American planning, is essentially *retardataire* in general conception, rather avowedly Swiss in its detail, and making use of a purely pictorial board and batten second story.

Mason's house, like his insistence upon a half-timber derivation for stick style work, is out of keeping with the general temper of the early seventies, which was nonantiquarian and antistylistic. American architectural thought in the early seventies was, with the exception of certain new forces which we shall discuss later, concerned on the whole with the immediate problems of the present and future and was little concerned with the past. When, in

Pl. 177

Pl. 177

Pl. 178

January of 1873, the *American Builder* published a large *Supplement* illustrating the Swiss chalet, it was immediately deluged with letters of complaint, accusing it of attempting to foster foreign building types to the detriment of the natural American development. The *American Builder* was consequently forced to explain that it was not advocating the Swiss chalet but merely desired

> to direct the thoughts of builders, for a moment at least into these channels . . . [to stimulate] new processes of construction, each of which should be a growth among ourselves, as they have been among the builders of Swiss chalets.

Concerned with the development of basic technique and with consequent new architectural growth, the best architectural thought of the early seventies had no love for antiquarianism and expressed itself in such words as these, used in an article entitled, "Americans vs. American Art," which appeared in the *American Builder* in 1873:

> Nothing so cramps invention as the trammels of tradition. The cold hand of the dead clasping about our throats will yet choke utterance. What we want is, not to further rivet upon us the chains of the past, but to rise up to the possibilities of our own times and country.

Pl. 179

It is in these terms that the best of the stick style houses of the early seventies must be understood. Such a house as the Jacob Cram, now Mary Sturtevant, on Indian Avenue in Middletown is an excellent example. Apparently built by Dudley Newton in 1871–1872 (although it exhibits many of the characteristics of the work of Peabody and Stearns), it represents a climactic moment in the first phase of that organic and basically nonstylistic development whose roots in America went back to Downing's time. This development had three basic principles which we have seen in operation to a greater or less degree since the forties. These were: 1) utility; 2) structural expression; 3) the picturesque. These three principles had consistently interacted and tended to reinforce each other, and can all be seen at work in the Sturtevant house. Utility had called for a certain number of rooms, different in function and thereby varied in shape, as can be observed in its plan. Since the halls are to pass through, they contain no fireplace and are not unduly developed, and the rooms themselves, although opening widely, are clearly separate volumes. This will contrast with later developments. Since the rooms are varied, the enclosing wall shapes are also varied, thus increasing the picturesque variety of the exterior. Moreover, high rooms are cooler than low rooms and, to the mid-century eye, more spacious. Consequently, the mass of the house will be vertical, expressive of its most important structural member, the vertical stud.

For this variety and verticality a flexible wooden frame system is perfectly adapted, and will naturally be expressed upon the exterior, as in the articulated wall stripping and gable trusses of the Sturtevant house. The stick expression, conversely, breaks up the wall and, as in the gables, casts a variety of shadows, all of which enhance the pictorial quality of the whole. This visual effect must further be developed by color which will not clash but will blend with the landscape and receive natural light with tonal richness, in this case a deep warm red. Similarly, high, light wooden truss roofs express the various changes in room shape and massing below, extend outward to protect the walls, and become an additional picturesque feature.

Yet in the picturesqueness of this stick style vernacular there is nothing quaint or cottagey, but rather a kind of harsh, jagged masculinity, which contrasts more than favorably with the tasty quaintness of some aspects of later development. It is only utilitarian and sensible to be able to move easily out of doors and also to be protected from the rain and the sun. This combines at the same time with a love of nature founded upon a sense of the picturesque. Consequently, as in the Sturtevant house, ample porches extend the interior volumes of the house and are reached through high glass doors set between structural studs. These porches become not only deep voids in the architectural composition, but are also natural expressions of wooden skeleton construction, with posts, horizontal plates and ties, and diagonal braces to extend the span and take the lateral thrust. In the stick work may be felt the influence of Japanese framing techniques which, like the Swiss chalets in the fifties, were becoming organic enrichments of the indigenous sensitivity toward frame construction.

Here is the same genius in operation which led to the development of skeleton construction in American nineteenth-century commercial architecture. It is the sense of the skeleton which vitalizes the commercial structural growth from Bogardus in the mid-century through Jenney in the eighties to Louis Sullivan's masterpieces in the nineties. While this story cannot be told in Newport, nevertheless one example of metal skeleton construction which did appear there dates from the same period as the Sturtevant house and was also by Dudley Newton. This was the Newport Gas Company building, 1874. Its cast-iron façade, Pl. 180 slim, open, and metallic, illustrates an expression of skeleton construction in metal which is comparable to the wooden skeleton expression of the Sturtevant house. The organic life which existed in the American architectural tradition in the early seventies is to be seen in each of these buildings.

HUNT IN THE EARLY SEVENTIES. Other aspects of the psychological atmosphere of the early seventies can be seen in the houses built during this period by Richard Morris Hunt. The first of these is the house Hunt built for himself in 1870–1871, and later sold to Colonel George Pl. 180 Waring. It is possible that this house was at least remotely "colonial" in inspiration. Symmetrical except for the slight projection of the window bay to the right, the proportions are unusually low and horizontal. The roof is a combination of gambrel and hip, and faintly classicistic columns screen the entrance. The awkward center gable with its fuzzy board and perforation work owes more to European "rustic" types than to the American stick style, while the more or less symmetrical plan may owe something to colonial precedent, as may the white walls, evidently original. If this colonialism was intended, although the mixed nature of the house makes it difficult to state so clearly, then it is the first built evidence of colonial reviv-alism to exist anywhere, as will become apparent later when we discuss the Colonial Revival. At any rate, the house is mincing and rather oppressively quaint, cottagey, and coy.

So also is the little house at 49 Bellevue Avenue, opposite the Redwood Library. This was built for Samuel Pratt in 1871, probably but not definitely by Hunt. It may possibly be a work of George Mason's, who illustrated it later in an article for *Harper's Monthly* and who certainly regarded Hunt as a master. The shape of its gable is similar to that on Hunt's own house, and a variation of the colored slates which sheath it was also used by Hunt in the next few years. With its tiny pictorial towers, here hardly justified by utility and structural expression, its lacy carving under the eaves, its colored slates, and its self-conscious air of the *mignonne*, this house also is evidence of a new quaintness. This tendency had been intent in the whole cottage development since Kingscote, but had never before been so overt. The plan here, however, is excellent, consisting of three interrelated spaces on a cross axis parallel to the street, with a kitchen placed centrally behind. The fireplace of the central living area acts as a pivot around which the space moves from living to service areas, and the axially open living space is extended through glass doors to a partially covered terrace. This is free small house planning of a high order, and it is further evidence of that flexibility of American nine-teenth-century domestic planning, from a later stage of which the plans of Wright, which sum up the development, were to take their point of departure.

Hunt's Marquand house of 1872, while much larger, is basically of the same type as the Pratt house. Owing something to the general stick style development, but much heavier, this house mixes stone, wood, and brick with diamond patterns of blackened headers in a way which is essentially turgid, rustic, and quaint. The heavy stick work of the walls, applied over brick, becomes meaningless and plastically confusing and represents a reversion from the organic logic of the stick style to what is now really a half-timber reminiscence. At the same time, it is also evidence of a partiality for stick expression which tends to impose itself even upon some masonry structures. Hunt's reversion to an inherent stylistic antiquarianism is even more apparent in the Travers Block of around 1875, a brick structure laced with the heaviest of chamfered half-timbering, nonstructural and clumsy in scale. A better building than the Marquand house, less stylistic and with more essential authority, was Hunt's T. G. Appleton house of 1875–1876, now unfortunately destroyed. Here the diagonally braced piazza was rough and ample and the whole massing of the house more decisive and solid. The braced balconies of the main gable were excellent examples of strong timber construc-tion, and the walls of the house were sheathed in variously colored and patterned tiles, an oblique and peculiarly Huntian indication of the new preoccupation with surface pattern and texture which by 1875 had already produced its first great monument in America, the Watts Sherman house.

This development is not our concern at the moment, however, and we should conclude

Pl. 181
Pl. 182
Pl. 181
Pl. 182
Pls. 187–191

our discussion of Hunt's work of the early seventies with a brief consideration of his altera- Pls. 183,184
tions and additions to the Wetmore house, carried out in 1872–1873. The opportunities afforded him here were entirely appropriate to the turgid romanticism which seems to have
been his primary characteristic during these years. To make the house more impressive,
Hunt raised the original concave French roof into a towering mansard of which the slope
is so steep that much of the original plasticity is lost. He further added a series of rooms and
complicated the mass with pictorial towers. Continuing the rough granite of the original
construction where he had to, he used where he could a smoother stone, as in the new porte-
cochere, window bays, and related detail. These are heavy in scale, in keeping with the
tremendous mass of the original house. Inside, Hunt produced his most expressive interiors.
If the misused word "Victorian," with all its connotations, has any meaning whatever, it
should be used to describe these rooms. They are massive, high, and dark. The stair hall
which Hunt added is a magnificent cavern wherein the solemn staircase, painted underneath with landscape scenes, mounts in dark and bemused majesty. Fortunately, the original
furnishings and hangings have been preserved, and they complete that sense of absolute im-
murement which the architectural setting provides.

The library is perhaps the most impressive single room. It is paneled in Hunt's own
version of that massive Eastlake oak to which Hunt's spirit must have risen when it first appeared in Eastlake's *Hints on Household Taste* (London, 1868; first American edition, New
York, 1872). To the notches, incisions, panelings, and chamferings of the Eastlake mode,
Hunt added in the Wetmore library curves, swags, and pine cones of his own. The diagonal
woodwork on the ceiling is a heavier version of the type he used in the living room of the
Griswold house of 1862. The room has power, and to enter it is to step inside an organ when
a note is sounded. Vying with it in effect is the dining room, not by Hunt but by the Italian
decorator, Frulini.

If the early seventies saw not only the apotheosis of the organic stick style but also some
occasionally eclectic and antiquarian work by Hunt, it also saw a brief flurry of outright
academicism, not to appear in force again for more than ten years. One of these academic Pl. 185
monuments was the George R. Fearing house, 1871–1872. This is, in Hitchcock's words, "a
rather careful imitation of the French chateaux of the eighteenth century." In actuality, the
Fearing house was designed in France by a French architect and the plans imported. Mason,
in *Newport and Its Cottages* (1875), says of it, with evident approval: "It is essentially a
French pavilion, carried out with a thoroughness and completeness that reminds one of the
country seats in the neighborhood of Geneva, which are so much admired by American
travellers on the continent."

Comparable to it in its static academicism was Red Cross, the C. J. Peterson house, built Pl. 185
about the same time. This was a brick block with symmetrically disposed porches and heavy
mannerist detail. Like the Fearing house, it was academic and dead in plan and, while its

roots were certainly archaeological, it seems most similar to the medium-sized chateaux published in the French architectural books of the mid-century. If academic, these "chateaux" are at least not overblown, but they express a new and disturbing point of view after the originality and willingness to experiment of the American mid-century development. The looting of European manorial farms which these represent, fed at that stream of cultural snobbery which had given Mason pleasure at the recognition of Genevan chateaux, was eventually to exert a pernicious effect upon American architectural invention.

CHAPTER TEN

The Shingle Style

IT WAS IN A PARTIALLY CLOUDED ATMOS-PHERE, compounded on the one hand of a vital tradition of experiment and growth and on the other of indications of a growing antiquarianism, that in the seventies there began to take shape what we may call the climax pattern in nineteenth-century American domestic architecture. This pattern was an eastern phenomenon until, by the late eighties, it lost its force in the east and shifted its center of gravity to the Chicago area where, at that time, the climax in commercial architecture had already begun to take place. In a brief period of little more than ten years, therefore, all the forces in American nineteenth-century domestic architecture, fusing with certain new forces and ideas, came together in the east and produced a domestic architecture of great vitality, originality, and quality. Yet in the synthesis which produced this architecture there were certain weaknesses, elements of antiquarianism and academicism which, after 1885, came forward and largely usurped the whole. To know the original domestic architecture of the early eighties and to be aware of the real threads of growth which came through from it into the twentieth century is vastly to enrich our cultural memory, since we have been cut off from the architectural energy which flourished in these years by the very antiquarians and academicians who destroyed it.

THE QUEEN ANNE AND COLONIAL REVIVAL. In this whole development, of course, Newport played a critical role. It was very likely for Newport that Henry Hobson Richardson intended his Richard Codman project of 1869. Basically of the developed stick style, like Richardson's own house of the previous year at Arrochar, Staten Island, it nevertheless made use of a kind of interior space which was new in American planning. This consisted of a large living hall, combining a great fireplace and a broad staircase, which opened out the interior

Pl. 186

153

volume of the house and connected with a smaller drawing room and dining room. In the use of this living hall, Richardson was undoubtedly influenced by late medieval types, some of which had recently been published in Robert Kerr's *The English Gentleman's House* (1864). Kerr had also published contemporary examples which made use of a pivotal hall, containing fireplace and stairs, off which the other rooms opened. One of the earliest and most skillful of these was Hinderton, Cheshire, by Alfred Waterhouse, 1859.

Pl. 186

In the England of 1869 the best use of such great hall planning was to be found in the work of Richard Norman Shaw. Since his partnership with Nesfield in the early sixties, at which time he had undoubtedly received some influence from Philip Webb, Shaw had been experimenting with the living hall plan. By 1869 he had already produced several of his manor houses, avowedly "old English" in evocation, of which Leyes Wood of 1868 was the most striking example. None of these had been published by 1869, however, and it is only by 1872, when Richardson built the F. W. Andrews house at Newport, now unfortunately destroyed, that he could have been very much aware of Shaw's houses. In 1871 a drawing of Leyes Wood, rendered in Shaw's beautifully textural sketch technique, had been reproduced by photolithography in the *Building News*, and others appeared in rapid succession. Not until 1874, however, was a Shaw plan published: that of Hopedene, Surrey. Shaw's houses, horizontally extended, tile-hung, half-timbered, with Tudor window bays and carved barge boards, can only be considered — and were so considered in England — as a break with the principles of the mid-century Gothic Revival, founded upon the structural integrity which had been demanded by Pugin and of which the greatest spokesman had been not the Englishman, Ruskin, but the Frenchman, Viollet-le-Duc.

One of the best expressions in England of these principles had already been seen in Philip Webb's Red House, Bexley Heath, built for William Morris in 1858–1860. Shaw's manor houses were of a different breed. With their tile hangings and half-timber over perfectly solid brick walls, they substituted stylistic evocation for structural integrity and made their appeal on two levels: first, through the powerful cohesion of their design, which was Shaw's gift, and secondly, through their implications of "Olde English," more or less Tudor precedent. Antiquarianism, therefore, was in their bones, and, once started on that path, Shaw began to recreate the progress of the English Renaissance. By the mid-seventies he had produced buildings which made use of a considerable amount of classicistic detail, such as New Zealand Chambers of 1872–1873 and Lowther Lodge of 1873. These were called "Queen Anne," in recognition of their movement toward a pseudo-eighteenth-century position, and the name immediately came to be associated also with Shaw's earlier, more medieval, really Tudor houses, such as Leyes Wood.

In his Andrews house of 1872, Richardson's use of shingles may have been an Americanization of Shaw's tile hangings, while his living hall may also have owed something to similar sources. In it the great stairs rise in a spectacular series of turns beside the massive

Pls. 187–191

fireplace, and the subsidiary rooms, here perhaps too many in number, modify with their smaller volumes the central volume of the living hall. In 1874, at any rate, Richardson built his closest adaptation of a Shavian manor house. This was the Watts Sherman house. As originally built, this was less horizontal and therefore less Shavian than it became when, in later years, Dudley Newton added the service wing. Nevertheless, with a stone first story and shingles above, its windows arranged in bays making use of half-timber, the house was always a strong evocation of Shaw's work and thereby of the late medieval manor house. Such was the drive toward this stylism that the eminently useful and very American piazza was omitted from the design. However, Richardson possessed the same power of coherent design which Shaw had, and the Watts Sherman house is a monument of considerable quality. Passing under the porte-cochere, which is just low enough so that one feels its presence as a palpable plane overhead, but high enough so that the scale is not unduly forced, one enters the vestibule, must turn right a little awkwardly to avoid the great stair, and comes therefrom into the living hall, off which open library, drawing, and dining rooms.

The relationship between the stair landing and the high, effectively freestanding fireplace, similar to those published by Viollet-le-Duc in his *Dictionnaire Raisonné*, is one of tension between two monumentally architectural elements. The beamed ceiling, unique in its time, emphasizes the ceiling plane and brings down the verticality typical of the mid-century into an expression of the horizontal, further developed by the spatial flow through the doorless openings on either side of the fireplace. A drawing of this hall, probably the work of the young Stanford White, who was in Richardson's employ between 1872 and 1878, was published in the *New York Sketch Book of Architecture* (1874). This drawing shows better than a photograph the window wall of the garden side, now masked by the later addition of a conservatory. The glass was by LaFarge, as was that on the entrance side, which can still be seen as originally intended. Stanford White also is probably responsible for the beautifully scaled shingle patterns of the exterior, as well as the flat half-timbering set in its panels of warm terra-cotta stucco. These increase and complete the horizontal continuity of the window bands, and this sense of surface and spatial continuity is further enhanced by the small-paned windows, as if the interior volumes were exerting an insistent outward pressure upon the thin skin which contains them. This too is new in the American development, this sense of surface continuity, expressive not only of the skeleton, as in the mid-century stick style, but also of the interior volumes enclosed by the thin structure. When the house was altered toward 1880, White turned the original drawing room into a library, and into his delicately scaled green paneling, picked out with gold, introduced not only colonial motifs but also over the doorways sinuous plant forms which are definitely proto-Art-Nouveau.

The Watts Sherman house, therefore, is an architectural monument of great quality but also a stylistic one. Its appeal to architects in the seventies was, as with Shaw's houses, at once as a sweeping and coherent design and at the same time as a Tudor manor house. Not yet was the antiquarian mental twist to take charge and claim quality for the Watts Sherman house precisely because it was a Tudor manor house, but the Watts Sherman house set the stage for such a development. The effect of the Watts Sherman house was immediate, and other "Queen Anne" designs began to appear in America. This trend was reinforced by the British Buildings at the Philadelphia Centennial of 1876. Built in a more or less "Queen Anne" style, these had a marked effect and were published with enthusiastic comment in the *American Builder* of 1876, which hoped that "the next millionaire to build a cottage at Long Branch . . ." would construct it in this style. One of the characteristics which most affected Americans in regard to the Queen Anne was that it purported to resurrect English "vernacular" building of the period just before the Renaissance began to take hold. As such it seemed to express the simple, the pure, and the unsophisticated. In the early seventies the United States had reached what seemed at the time a cultural nadir through corruption, financial scandals, governmental dishonesty, and industrial brutality. As a result, the yearning of many people for the fancied security of a simpler past was such that this old English vernacular became associated with what was supposed to have been the American vernacular at a similar stage of development — namely, the colonial.

Enthusiasm for early colonial building also reached its first peak at the Centennial of 1876, where a "New England Kitchen of 1776," low-beamed and stocked with colonial furniture and housewives in full regalia, vied as an attraction with the British buildings. Interest in colonial architecture, however, had been on the increase since the late sixties, nourished by the general rise of summer resorts which took place after the Civil War. In flight from a post-Civil War world grown, in one contemporary writer's words, "too large," the vacationists began to flee to Mt. Desert, Newburyport, Gloucester, and elsewhere, in search of elemental, more "natural" values. In many of these places a considerable amount of colonial architecture, in various stages of picturesque dilapidation, was still standing, and these ancient ruins came quickly to be associated with the cleaner and more simple dream world which the vacationing refugees were seeking. From the late sixties on, articles full of nostalgia for the old days and the old architecture began to appear in the popular magazines. One of the first of these was H. T. Tuckerman, "The Graves at Newport," *Harper's* (1869). This appropriately titled article derided the houses of modern date and saw these qualities in the old houses: "low ceilings, wainscot panels . . . snug and sunny window-seats . . . broad hall and easy staircase . . . high mantels and vast chimney. . ." While the author's intent is partially antiquarian, it should be noted that certain specifically architectural features move him here, and that these features are quite similar to those which appeared in the Watts Sherman house and which were to be the primary characteristics of the original architecture of the early eighties — low, horizontally extended space, expanse of window, and great fireplace masses.

It is appropriate that in this drive toward a new evaluation of colonial architecture,

Newport should have played a major part. At once a summer resort of long standing and an old colonial town of unique distinction, Newport was crammed in the early seventies with young architects who were capable of giving plastic expression to the new drives. Of these the most imbued with colonialistic enthusiasms was Charles Follen McKim, and at a very early date McKim added his bit to the revival. In 1872 he restored a room in the Thomas Robinson house on Washington Street, and this he made as "colonial" as possible, with a paneled wall and a large fireplace. A few years later, probably in 1876, McKim remodeled the interior of the Dennis house, now St. John's Rectory. Here he assembled more creatively those elements which had already been noted by Tuckerman as the primary architectural features of colonial architecture. Removing the stairs from their original position in the front hall, McKim remodeled the back room, enlarged it with a bay window containing a window seat, and reinstalled the stairs as a foil to the large fireplace. In other words, full of colonial enthusiasm and using elements colonial in derivation, McKim created a "Queen Anne" living hall which was essentially an original architectural manipulation of space.

Pl. 192

Pl. 192

This result must be understood, since it was from just such creative revaluation of diverse and partially antiquarian elements that the free shingled style of the early eighties was to grow. Its immediate inspirations were shaky — since they were partly antiquarian — but its deeper roots were strong and were founded in that flexible sense of space and wooden construction which we have seen as the vital force in the mid-century development. The early seventies, moreover, still looked at the colonial in order to admire its earlier, freer, more medieval phases. Bishop (then Dean) Berkeley's house at Middletown, for instance, the first colonial house to be reproduced photographically in a national magazine, was seen in the *New York Sketch Book* of 1874 as a picturesque pile, with the emphasis placed upon the rich texture of its shingled roof. The sketches which illustrated Junius Henri Browne's article on Newport, "The Queen of Aquidneck," *Harper's* (1874), were of the same textural, picturesque type.

Pl. 193

The seventies, therefore, for the most part preferred the colonial in its more medieval aspect, and though impelled by escapism and some antiquarianism, still looked at it with a creative and picturesque vision. A striking exception to this rule, one which looked forward to the stricter classicistic academicism of ten years later, was the Frederick Sheldon house of about 1875, now gone, which stood at the corner of Annandale Road and Narragansett Avenue. This house, ten years or more before its time, was obviously inspired by Palladian models and was a rigid box through which one bay window nevertheless managed to push itself. It was hailed by the always antiquarian-minded Mason with joy. He states: "Indeed, it was intended to embody the characteristic features and the attractive qualities of the stately old mansions of our fore-fathers, which have never yielded their place in the estimation of those who early learned to admire them." But the Sheldon house was by no means typical of the best energies of its time, as indeed Mason was not, and the creative synthesis of colonial

Pl. 193

and Queen Anne which was about to take place was to be for a time an original and non-stylistic one, founded upon the new sense of flowing, lower-ceiling interior volumes and of a richly textured surface continuity which would express those volumes.

The Queen Anne and colonial influences were discussed at great length in the new architectural magazine, the *American Architect*, founded in 1876. The magazine acted as spokesman for architects as a rising professional class, who were to be lifted high in dignity above the ordinary builder and to be protected by the American Institute of Architects, founded some years before. Some of the new architectural generation's later academicism and Beaux-Arts eclecticism can be traced to this social division, but that is not our concern at the moment. From the articles which appeared in the *American Architect*, it becomes apparent that the architects talked both "Queen Anne" and "colonial" interchangeably and were rapidly assimilating the two into a new point of view toward design. In the later seventies their houses were in general of a more or less "Queen Anne" or "old English" type, distinguished by the use of the new living hall with its consequent opening out of the interior space. While McKim's extraordinary Moses Taylor house at Elberon, New Jersey, 1876, was not of this type — echoing as it did Shaw's eighteenth-century classicistic detail of Lowther Lodge and looking forward to McKim's own later Palladianism of the eighties —

Pl. 193 nevertheless, his project for the Thomas Dunn house at Newport, 1877, was of the general run, though somewhat more stylistic than most. This was to have been placed near the site now occupied by the Naval Hospital, but it was unfortunately never built. Here is to be seen the large living hall with fireplace, opening toward the bay through wide glass doors. The massing of the project is comparatively low and horizontally extended, and the exterior, of stone below and wood above, groups its windows into bays and erupts into cratelike half-timbering and lush "Queen Anne" surface detail.

Pl. 194 Another development from the Watts Sherman house was the C. H. Baldwin (later Prescott Lawrence) house on Bellevue Avenue, by the New Jersey firm of Potter and Robertson, 1877–1878. Of brick, clapboards, and shingles, in that order from the ground up, the house opposes each to the other its variously timbered gables and extends the volume of its top story to receive the vertical chimney mass which penetrates it. The interior is wide open and spatially flowing, a great volume of space extended by piazzas which represent a greater Americanization of the Queen Anne than was accomplished by the Watts Sherman house. The problem of how to integrate subsidiary spaces with the parent space of the living hall, however, was by no means solved here, as can be observed in the incoherent organization of the various door and staircase openings.

Pl. 195 The C. C. Baldwin house of 1880–1881, wildly named "Chateau-Nooga," was built by George B. Post and is a rather later example of extensive half-timbering, which by 1880 had been generally discarded or transformed by the more advanced architects, although in the more eclectically English manor houses, which were unfortunately never to disappear, it was to continue for two generations. The J. Griffiths Masten house on Everett Place, built in 1883–1884 by Alexander G. Oakey of New York, is another late example of the half-timbered, more "old English" type. It has since, however, been rebuilt beyond recognition.

If in the late seventies there were architects who held on for some time to the more English side of the new architectural development, a side which was soon to be assimilated in the original synthesis of the early eighties, there were also those who tended to advance rapidly toward certain aspects of Palladian colonialism, which was also, in the early eighties, to be temporarily assimilated into the free design. Except for McKim, whose early Moses Taylor house was never published and seems to have had no direct influence at all, the most prominent of these was the firm of Peabody and Stearns, of Boston. It will be remembered that this firm had built the Nathan Matthews house of 1871–1872 in the developed stick style.

In 1877 Robert Swain Peabody published an article in the *American Architect* entitled, "The Georgian Homes of New England. Part I." This was signed "Georgian." The success of this piece emboldened Peabody, and when he produced Part II in January of 1878, he abandoned coyness and signed his own name. In his first article Peabody based his love for the colonial upon a desire for "cottagey" escape, now become hysterical: "we too want to live amid wainscoting, nestle in elliptical arched nooks, warm ourselves beneath the high mantels at blazing wood fires, and go up to bed over boxed stairs with ramped rails and twisted balusters. . . ." This utter embrace of the picturesque was one side of the new enthusiasm. On the other side was Peabody's second article, wherein he rediscovered the English Palladian books of the eighteenth century, which had, as a matter of fact, transformed American colonial architecture, in its earlier phases a basically medieval and organic expression of structure and function, by slipping over it a strait jacket made up of academic proportions and details. This Palladianism was eventually to cast a similar strait jacket over the new development as well, but the immediate effect of the colonial details, which from 1878 on were more and more in evidence, was the generally creative one of simplifying and lightening wood work in general after the heavy Eastlakian work of the early seventies.

An illuminating if exaggerated contrast is that between Hunt's library in the Wetmore house, of 1872, and White's library in the Watts Sherman house, of about 1880. Delicacy of scale, founded upon a creative revaluation of late colonial wooden detail, was an important feature of White's most original work of the early eighties. But for Peabody in the late seventies this dichotomy between the wildly picturesque and the chastely academic was too much to be immediately assimilated, and its effects are apparent in the first Breakers, built by Peabody and Stearns for Pierre Lorillard in 1877–1878. This was later sold to Cornelius Vanderbilt, was burned in 1892, and was replaced by Hunt's new "Breakers." In Peabody and Stearns' design, the plan was as monumentally symmetrical and imposing as the firm could make it, with a central hall, huge in size but spatially static. In massing there was obvi-

Pl. 196

ously a desire for Palladian formality in the flanking gables, adorned with eighteenth-century detail, which balanced each other. Yet these were so attacked by subsidiary masses as to create a very jagged series of relationships. A pictorial tower rose at the right of the entrance and was capped by a Renaissance arcade on stubby columns. Palladian windows and little pediments appeared, and most of the detail, inside and out, was decidedly "Georgian." The Palladian detail and intent conflicted here with Peabody's real vision, which, like that of his time, was basically picturesque. All that remains of this first "Breakers" is the children's playhouse on the grounds, well scaled for children and with a deep fireplace of smooth brick. Here the architects were not hampered by the monumental and academic preoccupations which obscured the design sense in the main house.

After 1880 — upon Richardson's return to wooden domestic design with a series of houses which were free in plan and picturesquely shingled, but coherent in formal organization, using wooden details of a simplicity which was not overtly colonial — Peabody and Stearns were for a time to achieve a similar integration in their domestic work, of which, unfortunately, no examples appear to exist in Newport. In public and institutional architecture Peabody and Stearns, like many other architects in the late seventies and early eighties, drifted for a while into a kind of semi-Palladian Queen Anne colonialism, using many classicistic details and inspired primarily by Shaw's New Zealand Chambers. An example of such work in Newport is George Mason's "Queen Anne Building" of 1882, now altered, where the façade of an old building was plastered with semi-eighteenth-century detail, including in the pediment over the central doorway a whole mass of Queen Anne sunflowers.

THE DEVELOPMENT OF AN INDIGENOUS STYLE. In the early eighties in general, however, domestic architects had temporarily fought their way through both "Queen Anne" as such and "colonial" as such. By the early eighties the first, and in a sense the real Colonial Revival, as a creative force, had done its work and was over. It had settled, naturally enough, into an architectural appreciation of colonial architecture of what might be called the middle phase — the plastic, gambrel-roofed types of the early eighteenth century, which Newport especially possessed in such quantities. It was inspired by the plasticity and warm surface texture of these houses, but had no desire to copy them, especially in plan.

In the new synthesis of the early eighties, domestic work of great originality and quality was accomplished by many eastern architects, freely developing what was now a coherent shingled style. The cottage architecture of the early eighties, nonstylistic and free, was most of all an orchestration of space and light. It was also a further expression — and for the nineteenth century the culminating one — of that organic wooden structure which had been the basic technical energy behind the whole nineteenth-century cottage development.

William Ralph Emerson of Boston achieved a design of easy adjustments, lightly picturesque in character, nonstylistic, and of infinite variety. His disciple, John Calvin Stevens of Portland, moved toward a regularization of the Emersonian formula and a stronger order, and expressed himself freely in print upon the relationship between democracy and a free design. Lamb and Rich of New York produced wildly inventive fantasies of an animistic vitality. Bruce Price of New York and Wilson Eyre of Philadelphia developed spatial extensions and simplifications which indicate the framework from which the great spatial rhythms of Wright, the basis of modern architecture, were to take their point of departure. No domestic work by any of these important architects appears to exist in Newport, but Wilson Eyre donated his services as designer of the Berkeley Chapel in Middletown, built in 1882–1883.

Most of the important shingled work of the early eighties in Newport was done by the rising young firm of McKim, Mead, and White. Charles Follen McKim and William Rutherford Mead had been loosely associated since 1872, when McKim, having spent some time at the Beaux-Arts and a year with Richardson, wished to strike out on his own. Mead had just returned from study in Italy. McKim and Mead did their own work and did not operate as a firm until 1877, at which time Bigelow joined them as junior member. It was in this year that these three, accompanied by Stanford White, made their celebrated trip in search of the colonial along the New England seaboard. In 1878 White left Richardson and spent the best part of a year in Europe, where he seems to have been impressed primarily by the *chateaux* of the Loire. Upon his return he joined McKim and Mead, and Bigelow retired from the firm. McKim and White were the designers of the new firm, Mead the engineer.

While this departmentalization of activity, coupled with the increasing number of draughtsmen employed, had eventually that deleterious effect upon organic design which has since been a common characteristic of the large American architectural office, nevertheless in the early eighties the arrangement seems to have worked well for a while. The free masterpieces produced by the firm during this period would seem to owe their quality to two sources: McKim's sense of order, not yet academic, and White's sense of space, light, and scale, always pictorial, but not yet purely decorative. The barn on the Fairchild estate built by McKim alone in the late seventies, shows the architectural vocabulary which they had to work with. Basically nonstylistic, the shingle sheathing nevertheless relates both to the Americanization of Shaw's tiles, as on the Watts Sherman house, and to old Rhode Island practice. Moreover, it is an excellent expression of light frame structure, the shingles expressing themselves as continuous protective covering over the light frame, and the continuity of surface which they provide further enhanced by the diamond-paned windows which keep to the plane of the wall. With these simple materials, the firm of McKim, Mead, and White was to accomplish more inventive and distinguished work in the early eighties than it was to produce later in marble.

The firm's first masterpiece in Newport was the Casino of 1879–1881. According to

Pl. 197

Pls. 197–199

legend, this was ordered by James Gordon Bennett in a fit of pique, but it really answered the need for a social center which had arisen with the great expansion of the summer colony. It is the first of those suburban and resort country clubs which were a new feature in the eighties and of which McKim, Mead, and White soon built other examples, such as those at Short Hills, New Jersey, and Narragansett Pier. Since the site was next to the Travers block on Bellevue Avenue, near the heart of the summer shopping center, McKim kept the street façade unobtrusive and simple. Symmetrical and ordered, it is not academic.

Above the smooth brick piers of the first story, between which shops are set, the shingled upper story, containing club rooms, corbels out beyond the plane of the piers and rides cleanly across them. The side gables produce controlled subsidiary gables which corbel out farther, and the center gable is hollowed by a deeply shadowed loggia from which a curving balcony projects. There is not only a variety of surface here in the shingle patterns of the wall, but also a subtle play between solid and void, open and closed, dark and light. The symmetrical order which controls the whole is given vitality by this movement. Behind the shops and the clubrooms, and reached through a flat arched passageway, is a courtyard surrounded by piazzas which curve out into an apsidal shape at the rear. This interior court is developed more picturesquely than the street façade. A fat shingled tower bulges near the entrance and represents those "Valley of the Loire" forms which were assimilated into the shingled style. Its bright yellow clock face contrasts with its textured shingle surface.

Pl. 198

The piazzas themselves are excellent examples of White's real genius at this time. They are partially enclosed spatial volumes, where the skeleton construction creates airy voids which are shadowed by spindle work screens. Japanese influence, especially important in America after the Centennial of 1876, appears in this organization of posts, plates, "open-work fascias," and pierced screens, as does also the whole mid-century tradition of the stick style. The total effect is similar to that of the twentieth-century constructivist experiments with space and light, such as those carried on by Moholy-Nagy. To the southeast of the piazzas is the tennis court with its spectator's grandstand, again a simple and expressive wooden structure. The theatre is some distance to the rear and is also an example of White's design skill at this period, with delicately handled and crisply detailed interiors. The lattice work in its piazza railings brings to modern minds not only the subtle scale of Japanese prints, but also the proportional relationships of Mondrian.

The Newport Casino, consequently, is one of the most distinguished buildings of the early eighties, controlled by a coherent spatial sense and a general sense of order, and opening out where possible into the most inventive kind of spatial, structural, and textural experiment. How much of this experiment was due to White may be seen in the dining room he added to Kingscote, 1880–1881. Here the service wing was moved away from the old house and the new dining room inserted in the space thus provided. In this room a molding passes continuously above the paneling of the walls, across the doors, across the Tiffany glass

Pl. 200

on either side of the fireplace, across the fireplace itself, and across the expansive bay window which opens to its left. By this means a serene continuity at human scale is created in the room, and a sense of the interpenetration of elements in space is achieved. The variety of materials in use here falls into a coherent pattern through the delicacy of its handling: the metal fireplace detail, the glass squares, the precise wooden paneling of the lower walls, and the thin cork strips of the upper walls and ceiling. It is a three-dimensional design which creates space by the interweaving of slender elements and in this it relates both to Japanese spatial organization and to the skeletal sensitivities of the stick style tradition.

More of this spatial sense, vital in the domestic architecture of the early eighties, is to be seen in the Tilton (now Hobbs) house of 1881–1882, also by McKim, Mead, and White. In exterior massing this house is a less distinguished version of their Cyrus McCormick house at Richfield Springs, New York, also of 1881–1882. It makes use of a similarly expansive single gabled volume with continuous window bands. In the McCormick house, the main volume was articulated by piazzas, but in the Hobbs house it is obscured by the awkward cross volume of the music room. The interior space, however, is extremely subtle, developed by a sense of plan in which the fireplace masses of hall, living, and dining rooms are solid elements around which the space flows, while the other walls take on the character of movable screens. The subdued light in the hall is manipulated in a very subtle way, the spindle screens breaking and splintering it. The ceiling plane slips across the whole and there is again this constant sense of spatial interpenetration and flow. The vistas in the house constantly change and modify each other, as in that from the living room with its semi-colonial and semi-Art Nouveau detail, back into the hall, shadowed on one side and flowing up the stairway on the other. The brightly lighted stairwell opens up the inside volume of the house vertically, so that the horizontal ceiling planes tend to become free elements, moving above each other in space. In the dining room, with its textured ceiling, its natural brick, and its stained wood, the fireplace wall sends its molding across the entrance to the music room, near which the space then slips outside through the glass wall. Here is that combination of open flow and subtle articulation which was basic in the work of the eighties and which was to become further orchestrated and developed in the work of Wright.

Southside, built for Robert Goelet, 1882–1883, was McKim, Mead, and White's next important work among their larger Newport cottages. It is perhaps too large and too manorial. Nevertheless, its interior, while somewhat pretentious, still opens freely around the great hall fireplace, and the galleries above create a movement in space at several levels. Through the sounding volumes of this hall the sea breeze blows with "force enough to make the gas-jets flicker," as a contemporary writer put it. These interior spaces open on the sea side to broad piazzas, above which the surface of the house bulges out in a shingled flow which is cut into by the shadowed voids of the loggias of the upper story. Set in the central bay is one of White's most elaborate plaster panels, which he was accustomed to stick full

Pls. 201, 202

Pls. 203, 204

of seashells, old rope, and broken bottles. Although wildly pictorial in conception, these often, as here, are a textural experiment of considerable vitality, used architecturally to create a visual continuity, differing from the rest of the shingled surface between windows. Notice how the light frame structure seems to expand with its volumes, evidence of the organic union at this period between flexible wooden structure and flowing interior space.

Pl. 205

Probably a better house than Southside, smaller and more unified, is the Isaac Bell house, 1882–1883, also by McKim, Mead, and White. Most striking here are the voids of the porches, supported by bamboo-like posts which White probably developed from similar work appearing in Viollet-le-Duc's "Fat Fau" house, from his *Habitations of Man in All Ages* (Boston, 1876). The open interior space of the Bell house is extended to the porches through glass doors. The living hall opens widely into both living and dining rooms, and, if somewhat heavier in effect than most of the best work of the period, its space is nevertheless expansive and calm. As in the Tilton house, it consists of interwoven areas of varying size and brightness. Like all the best work of this period, the Bell house blends into its surroundings with an appropriate warmth and textural richness. The dark shingles welcome the changing light from the surrounding foliage, and the porches create shadowed pavilions like the sheltered spaces under great trees. Architectural sensitivity to void, to volume, and to structure merges here with a sense of nature.

Pl. 206

Also of this period is McKim, Mead, and White's Samuel Colman house of 1882–1883. This is a simply massed, gambrel-roofed structure with a few dormers, contained loggias, and plaster panels. To the south it was extended, before later alteration, by flanking piazzas and a broad stone terrace. With a plan somewhat less distinguished and more cut up than those of the Goelet and Bell houses, the Colman house nevertheless represents a kind of mean in the work of McKim, Mead, and White in the early eighties and a kind of norm in the shingled style as a whole. It illustrates the capacity to use rough materials expressively and to build simply. Its rough stone base and its shingled upper stories exploit indigenous means of construction and develop them unself-consciously, but decisively.

Pl. 207

The energy within the cottage building of the eighties arises from this creative acceptance of basic techniques, the straightforward bones of building. This is not architecture conceived in an academic fashion, two-dimensionally upon a sheet of drawing paper, but architecture felt in the densities and properties of materials, in the reality of three-dimensional space. Appropriate to their place and climate and expressive thereof, these houses represent in their time a living architecture of originality and power. One of the most characteristic of these in the Newport area is the Lyman Josephs house in Middletown, by Clarence S. Luce, of Boston, 1882–1883. This house also represents the kind of design cohesion and order toward which the shingled style was moving. While its plan is inventive and horizontally extended, making use of a fireplace mass around which the space moves into a small study area, it is perhaps not so distinguished as the exterior mass of the house itself. Above

a rough stone base, wherein all the American stone walls which were ever built come naturally into their own, the volume of the upper story rides long and horizontal. The plane of
its projection above the stone picks up unbrokenly the sweep of the land upon which the
house is built and maintains serenely both constant scale and a oneness with the land.

From this nonstylistic energy only the most recalcitrant architects were exempt. Hunt,
especially, produced no shingled work at Newport, and his Shields house of 1883 was still   Pl. 182
basically a rather turgid exercise in his own stick style type, now unhappily stuccoed over.
His Busk house on Ocean Drive, however, built in 1891 when he was already engaged with   Pl. 207
his late palaces and when the free style itself had been largely overwhelmed, is perversely
enough, much more in the spirit of the early eighties, though somewhat heavy. Built entirely
of rough stone, it spreads between its flanking towers a deep slanting plane of shingled roof,
extending over a piazza below. Its horizontal extension and serene sweep express the power
of design which had resided in the organic development, nourished, as we have said, by a
sense of basic building techniques, of expanding space, and of unity with the land. Mont-
gomery Schuyler, in his review of Hunt's work published in the *Architectural Record* after
Hunt's death in 1895, was evidently somewhat appalled by Hunt's contemporary palaces
and dwelt therefore as long as he could upon the Busk house. It deserves attention and should
be remembered.

In the energy of the period, abstract plastic forms of considerable power were often
created. The Pavilion at Easton's Beach, dating from 1886–1887, was an example of
this. The deep roofs and round towers transformed the candle-snuffers of the Loire into a   Pl. 208
peculiarly American expression of shingled structure, and the ample shapes were given continuity by the surface flow. More exciting, before it lost its high roof, was the Bay View   Pl. 208
Hotel, in Jamestown, built about the same time. Here the sweep of the bulging tower was
girdled by the planes of superimposed piazzas, and the whole achieved a monumental amplitude by no means out of keeping with its flexible wooden structure. What was expressed here
was not mass but volume, as if the interior space were forcing its enclosing wall really to
"balloon."

An excellent, if unusual example of the formal invention of the time is the Flower
Shop on Bellevue Avenue, now considerably altered. This consisted of a gabled upper story
perched upon and deeply overhanging a first story, which was built out in a curving plaster   Pl. 208
cove. Meant as a delicate and amusing shape to catch the eye and advertise its purpose,
this little building, with its shingle patterns and ropework, had something of the quality
of a flower itself, its plaster cove expanding upward and the upper story lightly poised upon
it. If a little quaint, it is certainly expressive and is part of the same structural inventiveness
which produced the monumental amplitude of the Bay View Hotel.

Perhaps even more important than the achievement of this plastic power and invention was the development in the early eighties of a true vernacular of considerable quality.

Pl. 209

In 1882, McKim, Mead, and White built the Skinner (now Conron) house on Red Cross   *a*
Avenue. In this building they achieved the adaptation of their open planning to a small
house type. Behind an entrance sheltered by a deep overhang, a small and pivotal hall lighted
from the stair landing connects with a tiny study or reception room and opens into the free
cross volume of living and dining areas. These are oriented to the south and toward the
garden. Notice should be taken of how the double fireplace with a single hearth acts as a
spatial pivot between study and living areas. The exterior expresses the expansive flow of
the interior space and is also a small essay in the picturesque, almost undoubtedly by Stanford
White, who here flattens out the wall flow of the tower into a thin ribbon of window which
moves around the corner above the entrance porch. In the Skinner house, White went far
toward solving the problem of the small house in terms of open planning, a problem which
in 1885–1886 was to be further explored by Bruce Price in his cottages at Tuxedo Park and
one which was eventually to be most completely solved in the mature planning of Wright.

At any rate, so fully and naturally had the original shingled style permeated all levels
of suburban domestic architecture in the early eighties, that the average house, built by general builders, while it only occasionally solved the planning problem, nevertheless almost
always gave evidence of a pervading architectural sensitivity. A typical example is the Book-
Pl. 201
staver house in Middletown, 1885. This was built by J. D. Johnston, a local builder, from a
set of stock plans. Here, where both living hall with fireplace and living room are used,
the space, while open, tends to become overarticulated. Its organization around a central
fireplace mass in the Bookstaver house, however, is reminiscent, in plan at least, of Wright's
later solutions. Moreover, it is extended by the indigenous piazza and creates a flexible setting
for ample living which is expressed upon the exterior.

More striking as an example of the high quality of vernacular building are the Land
Pl. 211
Trust Cottages in Middletown near Easton's Beach. Easton's Point had been laid out for
development in 1885–1887 under the guidance of Frederick Law Olmsted, the distinguished
landscape architect, employed by a land company of which the trustees were John C. Bon-
croft, Benjamin Kimball, and Charles D. Wainwright. During this period the pavilion
at Easton's Beach, already mentioned, was built. In 1887–1888, E. B. Hall, a speculative
builder from Boston, constructed a group of small cottages on the Middletown side of the
beach. Laid out on a restricted plot of ground, they are arranged freely and with sensitivity
to ensure maximum sun, air, and space for all. Built in a variation of two types, they are all
of considerable distinction, and their plans are open, convenient, and extended by piazzas.
Their space is of that flowing, articulated, and expansive variety with which we have become
familiar, opposing the masses of fireplaces to the movement of open stairways and the penetration of window walls. Note should also be taken of the sensitive stone and shingle work,
the manipulation of voids and solids for movement and variety, and the subtle placing of
the window panel of the nearer cottage. Here is architectural design of greater assurance

than can be found in the average builder's project today. Although these houses are larger than it is possible to build today — an irrefutable economic problem for the modern builder — nevertheless their architectural quality is a question of basic sensitivities, not of economics. The level of the vernacular today represents what can only be considered a marked degeneration from the point it had reached in the developed shingle style.

THE ANTIQUARIAN REACTION. The academic reaction which began in the later eighties and overwhelmed most of American architecture in the nineties must be held largely responsible for the loss of basic sensitivities and creative techniques in domestic building. This reaction was a movement away from indigenous materials and techniques, away from a system of architectural creation three-dimensional in conception and thereby free in space, toward an architecture of the drawing board and the tracing kit. It was a movement also away from that invention whereby the earlier nineteenth century had created a whole new architectural environment. Because of this reaction, an antiquarian dislike of invention was soon to smother the living tradition under the rag-bag of the "traditional." The free tradition had not been on the whole a pretentious architecture. Although it had its large houses, nevertheless its origins were in the organic and the small, and as a result small houses developed easily from it as well. The academic reaction was to impose upon the vernacular a sense of pretension, in attempting to adapt itself to which the vernacular inevitably destroyed itself.

In this academic and antiquarian reaction, McKim, Mead, and White played a major part. It will be remembered that in the critical early days of the Colonial Revival McKim had approached the problem in a way which can only be called antiquarian, as in his colonial room of 1872 in the Robinson house. In 1876 he had furthermore made use of a flat, very linear decorative system of more or less eighteenth-century pilasters, inspired probably by Shaw's Lowther Lodge, for his Moses Taylor house at Elberon. In 1877 he had made that trip through New England with his colleagues, a trip afterwards claimed by the eclectic devotees of the firm as the "discovery" of the colonial. Although working for a time in a freer fashion, probably considerably under the influence of White, he again revealed what might be called his true colors in his Appleton house at Lenox, Massachusetts, of 1883–1884. Here he discarded shingles and used flat clapboarded walls painted red and set with various Palladian details painted white. The usual shingle style effect of volume was lost here, and the walls took on the look of stage flats, thin and rather brittle. The Palladian details were in a variety of scales, but the general effect was a rather positive one of abstract planes which ordered and defined a space. In plan, moreover, the Appleton house was still open and inventive, organized in a tightly knit series of diagonal axes which produced an interior space of both flow and direction. The obviously antiquarian intent and academic method had not affected the plan.

Pl. 212

In the Commodore William Edgar house, built at Newport in 1885–1886, this new mixture of antiquarianism and academicism began to take over free domestic design, or at least to war with it. The Edgar house presents an interior which is beginning to break up into cubes and lose the energy of its flow. The central hall is arbitrary and tight in shape, and the other rooms are more or less symmetrically arranged. In plan as well as in elevation, the asymmetrical elements which are produced, still expressing more or less freely the varying functions of the different areas, become somehow out of place in relation to the general scheme. They are not freely integrated elements in a free organism but awkward elements in a rigid composition. The smooth brick service wing with its one asymmetrically placed oculus is played off well against the void of the second story porch over the living room, but the window and door arrangements of the main block are inorganically conceived, and the scale of the whole, neither Palladian nor free design, is uncertain. In its beautifully laid brick, the wall surface is still alive, and the house has a strong, abstract dignity which was the chief positive quality of the new trend.

Pl. 213

In 1885–1886 at Newport, McKim, Mead, and White built the most important academic monument yet to appear. This was the H. A. C. Taylor house on Annandale Road. Consisting of a main block with the service wing disposed in a lateral ell, the plan is antiquarian in intention and static in effect. Set upon a surrounding terrace, it consists of a central hall with fireplace and straight stairway, off which four cubical rooms are placed. A clear geometry now totally controls the freely flowing spaces of the shingled style. This positive sense of abstract order tends, however, to be equated here with an antiquarian formula for order, an eighteenth-century semi-Palladianism. Planning of this nature, where a rectangle is drawn and the rooms symmetrically arranged within it, is in two dimensions, not in three. This spatial deadness of the interior is clear also upon the exterior elevations, here the proper word, of the H. A. C. Taylor house. Although it makes use of a very plastic roof, an antiquarian adaptation of the old Newport gable-over-hip, its walls are as flat as cardboard, thin planes which, even more than those of the Appleton house, give the impression of having been propped up, pinned into place by the otherwise unrelated porches, and joined loosely at the corners.

From close up to its entrance façade, the basic quality of the H. A. C. Taylor house is most apparent. The projecting side portions are thin planes, slightly behind which the exuberantly textured central portion is a contrasting plane. With these and with its colonialistic columns, the H. A. C. Taylor façade has the dignity of a good backdrop, delicate, elegant, rather abstract in scale. In its light yellow and gleaming white breaking with the rich autumnal colors of the free style, the Taylor house, the first of its long and as yet unended academic line, is still the best of all that line, and this is a significant thing. For what it offered was elegance but sterility. For architectural experiment, for those techniques and sensitivities which offered growth, it proposed, instead, "taste." In the mid-century romantic and rationalist sense of the word, which had been at the heart of the organic American development since Downing and Wheeler and which became the basis of Sullivan and Wright's architectural theory, this house no longer partakes of reality. It rejects the organic and denies the real.

Nevertheless, like the Edgar house or the Villard houses, the H. A. C. Taylor house has dignity, order, and calm. Its geometries are precise; its order is complete. After the shingled style it must have seemed to offer a cool purity, a monumental quietness. This feeling for order and monumentality in the best sense was to be absorbed from the academic reaction by Wright himself and to become a basic force in his mature design, as is analyzed by Henry-Russell Hitchcock in his article, "Frank Lloyd Wright and the 'Academic Tradition,'" *Journal of the Warburg and Courtauld Institutes*, VII (1944), 46–63. The Taylor house and its descendants in the East and eventually elsewhere, however, indicate a setting more for grandeur than for life. Moreover, with its outright academicism and antiquarianism it made possible a whole set of evocations of grandeur from the past, not only of Palladian grandeur, and it provided thereby a perfect tool of expression for a late nineteenth-century industrial aristocracy at once imperial-minded and unsure of itself.

The effect of the H. A. C. Taylor house was immediate. In 1886–1887, Clarence S. Luce of Boston, who had built the Lyman C. Josephs house of 1882–1883, built the Conover house, also in Middletown. By then Luce had seen the H. A. C. Taylor house, and his Conover house, while still shingled in surface and plastic if regularized in mass, has a semi-academic, tight, and spatially undistinguished plan: a narrow central hall with rooms opening, if still widely, on either side. Here is indicated the loss of that sense of total and flowing interior volume which had vitalized the free style.

Houses of the freer, more organic type were still built for a while longer and indeed tended to hang on, in one way or another, for some time, but, except in the West, their vital energy was gone. McKim, Mead, and White's Glover (now Howe) house in Newport, 1887–1888, is an example, although here the scale has become rather heavy. Similar to this is their Gordon King (now Manice) house of the same date. This is also heavy in scale and tends both toward the monumental and the stylistically evocative, using more eclectically not only the Valley of the Loire but also that Romanesque mass which is what the later eighties absorbed from Richardson's masonry city houses of the first part of the decade. Their Low house at Bristol, Rhode Island, also of 1887, but unfortunately outside the scope of this study, is a finer example, and one of the best the firm ever produced. Here, as in Wright's early work, the movement toward order, which had been developing in the shingled style itself, gives coherence and monumental dignity to the whole, without any antiquarian elements to corrupt and obscure the issue. Another late shingled structure was the Auchincloss house near Fort Adams, 1887–1888, which later suffered considerable additions.

In general, however, the new movement was toward Palladian regularity and evoca-

Pl. 213

Pl. 214

Pl. 214

tion, and "Althorpe," the Spencer house of 1889–1890, on Ruggles Avenue, is a revealing example. Here the old freedom seems to bulge hopelessly against the new rigidity which contains it. The Palladian shell, painted in light yellow with white trim, can be felt as squeezing in on the free style, which is still strong enough to expand in curved corner bays and to project in a veranda. The struggle between the real tradition of organic growth and the applied "traditional" strait jacket is made admirably clear. Some of this same quality is also apparent in McKim, Mead, and White's Edwin D. Morgan house of 1890–1891, east of Fort Adams. Here the entrance courtyard, bounded by projecting wings of brick

Pl. 214

making use of a white colonnade, is Georgian and very queer in scale, and, perched on its rocky bluff, the house creates a marvelous landscape of metaphysical incongruity, much like the paintings of Chirico. The plan consists of a decisive crossing of diagonal axes, making use of several richly articulated levels in space and interlocking superbly around the stair landing and the living hall. This plan, its openness and flow of space directed by a strong design order, recalls some of the characteristics of Wright's later planning. On the sea side the Georgian shell is ruptured by the curved living room bay with its brick columns, fortunately not painted white, and which, if somewhat out of scale with the rest of the house, are of great plastic power.

This is McKim, Mead, and White's last great plan. The rest of their story is one of academicism and of the eclectic pastiche. It would be pleasant to assume that, as family tradi-

Pl. 215

tion has it, the Bancroft (now Denham) house in Middletown, of 1893, was designed by Stanford White. It is not listed by Moore, the firm's court historian, as one of their works. While the house as a whole is not distinguished, it nevertheless has a light, articulated, and semi-oriental entrance pavilion which strongly recalls the late nineteenth- and early twentieth-century work of Maybeck and of Greene and Greene in California, and which serves as a link with their continuation and development of the organic tradition.

The true end of academicism and antiquarianism, so far at least as the colonial is concerned, can be seen in Dudley Newton's house of 1897 at Kay and Everett streets. Here

Pl. 215

Dudley Newton, who in 1872 had built a masterpiece of the organic stick style in the Sturtevant house, and who in his Gas Company of 1874 had moved in the main stream of organic American skeletal expression in metal, could do no better than to manufacture a rough copy of the eighteenth-century Longfellow house in Cambridge, Massachusetts. In its first phase in the seventies, the Colonial Revival, to give it a name which no longer accurately applies, had been capable of inspiring new growth. By the nineties it had become a totally antiquarian, academic, and reactionary phenomenon, qualities which it apparently retains to the present day.

In the H. A. C. Taylor house we had seen the Colonial Revival in its academic aspects coupled with an attempt at monumental grandeur, the expression of a new and perhaps more class-conscious point of view. In the late eighties this class consciousness was growing not only among the clients but among the architects as well. We saw the roots of this phenomenon in the early seventies when the *American Architect*, spokesman for the newly powerful American Institute of Architects, had begun a campaign to lift architects as a class above the common builder and to give them a recognized professional standing. The most important aspect of this move was an increasing respect for and dependence on schools of architecture, an educational snobbery whereby the architect could be set apart from the builder as an obviously educated man.

Schools of architecture at this period followed only one pattern, the French Ecole des Beaux-Arts by the late nineteenth century entering into its most corrupt and academic phase. The American schools which existed, M.I.T., Cornell, Columbia, were derivative therefrom and similarly rigid, academic, and classicistic in method, unconcerned with the facts of building, and culturally sterile. The climax of this new development came when, by 1895, McKim, Hunt, Burnham, Ware, and others, with financial assistance from J. P. Morgan, succeeded in establishing the American Academy in Rome. Beaux-Arts in method, archaeological and drowned in the monumental *projet*, this school turned out a generation of eclectics whose contact with the organic American tradition was nonexistent and whose proudest objective was the building of palazzi, civic, commercial, and domestic. When commissions for these were unobtainable, they were quite ready to turn out the colonialistic pastiche which became thereby what might be called a "Beaux-Arts Vernacular."

Of this new imperial eclecticism the first, the best, and the most qualified spokesman was Richard Morris Hunt. The first American to attend the Beaux-Arts, Hunt, as we have seen, had pursued an erratic course after his return to America. Involved early in the stick style, he had soon shown his desire for a heavier, more stylistic expression. In city building Hunt had begun to come into his own with the Vanderbilt house in New York, 1879. This was eclectically François Premier, if not strictly academic in type, and its descendants formed an urban countercurrent in the early eighties to the more organic shingled development of the rural, resort, and suburban areas. While Hunt during this period designed other buildings more Beaux-Arts and classicistic in type, and in their own way competent, his great opportunity in domestic architecture at Newport came in 1888, when he designed Ochre Court for Ogden Goelet. This was in building until 1891. If by 1888 the scales had already been weighted for both archaeology and grandeur, Ochre Court is the first full expression of these characteristics.

Pls. 216, 217

While purporting to be a late Gothic French chateau it is in actuality a tremendous Beaux-Arts *projet*, magnificently unconcerned with reality. Unlike Biltmore, Hunt's other great chateau — of which Hunt wrote to Vanderbilt that, "the mountains are in scale with the house" — Ochre Court is set not in miles of parkland, which its scale would seem to require, but rather upon what amounts to a small surburban lot. It has no relation to its site and offends it, and indeed the intention is to do so and to dominate it. Tremendous in size, it is yet cold and barren. Its featureless limestone reflects that preoccupation with the chastity of the drawing board which is another Beaux-Arts characteristic, for this is a *projet* which might as well have been modeled in plaster. Its plan is academically conventional. There is a great central hall, three stories in height, which mounts from the frigid whiteness of its lower floor to a heretofore unparalleled richness of Mannerist decoration in its upper zones. Hunt's point of view and his method of design are probably obvious here. He had been educated for this kind of building, and now a combination of economic and social forces had delivered into his hands a group of appropriate clients. As in his Marble House, of 1892, he could now create as he wished "projects" without stint, archaeological Gothic or classicistic, unrealistic and tremendous. At his disposal also were the richest and most expensive of materials, among them cold white marble, as here. For Hunt, then, toward the end of his life, his always tenuous contact with the simpler and more indigenous American culture could be completely loosed, and, with an opportunity unparalleled in history, he could withdraw into the dream world of the Beaux-Arts.

Pl. 218

Pls. 218–221

  It is in these terms that The Breakers, built for Cornelius Vanderbilt in 1892–1895, becomes explicable. Beaulieu of 1859, similarly monumental in intention, had been able to make a positive statement, essentially nonstylistic and expressed in the uncompromising solidity of its mass. But The Breakers casts about for Renaissance or Roman evocations and moves toward gigantism and the grandiose. It is idle to speculate as to the difference it would have made if Hunt had followed Vanderbilt's wishes and kept the mass to two stories. It might have made a house of more domestic scale but certainly a much less appropriate monument to its time, and it was Hunt's fated genius to produce such a monument. The Breakers beyond all doubt is the acme of the American palatial mansion of this period, and as such it should continue to be of very great historical interest. Modeled supposedly upon the Renaissance merchants' palaces of Genoa, its scale is in intent imperial. The quality of the design is uneven, since even Hunt could not sustain the imperial scale for long, and the applied orders of the entrance front are rather weak. Nevertheless, the façade toward the sea, set upon its deep terrace, attains something of the plastic richness which must have been Hunt's principal objective. The effect is attained by the contrast of massive end pavilions with a connecting loggia, a more or less Palladian method, and the details themselves are much in the Mannerist idiom. The plan, essentially static and academic, is of little importance except in its size and in the inevitable plastic weight of its structural piers. There is, as in Ochre Court, a great central hall, really more of a roofed cortile than a true hall. This is two stories in height and contains a monumental stairway. Various rooms open off it, and there is a constant sense of distance and of vista.

  Over and above the great size of the rooms, the most striking feature of the interior is the unequaled richness of the decoration. Most of this was designed by Hunt but executed by various firms of commercial interior decorators, whose importance on the Newport scene was rapidly increasing in the nineties. Many of the materials used are magnificent, the general effect rather lush. Blue marbles, luminous and cool, are overwhelmed by golden swags, cartouches, and festoons. The walls and the vaulted ceilings are crowded with decorative motifs thickly overlaid with gilt. The state dining room is most elaborate in this respect, with its variety of materials, shapes, and colors. In the billiard room, opening upon the loggia of the sea side, Hunt achieves a kind of submarine harmony of blue marbles and tawny alabasters, and this is perhaps the most successful room. The Breakers, consequently, culminates its kind. It is perhaps an even more significant monument of this eclectic moment than was Hunt's Administration Building at the World's Fair, Chicago, 1893, from which the impulse spread over the whole country.

Hunt's Belcourt, of 1892, the combined stables and house of Oliver H. P. Belmont, is also an interesting monument, somewhat similar to a Louis XIII hunting lodge and loosely resembling the first buildings at Versailles. Hunt let himself go here in a way which can hardly be called academic, but which was certainly eclectic. It might even be called surrealist, in its extraordinary juxtaposition of motifs. In the articulation of the brick structure of the exterior there are strange evocations of the earlier stick style, while the court, surprisingly enough, is heavily half-timbered. Pls. 222 , 223

The interiors especially, and in particular the great ballroom with its castellated fireplace topped by sculptured figures leaning over the battlements, seem to reflect, through a wild and distorting lens, the whole vigorous and living stream of the mid-century Gothic Revival. The Middle Ages of Viollet-le-Duc, which had once been capable of inspiring nineteenth-century invention, are essentially parodied here. The ballroom is a conglomerate of stained glass windows which serve as balcony doorways and open through what should be their structural members, of glass-filled trefoil windows opposed by trefoil gallery openings, and of flaccid plaster vaults which are too broad for the height of the room containing them. In all this the scale is thrown into incredible confusion. There are elements here of the tragedy of lost opportunities, both for a man and for a time, and Hunt, at the very end of his life, was heard to say that he hoped not to be known only as a "Vanderbilt architect," but wished to be remembered for his earlier wooden houses as well.

TWENTIETH-CENTURY ECLECTICISM. After the monuments by Hunt, the other eclectic houses at Newport are something of an anticlimax. It is more than possible that historians of the future may invent criteria whereby these houses would appear more meaningful, but to us today they are still "white elephants," a phrase coined by Henry James as he strolled along Cliff Walk in the early twentieth century and, remembering the informal shingled cottages of an earlier day, wondered how the palaces had ever come to be built. All of them, though differing in "style," seem of a piece, whether the Stuyvesant Fish house of 1898, by McKim, Mead, and White, with its overscaled colonial portico, or the Edwin Berwind house of 1900, Pl. 224

Pl. 225

by Horace Trumbauer, a copy of the Chateau Allière near Paris, with one of the more elaborate of the typical formal gardens. Most of them are huge in size, dry, and uninteresting, if "correct" in detail. None has any particular feeling for structure nor for architectural space, although they are in area so much more extensive than the earlier houses. The plans are rigid and two-dimensional, and the separate rooms represent the operations of interior decorators rather than architects.

Seen together, these houses constitute an exaggerated example of the super-suburb, which put a premium upon exclusiveness, pretension, and conformity, and which replaced the better integrated residential districts of the previous generation. In the atmosphere of these new suburbias, "adaptation," however absurd, was admissible, whereas any architectural invention, however organic, was suspect. It is Newport's distinction, as a place for the study of American domestic architecture, that the super-suburb created there remains so largely intact. To see the mansions massed together is to understand their effect in the early days of this century and to sense the cultural debilitation which they represented.

Pl. 226

Devised primarily as stage settings for lavish entertainment, the most successful of these houses are those which are most consciously theatrical and exploit their artificiality most frankly. Among these is Vernon Court, of 1901, by A. J. Hastings of Carrère and Hastings. Set in its green gardens, the chief one of which is a copy of a garden created by Henry VIII for Anne Boleyn, Vernon Court is a kind of sophisticated essay in esoteric taste. Its white stuccoed walls, now weathering into an appropriate texture, contrast sharply with the colors of its garden, and the terra-cotta ornament has an appropriately theatrical quality. Similar to

Pl. 227

this is McKim, Mead, and White's Rosecliff of 1901–1902. Here Stanford White's delicate decorative sense created a gleaming pavilion among the trees, a white pleasure house modeled after the Trianon. It is a decorative confection, appropriately inspired and without the architectural integrity of White's earlier houses.

The least successful of these houses are the latest in date, when the original impetus of the reaction against originality had departed and only a negative heritage of tasteful "correctness" remained. Such a house is Miramar, built in 1914. Here the scale is queer and confused.

Pl. 228

Set in a flat and extensive formal garden of the utmost rigidity, the house itself, only two stories in height, is a disoriented element aiming at a monumentality which it fails to attain. More typical of the early twentieth-century work in Newport, as elsewhere, are the more or less Palladian and somewhat more domestically scaled "colonial" houses, such as the Karolik

Pl. 228

house, built by Ogden Codman in 1910.

One of the sole echoes, however, of a continuing tradition of free architectural design in Newport is the Borden (now Davis) house, on Ocean Drive, completed by the firm of Angell and Swift in 1917. This house grows directly out of those basic energies which had been

Pls. 229, 230

behind the most productive aspects of the development which we have discussed — the sense of living space, the feeling for creative structural technique, the willingness to follow the analysis of the problem to a nonstylistic, inventive conclusion. The interior space is organized along a single axis and is further extended by verandas. The ceilings are low and the fireplace of the living hall is used as a massive element around which the space flows. Moreover, the natural materials, the spatial continuities, and the decisively organized horizontal planes of the overhangs indicate the close relationship of this house to work done at the same time and in the previous decade by Frank Lloyd Wright and other members of the Second Chicago School.

Although Newport is not rich in examples of inventive twentieth-century architecture, it should be Newport's pride that it is still, as in the nineteenth century, a unique town and a kind of microcosm of America. The problems which beset other American towns are exaggerated and brought into especially sharp focus here. The old eighteenth-century town presents the problem of intelligent restoration and preservation, while the question of the relationship between super-suburb and parent town is now particularly emphatic. The solution to these problems, as to the more common problems of mid-twentieth-century town planning, lies with the town of Newport itself and with those members of the summer colony who are able to span the two interests. For cultural integration and the direction of energies into creative channels, Newport, rich in the historical monuments of three centuries, must bend every effort to serve the purpose of cultural memory. And, in the intelligent appraisal of her architectural monuments, she must not lose sight of those cultural essentials of new invention and dynamic growth which are embodied in much of her nineteenth-century architecture.

---

a For "Conron" read "Dr. Carey."
b For "Allière" read "Château d'Agnès, by   Mansard, an early eighteenth-century château at Asnières near Paris."

PLATES

PLATES

PLATE 67

(upper)
Colony House. Original first floor plan. Measured by Isham. (N.H.S.)
(lower)
Colony House. Interior, the great hall. Photo, Meservey.

PLATE 68

(upper)
Colony House. The great hall, east wall. Measured by P. G. Gulbranson, *American Architect and Building News,* March 4, 1896.
(lower)
Colony House. Original second floor plan. Measured by Isham. (N.H.S.)

PLATE 69

(upper)
Senate chamber, south wall. Measured by P. G. Gulbranson, *American Architect and Building News,* March 4, 1896.
(middle)
Colony House. Senate chamber. Photo, Meservey.
(lower)
Senate chamber, west wall. Measured by P. G. Gulbranson, *American Architect and Building News,* March 4, 1896.

PLATE 70

(upper)
Colony House. Senate chamber, east wall. Measured by Isham. (N.H.S.)
(lower)
Colony House. Senate chamber, north wall. Possible original form. Measured by Isham. (N.H.S.)

PLATE 71

(upper)
Ninyon Challoner House, 1735. Ground plan by Benjamin Wyatt. From George Champlin Mason, *Reminiscences of Newport,* enlarged edition, in N.H.S.
(lower)
Daniel Ayrault House, 1739. Ground plan by Richard Munday and Benjamin Wyatt. Mason, *Reminiscences of Newport,* enlarged edition, in N.H.S.

PLATE 72

(upper)
James Gordon Farm. Half of the plan. Drawn on the back of Ann Franklin's Calendar of 1733.
(lower left)
Abraham Redwood House. Plan. Drawn by Bergner.
(lower right)
Abraham Redwood House, Thames Street, 1727. Drawing. Collection of Miss Pauline Weaver.

PLATE 73

(upper)
Wrought-iron gates from Abraham Redwood's estate. Now installed on the Redwood Library grounds. Photo, Meservey.
(lower)
House plans taken from Jahleel Brenton's study book dated 1712. Plan at left shows semicircular front steps. (R.I.H.S.)

PLATE 74

(upper)
Godfrey Malbone's town house. 1727. From Newell's lithograph.
(lower left)
Godfrey Malbone's town house. Marble mantel. Photo, Kerschner.
(lower right)
Godfrey Malbone's town house. Capital from door. Photo, Kerschner.

PLATE 75   *(upper)*
Jahleel Brenton House, Thames Street. About 1720. Old drawing. (N.H.S.)
(lower)
Jahleel Brenton House. Photograph by J. A. Williams, about 1870. (N.H.S.)

PLATE 76   *(upper)*
Jahleel Brenton House. Floor plan. Drawn by Bergner.
(lower)
Jahleel Brenton House. Stairs. Old photograph. (R.I.S.D.)

PLATE 77   *(upper)*
Jahleel Brenton House. Stairs. Measured drawings, *American Architect and Building News*, June 20, 1896.
(lower)
Jahleel Brenton House. Parlor paneling. Old photograph. (R.I.S.D.)

PLATE 78   *(upper)*
Jahleel Brenton House. Parlor. Paneling of the fireplace wall. Measured drawing, *American Architect and Building News*, June 20, 1896.
(lower)
Jahleel Brenton House. Paneling of the west wall.

PLATE 79   *(upper)*
Jahleel Brenton House. Details. Drawn by Bergner.
(lower)
Jahleel Brenton House. Molding sections. (H.A.B.S.)

PLATE 80   *(upper)*
John Gidley House, 1724. Formerly Thames and Gidley. North parlor, paneling. Photo, Bergner.
(lower left)
Paneling from the John Gidley House as installed in the Mason House, 31 Old Beech Road. Photo, Covell.
(lower right)
Thomas Robinson House. Dining room cupboard. About 1730. Photo, Covell.

PLATE 81   *(upper)*
William Redwood's country house, Mile Corner. Photo, Kerschner.
(lower left)
Benedict Arnold, Jr., House, Hammett's Wharf. Doorway. Photo, Bergner. (N.H.S.)
(lower right)
Metcalf Bowler country house, Portsmouth. Doorway. About 1760. Photo, Bergner.

PLATE 82   *(upper)*
Daniel Ayrault House, Thames Street at Ann. 1739. Richard Munday and Benjamin Wyatt. Photo, Bergner.
(lower)
Daniel Ayrault House. Doorway. Photo, Bergner.

PLATE 83   *(upper)*
Daniel Ayrault House. Doorway.
(lower)
Doorway, bracket. Measured by R. Kinnicutt.

PLATE 84   *(upper)*
Nathaniel Langley (Dr. King's) House, 32 Pelham Street. Doorway and mantel. Measured by J. B. Blair, *American Architect and Building News*, December 8, 1894.

(lower)
Henry Taggart (Fowler) House, 32 Second Street. Before 1763. Photo, Meservey.

PLATE 85   *(upper)*
Whitehall, Dean Berkely's house in Middletown, 1729. Photo, Meservey.
(lower)
Whitehall. Floor plan and elevation. Drawn by Isham. (C.D.)

PLATE 86   *(upper)*
Whitehall. Green parlor. Photo, Meservey.
(lower)
Red parlor. Photo, Meservey.

PLATE 87   *(upper)*
Abraham Rodrigues Riviera House, Washington Square. Photo, Meservey.
(lower)
Roof detail showing dormer windows. Photo, Meservey.

PLATE 88   *(upper)*
Deputy Governor Jonathan Nichols (Wanton or Hunter) House, 54 Washington Street. About 1748. Waterside view. From a stereoscopic view, 1870. (N.H.S.)
(lower)
Jonathan Nichols House. Washington Street side with doorway as restored at present. Photo, Kerschner.

PLATE 89   *(upper)*
Pediment from the waterside doorway of the Jonathan Nichols House, as installed on the Dennis House, 65 Poplar Street, from 1923 to 1950. Photo, Arnold.
(lower)
Jonathan Nichols House, pediment. Measured drawing. (H.A.B.S.)

PLATE 90   *(upper)*
Jonathan Nichols House. Detail showing construction of walls. Photo, Kerschner.
(lower)
Floor plan. Measured drawing. (H.A.B.S.)

PLATE 91   *(upper)*
Jonathan Nichols House. Arch in hallway. Measured drawing. (H.A.B.S.)
(lower)
Detail of stairs. Photo, Meservey.

PLATE 92   *(upper)*
David Cheeseborough House, Mary Street at Clarke, 1737. Arch and stairs. Photo, Bergner.
(lower)
Jonathan Nichols House. Stairs. Measured drawing. (H.A.B.S.)

PLATE 93   *(upper)*
Jonathan Nichols House. North parlor in 1950. Photo, Meservey.
(lower)
North chamber. Measured drawing. (H.A.B.S.)

PLATE 94   *(upper)*
Jonathan Nichols House. North Parlor, cupboard. Photo, Meservey.
(lower)
David Cheeseborough House. Detail, mantel wall. Photo, Bergner.

PLATE 95   *(upper)*
Christopher Townsend House and shop, 74 Bridge Street. Built between 1725 and 1750. Photo, Meservey.

(lower left)
Christopher Townsend House. Doorway and shop. Photo, Meservey.
(lower right)
Christopher Townsend House and shop. Plan. Drawn by Warren Oakley.

PLATE 96   *(upper)*
Christopher Townsend House. Mantel paneling. Photo, Meservey.
(lower left)
Job Townsend House, 63 Bridge Street. About 1729. Stairway. Demolished after 1952. Photo,
Meservey.
(lower right)
Christopher Townsend House. Molding sections. Bergner.

PLATE 97   *(upper)*
John Banister House, 56 Pelham Street. 1751. Photo, Meservey.
(lower left)
Stairs. Photo, Meservey.
(lower right)
West parlor. Measured by P. G. Gulbranson, *American Architect and Building News*, Vol.
LIV, No. 1089, adv.

PLATE 98   *(upper)*
Thomas Robinson House, 64 Washington Street. At right, St. John's Rectory (Dennis House),
65 Poplar Street. Photo, Arnold.
(lower left)
Thomas Robinson House. Dining room. Photo, Meservey.
(lower right)
Desk bookcase in the north parlor, by John Goddard. Photo, Meservey.

PLATE 99   *(upper)*
Dr. Hopkins House, 46 Division Street. Built between 1758 and 1772. Photo, Meservey.
(lower)
Crandall House, 59 Poplar Street. Before 1758. Photo, Meservey.

PLATE 100   *(upper)*
Erastus Pease House, 36 Church Street. Rear view. About 1785. Photo, Meservey.
(lower)
Mantel wall in kitchen. Photo, Meservey.

PLATE 101   *(upper)*
Wanton-Lyman-Hazard House. Paneling, south parlor. Photo, Meservey.
(lower)
South parlor, mantel wall. Measured by R. Kinnicutt.

PLATE 102   *(upper)*
Wanton-Lyman-Hazard House. South chamber, mantel wall. Measured by R. Kinnicutt.
(lower)
St. John's Rectory (Dennis House), 65 Poplar Street. Dining-room paneling. Photo, Meservey.

PLATE 103   *(upper)*
Metcalf Bowler country house, Portsmouth. About 1760. Paneling of parlor, as installed in
M.M.A., New York City.
(lower)
Metcalf Bowler country house. Parlor paneling. Measured drawing.

PLATE 104   *(upper)*
Redwood Library, Bellevue Avenue. Peter Harrison. 1748. Photo, Meservey.
(lower)
Redwood Library. Drawing by Eugène Pierre du Simitière. Du Simitière Collection, The

Library Company of Philadelphia.

PLATE 105
(upper left)
Casino for Sir Charles Hotham. William Rotch Ware. *Designs of Inigo Jones and others.*
(upper right)
Redwood Library. Detail, doorway. Photo, Kerschner.
(lower left)
Summer house from Abraham Redwood's estate in Portsmouth. 1766, Peter Harrison? Now on the Redwood Library grounds. Photo, Kerschner.

PLATE 105a
(lower right)
Beavertail Lighthouse, from Peter Harrison's *Map of Newport,* 1755.

PLATE 106
(upper)
The Brick Market in 1880, Washington Square at Thames Street. Peter Harrison, 1761. Stanhope photograph. (C.C.)
(lower)
The Brick Market. Elevation and section. Measured by R. Kinnicutt.

PLATE 107
(upper)
The Brick Market. Front elevation. Measured by R. Kinnicutt.
(lower)
Old Somerset House, London. Inigo Jones. From Colin Campbell, *The Vitruvius Britannicus,* 1727.

PLATE 108
(upper)
Touro Synagogue, Touro Street. Detail of portico. Peter Harrison, 1763. Photo, Meservey.
(lower)
Touro Synagogue. Interior. Photo, Meservey.

PLATE 109
(upper left)
Touro Synagogue. Interior, detail showing the present Ark of the Covenant. Photo, Bergner.
(upper right)
Ezra Stiles' sketch of the Ark on the margin of his diary for December 2, 1763. Yale University Library.
(lower)
Batty Langley, *Treasury of Designs,* 1750. Model for the lower part of the Ark of the Covenant as now executed.

PLATE 110
(upper left)
James Gibbs, *Rules for Drawing,* 1732. Pl. XXXV. Model for the system of superimposed orders for the Synagogue. This and the next two models from copy in the Providence Public Library.
(upper right)
Rules for Drawing. Pl. XVII. Model for the gallery balusters.
(lower)
Rules for Drawing. Pl. XLVII. Model for consoles of the door.

PLATE 111
(upper)
Customs Collector Charles Dudley House, Middletown. Peter Harrison. About 1750. Old photograph. (N.H.S.)
(lower)
Francis Malbone House, 392 Thames Street. Peter Harrison? About 1760. Photo, Bergner.

PLATE 112
John Banister country house. Formerly at Mile Corner. About 1756. Photo, Meservey.

PLATE 113
(upper)
William Vernon House, corner Clarke and Mary streets. Peter Harrison? Photo, Meservey.

American Architect and Building News, Vol. XV, #1098.)
(upper right)
Clarke House, Washington Street. Mantel. Demolished. Measured by Bergner.
(lower)
Newport mantels. Measured by P. G. Gulbranson. *American Architect and Building News*, #117, Adv.)

PLATE 136 *(upper)*
House built by Thomas Goddard between 1798 and 1802, 78 Church Street. Detail of west wall. Photo, Meservey.
(lower)
Swinburne House, 80 John Street. Built by Isaac Peckham. About 1807. Photo, Meservey.

PLATE 137 *(upper)*
Underwood House, 66 John Street. Built by John Tompkins. About 1811. Photo, Meservey.
(lower)
William Card House, 73 Division Street. 1811. Photo, Meservey.

PLATE 138 House built by John Kerber after 1790, 199 Spring Street. Doorway. Photo, Meservey.

PLATE 139 Joseph and Robert Rogers House, 33 Touro Street. About 1790. Doorway. Photo, Meservey.

PLATE 140 *(upper)*
Joseph Wood House, 27 Church Street. About 1810. Doorway. Photo, Meservey.
(lower)
Doorway, measured by P. G. Gulbranson. (From William Rotch Ware, *The Georgian Period*. Part IX, Pl. 31.)

PLATE 141 *(upper)*
Joseph Wood House. Detail of door. From Downing, *Early Homes of Rhode Island*. Photo, LeBoeuf. (R.I.S.D.)
(lower)
William Pain, *The Practical House Carpenter*, 1785. The Composite Order. Model for door at 27 Church Street.

PLATE 142 *(upper)*
Captain John Mawdsley House, 228 Spring Street. Doorway, about 1795. Photo, Meservey.
(lower)
Doorway. Measured by P. G. Gulbranson. (From William Rotch Ware, *The Georgian Period*, Part IX, Pl. 29.)

PLATE 143 *(upper)*
Robert Stevens House, 31 Clarke Street. Door, probably installed about 1800. Photo, Arnold.
(lower)
Samuel Hudson House, 23 Mary Street. About 1800. Doorway. Measured by P. G. Gulbranson. (From William Rotch Ware, *The Georgian Period*, Part IX, Pl. 28.)

PLATE 144 *(upper)*
Billy Smith House, About 1826. Door. 7 Oak Street. Photo, Meservey.
(lower)
118 William Street. Door. Measured by P. G. Gulbranson. (From William Rotch Ware, *The Georgian Period*, Part IX, Pl. 30. Demolished.)

PLATE 145 *(upper)*
Rhode Island Union Bank Building, Thames Street. Asher Benjamin, 1817. Old photograph. (N.H.S.)
(lower)
Rhode Island Union Bank Building. Central pavilion. Photo, Meservey.

(lower right)
Round House. Interior. Photo, Meservey.

PLATE 159   *(upper)*
Benjamin Marsh House, School and Mary streets. 1845. Stanhope photograph. (C.C.)
(lower left)
Andrew Jackson Downing, *Cottage Residences*, Fig. 40. A cottage in the bracketed style, 1844.
(lower right)
Galvin House, 417 Spring Street. 1850–1860. Moved from Fort Adams. Photo, Meservey.

PLATE 160   *(upper)*
Kingscote, Bellevue Avenue at Bowery Street. Richard Upjohn. 1841. Photo, Meservey.
(middle)
Kingscote. Drawing by John P. Newell. Courtesy of Mrs. E. Maitland Armstrong.
(lower right)
Kingscote. Plan of the first floor. Drawn by Warren Oakley.

PLATE 161   *(upper)*
Kingscote. Hall, looking toward front door. Photo, Meservey.
(lower)
Kingscote. Living rooms. Photo, Meservey.

PLATE 162   *(upper)*
Malbone, Malbone Road. Alexander Jackson Davis, architect. 1848–1849. Photo, Wayne Andrews.
(middle right)
Malbone. From the *Knickerbocker Magazine*, 1859.
(lower left)
Malbone. Plan from the office book of A. J. Davis in M.M.A., New York City.

PLATE 163   *(upper)*
Edward King House, Spring Street. Now People's Library. Richard Upjohn. 1845–1847. Photo, Meservey.
(lower)
Edward King House. Plan. From Andrew Jackson Downing, *The Architecture of Country Houses*, 1850.

PLATE 164   *(upper)*
Swanhurst, Bellevue Avenue. East side. Built by Alexander McGregor in 1851. Photo, Meservey.
(middle)
Swanhurst. Plan. Drawn by Warren Oakley.
(lower)
Swanhurst. West side. Photo, Meservey.

PLATE 165   *(upper)*
Chateau-sur-Mer, Bellevue Avenue. Seth Bradford, 1851–1852. Before alterations made in 1872. Photo, Frank Childs.
(lower)
Chateau-sur-Mer. Lithograph by John Collins. From *The City and Scenery of Newport, Rhode Island*, 1857.

PLATE 166   Charles H. Russell House. 185–1852. Demolished. From George Champlin Mason, *Newport and Its Cottages*.

PLATE 167   *(upper)*
Daniel Parrish House, Bellevue Avenue, 1851–1852. Calvert Vaux. Burned in 1855. Rebuilt in 1856 from original plans. Photo, Meservey.
(lower)
Daniel Parrish House. Plan and sea side. From Calvert Vaux, *Villas and Cottages*, 1855.

PLATE 168   *(upper)*
Beaulieu, Bellevue Avenue. Built by the Peruvian Ambassador, de Berreda. Entrance. 1856–1859. Photo, Meservey.
(middle)
Beaulieu. Sea side. Photo, Meservey.
(lower)
Beaulieu. Plan. Drawn by Warren Oakley.

PLATE 169   *(upper)*
All Saints Chapel, Church Street, 1852. Demolished. Stanhope photograph. (C.C.)
(lower)
The Chalet, Halidon Avenue. Leopold Eidlitz. 1854. Photo, Meservey.

PLATE 170   *(upper)*
The Chalet. Elevation. From Bullock, *American Cottage Builder*, 1854.
(middle)
The Chalet. Plan. From Bullock, *American Cottage Builder*.
(lower)
Chalet at Bailey's Beach. About 1855–1860. Stanhope photograph. (C.C.)

PLATE 171   *(upper)*
Hamilton Hoppin House, Miantonomi Avenue. Richard Upjohn. 1856–1857. Demolished after 1952. Photo, Meservey.
(lower)
Looking across hall into library. Photo, Meservey.

PLATE 172   *(upper left)*
Alexander Van Rensselaer House, Miantonomi Avenue. 1857–1858. Demolished after 1952. Stanhope photograph. (C.C.)
(upper right)
Charles Fearing House, 1853. Demolished. From George Champlin Mason, *Newport and Its Cottages*.
(middle left)
Fairbourne, Bellevue Avenue. 1853–1854. Demolished. From *Newport and Its Cottages*.
(middle right)
Edgewater, J. Frederick Kernochan House. 1864. Demolished. From Mason, *Newport and Its Cottages*.
(lower left)
Winan's first Bleak House, Ocean Drive. About 1865. Razed in 1894. Stanhope photograph. (C.C.)
(lower right)
Ogden Mills House, Bellevue Avenue. William R. Walker, architect, 1866. Photo, Meservey.

PLATE 173   *(upper)*
Sea View Cottages on the Cliffs. 1870. Stanhope photograph. (C.C.)
(lower)
Navy Houses, Goat Island, 1871. Photo, Meservey.

PLATE 174   *(upper)*
Showandasee, Train Villa, Bellevue Avenue. 1869. Stanhope photograph. (C.C.)
(lower)
J. N. A. Griswold House, Bellevue Avenue. Richard Morris Hunt. 1862–1863. Photo, Meservey.

PLATE 175   *(upper)*
J. N. A. Griswold House. Interior. Photo, Meservey.

(lower)
Plan. Drawing by Warren Oakley.

PLATE 176   *(upper)*
M. H. Sanford House, 72 Washington Street. Now W. King Covell. 1870. Stanhope photograph. (C.C.)
(lower)
M. H. Sanford House. Hall. Photo, Covell.

PLATE 177   *(upper left)*
Thayer Cottage, Bellevue Avenue at Wheatland Avenue. About 1870. Photo, Meservey.
(upper right)
Thomas Cushing House, Bellevue Avenue. 1870. From George Champlin Mason, *Newport and Its Cottages.*
(middle left)
Nathan Matthews House. 1871–1872. Burned 1881. From *The Architectural Sketchbook,* 1873.
(middle right)
Mrs. Loring Andrews House, 1872. Demolished. From Mason, *Newport and Its Cottages.*
(lower)
Thomas Cushing and Ogden Mills houses. Stanhope photograph. (C.C.)

PLATE 178   *(upper)*
George Champlin Mason's House, 31 Old Beach Road. George Champlin Mason. 1873–1874. Photo, Meservey.
(upper left)
George Champlin Mason's House. Plan. Drawn by Warren Oakley.
(lower right)
George Champlin Mason's House. Detail of façade. Photo, Meservey.

PLATE 179   *(upper)*
Jacob Cram House, Middletown. Dudley Newton. 1871–1872. Photo, Meservey.
(lower left)
Jacob Cram House. Plan. Drawn by Warren Oakley.
(lower right)
Jacob Cram House. Detail of piazza. Photo, Meservey.

PLATE 180   *(upper)*
Gas Company façade, Thomas Street. Dudley Newton, 1874. Now altered. Photo, Arnold.
(lower)
Colonel George Waring House, Catherine and Greenough streets. Richard Morris Hunt's own house. 1870–1871. Photo, Wayne Andrews.

PLATE 181   *(upper right)*
Samuel Pratt House, Bellevue Avenue. 1871. From a stereoscopic view taken about 1875. (N.H.S.)
(upper left)
Samuel Pratt House. Plan. Drawn by Warren Oakley.
(lower)
Travers Block, Bellevue Avenue at Bath Road. Richard Morris Hunt. About 1875. Stanhope photograph. (C.C.)

PLATE 182   *(upper)*
Linden Gate, Henry F. Marquand House, Rhode Island Avenue. Richard Morris Hunt. 1872. Photo, Wayne Andrews.
(middle)
T. G. Appleton House. Richard Morris Hunt. 1875–1876. Demolished. From George Champlin Mason, *Newport and Its Cottages.*

(lower)
Professor Shields' House. Richard Morris Hunt. 1883. From an old photograph. (S.P.N.E.A.)

PLATE 183   Chateau-sur-Mer. William S. Wetmore House, Bellevue Avenue. Enlarged by Richard Morris Hunt, 1872. Photo, Meservey.

PLATE 184   *(upper)*
Chateau-sur-Mer. Library. Photo, Meservey.
(lower)
Chateau-sur-Mer. Hall. Photo, Meservey.

PLATE 185   *(upper)*
George Fearing House, Narragansett Avenue. 1871–1872. From George Champlin Mason, *Newport and Its Cottages.*
(lower)
Red Cross, C. J. Peterson House. About 1872. Demolished. From Mason, *Newport and Its Cottages.*

PLATE 186   *(upper)*
Richard Codman Project. By Henry H. Richardson, 1869. Elevation. (Houghton Library, Harvard.) Plans. From Henry Russell Hitchcock, *H. H. Richardson and His Times.*
(lower)
F. W. Andrews House. H. H. Richardson, 1872. Architect's drawing. From Hitchcock, *H. H. Richardson and His Times.*

PLATE 187   *(upper)*
Watts Sherman House, Shepard Avenue. H. H. Richardson and Stanford White. 1874. Before Dudley Newton's addition. Photo by Frank Childs.
(lower)
Watts Sherman House. Drawing by Stanford White in *The New York Sketch Book of Architecture,* 1875.

PLATE 188   *(upper)*
Watts Sherman House. Photo, Meservey.
(lower)
Watts Sherman House. Photo, Meservey.

PLATE 189   *(upper)*
Watts Sherman House. Plans.
(lower)
Watts Sherman House. White's drawing of entrance and hall. From *The New York Sketch Book of Architecture,* 1875.

PLATE 190   *(upper)*
Watts Sherman House. Stairs. Photo, Covell.
(middle)
Hall, looking east toward LaFarge windows. Photo, Covell.
(lower)
Hall. Photo, Covell.

PLATE 191   Watts Sherman House. Library. Photo, Meservey.

PLATE 192   *(upper)*
Thomas Robinson House, 64 Washington Street. Fireplace wall by Charles Follen McKim. 1872. Photo, Meservey.
(lower)
Dennis House, 65 Poplar Street. Now St. John's Rectory. Living hall by Charles Follen McKim. 1876. Photo, Meservey.

PLATE 193   *(upper)*
Bishop (then Dean) Berkeley House. From *The New York Sketch Book of Architecture,* 1874.

(middle)
Frederick Sheldon House. About 1875. Demolished. From George Champlin Mason, *Newport and Its Cottages.*
(lower)
McKim's projected drawing and plan for the Thomas Dunn House (never built). From *American Architect and Building News*, July, 1877.

PLATE 194   *(upper)*
C. H. Baldwin (Prescott Lawrence) House, Bellevue Avenue. Potter and Robinson. 1877–1878. Photo, Meservey.
(middle left)
C. H. Baldwin House. Interior, looking across hall. Photo, Meservey.
(upper right)
Looking into turret. Photo, Meservey.
(lower)
C. H. Baldwin House. Plan. Drawn by Warren Oakley.

PLATE 195   Chateau-Nooga, C. C. Baldwin House, Belleville Avenue. George Post. 1880–1881. Photo, Meservey.

PLATE 196   *(upper)*
The Breakers, Pierre Lorillard, Ochre Point. Peabody and Stearns. 1877–1878. From an old photograph. (R.L.)
(middle)
The Breakers. Playhouse. Photo, Covell.
(lower)
The Breakers. Plan. From George C. Sheldon, *Artistic Country Seats.*

PLATE 197   *(upper)*
Barn of the Fairchild Estate, Second Street at Cherry. Charles Follen McKim. About 1878. Photo, Covell.
(lower)
Casino façade on Bellevue Avenue. McKim,, Mead and White. 1880–1881. Stanhope photograph. (N.H.S.)

PLATE 198   *(upper)*
Casino courtyard showing clock tower. Stanhope photograph. (C.C.)
(middle left)
Plan. From *A Monograph of the Work of McKim, Mead and White.*
(middle right)
Piazza. From a stereoscopic view. (N.H.S.)
(lower)
Piazza. From a stereoscopic view. (N.H.S.)

PLATE 199   *(upper)*
Casino. Billiard room. Stanhope photograph. (C.C.)
(middle)
Theatre interior. Stanhope photograph. (C.C.)
(lower left)
Detail, theatre piazza rail. Stanhope photograph. (C.C.)
(lower right)
Detail, theatre piazza rail. Photo, Meservey.

PLATE 200   *(upper)*
Kingscote. Stanford White. 1880–1881. Dining room. Photo, Meservey.
(lower)
Dining room. Photo, Meservey.

PLATE 201   *(upper)*
Samuel Tilton (now Louis Hobbs) House. McKim, Mead and White. 1881–1882. Photo,

Meservey.
(lower)
Plan. Drawn by Warren Oakley.

PLATE 202   *(upper)*
Tilton House. Hall. Photo, Meservey.
(middle)
Living room. Photo, Meservey.
(lower)
Dining room. Photo, Meservey.

PLATE 203   *(upper)*
Southside, Robert Goelet House, Narragansett Avenue. From the sea side. McKim, Mead and White. 1882–1883. Stanhope photograph. (N.H.S.)
(lower)
Southside. Photo, Wayne Andrews.

PLATE 204   *(upper)*
Southside. Plan. From George C. Sheldon *Artistic Country Seats.*
(lower)
Hall fireplace. Photo, Meservey.

PLATE 205   *(upper)*
Edna Villa, Isaac Bell House, Bellevue Avenue. McKim, Mead and White. 1882–1883. Photo, Meservey.
(middle left)
Isaac Bell House. Plan. From George C. Sheldon, *Artistic Country Seats.*
(middle right)
Isaac Bell House. Looking across hall to fireplace and stairs. Photo, Meservey.
(lower)
Isaac Bell House. Interior. From *The Century Magazine,* May, 1886.

PLATE 206   *(upper)*
Samuel Coleman House, 7 Red Cross Avenue. McKim, Mead and White. 1882–1883. Stanhope photograph. (C.C.)
(middle)
Samuel Coleman House. Plan. From George C. Sheldon, *Artistic Country Seats.*
(lower)
Samuel Coleman House. From *The Century Magazine,* June, 1886.

PLATE 207   *(upper)*
Lyman C. Josephs House, Middletown. Clarence Luce. 1882–1883. Photo, Meservey.
(middle)
Lyman C. Josephs House. Plan. From George C. Sheldon, *Artistic Country Seats.*
(lower)
Indian Spring. Busk House, Ocean Drive. Richard Morris Hunt, 1891. Stanhope photograph. (C.C.)

PLATE 208   *(upper)*
Pavilion at Easton's Beach. Stanhope photograph. (C.C.)
(middle)
Bayview Hotel, Jamestown. About 1885. Stanhope photograph. (C.C.)
(lower)
Flower shop, Bellevue Avenue. About 1883. Old photograph. (S.P.N.E.A.)

PLATE 209   *(upper)*
Skinner House, Red Cross Avenue. McKim, Mead and White. 1882. Old photograph. (S.P.N.E.A.)

(lower)
Plan. Drawn by Warren Oakley.

PLATE 210   *(upper)*
Judge Bookstaver House, Purgatory Road, Middletown. J. D. Johnston. 1885. Photo, Meservey.
(lower)
Plan. Drawn by Warren Oakley.

PLATE 211   *(upper)*
Land Trust cottages, Easton's Beach, Middletown. 1887–1888. Stanhope photograph. (C.C.)
(middle)
Land Trust cottages. Plan of the Rough House.
(lower)
Land Trust cottages. Plan of the May House. Drawn by Warren Oakley.

PLATE 212   *(upper)*
Commodore William Edgar House, Sunnyside Place. McKim, Mead and White. 1885–1886.
From the original drawing for *The Century Magazine*, July, 1886.
(lower)
Commodore William Edgar House. Plan. From George C. Sheldon, *Artistic Country Seats.*

PLATE 213   *(upper)*
H. A. C. Taylor House, Annandale Road. McKim, Mead and White. 1885–1886. Photo,
Meservey.
(middle)
H. A. C. Taylor House. Plan. From George C. Sheldon, *Artistic Country Seats.*
(lower left)
Conover House, Indian Avenue, Middletown. Clarence Luce. 1888. Photo, Meservey.
(lower right)
Conover House. Plan. Drawn by Warren Oakley.

PLATE 214   *(upper left)*
Gordon King House, Harrison Avenue. McKim, Mead and White. 1887–1888. Photo, Meservey.
(upper right)
Althorpe, Spencer House, Ruggles Avenue. 1889–1890. Stanhope photograph. (C.C.)
(middle)
Beacon Rock, Edwin D. Morgan House, Beacon Hill Road. McKim, Mead and White. 1890–
1891. Stanhope photograph. (C.C.)
(lower left)
Beacon Rock. Closer view. Stanhope photograph. (C.C.)
(lower right)
Beacon Rock. Plan. From *A Monograph of the Work of McKim, Mead and White.*

PLATE 215   *(upper)*
Bancroft House, Tuckerman Avenue, Middletown. 1893. Detail of entrance. Photo, Meservey.
(lower)
Dudley Newton House, Kay and Everett streets. Dudley Newton, 1897. Photo, Meservey.

PLATE 216   *(upper)*
Ochre Court, Ochre Point Avenue. Richard Morris Hunt. 1888–1891. Photo, Wayne Andrews.
(lower)
Ochre Court. Hall. Detail. Photo, Meservey.

PLATE 217   Ochre Court. Hall. Photo, Meservey.

PLATE 218   *(upper)*
Marble House, Bellevue Avenue. Richard Morris Hunt. 1892. Photo, Meservey.
(lower)
The Breakers, Cornelius Vanderbilt House, Ochre Point Avenue. Sea side. Richard Morris Hunt.

1892–1895. Photo, Meservey.

PLATE 219   The Breakers. Detail. Seaside loggia. Photo, Meservey.

PLATE 220   *(upper)*
The Breakers. Hall. Photo, Meservey.
(lower)
The Breakers. Grand staircase. Photo, Meservey.

PLATE 221   *(upper)*
The Breakers. State dining room. Photo, Meservey.
(lower)
The Breakers. Billiard room. Photo, Meservey.

PLATE 222   *(upper)*
The Breakers. Plan. Drawn by Warren Oakley.
(lower)
Belcourt O. H. P. Belmont House, Bellevue Avenue. Richard Morris Hunt. 1892. Photo, Meservey.

PLATE 223   Belcourt. Ballroom. Photo, Meservey.

PLATE 224   Crossways, Stuyvesant Fish House, Ocean Avenue. McKim, Mead and White. 1898. Photo, Meservey.

PLATE 225   *(upper)*
The Elms, Edwin Berwind House, Bellevue Avenue. Garden side. Horace Trumbauer, 1901. Photo, Meservey.
(lower)
Formal garden. Photo, Meservey.

PLATE 226   *(upper)*
Vernon Court, Richard Gambrill House, Bellevue Avenue. A. J. Hastings of Carrère and Hastings. 1901. Photo, Meservey.
(lower)
Garden. Copied from Henry VIII's garden for Anne Boleyn, Hampton Court. Photo, Meservey.

PLATE 227   *(upper)*
Rosecliff, J. Edgar Monroe House, Bellevue Avenue. McKim, Mead and White. 1901–1902. Photo, Meservey.
(lower)
Rosecliff. Architect's drawing of the staircase. (New-York Historical Society)

PLATE 228   *(upper)*
Miramar, A. Hamilton Rice House, Bellevue Avenue. Horace Trumbauer. 1914. Photo, Wayne Andrews.
(lower)
Maxim Karolik House, Bellevue Avenue. Ogden Codman. 1910. Photo, Wayne Andrews.

PLATE 229   *(upper)*
John Russell Pope's own house. Ledge Road. 1927. Photo, Meservey.
(lower)
Jerome Borden House, Ocean Drive. Looking across hall. Swift and Angell, 1917. Photo, Covell.

PLATE 230   *(upper)*
Jerome Borden House. Sea side. Photo, Meservey.
(lower)
Jerome Borden House. Plan. Drawn by Warren Oakley.

Washington Square in 1850. Showing from left to right: Charles Feke's House, Pitt's Head Tavern in original location, the adjoined Buttrick House, the Mumford House, and the Colony House. Taken from Walling's *Map of Newport, 1850.* published by W. H. Peek. (R.I.H.S.)

Overlooking the harbor. Made into a parking lot since 1952.
Photo, Meservey.

Drying Nets.
Photo, Meservey.

Through the arcade of the Old Stone Mill.
Photo, Meservey.

Spire of Trinity Church. Richard Munday, 1726.
Photo, Meservey.

The Colony House. Richard Munday, 1739.
Photo, Meservey.

The Brick Market at night. Peter Harrison, 1762.
Photo, Meservey.

Waterside view of Thomas Robinson, John Warren and Jonathan Nichols houses on
Washington Street in 1870.
Stereoscopic view by J. A. Williams. (C.C.)

Jonas Bergner's drawing of Thomas (and John) Goddard's house
and shop and Jonathan Easton's house when they stood on
Washington Street north of Willow. (N.H.S.)

Washington Street south of Bridge in 1948, showing the Isaac Dayton,
Edward Gladding, and Simeon Potter houses.
Photo, Meservey.

Bridge Street looking west in 1870, showing the Kendall Nichols House (demolished),
the John Townsend House (No. 70) and his gambrel-roofed shop (now rebuilt),
and the Christopher Townsend House.
J. A. Williams view. (C.C.)

Bridge Street looking east in 1948. Showing left, (No. 31) the Stephen Ayrault (Freeborn) House, and right, (No. 22) the Caleb Claggett, and (No. 16)
the William Claggett houses.
Photo, Ralph Arnold

Bridge Street looking east in 1880. Caleb Claggett House second from right.
Stanhope photograph. (C.C.)

Upper Thames Street looking south in 1948, showing from left; No. 18, David Braman, Sr., House (owned by Merriam Johnson before 1774); No. 24, moved here after 1850; No. 26, rebuilt by David Braman about 1813; No. 30, the John Stevens House, partly built in 1709. All restored since 1951.
Photo, Meservey.

North Baptist Street corner in 1870 looking north on Thames, showing the Job Bennett Shop (demolished) and House (No. 44), the two houses (Nos. 42 and 36) owned by Dr. James Keith, and No. 34, another John Stevens House.
J. A. Williams view. (C.C.)

John Stevens Shop, 29 Thames Street.
Photo, Meservey.

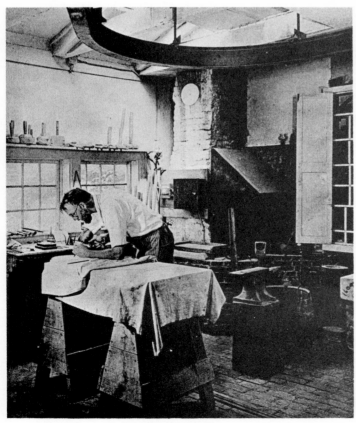

John Stevens Shop, interior.
Photo, Meservey.

Burial ground of the Governors, Farewell Street, showing at right, the George Lawton
House, home of Clarke Rodman in 1787, later, a Friends' School.
Photo, Meservey.

West Marlborough Street looking east in 1880, showing, left, Oliver
Ring Warner House, and right, Gervais Elam's Thames Street House
(both demolished.)
Stanhope photograph. (N.H.S.)

Marlborough Street looking east from Thames in 1870.
Stereoscopic view by J. A. Williams. (C.C.)

Marlborough Street looking east in 1948.
Photo, Arnold.

Thames Street at the southwest corner of Washington Square in 1870. Showing from left, the Thomas Durfey House (demolished), the Christopher Champlin House (now the Blue Moon Tavern) and the Christopher Almy House (demolished).
Stereoscopic view by J. A. Williams.
(John Howard Benson Collection.)

North side of Pelham Street above Spring in 1870, showing the Augustus Littlefield (Van Zandt) House.
Stereoscopic view by J. A. Williams. (C.C.)

North side of Pelham Street below Spring in 1870, showing from left: No. 32, the
Dr. King House, built by Nathaniel Langley before 1750; No. 48, built by John Gidley
in 1744, and No. 50 built by Daniel Vaughan between 1760 and 1777.
J. A. Williams photograph. (C.C.)

Pelham Street, the same view in 1948.
Photo, Arnold.

Michel Felice Corné House, 2 Corné Street.
Photo, Meservey.

Sailing vessels, wall paintings from the Corné House, painted by Corné after 1822.

Courtesy of the Newport Historical Society.   *Courtesy of John Howard Benson.*

Lucina Langley House, 43 Pelham Street, 1770.
Photo, Kerschner.

Governor Benedict Arnold Burying Ground, Pelham Street.
Photo, Meservey.

Bellevue Avenue in 1870.
Old photograph. (C.C.)

The Quaker Meeting House. Lithograph by John P. Newell, 1865, from an overmantel *View of Newport* painted about 1740.
N.H.S.

The Quaker Meeting House. From the overmantel painting, 1740. Originally in the Phillips House (demolished) on Mill Street. Now in Malbone Hall, Malbone Road. *Courtesy of Lewis G. Morris. Photo, Covell.*

First Meeting House, West Springfield, Massachusetts.
S.P.N.E.A.

The Stone Mill, Touro Park, 1675?
Photo, Meservey.

Governor William Coddington House, 1641. Demolished in 1835. From *John Gorham Palfrey, History of New England*, 1860, Vol. II, p. 62.

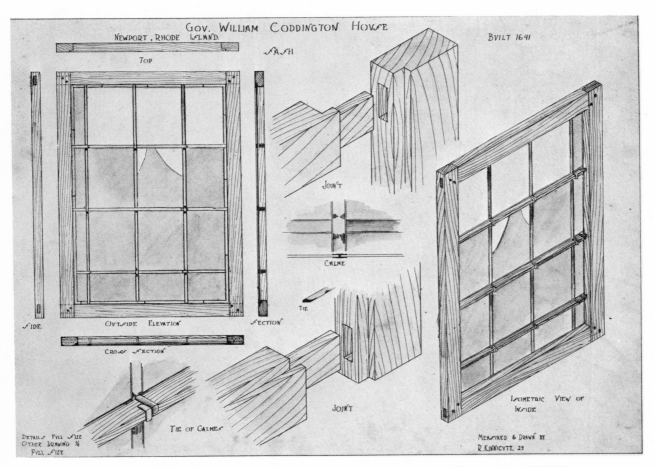

Governor William Coddington House. Drawing of the casement window now in R.I.H.S. *Measured by R. Kinnicutt.*

Henry Bull House, 1639. Burned in 1912. Old photograph. *N.H.S.*

The Sueton Grant House. Probably built by Jeremy Clarke before 1675. Demolished in
1898. From Edwin Whitefield, *Homes of our Forefathers, in
Rhode Island and Connecticut.* 1882.

Jeremy Clarke House, Restored. Drawing from Norman Morrison Isham,
Early Rhode Island Houses.

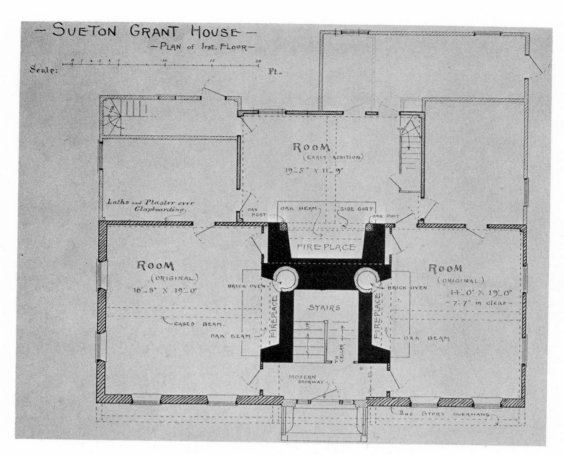

— SUETON GRANT HOUSE —
— PLAN of 1rst. FLOOR —

Scale: Ft.

ROOM
(EARLY ADDITION)
19'-5" X 11'-9"

Laths and Plaster over Clapboarding

OAK POST   OAK BEAM   SIDE GIRT   OAK POST

FIRE PLACE

ROOM
(ORIGINAL)
16'-8" X 19'-0"

BRICK OVEN

FIREPLACE

STAIRS

FIREPLACE

BRICK OVEN

ROOM
(ORIGINAL)
14'-0" X 19'-0"
- 7'-7" in clear -

CASED BEAM.
OAK BEAM

UP

TO CELLAR

OAK BEAM

MODERN DOORWAY

2ND STORY OVERHANG

Jeremy Clarke House.
Plan by Bergner.

Jeremy Clarke House. The chimney during demolition,
showing the arches of the stone foundation.
From an old photograph.
N.H.S.

Governor Caleb Carr House, Jamestown, about 1686. Burned about 1960.
From an old photograph.
N.H.S.

Captain Thomas Paine House, Jamestown. Drawing from Whitefield,
Homes of Our Forefathers.

Elder John Bliss House, Bliss Road at Anthony Place, before 1715.
Photo, Meservey.

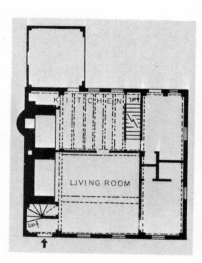

Elder John Bliss House, Plan.
Drawn by Warren Oakley.

Wanton-Lyman-Hazard House, 17 Broadway. Built by Stephen Mumford
between 1695 and 1700.
Photo, Meservey.

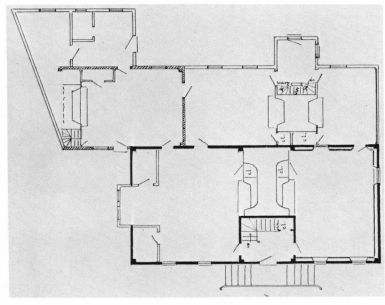

Wanton-Lyman-Hazard House. Plan before addition was torn off.
Drawn by Bergner.

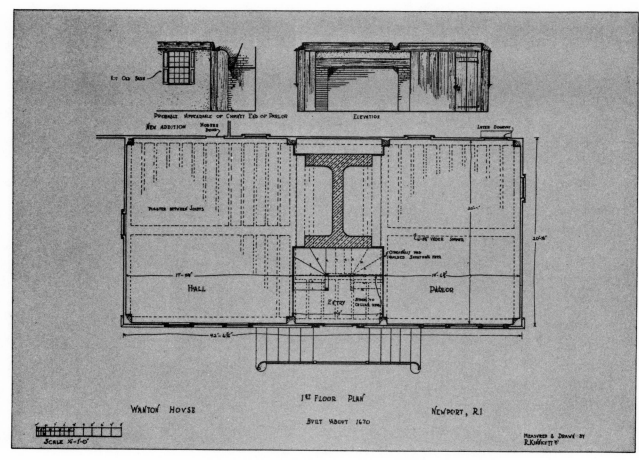

Wanton-Lyman-Hazard House. Plan, first floor.
Measured by R. Kinnicutt.

Wanton-Lyman-Hazard House. Scale model restoring house
to its seventeenth-century appearance.
Owned by Brown University.

Wanton-Lyman-Hazard House. Scale model.

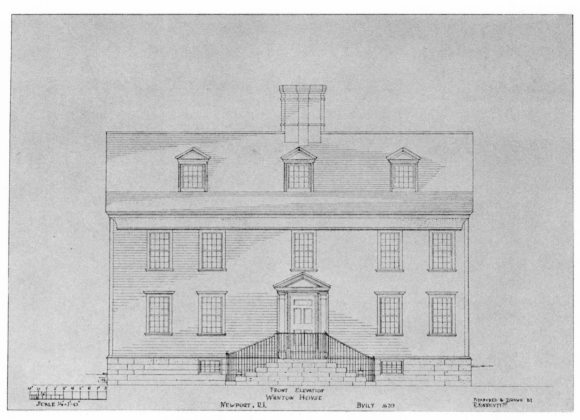

Wanton-Lyman-Hazard House, front elevation.
Measured by R. Kinnicutt.

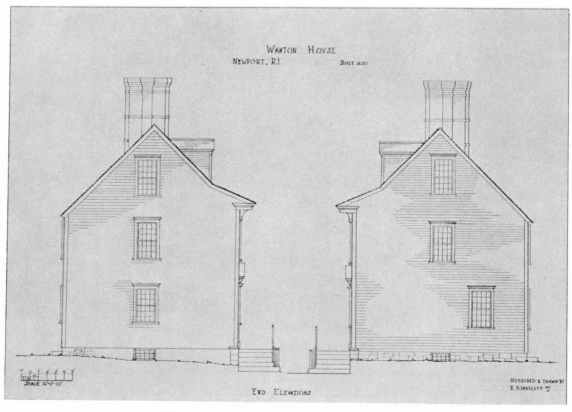

Wanton-Lyman-Hazard House, end elevation.
Measured by R. Kinnicutt.

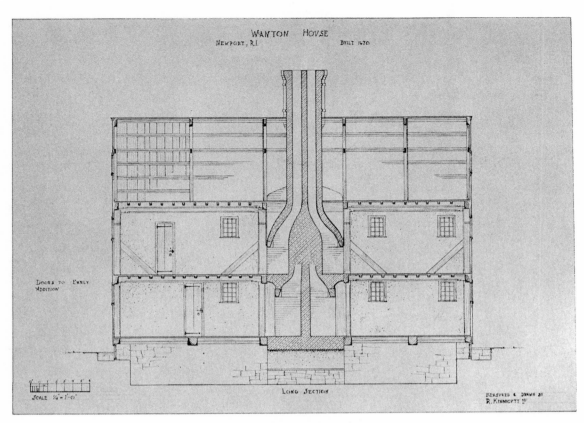

Wanton-Lyman-Hazard House, long section.
Measured by R. Kinnicutt.

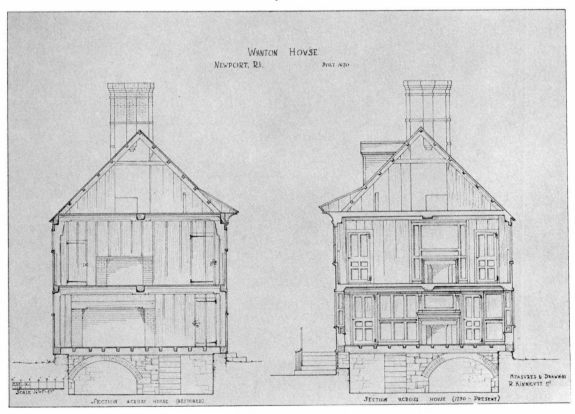

Wanton-Lyman-Hazard House, section across house.
Measured by R. Kinnicutt.

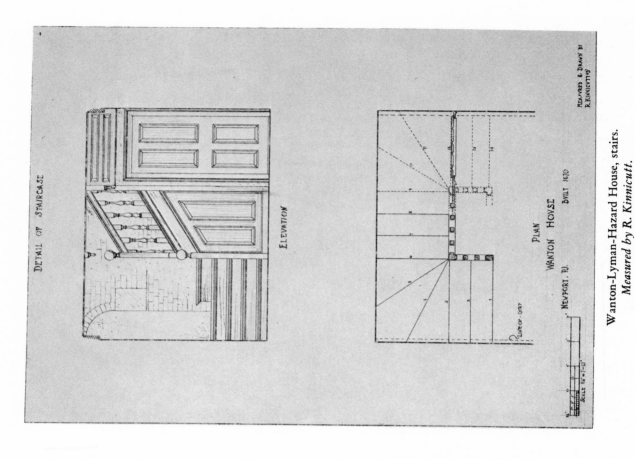

DETAIL OF STAIRCASE

ELEVATION

PLAN

WANTON HOVSE   NEWPORT. RI.   BVILT 1670

Wanton-Lyman-Hazard House, stairs.
Measured by R. Kinnicutt.

WANTON HOVSE
NEWPORT. RI.   BVILT 1670
FRAMING DETAILS

RAFTERS & RIDGE
PVRLIN

RAFTER & COLLER

CORNER POST &
WIND-BRACING

RAFTERS, COLL-
AR, & PVRLINS

2ND STOREY SVMMER & CHIMNEY GIRT

CHIMNEY GIRT, FRONT GIRT, & POST

SCALE ¾ = 1'-0"

Wanton-Lyman-Hazard House, framing details.
Measured by R. Kinnicutt.

Wanton-Lyman-Hazard House, stairway.
Photo, Meservey.

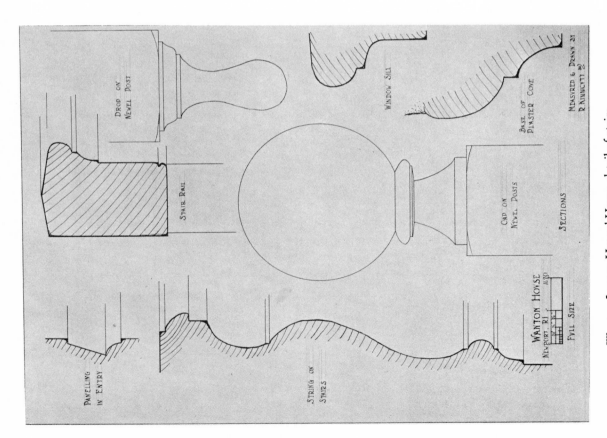

Wanton-Lyman-Hazard House, detail of stairs.
Measured by R. Kinnicutt.

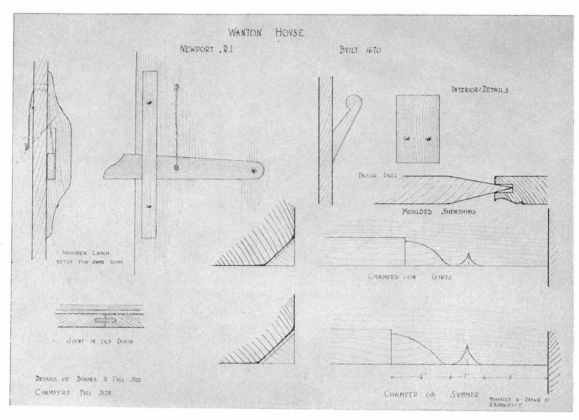

Wanton-Lyman-Hazard House, details.
Measured by R. Kinnicutt.

Wanton-Lyman-Hazard House, northwest chamber.
Photo, Meservey.

Wanton-Lyman-Hazard House, kitchen ell, after 1725.
Photo, Meservey.

Whitehorse Tavern, Marlborough Street, in 1870. Built by William Mays
before 1693. Enlarged by Jonathan Nichols before 1750.
J. A. Williams photograph. C.C.

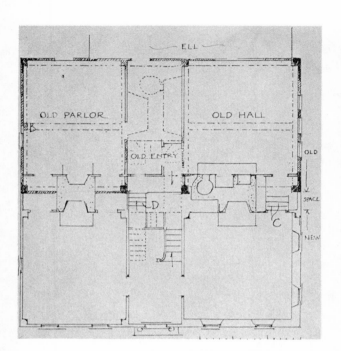

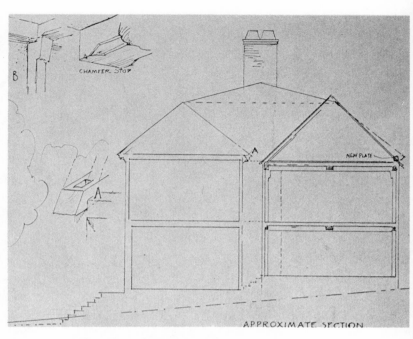

Captain John Mawdsley House, 228 Spring Street. Plan and elevation, showing how the two-room seventeenth-century Jireh Bull House was enlarged in the eighteenth century.
Drawn by Isham. S.P.N.E.A.

Jireh Bull, Jr., House, about 1680.
East part of Captain Mawdsley House.
Photo, Meservey.

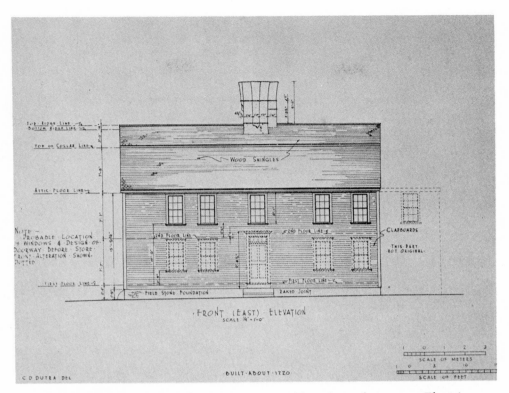

Thomas Richardson House, Thames Street, 1715. Torn down about 1940. Elevation.
H.A.B.S.

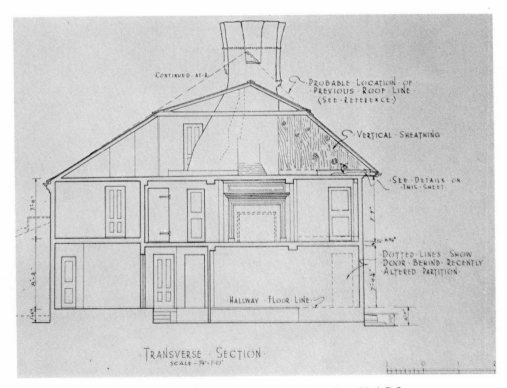

Thomas Richardson House, transverse section. *H.A.B.S.*

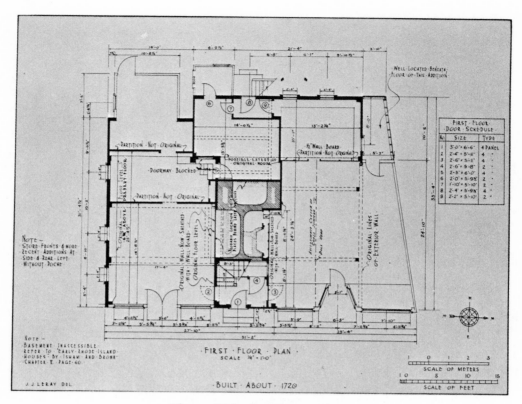

Thomas Richardson House. Plan.
H.A.B.S.
Note: The Thomas Walker House at 6 Cross Street, built between 1706 and 1713,
later The King's Arms, has a similar chimney plan. This house is now
being restored by *Operation Clapboard*.

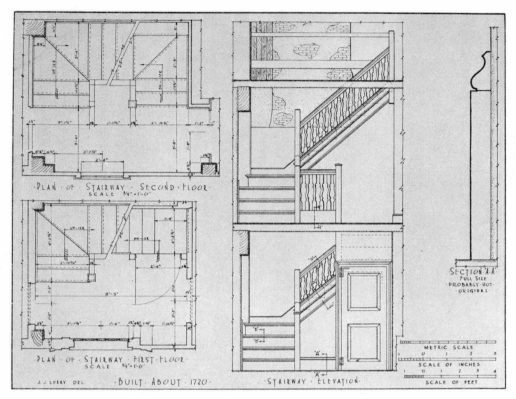

Thomas Richardson House, stairs. Measured drawing.
H.A.B.S.

Thomas Richardson House, stairs. From
Antoinette F. Downing, *Early Homes
of Rhode Island.*
Photo, LeBoeuf.

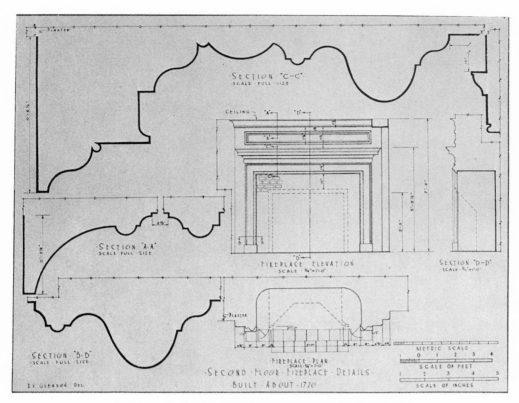

Thomas Richardson House, fireplace details. *H.A.B.S.*

Thomas Richardson House, mantel wall, north chamber. From
Antoinette F. Downing, *Early Homes of Rhode Island*.
Photo, LeBoeuf.

Pitt's Head Tavern, 5 Charles Street (now [1965] moved to Bridge and Second streets.)
Probably built by John Clarke before 1726; enlarged by Ebenezer Flagg,
nephew-in-law of Henry Collins, about 1744.
Photo, Meservey.

Pitt's Head Tavern, stairs. About 1726.
Photo, Meservey.

Pitt's Head Tavern, stairs.
Photo, Kerschner.

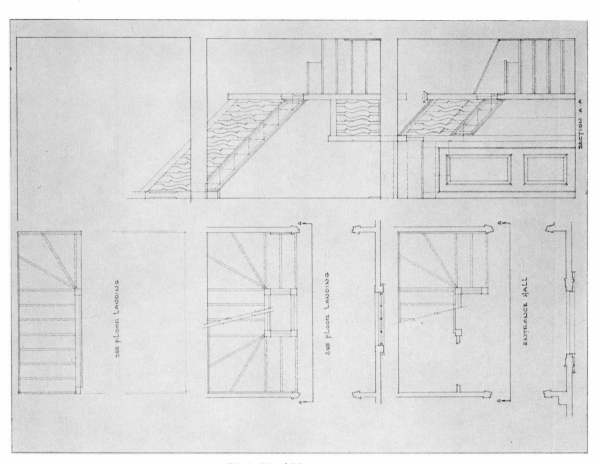

Pitt's Head Tavern, stairs.
Measured by Robert Hill. P.S.N.C.

Augustus Lucas House, 40 Division Street.
Rear stairs, before 1721.
Photo, Meservey.

Caleb Claggett House, 22 Bridge Street. Built soon after 1725.
Photo, Meservey.

Jahleel Brenton farmhouse, Harrison Avenue.
Before 1720. Stone and Brick
foundation vault.
Photo, Hopf.

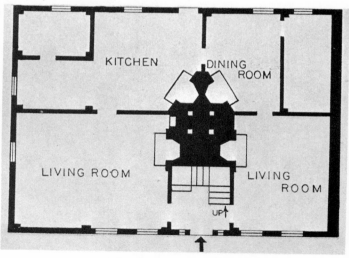

Caleb Claggett House, floor plan.
Drawn by Warren Oakley.

View of Newport in 1740 (before Long Wharf was extended). Showing from left, the
Quaker Meeting House, the Colony House, and Clarke Street, Trinity, and Mill Street
churches. The town schoolhouse can be seen in front of the Colony House.
From Newell's lithograph, 1865.
N.H.S.

Trinity Church, designed by Richard Munday, 1725.
Photo, Meservey.

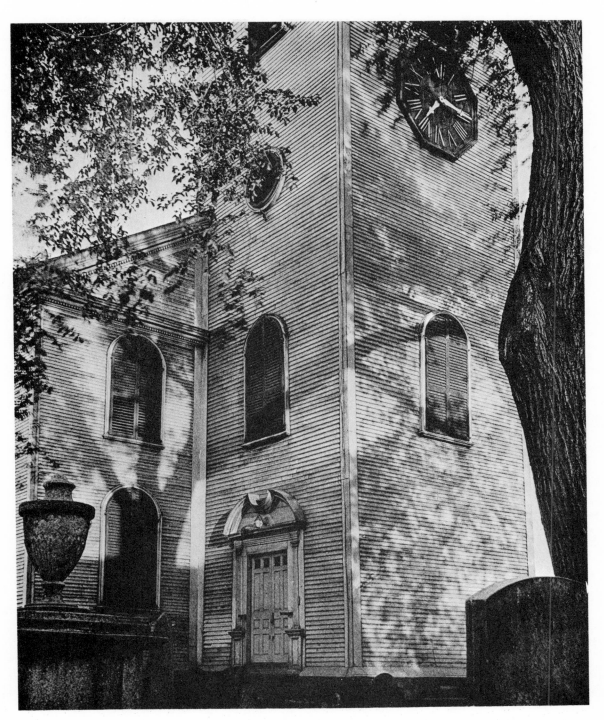

Trinity Church. Tower.
Photo, Meservey.

Trinity Church. Watercolors by John Gilpin, 1830. One shows
the church before it was lengthened in 1767; the other afterwards.
R.L.

Trinity Church. North door.
Measured by R. Kinnicutt.

Trinity Church. South door.
Measured by R. Kinnicutt.

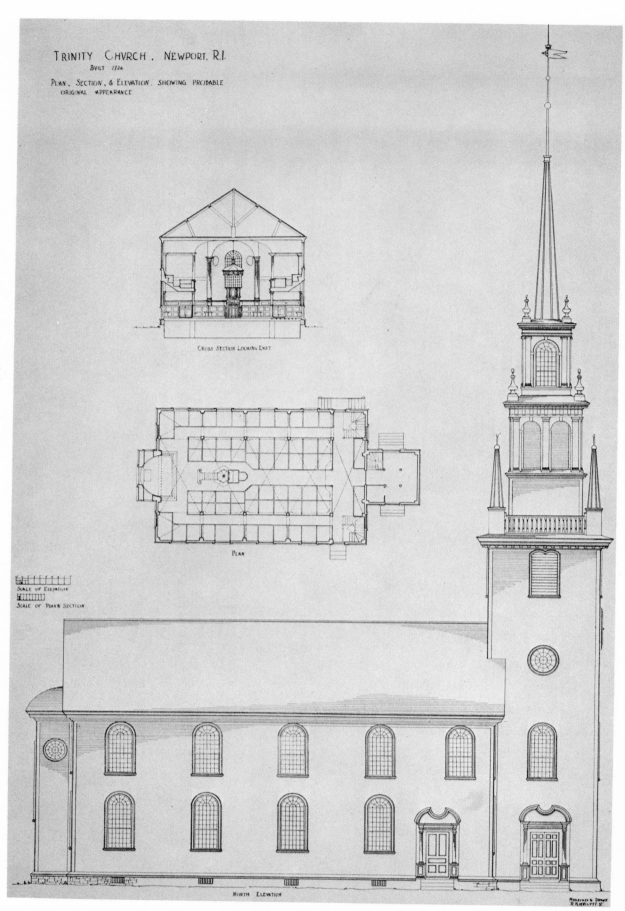

TRINITY CHURCH, NEWPORT, R.I.
BUILT 1726
PLAN, SECTION, & ELEVATION. SHOWING PROBABLE
ORIGINAL APPEARANCE

CROSS SECTION LOOKING EAST

PLAN

SCALE OF ELEVATION
SCALE OF PLAN & SECTION

NORTH ELEVATION

Trinity Church. Plan, section, and elevation, showing probable original appearance.
Measured by R. Kinnicutt. N.H.S.

Trinity Church. End section.   *Measured by R. Kinnicutt. N.H.S.*

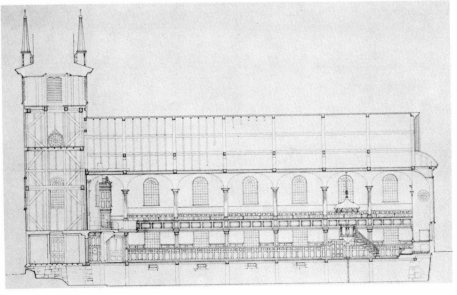

Trinity Church. Long section.   *Measured by R. Kinnicutt. N.H.S.*

Trinity Church. Interior section.   *Measured by R. Kinnicutt. N.H.S.*

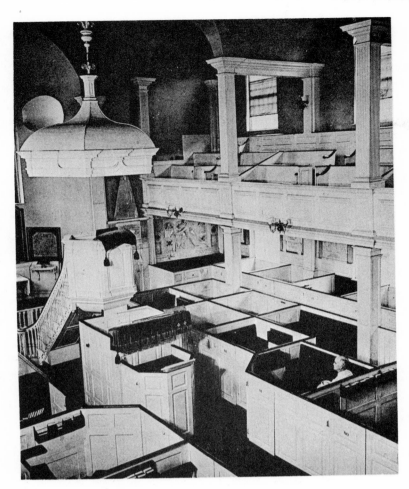

Trinity Church. Interior.
Photo, Meservey.

Trinity Church. Pulpit and reading desk.
Measured by R. Kinnicutt. N.H.S.

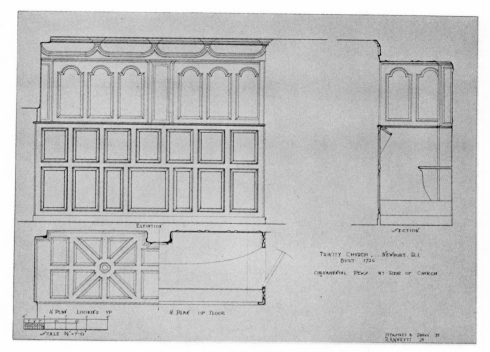

Trinity Church. Warden's pew.
Measured By R. Kinnicutt.

Sabbatarian Meeting House. Richard Munday? 1729. Engraving from
the *Seventh Day Baptist Memorial*, 1852.
N.H.S.

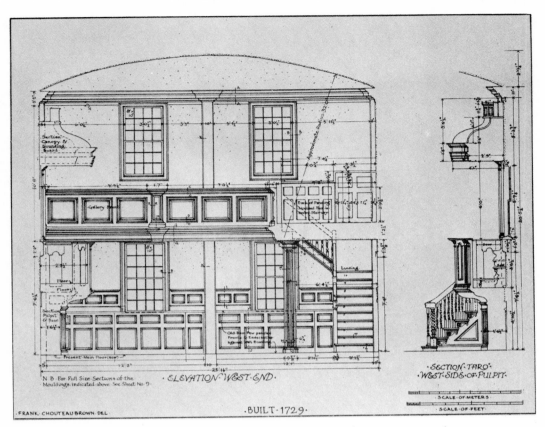

Sabbatarian Meeting House. Measured drawing, elevation, west end.
H.A.B.S.

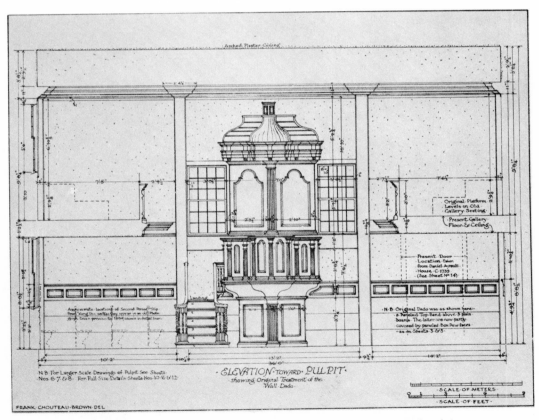

Sabbatarian Meeting House. Measured drawing, elevation toward pulpit.
H.A.B.S.

Sabbatarian Meeting House. Stairs and pulpit.
Photo, Meservey.

Sabbatarian Meeting House. Old view.
N.H.S.

Sabbatarian Meeting House. Detail of pulpit stairs.
Photo, Meservey.

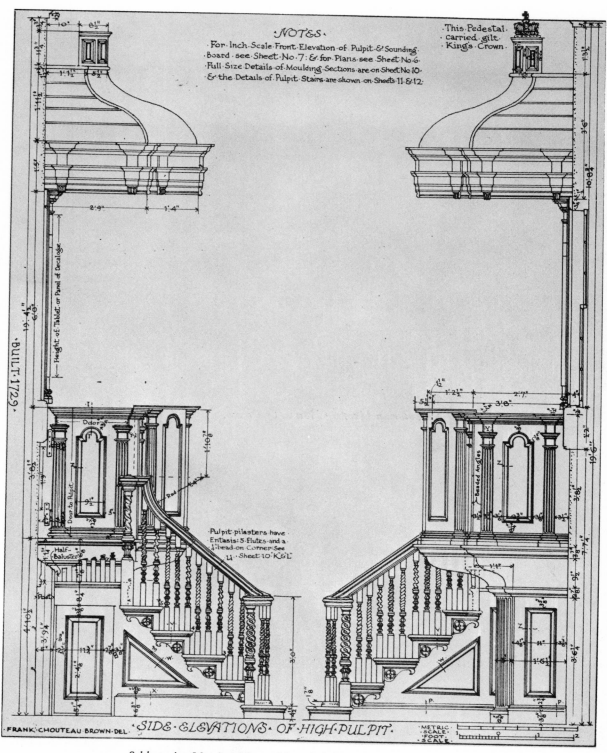

· NOTES ·
For · Inch · Scale · Front · Elevation · of · Pulpit · & · Sounding ·
Board · see · Sheet · No · 7 · & · for · Plans · see · Sheet · No · 6 ·
Full · Size · Details · of · Moulding · Sections · are · on · Sheet · No · 10 ·
& · the · Details · of · Pulpit · Stairs · are · shown · on · Sheets · 11 · & · 12 ·

This · Pedestal ·
carried · gilt ·
King's · Crown ·

· BUILT · 1729 ·

Pulpit · pilasters · have ·
Entasis · 5 · Flutes · and · a ·
⅓ · bead · on · Corner · See ·
Sheet · 10 · K · & · L ·

· FRANK · CHOUTEAU · BROWN · DEL · · SIDE · ELEVATIONS · OF · HIGH · PULPIT ·

METRIC ·
SCALE ·
FOOT ·
SCALE ·

Sabbatarian Meeting House. Measured drawing, stairs and pulpit.
H.A.B.S.

First Congregational Church, Mill Street, 1729. By Cotton Palmer
of Taunton. As it appeared in 1740.
From Newell's lithograph.

Second Congregational Church, Clarke Street, 1735. Cotton Palmer,
now of Providence. As it appeared in 1740.
From Newell's lithograph.

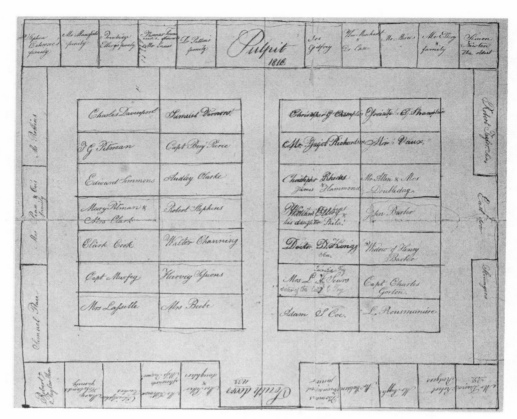

Second Congregational Church. Pew plan in 1816.
Courtesy, Miss Susan B. Franklin.

View of Clarke Street showing original spire of the Second
Congregational Church. Also, at right, French Hall.
Stereoscopic view by J. A. Williams, 1870.
S.P.N.E.A.

Colony House, Washington Square. Richard Munday, 1739.
Photo, Romano.

Colony House. Detail, door and balcony.
Photo, Romano.

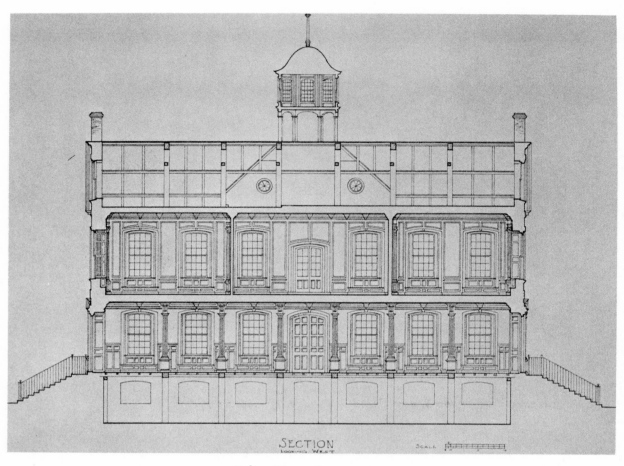

Colony House. Front section.
Measured by Isham. N.H.S.

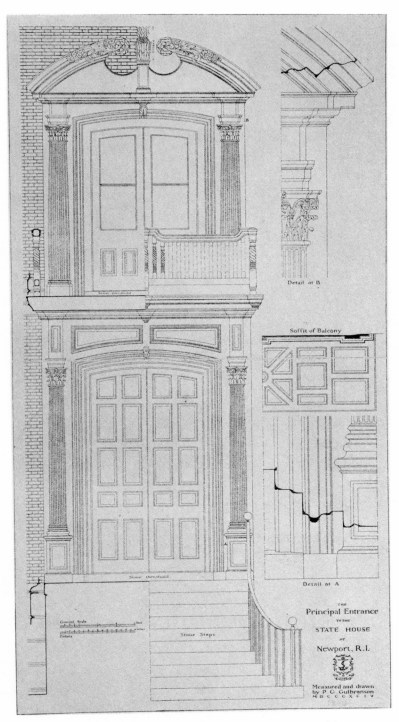

Colony House. Detail, balcony and door. Measured by
P. G. Gulbranson, *American Architect and
Building News*, April 27, 1895.

Colony House. Window detail.
Photo, Meservey.

Colony House. Detail, brickwork.
Photo, Meservey.

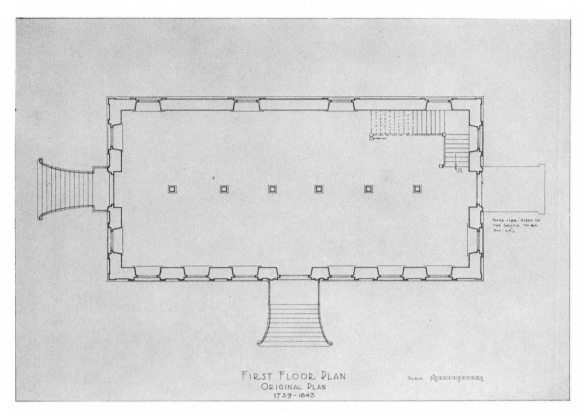

FIRST FLOOR PLAN
ORIGINAL PLAN
1739-1843

SCALE

Colony House. Original first floor plan.
Measured by Isham. N.H.S.

Colony House. Interior, the great hall.
Photo, Meservey.

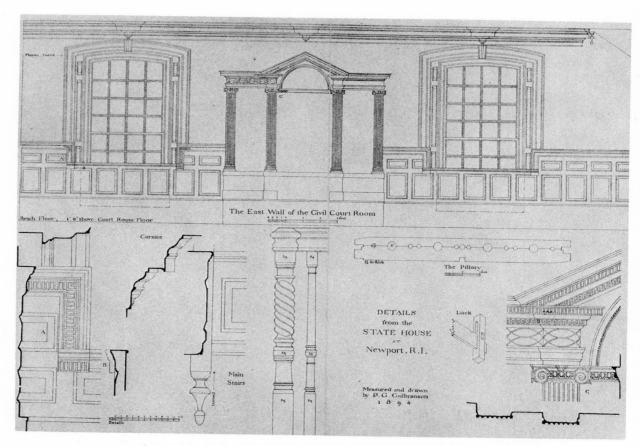

Colony House. The great hall, east wall. Measured by P. G. Gulbranson,
American Architect and Building News, March 4, 1896.

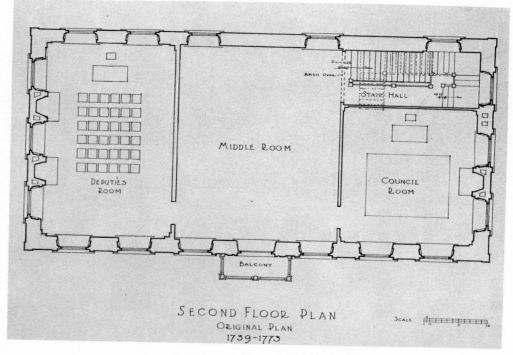

Colony House. Original second floor plan.
Measured by Isham. N.H.S.

Senate chamber, south wall. Measured by P. G. Gulbranson,
American Architect and Building News, March 4, 1896.

Colony House. Senate chamber.
Photo, Meservey.

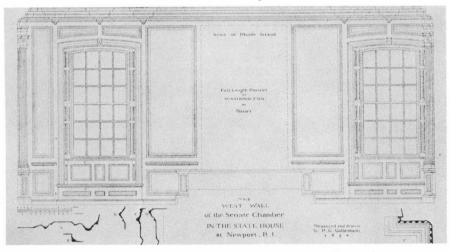

Senate chamber, west wall. Measured by P. G. Gulbranson,
American Architect and Building News, March 4, 1896.

Colony House. Senate chamber, east wall.
Measured by Isham. N.H.S.

Colony House. Senate chamber, north wall. Possible original form.
Measured by Isham. N.H.S.

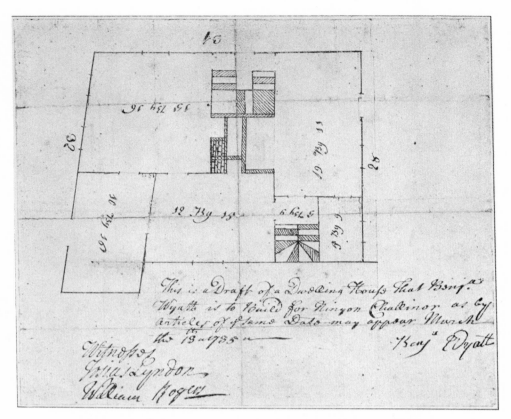

Ninyon Challoner House, 1735. Ground plan by Benjamin Wyatt.
From George Champlin Mason, *Reminiscences of Newport*,
enlarged edition, in the Newport Historical Society.

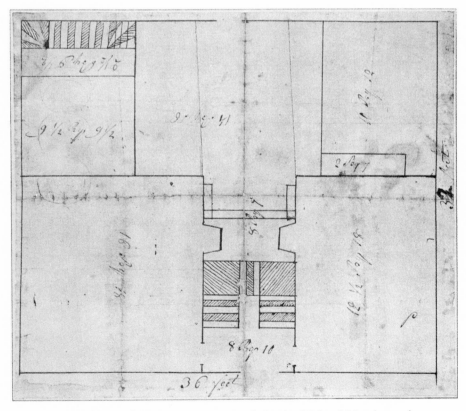

Daniel Ayrault House, 1739. Ground plan by Richard Munday and
Benjamin Wyatt. From Mason, *Reminiscences of Newport*,
enlarged edition, in the Newport Historical Society.

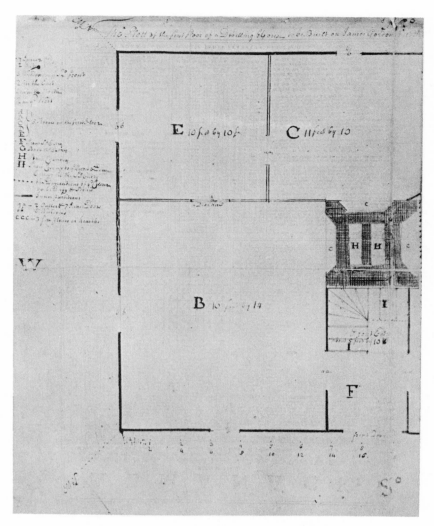

James Gordon Farm. Half of the plan. Drawn on the back
of Ann Franklin's Calendar of 1733.
R.I.H.S.

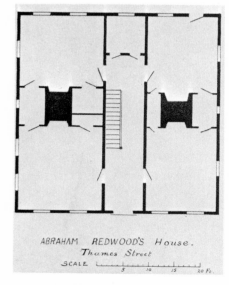

Abraham Redwood House. Plan.
Drawn by Bergner.

Abraham Redwood House, Thames Street, 1727.
Demolished. Drawing.
Collection of Miss Pauline Weaver.

[PL 72]

Wrought-iron gates from Abraham Redwood's estate.
Now installed on the Redwood Library grounds.
Photo, Meservey.

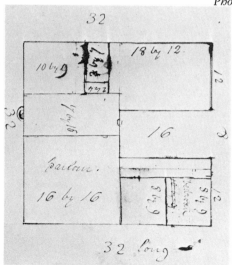

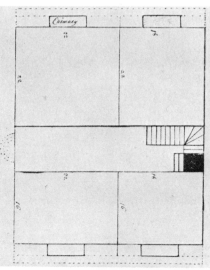

House plans taken from Jahleel Brenton's study book dated 1712.
Showing semicircular front steps.
R.I.H.S.

[PL 73]

Godfrey Malbone's town house. 1727. As it appeared in 1740.
From Newell's lithograph.

Godfrey Malbone's town house. Marble mantel.
Now in the Newport Historical Society.
Photo, Kerschner.

Godfrey Malbone's town house.
Capital from door. Now in
the Newport Historical Society.
Photo, Kerschner.

Jahleel Brenton House, Thames Street. About 1720. Demolished. Old drawing.
N.H.S.

Jahleel Brenton House. Photograph by J. A. Williams about 1870.
N.H.S.

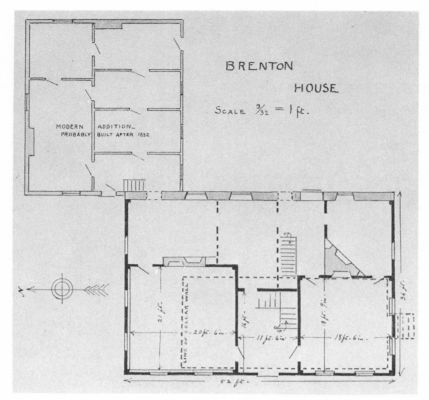

BRENTON

HOUSE

SCALE ³⁄₃₂ = 1 ft.

MODERN ADDITION
PROBABLY BUILT AFTER 1832

Jahleel Brenton House. Floor plan.
Drawn by Bergner.

Jahleel Brenton House. Stairs. Old photograph.
R.I.S.D.

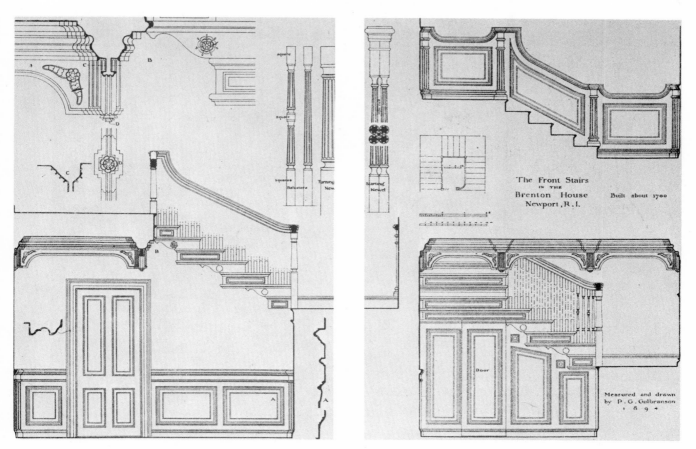

Jahleel Brenton House. Stairs. Measured drawings by P. G. Gulbranson,
American Architect and Building News, June 20, 1896.

Jahleel Brenton House. Parlor paneling. Now owned by the
Preservation Society of Newport County. Old photograph.
R.I.S.D.

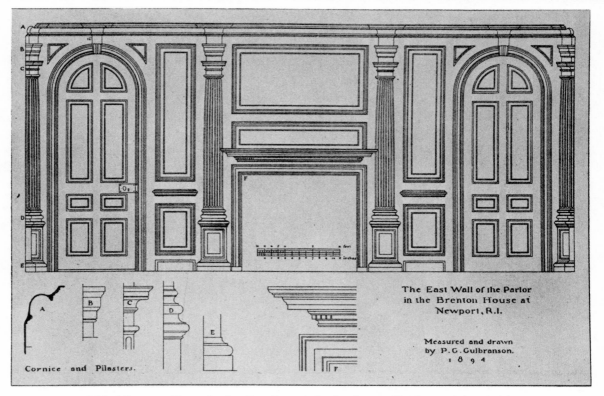

The East Wall of the Parlor
in the Brenton House at
Newport, R.I.

Measured and drawn
by P. G. Gulbranson.
1 8 9 4

Cornice and Pilasters.

Jahleel Brenton House. Parlor. Paneling of the fireplace wall. Measured drawing by
P. G. Gulbranson, *American Architect and Building News,* June 20, 1896.

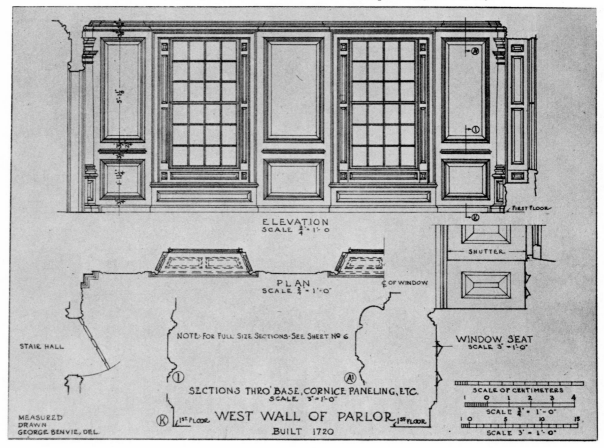

Paneling of the west wall. Measured drawing.

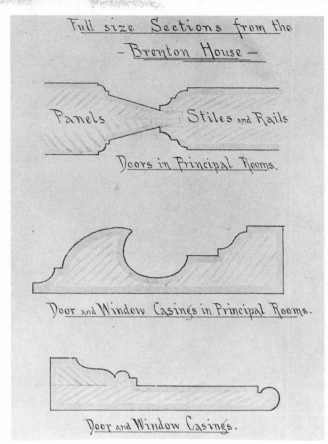

Jahleel Brenton House. Details.
Drawn by Bergner.

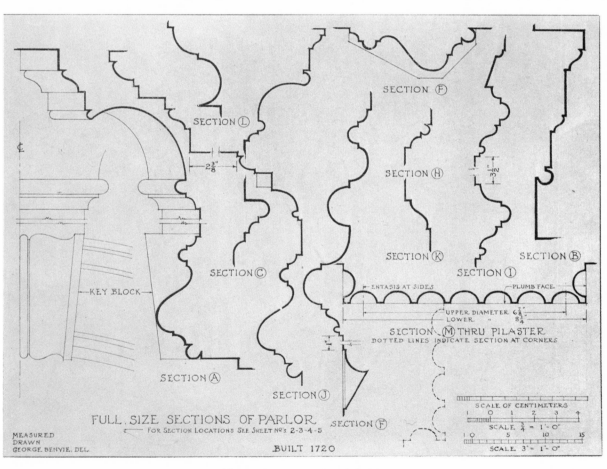

Molding sections. Measured drawing.
H.A.B.S.

John Gidley House, 1724. Demolished. Formerly Thames and Gidley. North parlor, paneling.
Photo, Bergner.

Paneling from the John Gidley House as installed
in the Mason House, 31 Old Beech Road. Now in
the Henry Francis du Pont Winterthur Museum.
Photo, Covell.

Thomas Robinson House. Dining room cupboard.
About 1730.
Photo, Covell.

William Redwood's country house, Mile Corner. Probably built about 1745
by Governor Joseph Whipple. Later, home of David Buffum.
Photo, Kerschner.

Benedict Arnold, Jr., House, Hammett's
Wharf. Doorway. Demolished in 1926.
Photo, Bergner.

Metcalf Bowler country house,
Portsmouth. Doorway. About 1760. Demolished.
Photo, Bergner.

Daniel Ayrault House, Thames Street at Ann. 1739.
Richard Munday and Benjamin Wyatt. Demolished.
Photo, Bergner.

Daniel Ayrault House. Doorway. Now
installed on the Barney Street entrance,
Newport Historical Society.
Photo, Bergner.

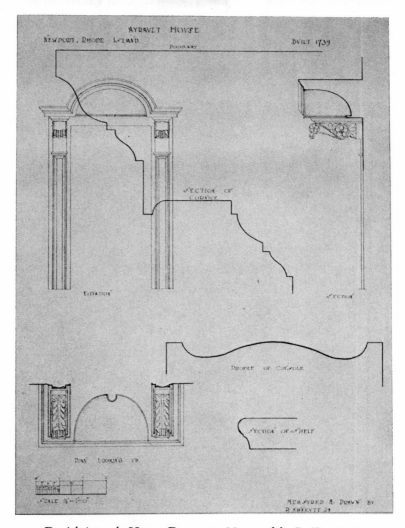

Daniel Ayrault House. Doorway. *Measured by R. Kinnicutt.*

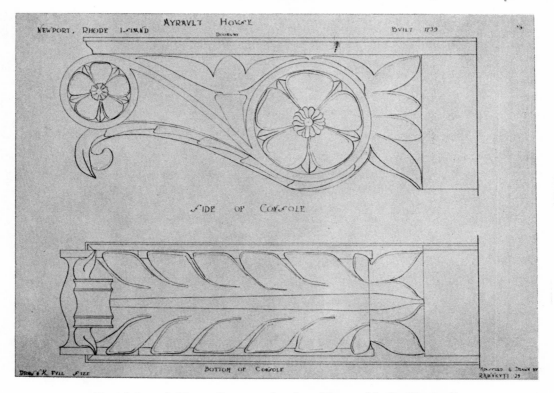

Daniel Ayrault House. Doorway, bracket. *Measured by R. Kinnicutt.*

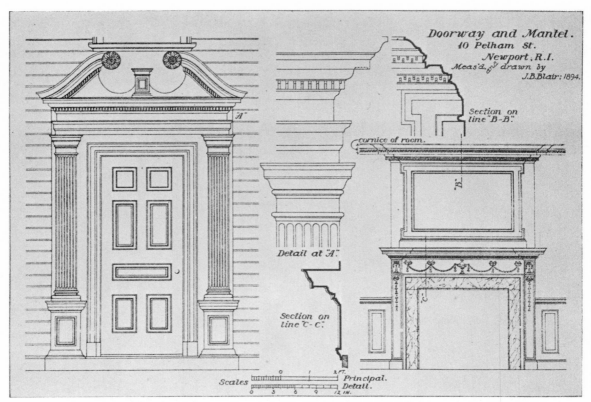

Nathaniel Langley (Dr. King's) House, 32 Pelham Street. Doorway and mantel. Measured
by J. B. Blair, *American Architect and Building News*, December 8, 1894.

Henry Taggart (Fowler) House, 32 Second Street. Before 1763.
Shows wide boxed cornice common in early eighteenth century.
Photo, Meservey.

Whitehall, Dean Berkely's house in Middletown, 1729.
Photo, Meservey.

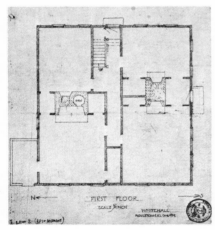

Whitehall. Floor plan and elevation.
Drawn by Isham. C.D.

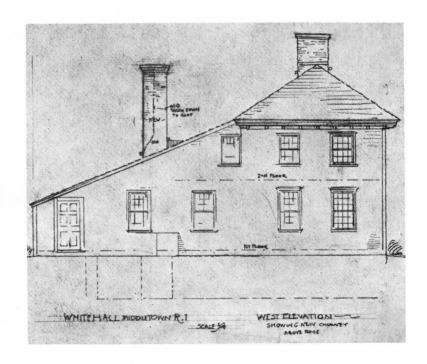

Whitehall. Green parlor.
Photo, Meservey.

Whitehall. Red parlor.
Photo, Meservey.

Abraham Rodrigues Riviera House, Washington Square. Built before 1722
by John Rathbun; enlarged before 1758 by John Gardner.
Home of the Newport Bank since 1804.
Photo, Meservey.

Roof detail showing dormer windows.
Photo, Meservey.

Jonathan Nichols (Wanton or Hunter) House, 54 Washington Street.
About 1748. Waterside view showing pedimented doorway and
segmental headed stair landing windows. Stereoscopic view
by J. A. Williams, 1870. (N.H.S.) See note
page 490.

Jonathan Nichols House. Washington Street side with doorway as restored at present.
Photo, Kerschner.

Pediment from the waterside doorway of the Jonathan Nichols House as
installed on the Dennis House, 65 Poplar Street, from 1923 to 1950.
Photo, Arnold.

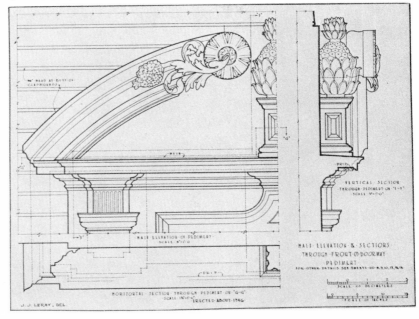

Jonathan Nichols House, pediment. Measured drawing.
H.A.B.S.

Jonathan Nichols House. Detail showing construction. The walls are brick filled, and this wall (south) is also plastered as in English half-timbering.
Photo, Kerschner.

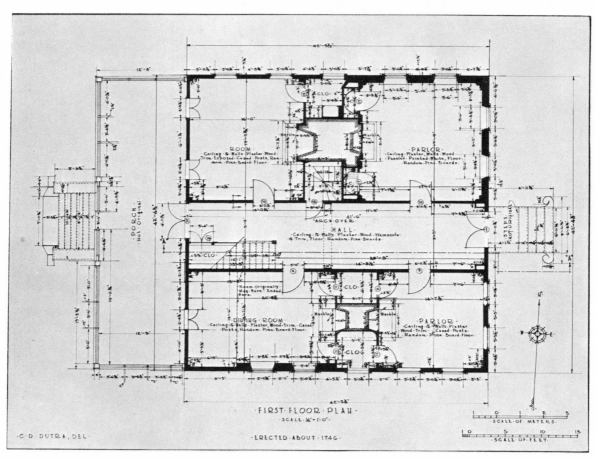

Jonathan Nichols House. Floor plan. Measured drawing.
H.A.B.S.

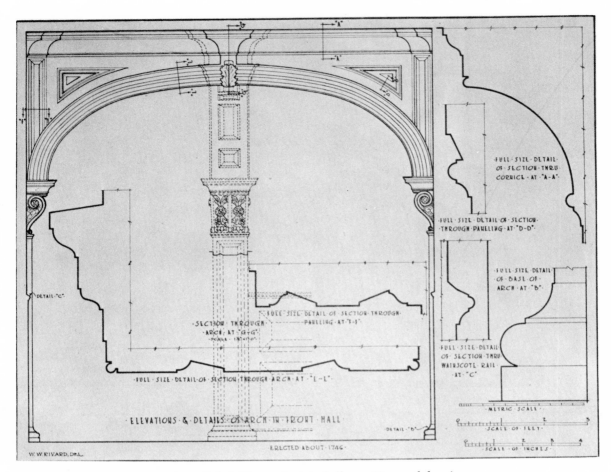

Jonathan Nichols House. Arch in hallway. Measured drawing.
H.A.B.S.

Jonathan Nichols House. Detail of stairs.
Photo, Meservey.

David Cheeseborough House, Mary Street at Clarke,
1737. Arch and stairs. Demolished 1908.
Photo, Bergner.

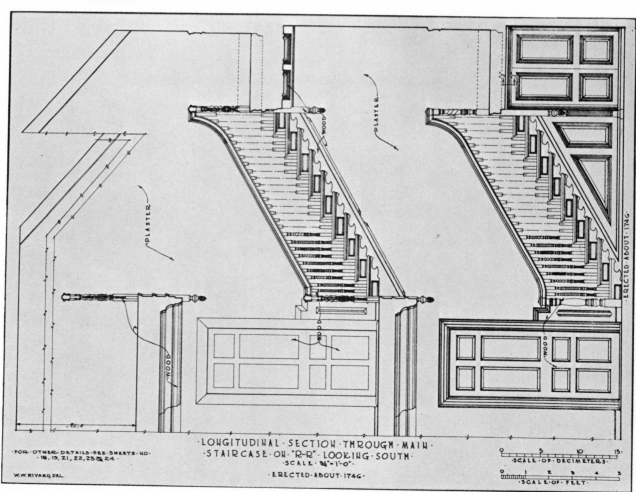

·LONGITUDINAL·SECTION·THROUGH·MAIN·
·STAIRCASE·ON·"R-R"·LOOKING·SOUTH·
·SCALE·¾"·1'-0"·

·ERECTED·ABOUT·1746·

·FOR·OTHER·DETAILS·SEE·SHEETS·NO·
·18, 19, 21, 22, 23 & 24·

W.W. RIVARD, DEL.

·SCALE·OF·DECIMETERS·

·SCALE·OF·FEET·

Jonathan Nichols House. Stairs. Measured drawing.
H.A.B.S.

Jonathan Nichols House. North parlor in 1950.
Photo, Meservey.

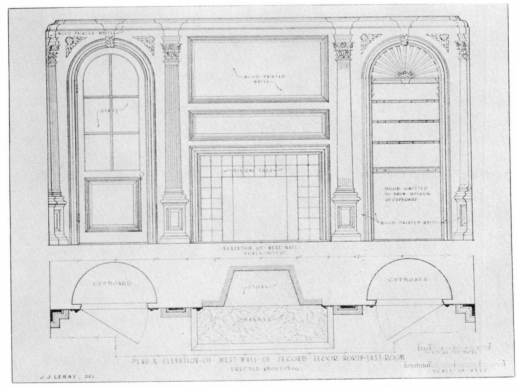

Jonathan Nichols House. North parlor. Measured drawing.
H.A.B.S.

Jonathan Nichols House. North parlor, cupboard.
Photo, Meservey.

David Cheeseborough House. Detail, mantel wall.
Photo, Bergner.

Christopher Townsend House and shop. 74 Bridge Street.
Built sometime after 1725, before 1750.
Photo, Meservey.

Christopher Townsend House. Doorway and shop.
Photo, Meservey.

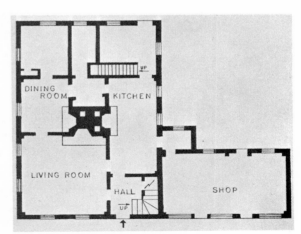

Christopher Townsend House and shop. Plan.
Enlarged at rear.
Drawn by Warren Oakley.

Christopher Townsend House. Mantel paneling.
Photo, Meservey.

Job Townsend House, 63 Bridge Street. About
1729. Stairway. Demolished after 1952.
Photo, Meservey.

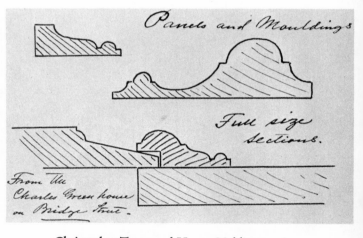

Christopher Townsend House. Molding sections.
Bergner.

John Banister House, 56 Pelham Street. 1751.
Photo, Meservey.

Stairs.
Photo, Meservey. P.S.N.C.

West parlor. Measured by P. G. Gulbranson,
American Architect and Building News,
Vol. LIV, No. 1089, adv.

Thomas Robinson House, 64 Washington Street. South part before 1736; north part
about 1760. At right, St. John's Rectory (Dennis House), 65 Poplar Street,
probably built by William Grafton about 1740.
Photo, Arnold.

Thomas Robinson House. Dining room.
Photo, Meservey.

Desk bookcase in the north parlor, by John Goddard.
Photo, Meservey.

Dr. Hopkins House, 46 Division Street. Built between 1758 and 1772. Dr. Hopkins was the hero of Harriet Beecher Stowe's *The Minister's Wooing*.
Photo, Meservey.

Crandall House, 59 Poplar Street. Before 1758. Owned by David Huntington before the Revolution. Thomas Chadwick bought it from Thomas Forrester's estate in 1796.
Photo, Meservey.

Erastus Pease House, 36 Church Street. Rear view, showing
curved roof line. About 1785.
Photo, Meservey.

Erastus Pease House. Mantel wall in kitchen.
Photo, Meservey.

Wanton-Lyman-Hazard House. Paneling, south parlor.
Installed by Martin Howard about 1750?
Photo, Meservey.

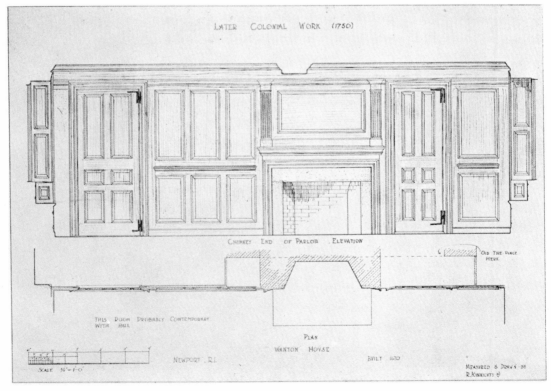

Wanton-Lyman-Hazard House. South parlor, mantel wall.
Measured by R. Kinnicutt.

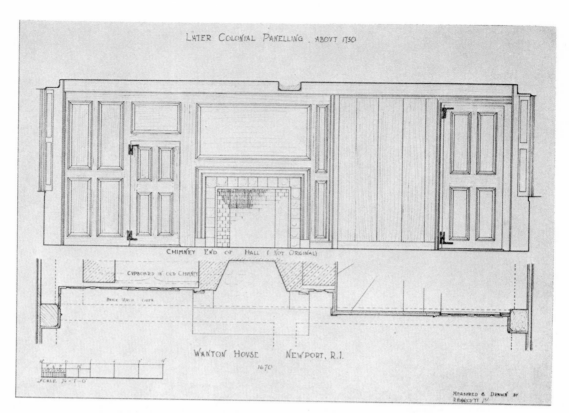

Wanton-Lyman-Hazard House. South chamber, mantel wall.
Paneling installed by Martin Howard?
Measured by R. Kinnicutt.

St. John's Rectory (Dennis House), 65 Poplar Street. Probably built by
William Grafton about 1740. Dining room paneling.
Photo, Meservey.

Metcalf Bowler country house, Portsmouth. About 1760. Demolished. Paneling of parlor, as installed in the Metropolitan Museum of Art, New York City.

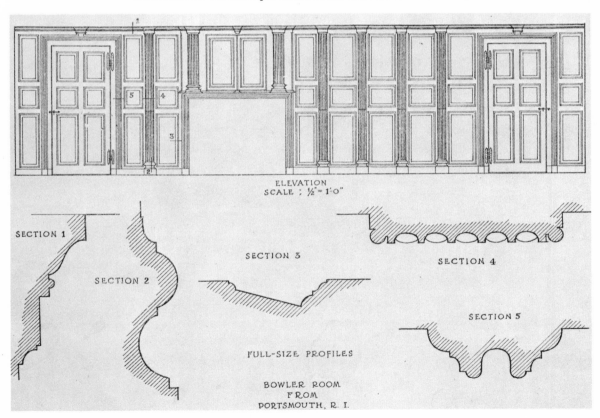

Metcalf Bowler country house. Parlor paneling. Measured drawing.

Redwood Library, Bellevue Avenue. Peter Harrison. 1748.
Photo, Meservey.

Redwood Library.
Drawing made by Eugène Pierre du Simitière, 1768. Du Simitière Collection,
The Library Company of Philadelphia.

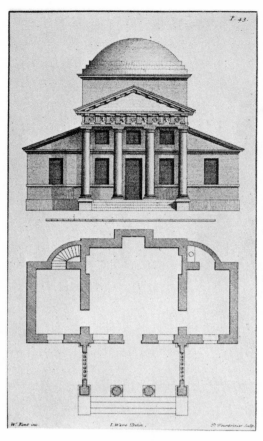

Casino for Sir Charles Hotham, Isaac
Ware, *Designs of Inigo Jones and
others*, First Edition, 1735?

Redwood Library. Detail, doorway.
Photo, Kerschner.

Summer house from Abraham Redwood's estate in
Portsmouth. 1766, Peter Harrison? Now on
the Redwood Library grounds.
Photo, Kerschner.

Beavertail Lighthouse, Peter Har-
rison, about 1755. From Peter
Harrison's Map of Newport,
Colonial Office, London. (Maps
N.A.C., R.I. 5.)

The Brick Market in 1880, Washington Square at
Thames Street. Peter Harrison, 1761.
Stanhope photograph. C.C.

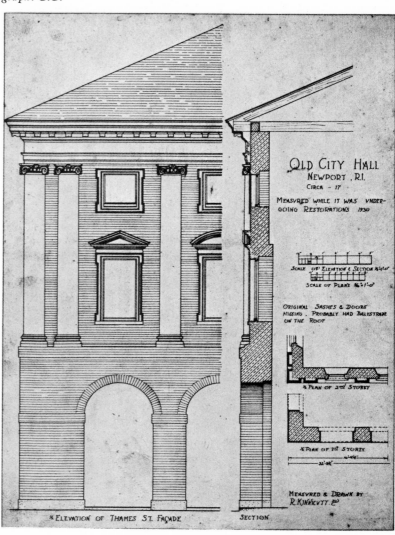

The Brick Market. Elevation and section.
Measured by R. Kinnicutt.

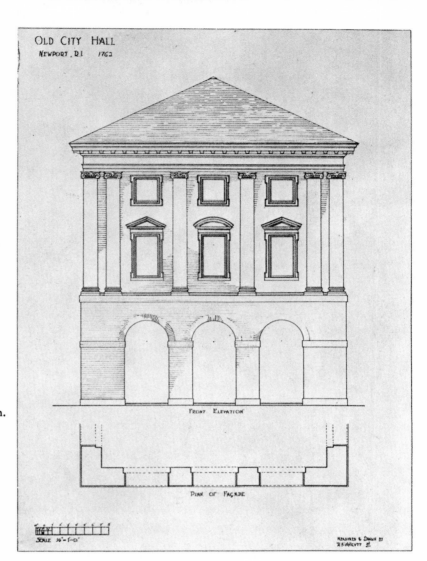

The Brick Market. Front elevation.
Measured by R. Kinnicutt.

Old Somerset House, London. Inigo Jones. From Colin Campbell,
The Vitruvius Britannicus, 1727.

Touro Synagogue, Touro Street. Detail of portico. Peter Harrison, 1763.
Photo, Meservey.

Touro Synagogue. Interior.
Photo, Meservey.

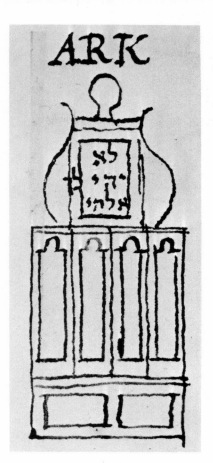

Touro Synagogue. Interior, detail showing the present Ark of the Covenant. Installed before the Revolution? *Photo, Bergner.*

Ezra Stiles' sketch of the Ark on the margin of his diary for December 2, 1763. *Courtesy of Yale University Library.*

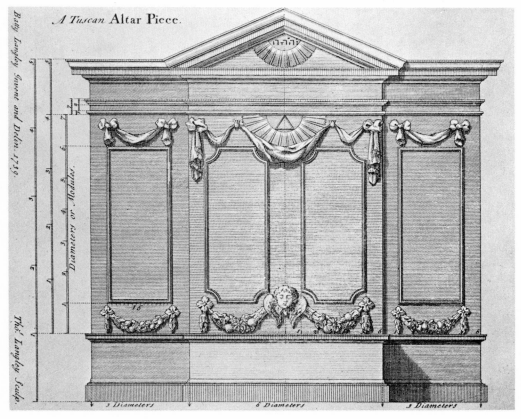

Batty Langley, *Treasury of Designs,* 1750, Pl. 35. Model for the lower part of the Ark of the Covenant as now executed.

James Gibbs, *Rules for Drawing*, 1732. Pl.
XXXV. Model for the system of super-
imposed orders for the Synagogue.
Providence Public Library.

Rules for Drawing. Pl. XVII. Model for
the gallery balusters.

Rules for Drawing. Pl. XLVII. Model
for consoles of the door.

Customs Collector Charles Dudley House, Middletown. Peter Harrison?
About 1750. Demolished. Old photograph.
N.H.S.

Francis Malbone House, 392 Thames Street. Peter Harrison? About 1760.
Photo, Bergner.

John Banister country house. Formerly at Mile Corner. About 1756. Demolished after 1952. Parlors and staircase now in the Henry Francis du Pont Winterthur Museum.
Photo, Meservey.

William Vernon House, corner Clarke and Mary streets. Owned by William
Gibbs before 1708. Enlarged about 1760 by Metcalf Bowler. Peter Harrison?
Photo, Meservey.

Vernon House. Detail showing window
and rustication.
Photo, Meservey.

Vernon House. Stairs and hall. From Downing, *Early Homes of Rhode Island*.
Photo, LeBoeuf. R.I.S.D.

Vernon House. Stairs, detail.
Photo, Meservey.

Vernon House. Northwest parlor. The paneling, dating about 1760, conceals frescoes of Chinese subjects painted about 1740 directly on the old plastered walls. The paintings imitate japanning and painted leather wall decoration.
Photo, N.H.S.

Frescoes under the paneling in the northwest parlor.
Photo, N.H.S.

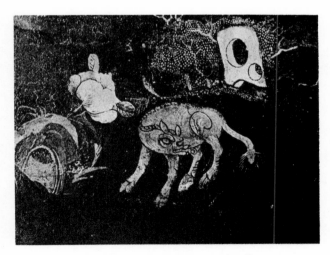

Northwest parlor. Fresco, detail.
Photo, N.H.S.

Peter Buliod House, 29 Touro Street. About 1755. Home of the Rhode Island Bank in 1795 and of Commodore Oliver Hazard Perry in 1818. House at far right was the home of Deputy Governor Josiah Lyndon after 1732. (Moved to 30 Edward Street and demolished since 1952.) Taken from a painting made before the Buliod House was altered.
N.H.S.

Captain John Mawdsley House, 228 Spring Street, 1760. Built in front, and
as part, of the Jireh Bull, Jr., House of 1680.
Photo, Meservey.

Southwest parlor, mantel wall. Measured by
P. G. Gulbranson, *American Architect and
Building News*, September 14, 1895.

Captain Mawdsley House. Southwest parlor, mantel wall.
Photo, Meservey.

Captain Mawdsley House. Southwest parlor, looking west.
Photo, Meservey.

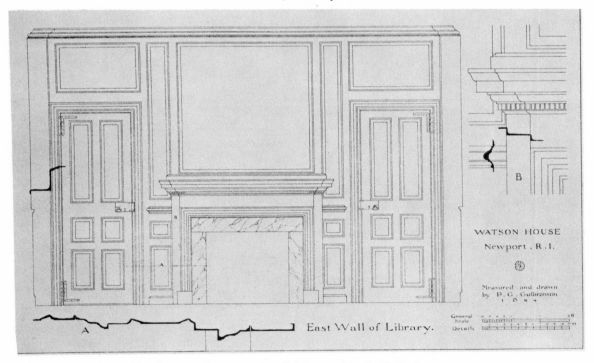

Northwest parlor, mantel wall. Measured by P. G. Gulbranson,
American Architect and Building News, September 14, 1895.

Captain Mawdsley House. Stairway.
Photo, Meservey.

The Wickham House, 32 Fair Street. About 1760. Demolished after 1952.
Photo, Meservey.

The Wickham House. Parlor mantel.
Photo, Meservey.

Pitt's Head Tavern, 5 Charles Street, in 1880. Built before 1726, enlarged by Ebenezer
Flagg about 1744. Originally on Washington Square. Moved to Bridge Street in 1965.
Stanhope photograph. C.C.

Pitt's Head Tavern. Doorway
during restoration of 1947.
Photo, Meservey.

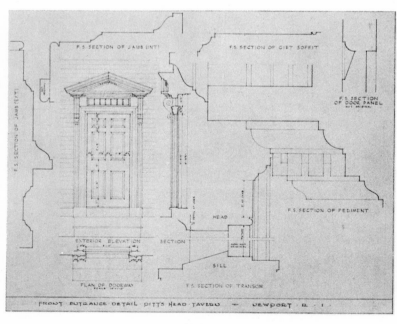

Door.
Measured by Robert Hill. P.S.N.C.

Captain John Warren House, 62 Washington Street. Built between
1736 and 1758, enlarged before 1775.
Photo, Meservey.

Captain Warren House. Dining room. Tiles from
William Redwood's Bridge Street house.
Photo, Meservey.

Captain William Finch House, 78 Washington Street. About 1770.
Photo, Covell.

Captain William Finch House. Mantel, northwest parlor.
Photo, Covell.

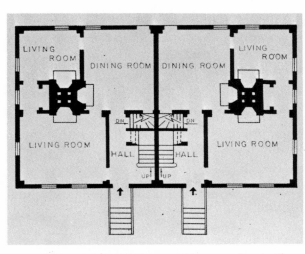

William and Joseph Cozzens House. 65 Farewell
Street. Known as the William Stevens House.
About 1765.
Plan by Warren Oakley.

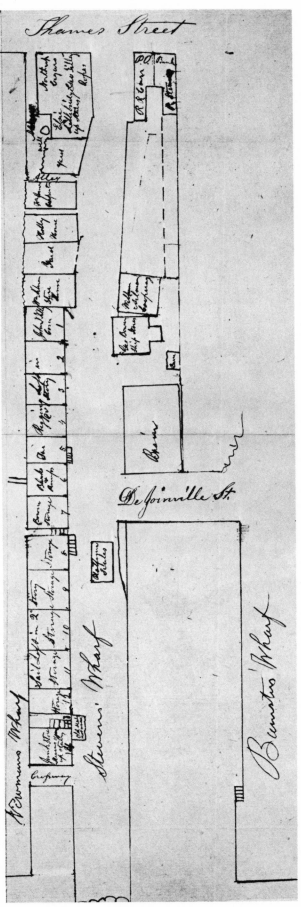

Plan of Bowen's (originally Stevens') Wharf,   [PL 125]
drawn by Arn Hildreth, who worked there
for sixty years as a block and pump maker.
Lent by George Piltz.

Old view down Bowen's Wharf.
C.C.

Bowen's Wharf in 1952. The shuttered building was the
Stevens ship chandler's store.
Photo, Meservey.

Robert Stevens' U-shaped double house, Bowen's Wharf
and Thames Street. About 1785? Rear view.
Photo, Meservey.

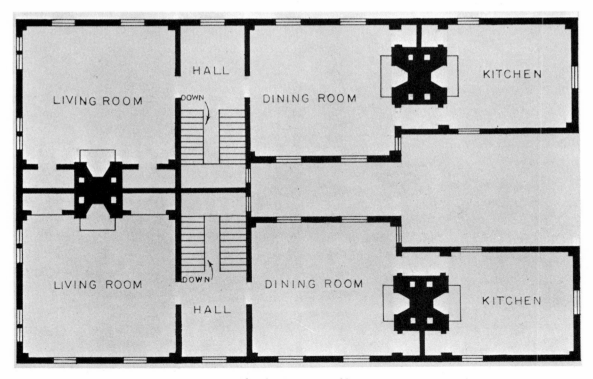

LIVING ROOM   HALL   DOWN   DINING ROOM   KITCHEN

LIVING ROOM   DOWN   HALL   DINING ROOM   KITCHEN

Plan by Warren Oakley.

Newport in 1818. Painting of Washington Square by a Hessian prisoner, showing, clock-wise, the Peter Buliod and Deputy Governor Josiah Lyndon (moved, demolished after 1952), houses, Philip Wanton's gambrel-roofed house, William Wanton's hip-roofed house, Isaac Gould's house (gambrel at left of the Brick Market). At right of Brick Market, the Job Lawton House (moved, demolished after 1952), the Charles Feke House, Pitt's Head Tavern (now on Bridge Street) with the adjoining Buttrick House, and the Mumford House.

The painting is owned by the Newport Bank.

Newport Jail, Marlborough Street. 1772. Before enlargement.
Stanhope photograph. C.C.

St. Paul's Methodist Church, Marlborough Street. 1806.
Photo, Meservey.

St. Paul's Methodist Church. Interior.
Photo, Arnold.

Mumford House, Washington Square. About 1796. Demolished, 1920.
Stanhope photograph. N.H.S.

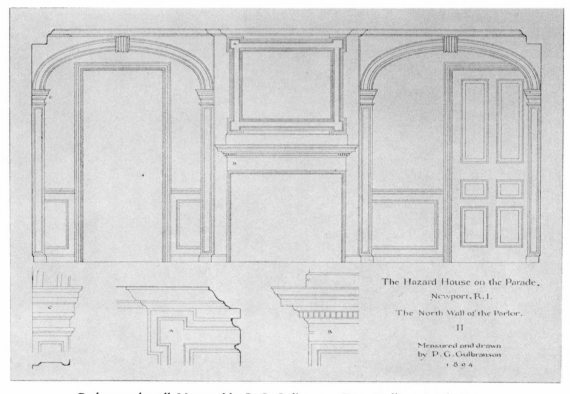

The Hazard House on the Parade.
Newport, R.I.
The North Wall of the Parlor.
II
Measured and drawn
by P. G. Gulbranson
1894

Parlor, north wall. Measured by P. G. Gulbranson. From William Rotch Ware,
The Georgian Period, Part 1, Pl. 23.

Vaucluse. Samuel Elam House, Portsmouth, 1803. Demolished.
Stanhope photograph. C.C.

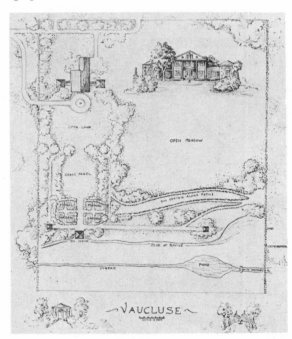

Elevation of house and plan of grounds. Re-
drawn from *Gardens of Colony and State*,
Garden Clubs of America, edited by
Alice G. B. Lockwood, 1931.

Bow window, from Charles Feke's Apothecary Shop, formerly Washington Square. This photograph shows it after it was moved to Dr. Johnson's shop between Marlborough Street and Washington Square.
C.C.

Bow window as now installed in the Newport Historical Society.
Photo, N.H.S.

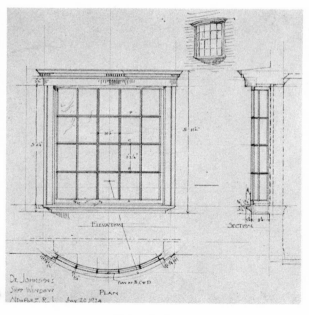

Bow window.
Measured drawing by Isham. N.H.S.

Robert Lawton House, 118 Mill Street. About 1809.
Photo, Meservey.

Samuel Whitehorne House, Thames and Dennison streets. 1804.
Photo, Meservey.

Christopher Fowler House, 29 Mary Street. 1800.
Photo, Meservey.

Mantelpiece in northwest parlor.
Photo, Meservey.

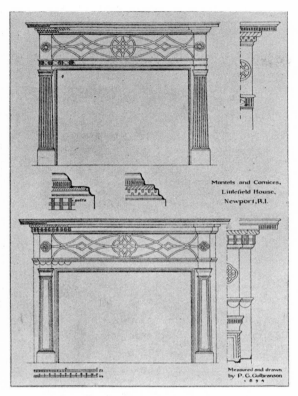

William Littlefield House, 12 High Street.
Mantels. Measured by P. G. Gulbranson.
From *American Architect and Building
News*, Vol. XV #1098.

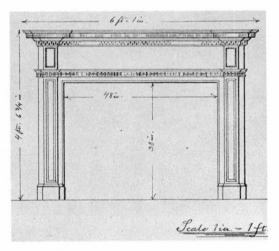

Clarke House, Washington Street.
Mantel. Demolished.
Measured by Bergner.

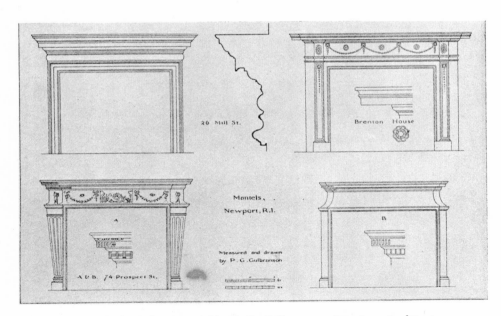

Newport mantels. Measured by P. G. Gulbranson, *American Architect
and Building News*, #117, Adv.

House built by Thomas Goddard between 1798 and 1802, 78 Church Street. Detail of west wall. *Photo, Meservey.*

Swinburne House, 80 John Street. Built by Isaac Peckham. About 1807. *Photo, Meservey.*

Underwood House, 66 John Street. Built by John Tompkins. About 1811.
Photo, Meservey.

William Card House, 73 Division Street. 1811.
Photo, Meservey.

House built by John Kerber after 1790, 199 Spring Street. Doorway.
Photo, Meservey.

Joseph and Robert Rogers House, 33 Touro Street. About 1790. Doorway.
Photo, Meservey.

Joseph Wood House, 27 Church Street. About 1810.
Doorway. Restored since 1952.
Photo, Meservey.

27 Church St.
Newport, R.I.

Measured and drawn
by P. G. Gulbranson
1894

Doorway. Measured by P. G. Gulbranson. From William Rotch
Ware, *The Georgian Period*, Part IX, Pl. 31.

Joseph Wood House. Detail of door. From Antoinette F. Downing,
Early Homes of Rhode Island.
Photo, LeBoeuf. R.I.S.D.

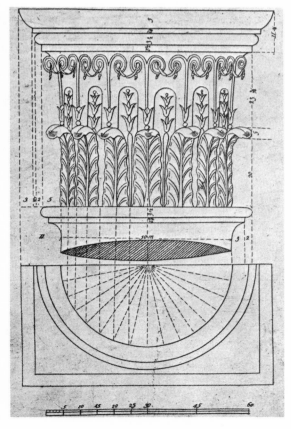

William Pain, *The Practical House Carpenter,*
1785. The Composite Order. Model for door
at 27 Church Street.

Captain John Mawdsley House, 228 Spring Street. Doorway.
Probably installed by Caleb Gardner about 1795.
Photo, Meservey.

Doorway. Measured by P. G. Gulbranson. From William Rotch Ware,
The Georgian Period, Part IX, Pl. 29.

Robert Stevens House, 31 Clarke Street. Door,
probably installed about 1800.
Photo, Arnold.

Samuel Hudson House, 23 Mary Street. About
1800. Doorway. Measured by P. G. Gulbranson.
From William Rotch Ware, *The Georgian Period*,
Part IX, Pl. 28. Demolished since 1952.

Billy Smith House, 7 Oak Street. About 1826. Doorway.
Moved from Broadway. Demolished after 1952.
Photo, Meservey.

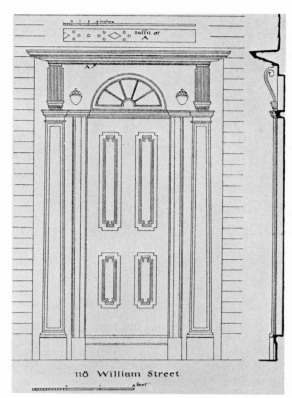

118 William Street. Door. Measured by P. G.
Gulbranson. From William Rotch Ware, *The
Georgian Period*, Part IX, Pl. 30. Demolished.

Rhode Island Union Bank Building, Thames Street.
Asher Benjamin, 1817. Demolished after 1952.
Old photograph.
N.H.S.

Rhode Island Union Bank Building. Central pavilion.
Photo, Meservey.

Fort Adams. Walls built in 1824 by Alexander McGregor under the supervision
of Major Joseph Totten, U.S. Army.
Photo, Eric M. Sanford.

Mill houses for Coddington Mill, Thames Street at Richmond Street.
About 1837. Demolished after 1952.
Photo, Meservey.

Zion Episcopal Church, Touro Street. Now Strand Theater.
Russell Warren, 1835. Old photograph.
C.C.

Levi Gale House. About 1834. Shown in its original location
at the head of Washington Square. Russell Warren.
Photo, Bergner.

Levi Gale House, as it appears today on Touro Street.
Now the Jewish Community Center.
Photo, Meservey.

Governor Van Zandt House, 70 Pelham Street. Built for Captain
Augustus Littlefield by John Ladd. About 1840.
Photo, Meservey.

Elmhyrst, William Vernon House, Mile Corner. Russell Warren,
about 1835. Attic story now removed.
Photo, Meservey.

Swinburne House, 115 Pelham Street. Before 1850.
Photo, Meservey.

House, 18 Mt. Vernon Street, built by John J. Allen about 1836.
Photo, Meservey.

Charles Sherman House (Judge Burke) House, 128 Mill Street. Before 1850.
Photo, Meservey.

William Spooner House, 11 Clay Street, before 1850. Once the home of
Royal Phelps Carroll. Now owned by Francis Flannery.
Photo, Meservey.

The Atlantic House. Formerly on Pelham Street near Bellevue Avenue.
About 1844. Partially demolished.
Lithograph by G. A. W. Endicott, N. Y. R.L.

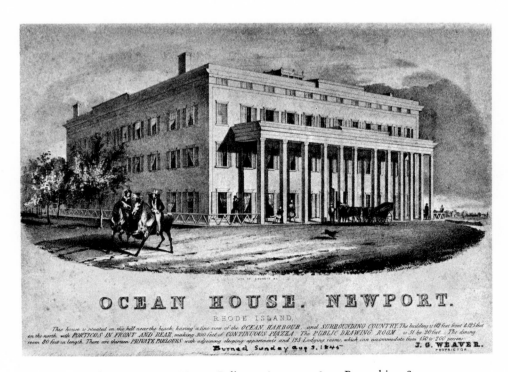

The First Ocean House, Bellevue Avenue, 1844. Burned in 1845.
Lithograph by G. A. W. Endicott, N. Y. N.H.S.

Second Baptist Church, North Baptist Street.
Russell Warren, 1834. Demolished. Old engraving.
N.H.S.

Second Ocean House, Bellevue Avenue. Russell Warren, 1845. Burned in 1898.
Stanhope photograph. C.C.

Second Ocean House. Detail of piazza.
Stereoscopic view by J. A. Williams. N.H.S.

Round House, Southwick's Grove, Middletown. Built by Christopher Southwick,
ship carpenter. About 1854. Demolished after 1952.
Photo, Meservey.

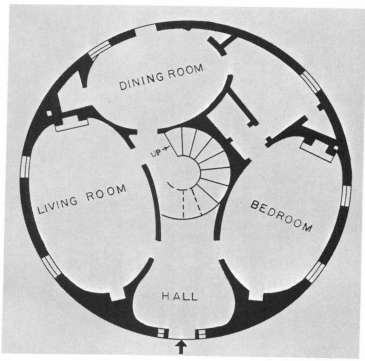

Round House. Plan.
Drawn by Warren Oakley.

Round House. Interior.
Photo, Meservey.

Benjamin Marsh House, School and Mary streets. 1845.
Stanhope photograph. C.C.

Andrew Jackson Downing, *Cottage Residences*,
Fig. 40. A cottage in the bracketed style, 1844.

Galvin House, 417 Spring Street. 1850–1860.
Moved from Fort Adams.
Photo, Meservey.

Kingscote, Bellevue Avenue at Bowery Street. Richard Upjohn. 1841.
Photo, Meservey.

Kingscote. Drawing by John P. Newell.
Courtesy of Mrs. E. Maitland Armstrong.

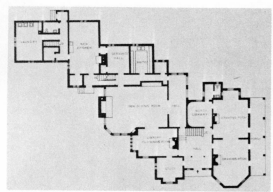

Kingscote. Plan of the first floor.
Drawn by Warren Oakley.

Kingscote. Hall, looking toward front door.
Photo, Meservey.

Kingscote. Living rooms.
Photo, Meservey.

Malbone, Malbone Road. Alexander Jackson Davis, architect. 1848–1849.
Photo, Wayne Andrews.

Malbone. From the *Knickerbocker Magazine*, 1859.

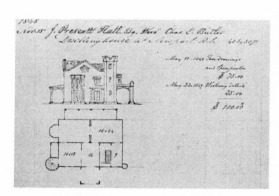

Malbone. Plan from the office book of
Alexander Jackson Davis in the
Metropolitan Museum of Art,
New York.

Edward King House, Spring Street. Now People's Library. Richard Upjohn. 1845–1847.
Photo, Meservey.

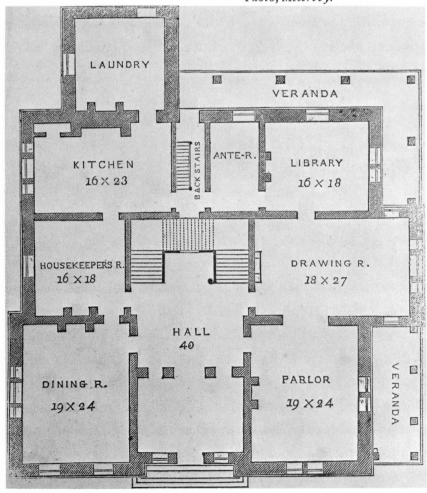

Edward King House. Plan. From Andrew Jackson Downing,
The Architecture of Country Houses, 1850.

Swanhurst, Bellevue Avenue. East side.
Built by Alexander McGregor in 1851.
Photo, Meservey.

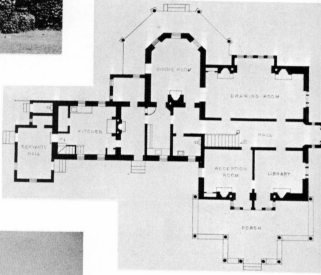

Swanhurst. Plan.
Drawn by Warren Oakley.

Swanhurst. West side.
Photo, Meservey.

Château-sur-Mer, Bellevue Avenue, Seth Bradford, 1851–1852.
Before alterations made in 1872.
Photo, Frank Childs.

Château-sur-Mer. Lithograph by John Collins. From *The City
and Scenery of Newport, Rhode Island,* 1857.

Charles H. Russell House, 1851–1852. Demolished. From
George Champlin Mason, *Newport and Its Cottages.*

Daniel Parrish House, Bellevue Avenue, 1851–1852. Calvert Vaux.
Burned in 1855. Rebuilt in 1856 from original plans.
Photo, Meservey.

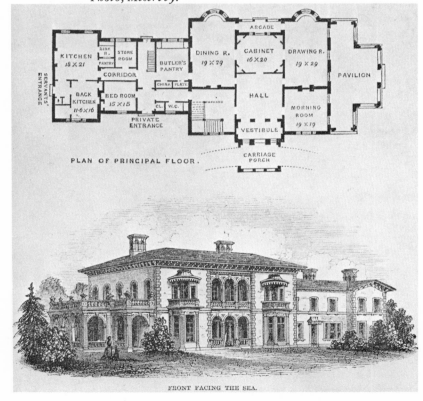

Daniel Parrish House. Plan and sea side. From Calvert Vaux,
Villas and Cottages, 1855.

Beaulieu, Bellevue Avenue. Built by the Peruvian Ambassador,
de Berreda. Entrance. 1856–1859.
Photo, Meservey.

Beaulieu. Sea side.
Photo, Meservey.

Beaulieu. Plan.
Drawn by Warren Oakley.

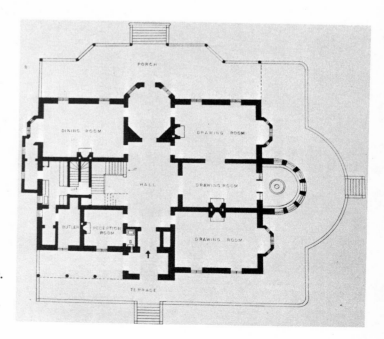

All Saints Chapel, Church Street, 1852. Demolished.
Stanhope photograph.

The Chalet, Hamilton Avenue. Leopold Eidlitz. 1854.
Photo, Meservey.

The Chalet. Elevation. From Bullock,
American Cottage Builder, 1854.

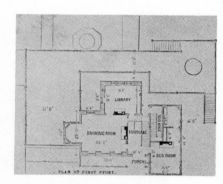

The Chalet. Plan. From John
Bullock, *American Cottage
Builder*, 1854.

Chalet at Bailey's Beach. About 1855–1860.
Stanhope photograph. C.C.

Hamilton Hoppin House, Miantonomi Avenue. Richard Upjohn.
1856–1857.
Photo, Meservey.

Hamilton Hoppin House. Looking across hall into library.
Photo, Meservey.

Alexander Van Rensselaer House, Miantonomi Avenue. 1857–1858. Demolished after 1952. *Stanhope photograph. C.C.*

Charles Fearing House, 1853. Demolished. From George Mason, *Newport and Its Cottages.*

Fairbourne, Bellevue Avenue, 1853–1854. Demolished. From George Mason, *Newport and Its Cottages.*

Edgewater, J. Frederick Kernochan House, 1864. Demolished. From George Mason, *Newport and Its Cottages.*

Winan's first Bleak House, Ocean Drive. About 1865. Razed in 1894. *Stanhope photograph. C.C.*

Ogden Mills House, Bellevue Avenue. William R. Walker, architect, 1866. *Photo, Meservey.*

Sea View Cottages on the Cliffs, 1870.
Stanhope photograph. C.C.

Navy Houses, Goat Island, 1871.
Photo, Meservey.

Showandasee, Train Villa, Bellevue Avenue. 1869.
Stanhope photograph. C.C.

J. N. A. Griswold House, Bellevue Avenue. Richard Morris Hunt, 1862–1863.
Photo, Meservey.

J. N. A. Griswold House. Interior.
Photo, Meservey.

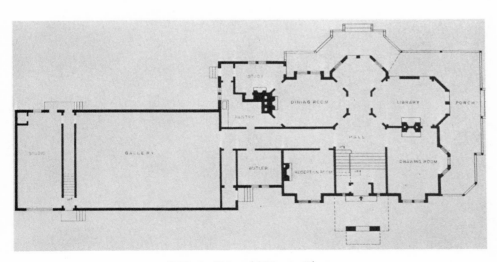

J. N. A. Griswold House. Plan.
Drawing by Warren Oakley.

M. H. Sanford House, 72 Washington Street. Now W. King Covell. 1870.
Stanhope photograph. C.C.

M. H. Sanford House. Hall.
Photo, Covell.

Thayer Cottage, Bellevue Avenue at Wheatland Avenue.
About 1870.
Photo, Meservey.

Thomas Cushing House, Bellevue Avenue. 1870. From
George Champlin Mason, *Newport and Its Cottages*.

Nathan Matthews House, 1871–1872. Burned 1881.
From *The Architectural Sketchbook*, 1873–1876.
Ed. Portfolio Club, Boston.

Mrs. Loring Andrews House, 1872. Demolished.
From Mason, *Newport and Its Cottages*.

Thomas Cushing and Ogden Mills houses.
Stanhope photograph. C.C.

George Champlin Mason's House, 31 Old-Beach Road.
George Champlin Mason, 1873–1874.
Photo, Meservey.

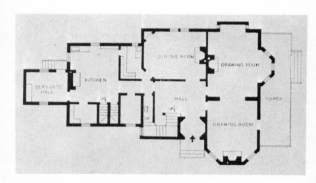

George Champlin Mason's House. Plan.
Drawn by Warren Oakley.

George Champlin Mason's House. Detail of façade.
Photo, Meservey.

Jacob Cram House, Middletown. Dudley Newton, 1871–1872. Derelict in 1965.
Photo, Meservey.

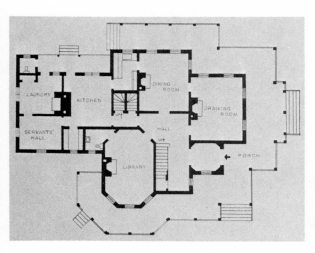

Jacob Cram House. Plan.
Drawn by Warren Oakley.

Jacob Cram House. Detail of piazza.
Photo, Meservey.

Gas Company façade, Thames Street.
Dudley Newton, 1874. Now altered.
Photo, Arnold.

Colonel George Waring House, moved from the site of the Viking hotel to Catherine and
Greenough streets. Richard Morris Hunt's own house. 1870–1871.
Photo, Wayne Andrews.

Samuel Pratt House, Bellevue Avenue. 1871. From a
stereoscopic view taken about 1875.
N.H.S.

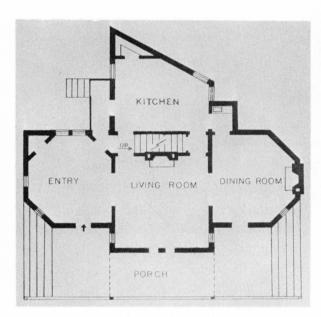

Samuel Pratt House. Plan.
Drawn by Warren Oakley.

Travers Block, Bellevue Avenue at Bath Road.
Richard Morris Hunt. About 1875.
Stanhope photograph. C.C.

Linden Gate, Henry F. Marquand House, Rhode Island Avenue.
Richard Morris Hunt. 1872.
Photo, Wayne Andrews.

T. G. Appleton House. Richard Morris Hunt.
1875–1876. Demolished. From George
Champlin Mason, *Newport and
Its Cottages.*

Professor Shields' House. Richard Morris Hunt. 1883.
From an old photograph.
S.P.N.E.A.

Château-sur-Mer. William S. Wetmore House, Bellevue Avenue.
Enlarged by Richard Morris Hunt, 1872.
Photo, Meservey.

Château-sur-Mer. Library.
Photo, Meservey.

Château-sur-Mer. Hall.
Photo, Meservey.

George Fearing House, Narragansett Avenue. 1871–1872. From
George Champlin Mason, *Newport and Its Cottages*.

Red Cross, C. J. Peterson House. About 1872. Demolished.
From Mason, *Newport and Its Cottages*.

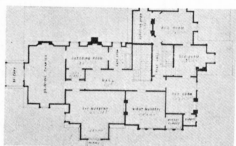
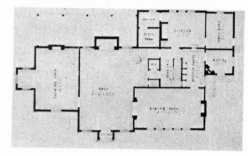

Elevation (Houghton Library, Harvard). Plans.
From Henry Russell Hitchcock, *H. H. Richardson and His Times.*
Richard Codman Project. By Henry H. Richardson, 1869.

F. W. Andrews House. H. H. Richardson, 1872. Architect's drawing.
From Hitchcock, *H. H. Richardson and His Times.*

Watts Sherman House, Shepard Avenue. H. H. Richardson and
Stanford White. 1874. Before Dudley Newton's addition.
Photo, Frank Childs.

Watts Sherman House. Drawing by Stanford White in
The New York Sketch Book of Architecture, 1875.

Watts Sherman House.
Photo, Meservey.

Watts Sherman House.
Photo, Meservey.

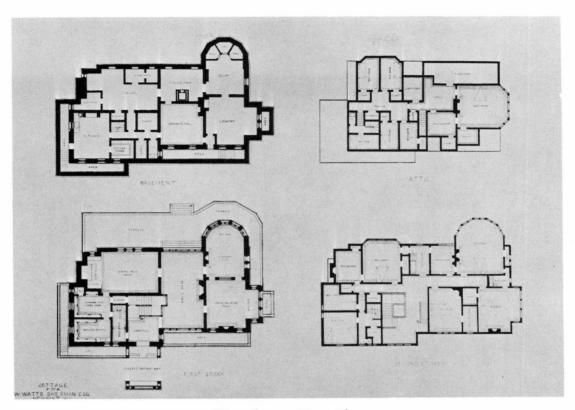

Watts Sherman House. Plans.

Watts Sherman House. White's drawing of entrance and hall.
From *The New York Sketch Book of Architecture*, 1875.

Watts Sherman House. Stairs.
Photo, Covell.

Hall, looking east toward LaFarge windows.
Photo, Covell.

Hall.
Photo, Covell.

Watts Sherman House. Library.
Photo, Meservey.

Thomas Robinson House, 64 Washington Street.
Fireplace wall by Charles Follen McKim. 1872.
Photo, Meservey.

Dennis House, 65 Poplar Street. Now St. John's Rectory.
Living hall by Charles Follen McKim. 1876.
Photo, Meservey.

Bishop (then Dean) Berkeley House. From *The New York Sketch Book of Architecture*, 1874.

Frederick Sheldon House. About 1875. Demolished. From George Champlin Mason, *Newport and Its Cottages*.

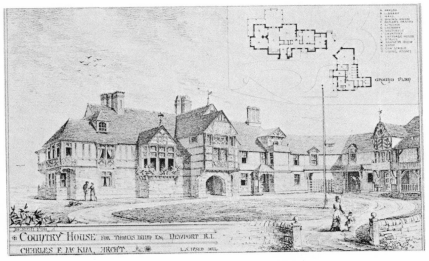

McKim's projected drawing and plan for the Thomas Dunn House (never built). From *American Architect and Building News*, July, 1877.

C. H. Baldwin (Prescott Lawrence) House, Bellevue Avenue.
Potter and Robinson. 1877–1878.
Photo, Meservey.

C. H. Baldwin House. Interior, looking across hall.
Photo, Meservey.

Looking into turret.
Photo, Meservey.

C. H. Baldwin House. Plan.
Drawn by Warren Oakley.

Château-Nooga, C. C. Baldwin House, Bellevue Avenue. George Post. 1880–1881.
Photo, Meservey.

The Breakers. Pierre Lorillard, Ochre Point. Peabody and Stearns.
1877–1878. From an old photograph.
R.L.

The Breakers. Playhouse.
Photo, Covell.

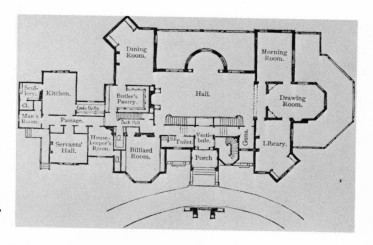

The Breakers. Plan. From George C. Sheldon,
Artistic Country Seats.

Barn of the Fairchild Estate, Second Street at Cherry.
Charles Follen McKim. About 1878.
Photo, Covell.

Casino façade on Bellevue Avenue. McKim, Mead and White.
1880–1881. Stanhope photograph.
N.H.S.

Casino courtyard showing clock tower.
Stanhope photograph. C.C.

Casino. Piazza. From a stereoscopic view.
N.H.S.

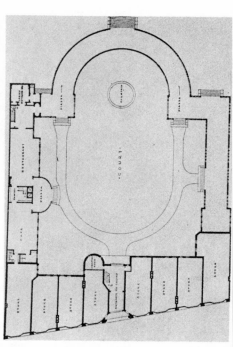

Casino. Plan. From *A Monograph of the Work of McKim, Mead and White*, Architectural Book Publishing Company.

Casino. Piazza. From a stereoscopic view.
N.H.S.

Casino. Billiard room.
Stanhope photograph. C.C.

Casino. Theatre interior.
Stanhope photograph. C.C.

Casino. Detail, theatre piazza rail.
Stanhope photograph. C.C.

Casino. Detail, theatre piazza rail.
Photo, Meservey.

Kingscote. Stanford White. 1880–1881. Dining room.
Photo, Meservey.

Kingscote. Dining room.
Photo, Meservey.

Samuel Tilton (now Louis Hobbs) House. McKim, Mead and White, 1881–1882.
Photo, Meservey.

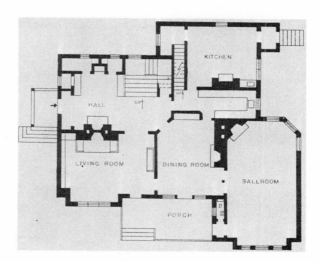

Tilton House. Plan.
Drawn by Warren Oakley.

Tilton House. Hall.
Photo, Meservey.

Living room.
Photo, Meservey.

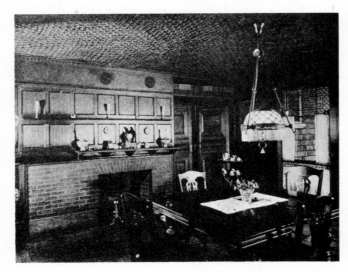

Dining room.
Photo, Meservey.

Southside, Robert Goelet House, Narragansett Avenue. From the sea side.
McKim, Mead and White. 1882–1883.
Stanhope photograph. N.H.S.

Southside.
Photo, Wayne Andrews.

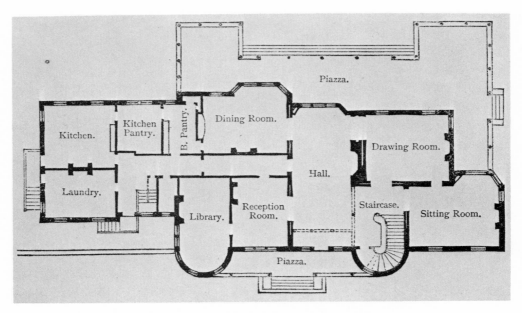

Southside. Plan. From George C. Sheldon, *Artistic Country Seats.*

Southside. Hall fireplace.
Photo, Meservey.

Edna Villa, Isaac Bell House, Bellevue Avenue. McKim, Mead and White. 1882–1883.
Photo, Meservey.

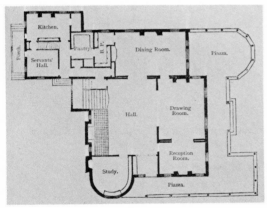

Isaac Bell House. Plan. From George C.
Sheldon, *Artistic Country Seats.*

Isaac Bell House. Looking across hall
to fireplace and stairs.
Photo, Meservey.

Isaac Bell House. Interior. From *The Century
Magazine*, May, 1886.

Samuel Coleman House, 7 Red Cross Avenue.
McKim, Mead and White. 1882–1883.
Stanhope photograph. C.C.

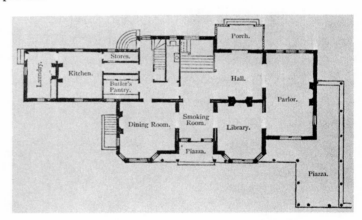

Samuel Coleman House. Plan. From George C. Sheldon,
Artistic Country Seats.

Samuel Coleman House. From *The Century Magazine*, June, 1886.

Lyman C. Josephs House, Middletown. Clarence Luce. 1882–1883.
Photo, Meservey.

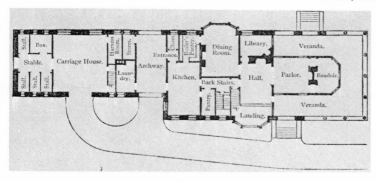

Lyman C. Josephs House. Plan. From George C. Sheldon,
Artistic Country Seats.

Indian Spring. Busk House, Ocean Drive.
Richard Morris Hunt. 1891.
Stanhope photograph. C.C.

Pavilion at Easton's Beach.
Stanhope photograph. C.C.

Bay View Hotel, Jamestown.
About 1885.
Stanhope photograph. C.C.

Flower shop, Bellevue Avenue.
About 1883. Old photograph.
S.P.N.E.A.

Skinner House, Red Cross Avenue. McKim, Mead and White, 1882.
Old photograph.
S.P.N.E.A.

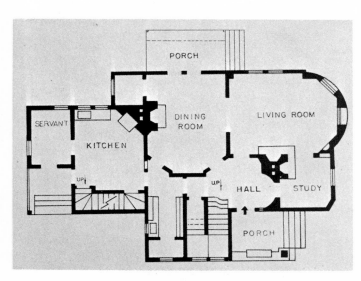

Skinner House. Plan.
Drawn by Warren Oakley.

Judge Bookstaver House, Purgatory Road, Middletown. J. D. Johnston. 1885.
Photo, Meservey.

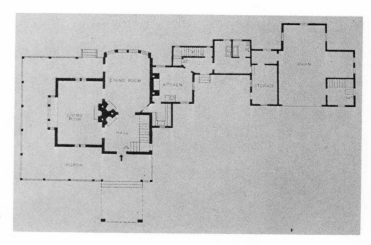

Judge Bookstaver House. Plan.
Drawn by Warren Oakley.

Land Trust cottages, Easton's Beach, Middletown. 1887–1888.
Stanhope photograph. C.C.

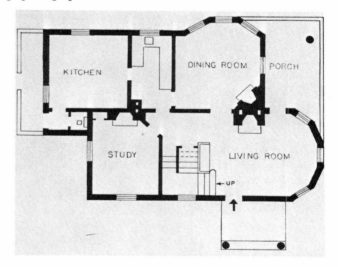

Land Trust cottages. Plan of the Rough House.
Drawn by Warren Oakley.

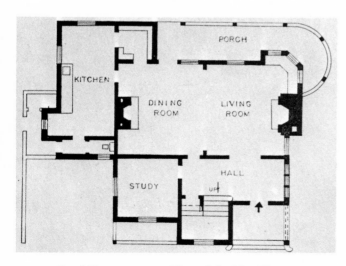

Land Trust cottages. Plan of the May House.
Drawn by Warren Oakley.

Commodore William Edgar House, Sunnyside Place. McKim, Mead and White.
1885–1886. From the original drawing for *The Century Magazine*, July, 1886.

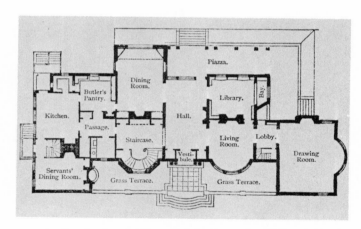

Commodore William Edgar House. Plan. From
George C. Sheldon, *Artistic Country Seats*.

H. A. C. Taylor House, Annandale Road. McKim, Mead
and White. 1885–1886. Demolished after 1952.
Photo, Meservey.

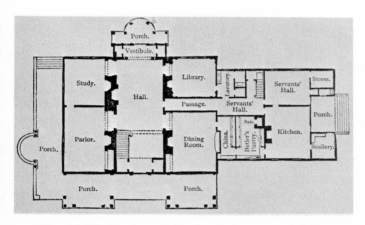

H. A. C. Taylor House. Plan. From George C. Sheldon,
Artistic Country Seats.

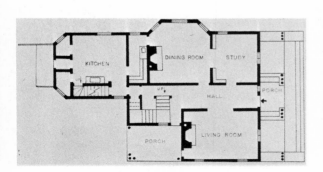

Conover House. Plan.
Drawn by Warren Oakley.

Conover House, Indian Avenue, Middletown.
Clarence Luce. 1888.
Photo, Meservey.

Gordon King House, Harrison Avenue. McKim, Mead
and White. 1887–1888.
Photo, Meservey.

Althorpe, Spencer House, Ruggles Avenue. 1889–1890.
Stanhope photograph. C.C.

Beacon Rock, Edwin D. Morgan House, Beacon Hill Road.
McKim, Mead and White. 1890–1891.
Stanhope photograph. C.C.

Beacon Rock. Closer view.
Stanhope photograph. C.C.

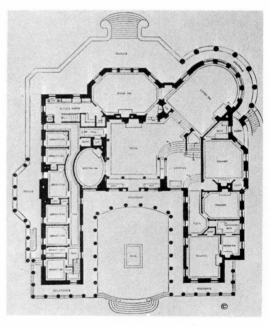

Beacon Rock. Plan. From *A Monograph of
the Work of McKim, Mead and White,*
Architectural Book Publishing
Company.

Bancroft House, Tuckerman Avenue, Middletown. 1893.
Detail of entrance.
Photo, Meservey.

Dudley Newton House, Kay and Everett streets. Dudley Newton. 1897.
Photo, Meservey.

Ochre Court, Ochre Point Avenue. Richard Morris Hunt. 1888–1891.
Photo, Wayne Andrews.

Ochre Court. Hall. Detail.
Photo, Meservey.

Ochre Court. Hall.
Photo, Meservey.

Marble House, Bellevue Avenue. Richard Morris Hunt. 1892.
Photo, Meservey.

The Breakers, Cornelius Vanderbilt House. Ochre Point Avenue. Sea side.
Richard Morris Hunt. 1892–1895.
Photo, Meservey.

The Breakers. Detail. Sea side loggia.
Photo, Meservey.

The Breakers. Hall.
Photo, Meservey.

The Breakers. Grand staircase.
Photo, Meservey.

The Breakers. State dining room.
Photo, Meservey.

The Breakers. Billiard room.
Photo, Meservey.

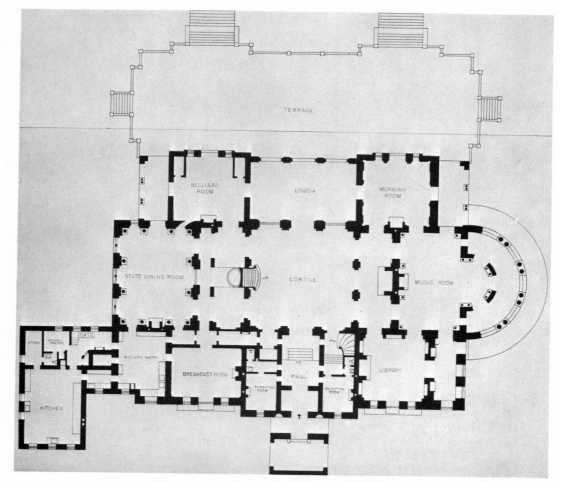

The Breakers. Plan. *Drawn by Warren Oakley.*

Belcourt, O. H. P. Belmont House, Bellevue Avenue. Richard Morris Hunt. 1892.
Photo, Meservey.

Belcourt. Ballroom.
Photo, Meservey.

Crossways, Stuyvesant Fish House, Ocean Avenue. McKim, Mead and White. 1898.
Photo, Meservey.

The Elms, Edwin Berwind House, Bellevue Avenue. Horace Trumbauer, 1901.
Garden side. Modeled after Mansard's Château d'Agnès at Asnières near Paris.
Photo, Meservey.

The Elms. Formal garden.
Photo, Meservey.

Vernon Court, Richard Gambrill House, Bellevue Avenue.
A. J. Hastings of Carrère and Hastings. 1901.
Photo, Meservey.

Vernon Court. Garden. Copied from Henry VIII's garden
for Anne Boleyn, Hampton Court.
Photo, Meservey.

Rosecliff, J. Edgar Monroe House, Bellevue Avenue.
McKim, Mead and White. 1901–1902.
Photo, Meservey.

1 SECTION "FF" LOOKING TOWARDS SALON 7

Rosecliff. Architect's drawing of the staircase.
New-York Historical Society.

Miramar, A. Hamilton Rice House, Bellevue Avenue. Horace Trumbauer. 1914.
Photo, Wayne Andrews.

Maxim Karolik House, Bellevue Avenue. Ogden Codman. 1910.
Photo, Wayne Andrews.

John Russell Pope's own house. Ledge Road. 1927.
Photo, Meservey.

Jerome Borden House, Ocean Drive. Looking across hall. Swift and Angell. 1917.
Photo, Covell.

Jerome Borden House. Sea side.
Photo, Meservey.

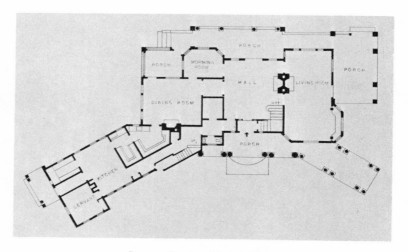

Jerome Borden House. Plan.
Drawn by Warren Oakley.

APPENDICES

a

APPENDIX A

Detailed Histories and Descriptions of Buildings

SOME SEVENTEENTH-CENTURY BUILDINGS

b   *Whitehorse Tavern.* The venerable Whitehorse Tavern on the northwest corner of Farewell and Marlborough streets has been in the Nichols family since 1700. Its story begins, however, with the days when William Coddington's sons and daughters were breaking up his original "six acre plot," granted in 1639, and selling it off in lots.

Pl. 37

    The land records show that the old part of the building, which is a two-room, two-story house with huge framing timbers and the remains of a central, pilastered brick chimney, was probably built before 1673. In that year William Mayes bought of Francis Brinley, who was Ann (Brinley) Coddington's brother, "one quarter of an Acre . . . now fenced with Pailes with the hous and housing," land which had been the southeast corner of William Coddington's garden lot.

    William Mayes died in 1692. His gravestone is illustrated in Erich A. O'D. Taylor's *Gravestones of Newport*, but Mr. Taylor has apparently confused him with his son William Mayes, Jr., who was the notorious pirate Lord Bellomont had set about to bring to trial in 1699. Mayes' return from pirating in the Red Seas "with vast wealth" had been an eagerly awaited event in Newport that year and Newport citizens showed no desire to help Lord Bellomont catch his man. Mayes therefore managed successfully to die unhanged.

    The house evidently became an inn before the Nichols family acquired it, for Mayes, Sr., had been granted a license to keep a tavern as early as 1687. In 1702 William Mayes the younger was granted a license to sell "all sorts of Strong Drink." In 1698 Mary, the sister of Mayes, Jr., married Robert Nichols, a descendant of Thomas Nichols, who had come from Wales via the Barbados in about 1650 to settle in Portsmouth on the farm now known as Overing's or the Page farm. Through this marriage, the Mayes house in Newport came into the possession of the Nichols family, who continued to own it, with the exception of a single year, for over two hundred years. The Robert Nichols family continued to keep the tavern. By 1708 the Town Council was "sitting at the house of Robert Nichols," and town records show that the cost of the Council dinners prepared by Nichols came out of the Town Treasury from 1708 to 1712. Mary Nichols kept the tavern after her husband's death, until their son, Mayes, took over in 1716.

c   In 1730 Jonathan Nichols, II, innholder, merchant, and later lieutenant-governor, who also owned and perhaps built the beautiful Hunter house at 54 Washington Street, bought the Farewell Street house. It was he who first hung out the sign of the Whitehorse. During the ensuing years the old building became so much a center of the town's affairs that when the new Colony House was being planned, the question arose as to whether it should not be built facing Whitehorse Tavern rather than the bay. While the Colony House was under construction, the General Assembly met at "Jonathan Nichols Inn," as did also a Criminal Court.

    After Nichols' death in 1754, his son Jonathan, III undertook to run the tavern. The *Mercury* of the sixties and seventies carries frequent references to the house as a place of meeting under the proprietorship first of Jonathan and then of Benjamin Nichols.

433

A letter in the Newport Historical Society written by Miss Matilda Nichols, tells that when the British soldiers arrived in Newport in 1777 and proposed to take over some of the rooms, her grandfather, Walter Nichols, the then incumbent of the house, replied to the officer who had made the demand: "Take it all, sir, take it all. Do you think I would permit my family to live under the same roof with British soldiers?" Whereupon he moved his family out of town for the three years of the British occupation. When Nichols returned to Newport in 1780, he made extensive changes in the house, put on the present broad gambrel roof, and later added the ell at the northeast corner. In 1782 he reopened the tavern under its old name.

Walter Nichols was a cabinetmaker. He and his son Joshua, apprenticed to him, were noted especially for making fine mahogany cases for tall family clocks. Miss Nichols' account says that he built the early nineteenth-century house which still stands next west of the Whitehorse Tavern for his own use as a cabinetmaker's shop. His grandson, William Nichols, who was a silversmith, also used the building for his shop.

Whitehorse Tavern remained in the possession of the family until 1901. No building could be more characteristic of colonial Newport or more palpably a part of its early history. Its gambrel roof, plain pedimented doors, and clapboarded walls that rise from the sidewalk's edge come straight from Newport's eighteenth-century past. Its seventeenth-century construction is somewhat concealed by additions, but its great chamfered girts and summer beams, its pilastered brick chimney, and its stairway butted against the chimney in the narrow front hall facing Farewell Street still take the visitor back to the days when William Mayes, Sr. bought the house from the Coddington family. It is shabby and neglected now, but it once played its part as that center of town life, the colonial tavern, and as the home of pirate, governor, patriot, innkeeper, cabinetmaker, and silversmith.

d

Abstract of deeds, Survey Notebooks.
Matilda Nichols, Whitehorse Tavern and the Nichols Family, Manuscript, Newport Historical Society.

Pl. 38
The Jireh Bull House. The old house which stands at 228 Spring Street has, because of its various owners, been known as the Mawdsley, Gardner, Watson, or Pitman house. From the outside, it looks like a typical mid-eighteenth-century dwelling, the home of some rich merchant, but the back half is a complete two-story two-room seventeenth-century house. Captain John Mawdsley, who bought the property probably very soon after his marriage in 1747, built an eighteenth-century addition a few steps lower down and in front of the early dwelling. He tied the two houses together under a Newport gable-on-hip roof so successfully that the seventeenth-century house was forgotten and was only rediscovered some twenty years ago.

The land deeds show that the early dwelling stood on property Benedict Arnold had bought after he came to Newport in 1654. In his will dated 1677, he gave his daughter, Godsgift, "that house and two acres of land that I bought of William Haviland . . . bounded on ye south and on ye east . . . by land . . . in the possession of Thomas Clifton." In 1680 Godsgift married Jireh Bull of South Kingstown, who was the son of Henry Bull, Newport's first sergeant and original settler, and the pair came to live in Godsgift's Newport house. In time it came into the possession of Ozias and Theodosia (Bull) Pitkin, who owned it from the 1730's and who soon began to divide their whole property into smaller lots. The deed for Mawdsley's purchase has not been found, but he probably bought his house and lot, the original homestead, directly from the Pitkins.

The original part of the house has a very heavy exposed and beautifully chamfered frame, complete with great summer beams in each room, which run perpendicular to the old chimney. This chimney, now removed, was probably built of stone, and stood, as Isham's restored plan shows, in the present back hallway between the two seventeenth-century rooms. The first steep stairway has also been removed, but the framing of the house is enough to indicate mansion-sized dimensions, probably too large to be the house that Benedict Arnold had bought of Haviland in 1654. It is more likely that Godsgift and Jireh built a new house on the same land soon after their marriage.

Abstract of deeds, Survey Notebooks.
Updike, *History of the Narragansett Church*, account of Henry and Jireh Bull. I, 519.
Henry Bull, IV, "The Bull Family in Newport," *Newport Historical Society Bulletin*, no. 81 (Newport, October, 1931).

Wanton-Lyman-Hazard House. The house at 17 Broadway is known as the Wanton-Lyman-Hazard house because of its successive later owners, the Wantons, Lymans, and Hazards. Its early history has until recently been unknown. But thanks to a newly found note in a Town Meeting record, we know now that Stephen Mumford probably built it just before 1700. In style it belongs to that phase of colonial architecture when baroque ideals were just beginning to supplant the old Gothic conception of building and when the seventeenth-century massive construction was occasionally being masked by molded and paneled work of archaic heavy scale. A two-story house, covered with a steeply pitched roof, as it was originally built, it had a typical Massachusetts and Newport ground plan of a single room on either side of a central chimney. This chimney was constructed of brick, not stone, but its pilastered top, mammoth size, and fireplaces with coves and rounded walls are typical of earliest Rhode Island practice. It rises from long stone cellar piers tied together by a brick vault, a form of construction in common use in Newport until 1750 or later.

The steeply pitched roof was kicked out across the front to take a huge plaster coved cornice of the kind shown in Moxon's *Mechanic Exercises*, published in London in 1698. A careful study of the roof framing has shown that this cove, an attempt at a classic cornice, was evidently part of the original construction.

In the interior evidence of changing style is equally apparent. The stairway, built against the chimney in three runs, is luxurious in comparison with the ladder-like steepness of other seventeenth-century stairs. Its Jacobean flavor is revealed by the closed string course ornamented with huge run moldings of cyma profile, by the squat and widely spaced turned balusters, and by the use of half balusters butted against the square posts. In common with early detail, the straight hand rail is molded only on the outer face, and butts directly into the posts, while the hand-turned newel caps are small and the drops are acorn-shaped. Another such stairway may be seen in the half of the old Taggart house now standing on Third Beach Road.

The framework in the Hazard house was originally all exposed in the interior, and the north chamber has been restored to show the chamfered ceiling beams and massive gunstock corner posts, sturdily braced. The vertical boarding of the sheathed walls is painted to imitate paneling, and is marbled in a kind of feather treatment in a color scheme of dull red and gray. Some early owner had decorated his wall in the newer style, an indication that the old seventeenth-century wide sheathing, tongued and grooved together, and then painted red, if at all, had gone out of fashion.

The walls of the kitchen lean-to (which had been built in the early eighteenth century) were painted in a diamond crossbar pattern in red on a dark ground. The back stair hall of Augustus Lucas' house at 40 Division Street has a similar diamond design. Such wall decoration is of early eighteenth-century date, interesting because so few examples have survived.

The present pedimented front door, the sash windows, and the mantel paneling are all the result of eighteenth-century additions, but the old house, with its massive seventeenth-century construction and its faint suggestion of Jacobean finish, is a fine example of our late medieval building.

Pls. 29–37,
101, 102

Pls. 29, 31

Pls. 34, 35

Pl. 37

The first historical mention of the house itself is in a deed dated 1721, when it was owned by Stephen Mumford. Among the papers in the State Archives, however, is the record of the Town Meeting for July 31, 1700, which reads: "The Comity haveing viewed the goodly building of Mr. Stephen Mumford on the lots granted him by the proprietors acts do agree no imposition should be imposed on him as to any further building or failure in not building so fully on both lots according to the acts and orders of building. . . ." As in other New England towns, the Newport proprietors had made regulations to insure the quality of buildings erected, and it seems safe to assume that the house Stephen Mumford owned in 1721 is the "goodly building" that had satisfied the demands of the "Comity" twenty years earlier.

In 1724 Mumford sold his house to Richard Ward, who later became Governor of the Colony. We do not know when Ward sold it, but Samuel Marryatt, tailor, owned it before 1749, the year he sold it to William Earl. In 1765, Martin Howard, Jr., bitter and outspoken author of the pro-British diatribe, *A Letter from a Gentleman at Halifax*, and friend of Dr. Moffatt and of the Stamp Master Augustus Johnston, was living in the house. By his own account he had refinished it at some expense. It was he who was probably responsible in 1750 or 1760 for the installation of the paneling in the south parlor and the chamber above. The parlor paneling resembles that of Metcalf Bowler's country house, now in the Metropolitan Museum in New York, and also the paneling in the dining room of the Dennis house, now St. John's Rectory, 65 Poplar Street.

Pls. 101, 102
Pl. 103
Pl. 102

When word reached Newport of the passage of the Stamp Act in August, 1765, an angry mob collected in front of the Colony House to hang in effigy three Tories: Howard, Moffatt, and Johnston. The mob first attacked Howard's house where they smashed doors, windows, the interiors, and the furnishings. Moffatt's house suffered a similar onslaught, but Johnston's house, which still stands on Division Street, survived almost unharmed. Moffatt and Howard made their escape to the British sloop of war, the "Cygnet," lying at anchor in the harbor, and never returned to Newport. A month later John Wanton bought Howard's house at public auction. He made the necessary repairs, which may have included the installation of the pedimented front door.

John Wanton's daughter was the Polly Wanton who captivated the French officers during their Newport sojourn in 1780–1781. A window pane taken from the house bears the words "charming Polly Wanton," which a young Frenchman is supposed to have scratched with his diamond ring. It may still be seen in the Historical Society. In 1781 Polly married young Daniel Lyman, a major in General Heath's army, and her father gave them the house. Their daughter, Harriet Lyman, married Benjamin Hazard, and the house remained in the Hazard family until it was purchased by the Newport Historical Society in 1927.

The building was restored in the same year by Norman Isham in such a way as to save as many interesting architectural features of the several periods as possible. It is necessary, therefore, to open the fireplace cupboard doors in order to discern the great seventeenth-century brick fireplaces, with their rounded side walls, and the curve of the seventeenth-century cove between mantel tree and chimney girt, masked behind the solid mid-eighteenth-century paneling.

A set of measured drawings was made when the house was restored, and another set drawn for the Historic American Buildings Survey is now on file in the Newport Historical Society Library, making it possible to study the construction of the house in detail.

Measured drawings, Library of Congress, Historic American Buildings Survey.

Drawings made by R. Kinnicutt for Norman Isham when the house was restored in 1927, in the Newport Historical Society.

Scale model made by the students of Brown University, together with information about the reconstruction, Brown University Art Department.

N. M. Isham, Manuscript notes in the Newport Historical Society, Isham file.

M. L. Stevens, "The Wanton-Lyman-Hazard House," *Old Time New England*, XXI, no. 2, 51ff.; "The Old Hazard House," *Newport Historical Society Bulletin*, no. 33 (July, 1920); "Papers relating to the Wanton-Lyman-

Hazard House," *Newport Historical Society Bulletin*, no. 66 (1928), pp. 7–30; M. L. Stevens and Jonas Bergner, "Two papers on the Wanton-Lyman-Hazard House," no. 59 (October, 1926).
Abstract of deeds, filed under Broadway, Survey Notebooks, Newport Historical Society.
Alice Brayton, *Gardens of Colony and State*, I (New York, 1931), 225.

The Daniel Wightman House. The house standing at 2 Coddington Street has been so changed on the outside that the huge chamfered beams of seventeenth-century construction come as a surprise when one steps inside. The history of the building is given here for the first time.

The Reverend Daniel Wightman, house carpenter turned minister, came to Newport from Kingstown in the early 1690's to become the second pastor of the Six Principles Baptist Church, organized in 1656. The Wightman genealogy states that when he bought a lot of land in Newport in 1694 he was called "joyner." The deed for this transaction has not been located, but a plat of John Coddington's land made by Samuel Easton in 1744 shows that Daniel Wightman then owned all the land between Thames and Charles streets on the north side of Coddington Street in the ancient heart of Newport. Newport deeds show that he had bought the piece of property just west of Charles on Coddington Street from Francis Brinley in 1721.

The two-story, two-room central-chimney house was probably built by the carpenter-minister himself soon after his arrival in 1694. Flared gunstock corner posts support massive chamfered ceiling beams. The summer beams are large and exposed in all four of the original rooms, and the small stair entry opens in front of a large brick chimney set on a foundation of stone. Unfortunately the mantels, windows, and doors have all been changed, and the exterior has been so modernized that it gives no clue to the age of the house. As a result, one of Newport's most interesting seventeenth-century buildings has long been unrecognized.

Daniel Wightman's daughter Elizabeth married Captain Stephen Hookey in 1724. In time Stephen and Elizabeth came into possession of the mansion house which they gave to their son Daniel Hookey in 1770. It remained in the Hookey family until 1833.

Information filed under Abstract of deeds, 2 Coddington Street, Survey Notebooks.

6 Coddington Street. In 1748 Daniel Wightman gave his daughter and son-in-law the adjoining property at Charles and Coddington streets that he had bought of Francis Brinley in 1721. By 1770 their second son, William Hookey, the goldsmith, was in possession of the little house on this corner, now numbered 6 Coddington Street. Here he lived until his death. His will, probated in 1812, reads, "I give, devise and bequeath unto Elizabeth Kirber, the young woman who lived with me and has lived with me a number of years for her kindness and faithful service to me in sickness and in health my dwelling house where I now live . . . I also give her the bed, bedstead and bedding . . . not thinking it too much for the care and pains she has taken of me at all times."

The quaint little house that William gave to Elizabeth is of the seventeenth-century type known as the Rhode Island story-and-a-half house. These houses, more common in northern Rhode Island than in Newport, were built with a three-foot half story above the first story to give additional head room in the garret. As a result, the outside window caps do not come directly under the eaves, as they do in Cape Cod houses, but are set three and a half feet or so below the roof line. William Hookey's house may be the only one left in Newport of this characteristic early Rhode Island type, but the frame is made of such light timbers that it cannot be of seventeenth-century date. More likely the Reverend Daniel Wightman, following Kingstown tradition of some fifty years earlier, built the house in the 1720's soon after he bought the land from Francis Brinley.

The Perry Weaver House. The house generally known as the Perry Weaver house, No. 8 Coddington Street on the northeast corner of Coddington and Charles, is of seventeenth-century construction, although the deed record has only been taken back to 1750. In that year the house, which then belonged to Zebulon Spinney, mariner, was sold for debt to Jonathan Sheldon. Perhaps built by one of the members of the Coddington family, it occupies part of William Coddington's six-acre plot. It is a two-room, two-story pitch-roofed house, and its system of framed and chamfered beams indicates that it must have been built in the last years of the seventeenth century. The central chimney has long since been removed, as have the stairs and other early finish, but a good mantel piece of raised paneling belonging to the period of about 1740–1750, and similar to the mantels found in the Augustus Lucas house, has remained, hidden in a modern closet.

Abstract of deeds, 8 Coddington Street, Survey Notebooks.

The Weston Clarke House. The double house which stands at 18 and 20 Marlborough Street, like many other early Newport houses, took on its present appearance in the mid-eighteenth century, but there are still one or two gunstock posts to indicate the presence of an earlier dwelling, probably the one that Weston Clarke gave his son Jeremiah in 1727. The land was originally William Coddington's, but deeds show that Weston Clarke owned this particular lot as early as 1704. Jeremiah Clarke sold the house to John Fryers in 1750, and under that name frequent references are made to the property in various issues of the *Mercury* of 1758 to 1800.

The dividing wall between the two houses is shared by both and in point of fact is not a complete wall. The east bed chamber of the west house extends beyond into the eastern house, while in turn the west parlor of the east house extends over into the western part, an arrangement which is probably the result of an early eighteenth-century enlargement.

Abstract of deeds, 18 and 20 Marlborough Street, Survey Notebooks.

HOUSES BUILT BETWEEN 1725 AND 1750

Pls. 85, 86, 193

Whitehall. "Yonder is one of the worthiest, most learned men in the three kingdoms who has met with the wretchedest usage ever was heard of." The Earl of Egmont, who made this statement in 1732 was speaking of George Berkeley, Dean of Derry, one of England's most celebrated metaphysicians, the friend of Dean Swift, of Pope, Addison, and Steele, author, poet, and one-time contributor to the *Guardian.* The Irish Dean had just returned to London from a three-year stay in Rhode Island. There he had waited in vain for the funds voted by Parliament with which to found St. Paul's College in Bermuda for the education of colonials and the New World Indians.

In September, 1728, the man of whom Alexander Pope had written "unto Berkeley every virtue under heaven" had set sail for Rhode Island, his ship loaded with his goods and chattels and a promise of £20,000 for his cherished Bermuda project ringing in his ears. He was accompanied on his adventure by his bride, her friend, "my lady Handcock's daughter," Sir John James, the architect, Richard Dalton, and the painter John Smibert.

Four months later, on Thursday, January 23, 1729, when their ship weighed anchor in Newport harbor, they were met by the Reverend James Honeyman who welcomed the Dean and his wife as guests in his home. In February, Berkeley bought a farm and small house of Joseph Whipple in Middletown with the intention of raising produce for the college until the endowment arrived. He built his first real home in a valley because, as he wrote, "to enjoy what is to be seen from the hill I must visit it only occasionally." The house was an unpretentious, hip-roofed building with a long, sloping, lean-to across the back, two big chimneys, a modillion cornice of flat blocks, and a pedimented front door, as well as a side door which led to the garden. He named it "Whitehall," "in loyal remembrance of the palace of the English Kings from Henry VIII to James II," and here he maintained the idyllic existence reflected in the pages of *Alciphron, or the Minute Philosopher*, which he composed in Middletown.

Berkeley's personal charm was such that Swift's Vanessa, though she met him only once, bequeathed him half her property. Newport not only gave him the respect due a celebrated visitor, but also the affection which he invariably won wherever he went. He preached at Trinity Church and sometimes at Tower Hill in Narragansett for the Reverend Dr. James McSparren. He drew around himself a conference of clergymen, as well as the members of the Philosophical Society which later grew into the Redwood Library, two groups suited to his scholarly tastes. The notables of the day came to Whitehall to call, but his time was largely absorbed in his studies and his writing, while he found his chief pleasures in his family, in philosophical discourse, and in enjoyment of his natural surroundings. He wrote his friend Tom Prior that Newport "exhibited some of the softest rural and grandest ocean scenery in the world," and he deliberately arranged his days to allow time for the enjoyment of the world around him, an enjoyment which accorded with an essay on *Pleasures Natural and Fantastical* that he had written for the *Guardian* years earlier.

"Fair weather is the joy of my soul," he said, "about noon I behold a blue sky with rapture, and receive great consolation from the rosy dashes of light which adorn the clouds of the morning and evening. When I am lost among green leaves, I do not envy a great man with a crowd at his levee. And I often lay aside thought of going to an opera, that I may enjoy the silent pleasure of walking by moonlight, or viewing the stars sparkle in their azure ground, which I look upon as part of my possessions, not without a secret indignation at the tastelessness of mortal men, who in their race through life overlook the real enjoyments of it."

The Berkeley's first child, a son, was born at Whitehall in June of 1729. Their second child, a daughter, died in infancy and was buried in Trinity churchyard on September 5, 1731. Sorrow had followed disappointment. In 1730, Lord Percival wrote that Sir Robert Walpole had admitted in private that the college money would never be paid. It was a bitter blow for the poor Dean. He wrote from Newport sadly, "As for the raillery of European wits, I should not mind it if I saw my college go on and prosper."

Berkeley set sail for home in September of 1731. On Friday, the 18th of February, 1732, he was again in London, where he gave the annual sermon before The Society for the Propagation of the Gospel in Foreign Parts in the Church of St. Mary-leBow. He gave his house and his library to Yale College on July 26, 1732, the annual rents and profits of which were to be applied to the maintenance of three resident scholars, scholarships which continue to this day. The same year he sent an organ to Trinity Church as a farewell present. In 1734 he was raised to the Bishopric of Cloyne, where he ministered for eighteen years. A request to resign was denied by the King who declared that "George Berkeley should die a Bishop in spite of himself," but granted him liberty to reside where he pleased. He removed to Oxford with his family, where he died in 1753.

Twelve years after the Dean had set sail for London, his Middletown home was serving as an inn; the proprietor was already capitalizing on the name of its distinguished builder. Dr. Alexander Hamilton stopped here in 1744 and thus described his visit in his *Itinerarium*: "We called at a public house which goes by the name of "Whitehall" kept by one Anthony, about three miles out of town, and the dwelling here of the famous Dean Barclay, when in this Island, and built by him. As we went along the road we had a number of agreeable prospects. At Anthony's we drank punch and tea and had the company of a handsome girl, his daughter."

This handsome girl, or one of her sisters, was to become the mother of Gilbert Stuart.

The Newport *Mercury* of the sixties and seventies continued to advertise Whitehall as a tea house. A picture of the old landmark, drawn by Lieutenant Harwood, U.S.N. (*circa* 1840), was included in a book called *Picturesque Illustrations of Rhode Island and the Town of Newport*. Whitehall, now in the hands of tenant farmers, was invariably pointed out to visitors as an historic place. But Yale, its absentee landlord, had little use for a Middletown farm. By the end of the nineteenth century it had fallen into ruin. In 1899 the Colonial Dames secured a 999-year lease in order to establish a perpetual memorial to the Irish Dean, and they succeeded in saving the house. In 1936, the tercentennial year, they undertook a careful restoration of two rooms under the guidance of Norman Isham.

Because of its immediate English origin, an original oddity of plan, and later changes, the building presents certain unsolved problems, but it is one of the very fine restorations of the state. The two-story house with its central chimney, high roof hipped back to a ridge, and long lean-to has been painted the old Spanish brown color common to early eighteenth-century dwellings. The peculiarity of the wide divided front doorway, half of which is false and extends beyond the parlor wall at the left is still unexplained. The change must have been made early because Harwood's drawing shows that the arrangement was in existence then. The original modillion cornice was replaced in 1900. The new one is slightly smaller in scale, and is unusual in that the windows are set some six inches below it and do not break into it.

The space in the entry hall where the stairway normally should be is not supposed to be large enough to allow stairs, but a back side hall between the east parlor and the so-called Dean's study has evidently served as a stair hall for many years. Ninyon Challoner's house of 1735 had such a side-hall plan. The staircase now installed here is not original, but it came from an old Newport house. The red parlor at the right and the green room at the left have been restored to their early appearance, with their early bolection paneled chimney breasts. The seventeenth-century tiles surrounding the fireplace in the red room came from Holland. The framed green tree tiles in the green room were part of the original fireplace tiles that the Berkeleys installed. The old paneling in the study was installed in the 1900 reclamation, but the tiles around this fireplace are original. The present kitchen, with its mammoth brick fireplace in which the oven is set in the back wall, may be the house Joseph Whipple sold the Dean in 1729. The slave quarters for the three slaves Berkeley bought in Newport, and a kitchen fireplace, were located in the cellar. There is also evidence that the Dean's library was housed in a little separate building, the one that the Reverend Andrew Burnaby, writing in his diary in 1759, reported was then being converted into a dairy.

The furnishings of the house have been limited to pieces of Berkeley's day and earlier. On the table in the green room lies the large 1784 edition of Berkeley's collected writings, open to the pages containing his description of Newport. There is a library of eighteenth-century books in keeping with his scholarly tastes, as well as pictures of his English and American friends. The house, set far back of its stone wall, with the boxwood growing by the doorway is redolent of the Berkeleys' brief tenure. It is easy to imagine the Dean walking in his garden, writing in his study, or discoursing with the visitors who found their way to his door, while his young wife, taught by Smibert, painted pictures when she could, tended to household duties, and cared for their Rhode-Island-born son.

Stanley Hughes, "Very Rev. Dean George Berkeley, DD.," in *Early Religious Leaders of Newport* (Newport, 1918), pp. 79–96.

Bull, "Memoir of Rhode Island" (Hammett, II, 87–98).

Records and notebooks kept for the house by the National Society of Colonial Dames in Rhode Island, Whitehall Committee, in the keeping of Miss Ruth Davenport.

Alice Brayton, *Gardens of Colony and State*, "Whitehall," I, 187–189.

The Jonathan Nichols House and the David Cheeseborough House. The handsome Deputy Governor Jonathan Nichols house, famous as the home of two governors, of an ambassador to Brazil, and as the Headquarters of Admiral de Ternay, first in command of the French Navy during the Revolution, was once part of the complex of home, garden, wharf, and shops that made up the waterside property of an important eighteenth-century Newport merchant.

Pls. 88–94

Although the house probably took its present form after 1758 and should be known as the Joseph Wanton house, the history of the property goes back to 1719 when Nathaniel Sheffield gave his son James a lot of land by the "Bay or salt water, with the warehouse and wharf built thereon," which was almost certainly the house lot (#14 of the Easton's Point Quaker lands of the First Division). James bought the garden lot (#13) next south in 1725.

In 1748, Sheffield sold lots #13 and #14, together with all "buildings and edifices thereon erected and now standing, the wharfs, the fish (?), etc." to Deputy Governor Jonathan Nichols, the son of the Deputy Governor Jonathan Nichols who had died in 1727. Nichols, Jr., was a prosperous merchant, the proprietor of the Whitehorse Tavern, and the owner of at least one privateer.

In old Newport deeds it was customary to specify a house as a "messuage or mansion house," and the warehouses and shops as "buildings," and therefore it has generally been assumed that Jonathan Nichols built the house itself sometime between 1748 and his death in 1754. But Ezra Stiles' map of 1758 shows a house with only one chimney, and the original construction of the west façade, which, as shown in an old stereoscopic view, had two unique segmental-headed stair landing windows and the off-centered doorway is asymmetrical and early in appearance. This façade itself shows evidence of being an alteration. It is possible that James Sheffield built a house soon after 1719, and that Lieutenant Governor Wanton rather than Nichols enlarged it, adding the southern part. The door with the broken pediment originally on the water front entrance, as well as the hall and stair detail and the interior paneling date, however, about 1740 in type.

In 1756, Colonel Joseph Wanton, Jr., Deputy Governor in 1764 and 1767, whose father also was a Governor, bought the "wharf and mansion house, warehouse, stables and buildings." He bought mahogany furniture from Job Townsend, as Townsend's account books show, and he was probably responsible for the unusual painted decoration found underneath many coats of paint in the right hand parlor. He continued the tradition of hospitality which Nichols had already established, but his loyalist sympathies made it "convenient for him to go to New York" when the Revolutionary war broke out. He went with his father, who because of his political views had been deposed as governor in 1775. A few years later the Wanton estates were confiscated, and by 1781 both father and son were dead.

The chapter of this branch of the Wanton family in Newport had drawn to a close, but their house successfully survived the British occupation of 1777-1779, when Henry Collins' house next door and many others went down for fuel. This is the house, as mentioned above, where Admiral de Ternay, First in Command of the French Navy, was quartered and where he died. In 1786 the Treasurer of Rhode Island sold the confiscated property to John Innes Clark and Joseph Nightingale, prominent Providence merchants. These investors sold to John Faxon who in turn sold to Seth Barton, the younger brother of the William Barton, hatter and continental Major, who was noted for his daring capture of General Prescott in 1777.

In 1805 the house was sold at auction to William R. Hunter. A graduate of Brown University and a brilliant lawyer, he was the son of Dr. William Hunter and the brother of the three Misses Hunter whose charm and beauty delighted the young French officers in 1780-1781. In 1804 he married Mary Robinson, daughter of the doughty New York Quaker, William T. Robinson, and a relative of the Thomas Robinsons who lived just down the way at 64 Washington Street. Mary's father had objected strenuously to her marriage outside the Quaker faith, and the letters the young pair exchanged, published by Anna Wharton Wood in the *Newport Historical Society Bulletin*, "A Newport Romance of 1804," tell a charming story of the young man's successful courtship in the face of family opposition.

The Hunters lived in their Water Street mansion from the time of purchase in 1805 until they were called to Washington, when they offered the house for sale again, advertising it as one of the best in Newport.

"Newport Mercury, 1826

"The Estate lately occupied by the Subscriber, situate on Washington street, formerly called the Wanton Estate — It consists of large Lot, an ample elegantly finished Dwelling House in perfect repair a suitable Garden etc. with the remains of what was once the best wharf in Newport. The water and wharfing privilege is unequaled, extending upwards of 400 feet to the channel, with room enough for the erection of Twenty Stores. In the year 1799 Two Ships of War of the U. S. the *George Washington* and *General Greene* were careened at the same Wharf, then in good repair and in profitable use. This Estate is particularly suited for large Ships; the East India or Whaling business — it will be sold cheap, and on liberal Credit. For terms apply to Nicholas G. Boss, Cashier of the R. I. Union Bank or to the Subscriber in Providence. William Hunter.

"If not soon sold, it will be Let for the Summer. It is a most elegible residence for a Southern family."

That it was not sold for nearly thirty years reflects the low ebb of Newport shipping affairs. In 1834 Hunter was appointed Chargé d'Affaires and later United States Minister at the Court of Don Pedro the First, Emperor of Brazil, where he served for ten years. He returned to Newport in 1844 and died in 1849.

In 1854 The Old Colony Steamboat Company bought the house and from then on it served as a genteel boarding house. According to Miss M. E. Powel, The Town and Country Club sometimes met there, and Colonel Thomas Wentworth Higginson, who wrote *Malbone* and *Old Port Days*, lived in the house for several seasons.

In the 1870's Dr. Milton Mayer ran the house as a convalescent home, and it was at this time that damaging exterior and interior changes were made, the chief of which were the widening of the entrances, the building of a rear porch and the removal of the front and rear pedimented doorways. The street front or eastern doorway, which was probably the simpler of the two, was allowed to disappear and Colonel Higginson's phrase, "the high front door still retains its Ionic cornice," written in 1869, is all we know of its original appearance. The water-front door is the one which has until recently been on St. John's Rectory and which resembles the balcony door of the Colony House. The building of the rear porch also necessitated the removal of the two segmental-headed stair landing windows mentioned above. Fortunately the stereoscopic view by J. Appleby Williams shows the water-front entrance before these changes were made. After 1881, when Dr. Horatio Storer bought the place, no further changes were made. Miss Agnes Storer sold it to the Sisters of St. Joseph's in 1915. The Preservation Society of Newport County bought it in 1945, and it is now in process of restoration.

If Stiles' map is correct, and the southern part of the house was added after 1758, the interior woodwork belongs to an earlier period. As restoration progresses, evidence in the house itself suggests that the explanation may lie in the fact that if Wanton enlarged the house he installed the stairway and perhaps some of the paneling from earlier Newport houses. The stairway shows signs of having been originally designed for a higher ceiled building, and Mr. Thomas Marvel, now in charge of the restoration, suggests that the stairs of Malbone, burned in 1766, may have been saved to reappear here, cut down to fit. The two old segmental-headed windows, typical of stone rather than wood construction, do not fit the landing space properly and actually were partially simulated in paint on the interior. They too may have come from Malbone. Whatever the true story, however, this house, like many others in Newport, is the product of eighteenth-century alterations.

Pls. 92, 94

As it stands, it is linked architecturally with Richard Munday's public buildings, Trinity Church and the Colony House. It is even more closely related to the house David Cheeseborough built on part of Peleg Sanford's orchard lot on Mary Street. The latter house was built soon after 1737 when, as land records show, Cheeseborough acquired the lot. This date is further verified by the numerals, 1737, which Jonas Bergner saw scratched in the lead on one of the dormers. When the house was torn down in 1908, Bergner made drawings and took photographs, and wrote a detailed description of its construction. Like the Nichols house, it was built of heavy stud construction with brick filled walls, plastered over in true English half-timbered tradition. Horizontal ship lapped sheathing boards were laid over the half timbering. These boards were of pine in the Cheeseborough house and oak in the Nichols house, and they were in turn covered with beaded ship lapped clapboards. Such construction accords with what is known of other early Newport building. Its use in these two houses proves the long continuing medieval tradition of building methods.

The Nichols house was evidently left unpainted for many years, since the remaining old split and ship lapped clapboards on the north wall were weathered a very dark gray underneath the paint. The color next to the wood, an off-white, was probably put on in the early nineteenth century. When the house was painted recently, the first off-white color was selected, since it was impractical to strip off all the old paint or to leave the wood exposed.

Both houses were built on the typical mid-eighteenth-century floor plan of four rooms, two on either side of a wide central hallway running through the house. In each main hall a mahogany staircase with curved and ramped rails and richly carved, twisted balusters was set back of a low dividing arch. The double twisted newel post of the Cheeseborough stairs, like that of the Hancock house in Boston, built in the same year, is evidence of the use of similar features in important houses in different geographical areas. The curved bottom step and the newel post of the Nichols stairs, now removed, were undoubtedly like those of the Cheeseborough house.

Six of the rooms in the Nichols house are wainscotted from floor to ceiling with raised or bolection paneling of the type used for the gallery breasts of Trinity Church, the Council Chamber of the Colony House, and the Cheeseborough house parlor. The two northwest parlors, one upstairs, one down, both paneled from floor to ceiling, are ornamented with Corinthian pilasters set on high pedestals. Fireplaces surrounded by Dutch tiles are flanked by arched shell cupboards and finished with angel heads set in the spandrels of the arches. The parlor of the Cheeseborough house followed the same scheme, but lacked the shell cupboards and the decorative angel heads. This popular scheme, described more fully earlier, probably appeared for the last time in these two rooms of the Nichols house. The large windows are complete with inside shutters and deep window seats made of mahogany.

The floor in the northwest downstairs room of the Nichols house is made of pine boards about eight inches wide. These are tenoned together with slats that go all the way through one board and half way through the adjoining boards. The tenons are set about ten inches apart, and spaced alternately down each board. This construction makes a webbing of remarkable strength. Jonas Bergner noted that the Cheeseborough house floors were constructed in the same manner, made of pine floorboards eighteen inches wide.

As the rooms have been stripped of their incrustation of paint, interesting information concerning the original finish and the installation of the cupboards has been brought to light. The cupboards and paneling in the northeast parlor show architectural evidence of having been made for different places and the first level of painting seems to bear out this fact. The parlor, which has recently been taken back to the natural wood, was evidently first painted or stained a reddish tone with a very powdery paint. This original color came off almost completely when the second level of color, a hard yellow grey-green was removed.

The second level of paint appeared on all walls and doors, as well as the glazed cupboard doors. To go with this second level of yellow grey-green, mentioned above, the pilasters of the room, the baseboards, under-window-seat moldings, cupboard shelves, and the cupboard pilaster tops were all marbled in a close-veined spiral pattern in ochre on black. A small section of this marbling has been saved. The cupboard pilasters were marbled with dark veining on an ochre ground, while the cupboards themselves and the insides of the cupboard doors were first painted a dark blue-green. The cherub faces in the arch spandrels were polychromed naturalistically in shades of Venetian red. The wings were tinged very thinly with a *terre vert*, and a yellow-green, dark blue, and Venetian red. The cupboards have been repainted the old green and the two angels at the left of the mantel still retain their original eighteenth-century coloring. The angels in the cupboard were also painted naturalistically, but the wings had a deeper green, which toned in with the blue-green of the cupboards. The shell cupboards, glazed cupboard doors, angel heads, and the marbled decoration were all part of the room when it received its covering of yellow green paint. It seems likely that Joseph Wanton installed some of the various parts, and supervised their decoration soon after 1758.

The third level of painting, a light stone or sand color, which covered the whole room, except for the mahogany window seats, including pilasters, angels, and cupboards, may have been contemporary with the painting of the Colony House Council Chamber in 1784, also painted a light stone color.

The northeast chamber, which is almost like the parlor below, seems to have been left unpainted for a longer period of time and never had so elaborate a scheme. Its first color was the common reddish tone. The paneling of the southeast room was stained and grained to look like mahogany, and for many years visitors reported that the walls were paneled in mahogany. As said elsewhere, the southwest room was "spreckled." The hall wainscotting was painted bluegreen; the walls above were probably whitewashed, unless they were once papered or hung with "printed canvass." Other rooms were painted an apricot color, and some of the chambers were painted a fairly strong dark green.

The study and restoration of the rooms in the Nichols house has helped bring to light the kind of decoration in vogue during the years when first Jonathan Nichols and then Joseph Wanton's cargo-laden ships weighed anchor by the wharfside. "I know no finer specimen of these large colonial dwellings," Colonel Higginson wrote in the opening pages of *Malbone*, "in which the genius of Sir Christopher Wren bequeathed traditions of stateliness to our democratic days. Its central hall has a carved archway; most of the rooms have painted tiles and are wainscotted to the ceiling; the sashes are red-cedar, the great staircase mahogany; there are cherub's heads and wings that go astray and lose themselves in closets and behind glass doors; there are curling acanthus-leaves that cluster over shelves and ledges, and there are those graceful shell-patterns which one often sees on old furniture, but rarely in houses . . . the western entrance, looking on the bay, is surmounted by carved fruit and flowers, and is crowned, as is the *roof*, with that pineapple in whose symbolic wealth the rich merchants of the last century delighted."

The part of *Jonathan Nichols' Inventory* concerning his household effects, taken from the Town Council Book 12 (page 59) in the Newport Historical Society, is printed here for the first time.

Inventory of the Personal estate of the Honble
Jonathan Nichols Esq. Late of Newport dec'd taken
by us ye subscribers September 14, 1756.

pg. 60

2 Marble Side boards 2 Waiters £ 8	268
Looking Glasses @ £ 100 £ 200 1 Carpet on ye floor £ 20 3 doz China Plates £ 72	292
odd China Plates £ 11 2 China Bowls one cracked £ 10 6 China Bowls pint ones @ 40/ £ 12	33
2 Large Glass Bowles 80/ 5 Coffee Bowles & Saucers £ 11 one doz Coffee Cups with handles 100/	20
one sugar pot 2 Pints and 1 Spoon Boat 100/ four Glass Bowles with handles 60/	8
1 Lignumvitae Stand with Cruets and Salts tipt with Silver £20 2 Glass Candlesticks	22
9 Drinking Glasses and 1 Glass Cup 55/ one Shagreen Case of Knives and Forks £70	72.15
1 do smaller £35 oz pwt gn	
435 6 5 of plate @ u o/ £2393	2864.17.6
parcell of Plates and Dishes in ye Closet £60 5 Leather Chairs @ 60/ £15 1 Great Chair 100/	80
1 pr Tongs, Shovel and Andirons £10 one Quadrille Table £25 1 small mahogany Table £15	50
1 Looking Glass £40 1 Mahogany Desk £40 1 Picture 5/ 1 pr Pocket Postols £14	94:5
1 fowling pc. £12 Parcell Books and a Bible £12 three Brushes @ 2/	24:12
6 Doz. Hard Mettle plates @ £16 is £96 15 Pewter Dishes £45	141
1 Doz. Knives and forks £8 2 old Cases with Some Bottles £6	14
Some fishing Lines and horse shoes in a Basket and some squares of Glass 100/	5
1 Bed Bedsted and furniture £90 1 Single Bed £35 one Bedsted, bed and beding £65	190
10 Old Chairs £10 2 Maple Tables £16 2 small Mahogany Tables £16 1 Looking Glass	62
1 pr. Andirons Shovel and Tongs, Bellows 2 pr Snuffers and 2 Old Brushes £30	30
Parcell Glass on ye shelf 100/ 44 Pewter Plates @ 10 p doz. £36.16 8 Pewter Basons	51:16
1 Brass Coffee Pot £7 3 Pewter Pint pots 40/ Parcell of Earthen £15 3 old Teapots £6	30
1 Stone Jug and Candle box 40/ one Doz Knives and forks and 5 other knives £ 6 black chairs 100/	13
One Easie Chair and 8 bottoms for Comm £30 1 Bed and furniture £100 1 bed and furniture £130	270

1 Small Pallet Bed and Bed Stead £50 16
Earthen Plates 1 Platter 1 Decanter ye
same glass ware £30 8 Chairs Red Harrateen
Bottoms @ £15

1 Easie Chair £40 Bed and furniture £140 1 tea table £10 1 Looking Glass 70	260
Parcell China on ye Table 1 Large Bowl £30 1 Large Case of Bottles £45	75
1 Shovel & tongs & 1 pr Andirons £6 1 pr. Tobacco Tongs 5/ 1 Carpet £7	13:5
1 old Desk £15 1 large Glass £100 1 Small do £10 1 Mahogany Dressing Table £20	145
1 Maple Table £10 1 high case of Draws £80 1 Bed and furniture £120 1 empty case 5/	210:5
1 Bed and furniture £115 one case of Draws £20 Glasses thereon £20	155
Old Chest & trunk £2 4 little trunks 80/ Glas 20/ 2 beds beding and Bedsteads £120	127
1 Bed & Bedding £60 1 Gun £10 Number of Baggs £80 2 Carpets £80 2 Brass Sconses 60/	233
1 Bed and Beding £60 4 Old Trunks 80/ Wearing Apparell £500	564
Blankets & Coverlid £46 3 Doz. Sheets £120 8 Tablecloths Damask & Diaper £30	196
19 Diaper Napkins old £9.10 29 Towels £20 7 Window Curtains & Vallance £20	49:10
10 Pillow Cases £12.8 Bolster Cases £6 4 Ozenbrigs Table Cloths £10 2 pr Callico & 6 pr Tape £110	138
1 Table 20/ 6 old chairs 20/ 10 old Platters £25 16 Plates 2 Basons & 1 Porringer £12	39
1 Callender & 4 Spoons 60/ one Tin Oven £5 1 Tin Can 1 Skimmer 1 Ladle & Formenter 80/	12
4 Belmettle Kettle & 1 Skillet £24 3 Brass Skillets 100/ 2 Chafing dishes £6	35
1 Stone pot and 2 Tea Kettles £20 1 Warming pan 90/ 7 pails 60/ 12 Bowls and 3 trays 45/	29:15
1 Morter & Pestle 15/ 10 Bake pans £15 3 pr flats and 2 Box Irons £12 1 Jack Spit & Saucer 80	107:15
1 pr Andirons 4 Trammels 1 Driping pan & fender Slice & tongs £40 1 GridIron 3 Wedges 1 pr Broken Andirons & 1 Spider £2 1 pr Stilyards 1 Choping knife and 1 Bread Toster £5	57
one Maple Stool 30/ 9 Candlesticks £11 one frying pan 50/ 9 knives and forks 30/	16:10
One tunnel Augur 20/ 7 Iron pots & 3 Iron Kettles £35 2 Brass Kettles £35 3 axes & 1 basket 100/	76
One Pump hook & 1 Scoop Shovel 80/ 1 seive & 1 Keelen 15/ 4 Rakes & 1 Pitch fork 50/	7:5

2 Iron Barrs 2 Chains and 1 Yoak £22 a
parcell nutcrackers & a Burning Glass 70/   25:10

1 Silver Watch £70 1 Bond Walter Cornell
£550 A parcell Silver Buttons, 1 pr Gold
Buttons & 1 pr Shoe Buckles   30

17 @ 6 12 chain @ 60. £36
1 large Mahogany Table £55 1 smaller do
£25 1 Looking Glass £70 1 Clock £200   350

4 Pictures £12 1 pr. andirons Shovel and
Tongs Brass £18 one carpet on ye floor £6   36

Abstract of deeds, Survey Notebooks, Newport Historical Society.

Notes on the construction of the house and progress of its restoration, Survey Notebooks.

Jarvis Morse, "The Wanton Family and Rhode Island Loyalism," *Rhode Island Historical Society Collections*, XXXI, no. 2 (April, 1938).

A. W. Wood, " Newport Romance of 1804," *Newport Historical Society Bulletin*, no. 61 (April, 1927).

Bull, "Memoir of Rhode Island," II, 114.

Measured drawings, Library of Congress, Historic American Buildings Survey.

n *The Banister Town House.* John Banister, prominent merchant, inveterate smuggler, and the irascible brother-in-law of Peter Harrison, owned houses and warehouses on Thames Street, a mansion house on Spring Street, and two houses at Mile Corner, one of which was burned by the British. His letters and account books furnish an invaluable account of his business affairs, from his heavy engagement in "free trade" to his household accounts. Pl. 97

The history of the Spring Street property is important, among other reasons, because of the fact that Banister recorded in these account books the year the house was begun, 1751. In 1740, his wife, Hermione Pelham, had inherited from her father, Edward Pelham, part of Governor Benedict Arnold's original Mill Field, known as the upper Mill Field. An old plat shows that in the following year, 1741, Pelham Street was cut through from Thames to Spring Street. In the same year Banister's accounts began to list items concerned with building the brick wall which once enclosed the Spring Street lot between Pelham and Mill. James Mauran's manuscript (Newport Historical Society, MS 1240) records that the bricks for the wall were imported from Holland, and that a wooden gate once closed the passageway at Pelham and Spring streets.

In 1751 the accounts show that Banister had begun to build his Spring Street house behind his fine brick wall. His will, dated 1767, gives his son John "my dwelling house and garden in Newport which I built on the field commonly known by the name of the Mill Field, upper field or Meeting House field brick wall." Since the house is one of the few dated so exactly, its architectural features are especially important in the history of Newport building.

Like the Cheeseborough and Hunter houses, it is a broad gambrel-roofed building with two interior chimneys and a central hallway. The stairway placed at the back of the hall has ramped molded rails and very delicate twisted balusters which reflect the lateness of the date. The paneling does not extend from floor to ceiling, as in the Hunter house, and is no longer made with raised bolection moldings, but is beveled and flat and belongs to the simpler style of paneled work which was by this time supplanting the lavish earlier eighteenth-century raised type. But the huge coved molding that forms part of the stair hall cornice is similar to that employed for the hall cornice moldings of both the Hunter and the Cheeseborough houses.

General Prescott, the unpopular commander of the British forces, was quartered in this house during the British occupation. He was harsh tempered and domineering and, according to Newport tradition, the Quakers found his order that all citizens remove their hats in his presence especially hard to bear. He is purported, among other things, to have had a walk laid from the

Banister house to his guard house on Mill Street made from the house doorsteps which projected onto the sidewalks. These, it is said, he had ordered taken up so that his drunken officers would not fall over them at night. Local historians, such as Dr. Turner, record that the citizens, thus bereft of their front steps, many of which were never replaced, had to enter their houses by short ladders until such time as they could manage to repair the damage. This procedure is supposed to explain the prevalence of recessed doorways in Newport. They were more likely recessed, as was the Banister doorway, in order to afford some slight protection against the weather.

The old house remained in the Banister family until 1821, when it was sold to Joshua Sayer. The Sayer family owned it until 1906. Now run as a boarding house, it is still one of the finest gambrel-roofed mansions of Newport's prosperous years.

Banister Account books, Newport Historical Society.
Banister Letter books, Newport Historical Society.
Bridenbaugh, *Peter Harrison, First American Architect* (Chapel Hill, 1949).
Judge Darius Baker, "The Newport Banisters," *Newport Historical Society Bulletin*, no. 43 (January, 1923).
Abstract of deeds, Survey Notebooks.
John Stevens Account Books, owned by John Howard Benson.
B. J. Lossing, *The Pictorial Field Book of the Revolution* (New York, 1852), II, 64–65.

Pl. 45

The Augustus Lucas House. The story of the square gable-on-hip roofed house standing on the corner of Division and Mary streets goes back to the first years of the eighteenth century. In 1700 Augustus Lucas, a French Huguenot, arrived in Newport via the Channel Islands from St. Malo near Mont St. Michel. By 1711 the *Boston News Letter* was carrying advertisements of Indian and Negro slaves for sale at the Newport Colony House, to be seen at the house of Augustus Lucas. In that same year Lucas purchased from Walter Clarke the property at Division and Mary streets which had been part of Jeremy Clarke's original 1639 grant of land. In 1713 he bought an adjoining lot. When this transaction was finally completed in 1721, buildings were mentioned, although a "messuage" or "mansion" house was not specifically named. The lots included the garden and the land where Lucas later planted his orchard and carried on his experiments in grafting fruit trees. The date of 1721 is too early for the front part of the house, but the stairway in the rear entry, which has already been discussed in Chapter 2, was undoubtedly the original front staircase of an earlier house built to face east.

Architectural features indicate that sometime before 1750 the old house must have been rebuilt into the structure we see facing Division Street today, a square central-chimney house with an Ionic pedimented doorway and a modillion cornice composed of flat blocks which break out around the windows. The main stairway set against the chimney in the central hallway is fitted with ramped railings and handsome spiral balusters. Such balusters had begun to go out of fashion by 1760. The parlors on either side of the chimney on both the upper and lower floors have retained their original mantel breasts made up of raised paneling. Mantels of this type are composed of one narrow and one wide panel above a fireplace, which in turn is enclosed by the same raised moldings used to frame the panels. They, too, belong to the years before 1760.

Augustus Johnston, Lucas' grandson and the son of George and Bathsheba (Lucas) Johnston, came into possession of the house sometime before 1765, and was probably responsible for its enlargement. Johnston, who was a lawyer, had once been so popular personally that the town of Johnston was named in his honor. Unfortunately, in 1765 he had accepted the post of Stamp Master in Newport. In the same year he paid the price for holding an office which had become a symbol of the tyranny of the British Crown. With Martin Howard and Dr. Moffatt, he suffered violence against his property at the hands of a mob in the Stamp Act riot of 1765. When the rioters arrived at his house, after their attack on Howard's and Moffatt's, Johnston had taken refuge in the cellar. He resigned the hated office soon afterward and left Newport to settle in Charleston, where he became Judge of the Vice Admiralty Courts.

In 1766 Johnston's stepfather, Matthew Robinson, who had married Bathsheba Johnston after her first husband's death, bought the house, but because of his own Tory views he was allowed freedom from jail after the Revolution only on condition that he stay at Hopewell, his Kingston home. Samuel Freebody bought the Lucas house in 1788. Miss Susan Braley Franklin has given an interesting account of the admirable old building in her account of Division Street, no. 104 of the *Newport Historical Society Bulletin*. The house, in spite of its present covering of tar paper bricks and its changed front steps and railing, is basically little altered. It is a fine example of the home of the moderately well-to-do eighteenth-century solid citizen.

S. B. Franklin, "Division Street," *Newport Historical Society Bulletin*, no. 104 (March, 1948), pp. 14–21.

Pitt's Head Tavern. The history of the broad two-story gambrel-roofed house known as Pitt's Head Tavern, now located at 5 Charles Street, is an important one for Newport. Originally it stood on the northeast corner of Charles and Washington Square, formerly the Queen Street, where recently studied land records place it before 1726. In that year, John Clarke, mariner, sold "a lot of land with a messuage or dwelling house" on it to Jonathan Chace, mariner. The present house, a typical gambrel-roofed building, was doubled in size before 1765, but the framing for the former mammoth chimney and fireplaces and the little stairway with its tight three runs and its S-shaped balusters all belong to this earlier period.

Pls. 143–45, 122, 128

In 1742 Jonathan Chace sold the Queen Street property to Henry Collins, long called the Lorenzo de Medici of Rhode Island because of his patronage of art and letters. Just the year before, in 1741, Henry Collins' young niece, Mary Ward, daughter of Governor Richard Ward, had married Ebenezer Flagg, son of John and Abiah Flagg of Boston. Collins may have given them the house as a wedding present. At any rate, soon after 1742 they were established in the dwelling which was to be their home until 1765. They named their first child Henry Collins in honor of their relative, friend, and partner in business.

In 1744 John Stevens, mason, was laying steps and paving for the Flaggs' house. He altered the chimney and fireplace and set ninety-five tiles, some of them probably the Dutch tiles then much in vogue for fireplace decoration. Perhaps at this time the original end-chimney half-a-house was enlarged to the five-room house with central chimney and entry which we see today. That this had been accomplished by 1765 was clearly indicated by the inventory of Ebenezer Flagg's personal property, which listed the contents of the house room by room.

Ebenezer Flagg was a founding member of the Redwood Library. He engaged in the manufacture of cordage and became associated in business with Collins. During these years Newport was competing for commercial supremacy with New York and the prosperous firm of Collins and Flagg, later Collins, Flagg, and Engs, was known to have a ship for every letter in the alphabet. But trade difficulties of the 1750's occasioned by the Seven Years' War, and the stricter enforcement of the Admiralty Rules finally forced the firm into bankruptcy. The loyalist George Rome took over the affairs of Collins and Engs in 1762. Ebenezer Flagg died that same year. Henry Collins died two years later and lies buried in the Flagg family plot in the town burial ground.

In 1765 the Flagg family sold their mansion house to Robert Lillibridge and in the next few years their name disappeared from Newport annals. Both sons of Ebenezer and Mary Flagg entered the service of the Continental forces early in the War for Freedom. Ebenezer Flagg, Jr., was killed with his commanding officer, Christopher Greene, in a surprise attack by the British in Westchester County, New York.

Henry Collins Flagg headed the Medical Department of the Southern Division with the title of Apothecary General. After the war he settled in Charleston where he married Rachel Moore Allston, widow of Captain Allston and mother of the painter, Washington Allston, who later lived on Clarke Street.

The Flagg inventory lists seventeen pictures among the family possessions in the Queen Street house. Probably some of these came from Henry Collins' own collection. When Henry Collins Flagg moved to Charleston, he is known to have taken the family portraits with him. They included portraits of his father and his mother, Gershom Flagg, and the Sabbatarian minister, the Reverend Hiscox, all by Robert Feke; Henry Collins by John Smibert; and his grandfather, Richard Ward, by an unknown artist. These portraits were brought north by William Flagg years later, who left them at his death to Mrs. Cornelius Vanderbilt, a lineal descendant of Richard Ward. They are now in the possession of the Countess Laszlo Szechenyi. The "black walnut chairs," the clock, mahogany desks and tables, and many other household possessions listed in the inventory of a once quietly well-to-do family have long since been scattered.

Soon after Mary Flagg sold the house to Robert Lillibridge, he hung out the "Sign of the Right Honorable William Pitt's Head," and the house entered on a long and colorful career as a famous coffee house. The likeness of the popular William Pitt, "the Great Commoner," had come originally from an establishment opened in Thames Street in 1759 by a James Brooks from England. He allowed his coffee house to lapse within a year or two but the new Pitt's Head thrived under Lillibridge's management, and became one of Newport's most successful taverns. He had a good eye for business, and ran ingenious notices in the *Mercury* like the following one designed to suggest pleasant ways for Newport's summer visitors to spend their leisure time:

"Robert Lillibridge, Jun., At the Sign of PITT'S head, near the Courthouse, NEWPORT Hereby informs the public that he now has in good order, A Genteel COACH, coachman, and two good horses, for carrying out gentlemen and ladies, on parties of pleasure,—The coachman understands driving well, and waiting on company in the best manner; and will attend at the houses of any gentlemen and ladies with the coach, at any hour they may chuse."

That he ran the risks involved in dealing with the public at large is shown by the following notice of combined warning and outrage that he put in the *Mercury* of September 7, 1767:

"This is to warn all People to take Care, and not be imposed on by one Robert Jameson, a Scotchman, as I have been; he endeavours to pass for a Commissioner sent from England by the Parliament to take a Survey of America, he draws Bill of Exchange, and shows Notes of Hand against several People, and endeavours to sell them: and through his insinuating Stories I have trusted him twenty-two dollars, and Yesterday Morning he went out under a Pretence to dine abroad, and is run away, it is supposed he went up the River in a Prudence Boat and so to go to Boston;—He has been in Goal in Philadelphia for borrowed Money on the Strength of his telling about that he owned a Ship, which proved to be false. He had on a brown snuff colour's Coat and Jacket, old stocking Breeches, his Hair something curled, almost black, his Hat something rusty, square silver carved shoe Buckles, and metal Knee Buckles, he is of short Stature, I shall be able to give the Public, in a few days a large Account of said Person."

During the British occupation the house was used by Commander Cole as headquarters to recruit soldiers into his Majesty's Army. The *Journal* of John Trevett, U.S.N., published in Vol. 6, page 197ff., of the *Newport Historical Magazine*, gives an interesting account of his secret and disguised visit to the house in 1777 while it was in British hands.

"I went to Capt. Lillibridge's on the Parade. It was then about 11 o'clock. He kept a tavern and I went in and called for a sling. The room was crowded with British and Hessian officers, and I immediately went into the kitchen where the family was, knowing that Capt. Lillibridge had been treated ill by the British and had no regard for them. In a short time I followed him out to the barn, and no one being near, I made myself known to him. He immediately left the barn and we went into the east room by ourselves. He gave me what refreshments I wanted; and then I could see all the British officers and soldiers, and old refugee Torys walking about the Parade. Capt. L. could not help shedding tears for my safety, for fear of one of our townsmen who visited his house all times a day. I was reviewing the Parade when one of the villains (his name was Will Crozen), came running up the steps and came right to the east door where we were. He was not soon enough, however, for I stepped to the door and put my finger on the latch, and he supposed it fast, and went immediately through the bar-room into the kitchen. I did not bid my friend Lillibridge goodbye, but stepped out on the Parade and directly before me was Mr. John Wanton."

The tavern also served as Hessian headquarters and later, when the French were in Newport, the French billeting list indicated that Inspecteur Duval was quartered there. In 1815 the building housed the Offices of the Collector and the Naval Officer for the Port of Newport. In that same year Edward Lawton bought it and it remained in possession of the Lawton family until the Independent Order of Odd Fellows purchased it in 1877, and moved it to its present location at 5 Charles Street to make room for their new hall. It is now owned by the Preservation Society of Newport County.

The stairs and hall have been restored to their original appearance by John Perkins Brown. The chimney, now gone, originally was sprung from a stone vault in the cellar (which was described in the Flagg inventory as a storage place). Old gray-green sheathing in the kitchen chamber, and two panel doors painted to imitate marbling and hung with long pin hinges, are other indications of early eighteenth-century date. The bolection paneling and woodwork of the south parlor may have been installed in 1744 when other changes were being made. Its first color was green wainscot color and in the Flagg inventory it was listed as the green room.

The north wall of the house still retains some of the early shiplapped clapboards. The first color on these clapboards, a light creamy tone, was laid next to the clear unweathered yellow of the pumpkin pine. This suggests that Pitt's Head Tavern was painted a near-white at that date. The doorway also displays, underneath its many coats of paint, the same off-white color. The rear of the old part of the house was shingled and was first painted Spanish brown.

The fine exterior doorway resembles the scroll bracketed doors of the Redwood Library and the Jewish Synagogue and calls to mind the name of Peter Harrison. The cornice of shaped modillions, which does not break around the upper windows, is of the later type employed for the Metcalf Bowler house of 1760. Wall paper discovered behind the plastering on the chimney wall in the hall belongs to the period of about 1815, put on perhaps when Edward Lawton bought the house. The detail of the north room dates from the latter part of the nineteenth century.

A *Gazette* containing the story of Pitt's Head Tavern has been published by the Preservation Society, and measured drawings of the ground plan, elevation, and some of the details have been made. In time the Society hopes to restore this old house as a monument to Newport's tavern life and mercantile past.

Abstract of deeds and notes, Survey Notebooks.
John Stevens' Account Books.
A. F. Downing, "An Account of Pitt's Head Tavern," in the *Newport Gazette*, I, no. 1 (Newport, 1947).
Ernest Flagg, *The Founding of New England*, pp. 142–143.
Journal of Lieutenant John Trevett, U.S.N., 1772–1782, from the *Rhode Island Historical Magazine*, VI (Newport, 1885), 197.

The Thomas Robinson House. The broad gambrel-roofed house at 64 Washington Street is famous as the Newport headquarters of the Vicomte de Noailles during the Revolutionary war and this part of its history has already been recounted in Chapter 6. Architecturally it ranks among the most interesting houses standing in Newport today. It is shown on Stiles' map, where it is marked as a two-story dwelling with one chimney. The southern part was known to have been standing in 1736 when Walter Chapman sold lot #61 of the Easton's Point lands to Benjamin Hazard of South Kingston, and family tradition claims that this part was even earlier. It may have been built about 1725 when deeds show that Chapman was already paying the annual quitclaim rental required by the Quaker proprietors. The architectural style of the corner cupboard, discussed in Chapter 4, agrees with this early date. This old part of the house was built on the same three-room plan employed for the Christopher, Job, Thomas and Solomon Townsend houses, three of which were built soon after 1725.

In 1754 Thomas Robinson married Sarah Richardson, daughter of Thomas Richardson, whose house formerly at 87 Thames Street has been discussed in the early part of Chapter 4. In 1760 Robinson bought the Washington Street house, then known as "The Old Tavern," and it has been in the Robinson family since that year. Quaker Tom and his bride soon built an addition to the north, converting the whole into the big gambrel-roofed building we see today. Their new rooms were wainscotted to the chair rails with the flat paneling which had now superseded the heavy bolection type. The mantel walls were paneled from floor to ceiling, but the over-mantel panels were plain, a treatment as popular at this time as were the elaborate pedimented two-story mantels to be found in the Francis Malbone and Mawdsley houses. The new stairway with its ramped rails and turned balusters was built in three runs and resembles the ones in the Mawdsley and Stevens houses, all being constructed about this time.

The young Robinsons ordered handsome new furniture for their house from "neighbor" Thomas Goddard, but Sarah had also brought with her the furniture she had inherited from her mother, some of which Edward Wanton had brought with him from England before 1658. By the rare good fortune of continued family ownership, much of this old furniture remains in the house. As a result, the interiors present a more authentic picture of the mid-eighteenth century than any other in Newport today.

Fortunately, too, only a few architectural changes have been made since the addition of 1760 was built. The windows still have their inside shutters, the doors their wrought iron hardware and the fireplaces and mantels are unaltered, except for the one in the old kitchen. In 1879 Charles Follen McKim converted this room into a back living room, treating it in the same "colonial" or "Queen Anne" manner he employed for the back living room of the Dennis House across the street. This room too, has now become a period room in its own right. McKim also replaced the original turned drops for the stairway finish with carved flame drops copied from the earlier detail found in buildings like the Jonathan Nichols house. A porch has been built across the rear of the house. Otherwise it is much as the Robinsons, their friends, and the Vicomte de Noailles knew it.

Recently, when the paint in the southern chamber was cleaned, paintings next the wood on the over-mantel were discovered. They are being carefully brought to light; the subject has proven to be an autumn scene of burning leaves.

Anna Wharton Wood has given an excellent account of the Thomas Robinson family, the history of the house, and particularly the story of the stay of the Vicomte de Noailles in Newport in her paper on the "Robinson Family and the Vicomte and Vicomtesse de Noailles," published in Bulletin, No. 42 (October, 1922) of the Newport Historical Society.

Abstract of deeds, Washington Street, Survey Notebooks, Newport Historical Society.

HOUSES BUILT BETWEEN 1750 AND 1775

The Vernon House. The historic house at the corner of Clarke and Mary streets is famous not only for serving as Rochambeau's headquarters, but as the meeting place of General Washington and the French chief-in-command. As we have seen, its classic rusticated exterior has been attributed to Peter Harrison, but the discovery in 1937 of frescoes of Chinese character on the plastered walls back of the paneling in the northwest parlor has proven the existence of a much earlier house.

Deeds in the Newport Historical Society show that William Gibbs, a painter, owned a house on this spot before 1708, and internal evidence indicates that the frame of the north half of the present building belongs to the late seventeenth, or beginning of the eighteenth century. The Gibbs-Gardner family owned the property until after 1744, and there are two fragmentary deeds in the Newport Historical Society; one, William Gardner to Patrick Grant, the other, Patrick Grant to Charles Bowler, which concern the property, but the dates and boundaries are missing. The arrival of Charles Bowler in Newport and the description of his Portsmouth house and garden have already been discussed in Chapter 3. He probably bought the Clarke Street house about the time he received his appointment as Collector of Revenue in 1753. In 1759 he sold the building to his son, Metcalf, now a successfully established merchant engaged in shipping and the West Indies trade. Politically important, Metcalf Bowler served as a member of the Assembly for over nineteen years. In 1768 he was put on the committee to prepare an address to King George setting forth the grievances of the colonies. He was also appointed Chief Justice of the Supreme Court in 1776, a post he retained for a year, even while he was in the employ of the British Crown as a secret agent.

The building that Metcalf Bowler bought of his father faced Mary Street and, as shown on Ezra Stiles' map of 1758, was two stories high with one chimney, still only half the size of the present house. It was in this older part, behind the paneling Bowler probably had installed when he enlarged the house and changed the size of the north room, that the wall paintings were discovered. Painted on the smooth plastered surfaces of the two exterior walls, these decorations are of extraordinary architectural and historic interest. As we have already said, they were intended to simulate a wood-paneled room of the raised or bolection type, like the parlors of the Brenton, the Cheeseborough, and Nichols houses. The moldings, stiles, and rails were carefully depicted and then marbled, and the panel faces were reserved for pictorial scenes. The Chinese style in which these were done was at the height of its popularity in the early and mid-eighteenth century. The clock William Claggett made for the Sabbatarian Meeting house in 1731 is also adorned with little Chinese birds and flowers. But the subject matter of at least two of the Clarke Street paintings, which indicates an acquaintance with scenes in the cycle of the Buddhist Hell or with the Chinese courts of punishment, is so unusual that it has led students to believe they may have been executed by someone who had visited China.

As we have seen, rooms wainscoted with bolection paneling and then decorated with marbling and with pictorial scenes belong to the first half of the eighteenth century. The decoration of this room belongs in this tradition and was probably put on sometime about 1730 to 1740, while William Gibbs or his family still owned the house. The upstairs north rooms were also originally painted. In 1879, when repairs were being made, a West Indies scene was discovered behind the mantel breast in the northwest chamber, which James E. Mauran described in the Newport *Mercury* of October 18, 1879. The painting was subsequently removed from the house and has since disappeared.

When Metcalf Bowler bought the house in 1759, he added the present hall and the rooms on the south, transforming it into a two-story rusticated mansion with a wide classic doorway, a modillion and dentil cornice, and low hipped roof, with a flat deck and a double row of balustrades.

The interior, laid out on the old four-room central-hall plan, is more traditional. The fine stairs retained the ramped rails and twisted balusters of an earlier day and were set at the back of the broad central hall behind a low dividing arch sprung from brackets. The landing opening was treated as a window of Palladian form like those to be seen in the Banister country house and Francis Malbone's Thames Street house.

Since Bowler was wealthy and had no need to paint imitation paneling on plastered walls, he now installed paneled mantel breasts and wainscotted all four walls in the north parlor. This room, with its flush paneling, modillion and dentil cornice, and two-story mantelpiece topped by a broken scroll pediment, is much like the parlors in the Francis Malbone and the Mawdsley houses, both finished about the same time.

Bowler owned the Clarke Street house until 1773, when he sold it to William Vernon and retired to his country estate. William Vernon, who was an ardent patriot, belonged to one of the most successful merchant families of Newport's golden years just before the Revolutionary war. At the war's outbreak, he left Newport, as did many other patriots. When the French arrived in Newport in 1780, General Rochambeau was quartered in the house. William Vernon returned to Newport in 1782, after the war was over.

At this time he made repairs to the house, including painting the exterior. A letter from Samuel Vernon to his father gives directions for this process. He ordered "white with a little red lead mixed in" to give a pinkish stone color. William Vernon replied, with a view toward economy as well as toward reproducing the effect of stone, that "Barry can throw the sand on as well as a painter." This sanded surface was without doubt a repetition of the original treatment.

William Vernon continued to play an important part in Newport affairs until his death in 1806; he was instrumental in establishing the Newport Bank, the third bank of Newport, which according to *Mercury* notices, opened its doors in November, 1805. After his death, his son, Samuel, continued to live in the house. By now Samuel Vernon was accounted the richest man in Newport. He also became president of the new bank, and with the Champlins, was foremost in the town's struggle to regain its prewar commercial position, a struggle doomed to failure by the events preceding the War of 1812.

Samuel's brother, William Jr., spent many years abroad. When he returned to Newport he brought back a notable collection of paintings, one of which, a copy of the Mona Lisa given him by Marie Antoinette, has received periodic publicity as possibly painted by Leonardo da Vinci himself. The collection was hung on the walls of the house, where it remained until the house was broken up and sold at auction after William's death in 1839. When Harwood Read bought the house and property in 1872, it had been in the Vernon family for a hundred years. In 1912 the Charity Organization Society, in order to save Rochambeau's headquarters, bought the house and made a partial restoration of it.

Architecturally, the Vernon house is one of Newport's most interesting buildings. As it stands today, doubled in size, it is an excellent example of the fully developed Georgian mansion house. The old building which housed General Rochambeau for a year and where George Washington conferred with the French commander is, with its Chinese frescoes, a unique document of two important building periods.

Abstract of deeds, Survey Notebooks.
Correspondence concerning the paintings in the north parlor, Newport Historical Society.
Maud Lyman Stevens, *The Vernon House* (Newport, 1915).
Elton Manuel, Clarke Street, manuscript.

Pl. 111 *The Francis Malbone House.* The Francis Malbone house, now St. Clare's home which stands between Brewer and Young on Thames Street, has frequently been confused with Godfrey Mal- *u* bone's gambrel-roofed town house, formerly on the northeast corner of Cannon and Thames streets. Francis Malbone's house is a severe square three-story Georgian mansion of brick with a sandstone basement, double belt course, heavy window caps (now removed), and a fine Ionic doorway very similiar in detail to the Ionic portico of the Synagogue. In fact the entire exterior resembles that of the Synagogue. Peter Harrison might well have designed such a building, but his name cannot be definitely connected with it, except for its style, and the fact that it is known that two of the carpenters, Samuel Greene and Wing Spooner, who worked on Redwood Library, also worked on the house.

v

The history of the building, recently traced back to its first ownership, establishes its date of building. In 1758 Mary Wickham sold a lot of land on the east side of Thames Street at Brewer to Francis Malbone, a member of the rich Malbone family and like his cousin Godfrey, a merchant and slave trader. Malbone probably started to build his mansion house soon after he bought the land, since the architectural style accords with this date. The plan is the typical one, based on a broad central hall with a pair of flanking rooms on either side. The hall scheme repeats that of the Vernon house. It has a low dividing arch set on brackets, the stairs are fitted with ramped rail and twisted balusters, and the stair landing is lit by a window of Palladian form.

The front parlors, paneled on all four walls with flush paneling, have dentil cornices and "eared" mantel panels. Two-story pedimented mantels adorn the fireplace walls and the one in the northwest parlor is topped by a broken scroll. The northwest parlor of the Vernon house and the southwest parlor of the Mawdsley house are very similar in character.

Subterranean passages found in the cellar have been traced to a subway leading to the waterside. Such passages were probably used to smuggle dutiable merchandise in the house without benefit of payments to the King's customs, a practice common in the Free Port of Newport, and one upon which many Newport fortunes were founded.

The French billeting list shows that Desandrouins, commanding colonel of the Engineering Corps was quartered with "Captain John Malbone" at 28 Thames Street. This was the Francis Malbone house. Francis Malbone II, elected United State Senator in 1804, just a few months before his death, was the best known later occupant of the house. It was sold out of the family in 1827. In 1833, Joseph Totten of the U. S. Engineers, in Newport at this time to enlarge and rebuild Fort Adams, bought the house. It changed hands a number of times in the ensuing years and in 1910 was taken over by the White Sisters to become St. Clare's home.

Abstract of deeds, Survey Notebooks.
The Reverend Edward Peterson, *History of Rhode Island* (New York, 1853), pp. 134–135.

w

The Banister Country House. One of John Banister's country houses is still standing, set back from the West Main Road at One Mile Corner. Built about 1756, it is a stately gable-on-hip-roofed building with two interior chimneys and a spacious hallway running through the center of the house. A fine stairway with twisted balusters is set at the back of the hall and a round-headed Palladian window lights the broad landing. This detail, together with the fact that the exterior of the building is wood, rusticated to resemble stone, has given rise to the surmise that Peter Harrison may have helped design the house. Since he was John Banister's brother-in-law, although not on good terms with him, it is possible that he may have had a hand in the building. A porch extending around the house is a late addition.

Pl. 112

The house is now unoccupied and it is to be hoped that this once beautiful building may somehow be saved from the fate of Vaucluse, which fell down from neglect, or of Charles Dudley's fine house (almost certainly designed by Harrison) which was only recently pulled down.

Banister's town house and his country house are both sturdy examples of mid-eighteenth-century colonial building. They take on added historic significance in a review of the growth of a town and of a society, since they are almost the sole remaining examples of the pairs of town and country estates which helped give the life of Newport merchants a patrician and a country air. If the gardens were again in order and Banister's wharf, warehouses, and stores at the foot of Pelham Street and his house on Thames Street were still standing, they would give an even truer picture of the expansive living maintained by a wealthy colonial merchant.

Pls. 38, 117–120, 142

Mawdsley-Gardner-Watson-Pitman House. Captain John Mawdsley, who was born in England in 1721, arrived in Newport in young manhood, where he acquired a large fortune in commercial pursuits, was for a time a commander of a privateer, and became prominent in Newport affairs. In 1747 he married Sarah Clarke, descendent of Walter Clarke, one of Rhode Island's early governors. It is not known when he came into possession of the old Jireh Bull House at the corner of King (Franklin) and the old Back Street (Spring), already discussed in the seventeenth-century section of this Appendix, but he probably bought it from Godsgift and Osias Pitkin soon after his marriage. It was just about this time that they were dividing into lots for sale the property that Godsgift Bull Pitkin had inherited from her father Benjamin Bull.

As befitting Mawdsley's affluent position, he soon set to work to enlarge the two-room seventeenth-century house by building a two-room two-story house in front of it and tying the two buildings together with a Newport gable-on-hip roof. The exterior, with its wide, heavily capped windows, modillion cornice, and three pedimented dormer windows, conceals all trace of the earlier building. In the inside, the new stairway, set on the back wall of the new house, was fitted with ramped rails and turned balusters. The southwest parlor was paneled from floor to ceiling on all four sides, and the walls were furred out to allow for the deep window seats and inside shutters considered almost a prerequisite for fine houses of the mid-eighteenth century. The dentil cornice and two-story mantelpiece with its "eared" panel and broken scroll pediment completes the finish of the room and suggests a date of about 1750 or 1760, since the parlor of the Francis Malbone House has a similar mantel and cornice. Mawdsley installed somewhat simpler paneling in the northwest parlor and redecorated the northeast room in the old part of the house. With his house now finished in the best taste of the day, he entertained frequently, and as contemporary accounts had it, "hospitality and urbanity marked his steps."

In her paper on the "Mawdsley House," published in the Newport Historical Society Bulletin, No. 97 (July, 1936), Miss Maud Lyman Stevens gives an excellent and full account of Mawdsley's last years, of life in the house during the years of 1780 and 1781 when it served as the headquarters of François Jean, Marquis de Chastellux, and of its later owners.

Caleb Gardner, another of Newport's prosperous merchants, a Revolutionary war hero, and a friend and correspondent of General Washington, bought the house in 1795, after Mawdsley's death. Gardner installed the handsome fanlight doorway and probably also imported the marble front steps and walk which tradition says were "in honor of a bride." Dr. Daniel Watson bought it in 1827, and it remained in his family for nearly seventy years. In 1902 Theophilus Pitman bought the old house and continued the tradition for gracious living which has saved this building from the fate of so many others in Newport. He installed the mantels in the chambers in the eastern part of the house, which he had brought from the old Benjamin Pitman house on Broadway, torn down at this time. Benjamin Pitman, master builder, who had erected St. Paul's Methodist Church, has been credited with carving these mantels. He also removed the door from the John Pitman house across the street and installed it on the north side of the Mawdsley House.

The house is now owned by the Society for the Preservation of New England Antiquities and serves as headquarters for the Girl Scouts.

Maud Lyman Stevens, "The Mawdsley House," *Newport Historical Society Bulletin*, No. 17 (June, 1936).

Files, Society for the Preservation of New England Antiquities, 4 Lynde Street, Boston, Mass. Notes, elevation and ground plans.

Survey Notebooks, The John Mawdsley and Jireh Bull house. See both Franklin and Spring Streets, Newport Historical Society.

a Deed records and other documentary data are filed in the *Survey Notebooks* in the Newport Historical Society. Referred to hereafter as *Survey Notebooks.*

b Now owned and restored by the Preservation Society of Newport County.

c For "and later lieutenant-governor, who also owned," read "son of Benjamin Nichols and cousin of the lieutenant-governor who," etc.

d Demolished after 1952.

e Demolished after 1952.

f *The Thomas Walker House,* 6 Cross Street, built between 1706 and 1713, should be added to this list. See *Supplement, Key to Map,* under *6 Cross Street,* page 492, for description.

g For "merchant, the proprietor of White Horse Tavern" read "merchant and cousin of," etc.

h For "right-hand parlor" read "throughout the house."

i Additional information about the structural changes in the Jonathan Nichols House.

The 1952-1953 restoration proved that the rear wall had undergone at least three separate alterations. The stereoscopic view of the house made about 1870 by J. Appleby Williams reproduced on Plate 88 shows two segmental headed windows at the stair landing level. When the nineteenth-century porch and bull's-eye window were removed with the intention of restoring these windows it was discovered that the south window did not fit with the stair landing paneling. Even earlier second-story windows framed in and capped as a part of the eaves cornice were also revealed.

Furthermore, the interior staircase, which does not work with either of the window schemes revealed during restoration, shows evidence of having originally been designed for a higher-ceiled house. It has been suggested that this beautiful staircase may have been made for another fine house (such as Malbone Hall, burned in 1766) and was installed here at an early date, perhaps by Joseph Wanton. The photograph on page 292 shows these changes.

j Read "four" for "six."

k Final analysis of the architectural detail and the paint colors indicated that all the paneling and trim in this room were installed at the same time, but that the fireplace opening had originally been larger, and evidently belonged to an earlier treatment of the room.

l Read "walnut" for "mahogany." See note l on page 77 for other color treatment. The downstairs hall was painted a dark grayed blue green, the upper hall a dark olive.

m Read "3 looking glasses."

n 56 Pelham Street.

o 40 Division Street. Restored after 1952. Deed abstracts are in the *Survey Notebooks.* A very large fireplace with the oven located in the back wall was discovered in the old part of the house during restoration.

p Moved to Bridge Street, west of Second in 1965. To be restored.

q The shingles cover the original clapboards.

r 64 Washington Street.

s Read "1872" for "1879."

t See illustrations for the proposed Clarke Street Restoration, page 464 and also Pls. 113–115.

u 392 Thames Street.

v Line 8. See note g on page 91.

w Demolished after 1952. Stair hall and parlors now installed in the Henry Francis du Pont Winterthur Museum.

x No. 228 Spring Street.

Spot Restoration Program Recommended for

HISTORIC NEWPORT

From the findings of the Survey reported in the foregoing pages, the Committee has drawn up a plan for a "spot" or "unit" method of precedure to help preserve Newport's colonial buildings. In this plan, some thirteen areas, all rich in historic houses, have been recommended for future restoration. Routes connecting them have been mapped out, and they have been arbitrarily numbered in terms of their importance, dangerous condition, or location. A single building restored in any part of the town becomes a step in the accomplishment of the whole plan. The areas and buildings so designated are:

1. Clarke Street because of the Vernon house and ten other colonial and early nineteenth-century buildings.
2. The block between the Colony House and Stone Street because of the Wanton-Lyman-Hazard house, a seventeenth-century survivor in the center of the city.
3. The Jonathan Nichols house and Washington Street as a section where merchant princes built their homes, shops, and wharves.
4. The Quaker Meeting House, as the most important seventeenth-century religious building in the state.
5. Division Street, as a street filled with characteristic little houses.
6. Coddington Street, where three almost unknown houses of seventeenth-century construction still stand. *a*
7. The Whitehorse Tavern, and Marlborough Street between Farewell and Thames, with its row of early buildings on the north side. *b*
8. Bowen's Wharf, as the wharf owned by Peter Harrison, and as an example of one of Newport's eighteenth-century shipping centers. Also the old ship chandler's shop, and Robert Stevens' double dwelling house are unique.
9. John Stevens' shop and the row of houses on upper Thames Street, as examples of small shops and homes. *c*
10. Bridge Street, where the houses of Christopher and Job Townsend, John Townsend, Caleb and William Claggett, and Captain Peter Simon stand. *d*
11. The group of little houses along Poplar at Second Street.
12. "The Court End of Town," where Francis Malbone's house of 1760 stands and where Samuel and John Whitehorne, distillers, built their fine houses.
13. The Mawdsley house at John and Spring streets, with its two seventeenth-century and eighteenth-century parts, and the row of early nineteenth-century houses on upper John Street.

Because of its central location, and the Vernon house, Clarke Street has been placed first on the foregoing list. Plans to restore its buildings and gardens have been drawn up. The history of the little street is set forth briefly here.

Clarke Street, a block-long lane laid out in the shadow of the Colony House was named for its earliest owners. The French, however, called it New Lane, and it saw a year of brilliant life in 1780–1781 when General Rochambeau established his headquarters at the Metcalf Bowler house, then in possession of William Vernon. In that same year the French commander had a ballroom built in the garden just north of the house, where the young officers could assemble for dinners, dances, and recreation. In this room, Washington was entertained at a brilliant ball on the evening of March 7, 1781, when he came to Newport to consult with General Rochambeau. He had landed on the Long Wharf the day before and had been received in a splendid military pageant by the army of the allies "drawn up in double lines all the way from Long Wharf past the State House to the Vernon house."

Long before that historical event, however, the land of Clark Street had been part of the original grant made in 1639 to Jeremy Clarke, third governor of the colony. In 1700, a lane was cut through to Peleg Sanford's orchard by Jeremy's son Walter, who was elected Governor three times, and for whom it was named. For many years kept strictly a family affair, its lots were sold off to relatives of the Clarkes, the Rodmans, and the Harwoods. Many of the first buildings are still standing and several have seventeenth-century beginnings, but the street's importance in Newport history belongs to the eighteenth and early nineteenth centuries, when a colonial church and parsonage were built, an artillery building went up (in 1835), and a church school and an academy flourished.

Here lived, side by side with colonial governors, rich merchants, artists, a judge, and an eminent divine, artisans and craftsmen, a list of whose occupations gives a cross section of the ways in which colonial citizens earned their livelihoods. On this short block were once to be found a "tinn man" who made a trumpet for Fort George, a postmaster, a carman (carter), a clothier, an innkeeper, a sadler, a painter, and a brewer. Newport's early leather industry is reflected by the several tanners and cord-wainers (shoe makers) whose homes were on Clarke Street, where also lived housewrights, blacksmiths, schoolmasters, manufacturers, merchants, and mariners.

A brief sketch of each of the individual buildings is included here. Elton Manuel has prepared a fuller account of the denizens of Clarke Street.

See also Plate 62.

THE BUILDINGS ON THE EAST SIDE OF CLARKE STREET

51 Touro Street. In 1800, Joshua Wilbour, housewright, bought from John Rogers, Stephen Hopkins, and William Rodman a lot of land that the Rodman family had owned since Hannah Rodman inherited it from her father Walter Clarke in 1711. In 1802, Wilbour sold the lot with a house built on it to John Wood, a mariner, who in turn sold it in 1809 to William Ellery, III, son of the signer of the Declaration of Independence. It remained in the Ellery family until Issac Gould bought it in 1852. Miss M. E. Powel, in her notes on the Parade, has described the house as her family knew it during the 1840's when they rented it for several Newport summer seasons. William Sherman bought it in 1877 and it has been in the Sherman family since then. It is a three-story wooden mansion house with two interior chimneys, a low hipped roof and characteristic detail of the first years of the nineteenth century. The doorway has been altered.

The proposed restoration removes additions in the rear, replaces the sash for the windows, and substitutes for the present late recessed doorway one drawn from the pages of William Pain, whose books were used as sources for several Newport doors of this period. The lot south of the house would be restored to a garden in accordance with Miss Powel's description of it.

14 Clarke Street, Ezra Stiles' House. In 1756 the Second Congregational Society voted to build a house for the use of the ministry on land given by William Ellery and Peter Coggeshall opposite the meeting house in Clarke Street. In 1765 it was voted that the parsonage house in Clarke Street "together with the lot and garden thereunto belonging is hereby forever appropriated to and for the use of the minister of the Second Congregational Church in Newport."

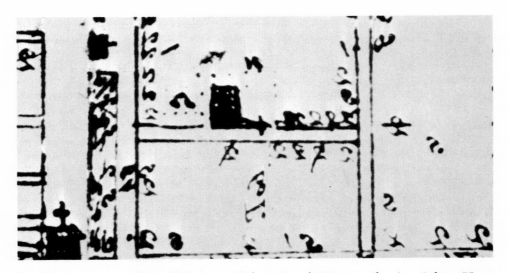

Clarke Street in 1758. Detail from Ezra Stiles' *Map of Newport,* showing Colony House at upper left, the School House in Ann Street at lower left, the Second Congregational Church in Clarke Street. Ezra Stiles own house is across from the church shown as a two story house with a bar, representing two chimneys. The Vernon House is shown as a two story house with one chimney, before enlargement. The Cheeseborough House is shown across Mary Street at the right.

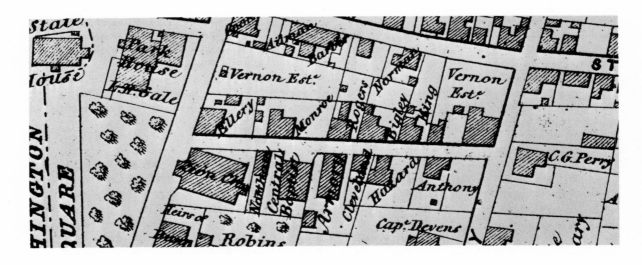

Clarke Street in 1850. Detail from Dripp's *Map of Newport,* showing Zion Church, the Second Congregation Church, now Central Baptist, the Armory, and, on the Vernon estate, the ballroom built by the French. The Cheeseborough House now belongs to C. G. Perry.

Here Ezra Stiles, minister of the Second Congregational Church, lived during his Newport years. In his garden to the south of the house the learned doctor raised the white mulberry trees for his experiments in silk worm culture, and here Mrs. Stiles spun and sent to London for weaving almost enough silk to make a gown, which became a treasured family heirloom. Here Dr. Stiles made his astronomical calculations, and on the evening of June 3, 1769, watched the transit of Venus in company with Henry Marchant and William Vernon, who already lived in the Bowler house down the street.

The parsonage, a great gambrel-roofed building with central doorway and hall, was originally turned end to the streets, with the main door opening on the south into the garden. In 1834, when the Congregational Society sold it to Peter Munro, he turned the house south side to the street, "improved" the porch and entry, and added the Greek Revival detail. The building is now used as the Henderson Home.

In the partial restoration recommended, the bay windows would be removed, the early sash replaced, and the exterior detail of the house taken back to the time of its building in the 1750's. A typical doorway of that date with a pediment and double flight of steps has been chosen to replace the present Greek Revival entry.

The original garden south of the house has not been reconstructed in accordance with the old bounds, but the "pare" trees Stiles mentioned in his diary and the white mulberry trees have been allotted their space in the planting.

No. 26 Clarke Street. Not many years ago a house known as the Jonas Elias house stood on the lot south of Ezra Stiles' garden lot. This old gambrel-roofed house was torn down in 1926, but a history of the property is sketched here. Ebenezer Richardson owned the land in 1725. Years later, in 1818, Daniel Rogers, a manufacturer, sold house and lot to Robert Rogers, Jr., merchant of Bristol. In 1863 the house was sold to William Langley. In the restoration the now empty lot would be gardened. It is possible that an old building moved from elsewhere could be placed here.

No. 28 Clarke Street. Part of this stark high gambrel-roofed house may go back to the first years of the eighteenth century. In 1701, Thomas Mallet, innkeeper, sold the lot to Caleb Hollingsworth, sadler. Five years later Hollingsworth sold it with a dwelling house to Simon Ray of New Shoreham. Ray's deed was delivered in 1707 in the presence of John Carr by "turf and twig," ancient procedure for absentee land transfer. Peter Easton was in possession of the property by 1712, and it remained in his family until after 1727. In 1755, John Bennett sold the house to Joseph Burrill, who was recorded in the early deeds as a "Tinn man" and who was paid "twelve shillings lawful money" out of the General Treasury in 1774 for making a "large speaking trumpet" for use at Fort George. His son Joseph, also a "Tinn plate worker," inherited the house in 1701.

By the time Burrill had willed the house to his son, it had long since taken on its present appearance, but uneven floor levels suggest that part of the older house was built into the newer one. In the proposed restoration small-paned sash windows and an early door have been drawn in to replace the present modern ones.

No. 32 Clarke Street. The history of this property goes back at least to 1722 when Samuel Rhodes, yeoman, sold a dwelling house and lot of land to Simon Pease, mariner. Ezra Stiles' map of 1758 shows a building in this location, but it had disappeared by the time Blascowitz made his map in 1777. Probably the house was rebuilt after the Revolution by Simon Pease, in whose family it remained until Edward Peterson acquired the property in 1799 and sold it almost immediately to the stepfather of Charles Bird King, "limner," one of Newport's native artists, noted for a series of portraits of the Indian chiefs who came to see "the Great White Father" in Washington. He inherited the house from his mother in 1802. Here he lived for many years until he moved to Washington.

In the proposed restoration it has been suggested that the nineteenth-century balcony and the third story built on by Mr. King to serve as his studio both be removed. The house would be restored to a plain two-story building with a gable roof and an ell at the rear. The small paned windows would be put back and the present door replaced by one of a type common to the middle years of the eighteenth century.

Pls. 113–115

The Vernon House. This historic house, architecturally one of the most outstanding buildings in Newport, has been described in Chapter 7 and Appendix A. The proposed restoration advocates replacing the window sash with small-paned glass and replacing the present shutters with ones of early date. It also recommends complete restoration of the interior and careful furnishing with the best of Newport's eighteenth-century furniture.

Pl. 62

French Hall. In 1767 William Vernon purchased the lot just north of the Vernon house for a garden. It was on this garden lot that General Rochambeau caused the ballroom to be built for his officers. Although the Vernons had offered the French general whatever assistance possible, this elicited a complaint from William Vernon in a letter to his son Samuel, written in 1781, "I understand General Rochambeau had not your leave for building an Assembly-room in the garden. I can't think it polite of him." "French Hall," a square rusticated building resembling the main house, stood until 1894, when it was torn down to allow for the present building. Because of its historic interest, it has been recommended that the Assembly Hall built by the French be rebuilt. This could be accomplished from information based on descriptions and photographs.

Southwest Corner Lot. In 1782, Samuel Vernon bought a lot with a partially demolished house on it on the west side of Clarke at Mary Street and converted it into an additional garden, the broad central path and attractive beds of which are still remembered by old Newporters. Part of this lot would be restored as a garden.

THE BUILDINGS ON THE WEST SIDE OF CLARKE STREET

Pl. 147

The Zion Episcopal Church. In 1701, Walter Clarke sold the land (fenced), on which this church was to be built years later, to John Headley, a brewer. In 1759, Thomas Cranston sold the lot with a house on it to Peleg Barker, Esquire, a schoolmaster. The house was gone by 1832 when John Lyon sold the lot to the Building Committee of Zion Church with the "foundation stone of a cellar." In the following year, Russell Warren, who also designed the Levi Gale house was employed to build the church in the correct Greek Revival manner of an Ionic prostyle temple. It served as an Episcopal Church until it was sold to St. Joseph's Church in 1885. It now serves as a motion picture theatre.

The proposed restoration, which is based on an old photograph, would restore the Ionic portico.

No. 11 Clarke Street — The Bell or Richmond House. The gable-roofed house at 11 Clarke Street was raised some years ago to allow room for a garage underneath. Old pictures show it as a two-story house with a plain central doorway which opened into a small stair hall in front of the central chimney. Little houses like this one were the characteristic homes of Newport's early artisans and workers. In 1780 "Peleg Barker Esq." owned the house. He advertised in that year in the pages of the *Mercury,* "an evening school for teaching reading, writing and arithmetic." In 1789 he sold house and lot to Matthew Barker, blacksmith. Matthew and his wife owned it until 1796, when they sold it to Gideon Richmond, "carman." In 1829 Gideon's son, Gideon, a cordwainer, sold part of the house of Dr. Benjamin Case. Sometime thereafter the house was divided in ownership, and remained divided until 1879, when it was sold at auction to Isaac Sherman. It is now owned by Elizabeth Bell.

The restoration proposed suggests dropping the house down to its original height, removing an addition at the north side and replacing the central doorway. A plain board fence has been chosen to enclose a garden laid out at the side and rear of the house.

Pl. 61

The Second Congregational Church. This building, built by Cotton Palmer in 1735, has been described at length in Chapter 5. The Central Baptists bought the building in 1847, at which time they made extensive changes which included lengthening the house to ninety-three feet and enclosing the tower in the body of the church. They also added the Greek Revival exterior and interior detail, but Cotton Palmer's spire above the tower was allowed to keep its old appearance. A view of Clarke Street made by J. A. Williams before 1874 shows it still unchanged. In 1874–1875 wings were added and the Victorian detail was encrusted on the façade and spire, although the basic lines of the original spire remained unaltered until it was taken down in 1946.

The present restoration suggests rebuilding the spire in its original form, but keeps the Greek Revival detail and the wings in accordance with the last enlargement in size. Photographs, old views of Newport, internal evidence, and the church records would make possible, at least on the exterior, a complete restoration of Cotton Palmer's original house.

The Newport Artillery. In 1835, the Newport Artillery, now the oldest active military organization in America, voted to build a new "armoury." The year before, Audley Clarke, Newport merchant and benefactor, had given the land on Clarke Street "in consideration of my feeling of attachement and good will towards the Artillery Company of Newport, a military company chartered by the Assembly in A.D. 1741." Enoch Hazard gave the stone.

Alexander McGregor, a stone mason who had come to Newport from Scotland and who had worked under Major Joseph Totten on the 1833 part of Fort Adams, was contractor for the building. As finished in 1836, it was one story high with a gable roof. In 1906 the house was raised a story. In 1880, Colonel John Hare Powel presented the Society with the emblems from the paddle-box of the S.S. "Metropolis," dismantled in Newport harbor in 1878, and these now decorate the front gable end of the building.

In the proposed restoration it is recommended that the building be restored to its original height of one story and that the flagpole which once stood in front of the Armory be replaced.

No. 27 Clarke Street — Cuthbert Campbell Lot. Although the house standing on the lot south of the Artillery lot is late (the third to be built on the property), the story of the lot is an interesting one.

In 1699 Walter Clarke sold it, designated then as the "fifth lot" north of Peleg Sanford's orchard, to William Rhoad, cordwainer. In 1716, John Wright, clothier, owned it. A house had been built there by that time because in that year Wright sold the lot with "dwelling house" to Cuthbert Campbell, one of Newport's first postmasters. Here the man who was responsible for the care of the eagerly awaited weekly *Boston News Letter* and other mail "by post" lived for many years. The house remained in his family until his granddaughter, Elizabeth Hargill, widow of the tanner, Barnabas Hargill, sold it in 1779 to Robert Stevens, East Greenwich merchant.

By 1837 this first old house was gone. Seth Cleveland bought the lot of land in 1842, and probably built very soon after the little one-story Greek Revival house which shows in some of the old views of Clarke Street. This house has been moved back and built into the ell of a large rooming house, the old Cleveland hotel, which now stands on the spot where lived one of Newport's first postmasters, and one after the other of her artisan tradesmen, cordwainer, clothier, tanner, and merchant.

The Newport Academy. In 1786 Robert Rogers, a graduate of Brown University and a lieutenant in the Revolutionary war, advertised in the pages of the *Mercury* that a "considerable addition had been made to the Academy lately erected in this city in order to accommodate a larger number of pupils entrusted to his care."

This Academy stood back of Cuthbert Campbell's house just south of the Artillery lot, and a way ten feet wide was laid out to it to be kept open "forever." It was a plain one-story building set on a high foundation. A flight of six wooden steps led to the entrance on the northeast corner, and the addition Mr. Rogers advertised, built on the east, was used for a girl's school.

In 1803 when Mr. Rogers retired, Levi Tower, also a Brown graduate and one of Rogers' assistants, took over the duties of master. The school was discontinued about 1840, and the building is now gone, but part of its history is included here. Miss Ruth Franklin, in her paper, "Some Early Schools and Schoolmasters of Newport," describes vividly the conduct of the school under Mr. Tower.

"The room was as cold as a barn — the only heat from a wood stove — and illustrated all the climates of the globe. In close proximity to the stove, it was torrid; a few feet away, temperate; around the sides, frigid. Scholars were allowed to stand near the stove as long as they could manage to stand on one foot and hold the sole of the other up to it. Mr. Tower said — 'if you are cold you can do it without wavering, if you can't, go back to your seat.' There were long wooden desks arranged on a terraced platform, the back row for older scholars, the second for those less advanced, the lowest for beginners. In the flat part of each desk a hole was bored to hold the ink horn. The ink was made by the teacher from powder, and kept in a jug which was filled on Monday and emptied back on Friday. Red ink was made from 'pigeon berries.' A terrestrial and a celestial globe completed the equipment. The teacher had a stand up desk on which were kept the ruler and the cowhide, which were

Clarke Street today. Looking north from Mary Street, showing left,
the John Odlin House and right, the Vernon House.
Photo, Ralph Arnold.

Clarke Street in 1870. Looking north from Mary Street, showing left, John Odlin and
Robert Stevens houses, Newport Artillery, Second Congregational Church, and part of
the Zion Episcopal Church; right, the Vernon House and French Hall.
Old photograph by J. Appleby Williams. (N.H.S.)

Robert Stevens House, 31 Clarke Street, about 1709.
Enlarged in the mid-eighteenth century.
Photo, Ralph Arnold.

View of the east side of Clarke Street. Proposed restoration. Showing left to right,
the Joshua Wilbour, Ezra Stiles, Joseph Burrill, Simon Pease houses,
French Hall, and the Vernon House.
Rendered by Edward Doyle.

John Odlin House, 41 Clarke Street.
Restored sketch.

Robert Stevens House, 31 Clarke Street.
Sketch.

Newport Artillery. Restored sketch

Plan for gardens in Clarke Street.
Drawn by Philip D. Creer.

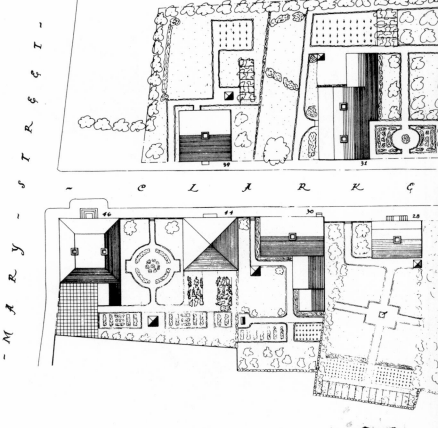

Vernon House,
Rochambeau's Newport Headquarters. Restored sketch.

Simon Pease House, 32 Clarke Street.
Restored sketch.

Joseph Burrill House, 28 Clarke Stree
Restored sk

Second Congregational Church.
Partially restored sketch.

Peleg Barker House, 11 Clarke Street.
Restored sketch.

Zion Episcopal Church. Restored sketch.

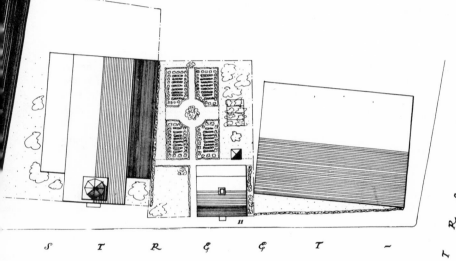

SKETCHES FOR
THE PROPOSED CLARKE STREET
RESTORATION.

Prepared by Philip D. Creer.

Ezra Stiles House, 14 Clarke Street.
Partially restored sketch.

Joshua Wilbour House. 1802. Restored sketch.

frequently required for punishment. Discipline was harsh and penalties severe. There were no vacations. School hours were from nine to twelve and from two to five. . . Each scholar had to provide himself with an English Reader, Murray's Grammar, a Spelling book, a Geography, Daholl's Arithmetic, a slate, goosequills for pens, one-half quire of Fool's cap paper, and a piece of lead for a 'plummet' to rule his writing book. No lead pencils were allowed. Ciphering and writing books were made by the teacher from the paper furnished by the pupils and had paper covers."

In 1851, the town of Newport bought the Academy and built in its place the old Clarke Street School, This building, like the earlier one, has disappeared, and the land now forms part of the grounds of the John Clarke School. Because of practical considerations, this land has not been included in the proposed restoration, although the story of the Academy rightfully belongs to Clarke Street.

31 Clarke Street — The Robert Stevens House. The two-and-a-half-story gambrel-roofed house with its end set to the street and its fanlight doorway opening into a south garden must look much as it did in 1780–1781 when Rochambeau's young aides-de-camp, Conte Axel de Fersen and the Marquis de Damas were quartered there. The officers were among the most colorful figures in the French Army, and Axel de Fersen had a particularly romantic career, described more fully in Chapter 6.

Robert Stevens, upholsterer, and father of the merchant of the same name who owned the old Stevens wharf off Thames Street, was in possession of 31 Clarke Street during these years. He had bought the house in 1742 from Comfort Hatch, the widow of Nathaniel Hatch. Although early deeds show that a house was built on the property as early as 1709, the present building is mid-eighteenth-century in character. The interior is severely plain, and the chief ornamental feature of the exterior, the door, belongs to the last years of the eighteenth century. Robert Stevens probably remodeled the widow Hatch's house extensively or built a new one soon after he purchased the property in 1742.

In 1815 Robert Rogers bought the house and was living in it when Washington Allston, the painter, boarded there while he attended the Clarke Street Academy and studied art with Samuel King. The only change suggested in the proposed restoration is the substitution of small paned sash in place of the larger paned windows installed at the present time.

39 Clarke Street — The Melville House. As mentioned in Chapter 6 the Comte de Laberdiere and the Baron de Closen were quartered with "Henri Potter" at what is now No. 39 Clarke Street. The history of the property goes back to the end of the seventeenth century, when John Odlin owned a house and lot in Clarke Street. He left both to his great-grandson, Henry Potter. Odlin's old house, according to Henry Bull, was still standing in 1841, but when the Melville family bought the property in 1869, they moved the house they owned on Frank Street to the Clarke Street lot. The narrow, high pitch-roofed house standing there today is probably the Frank Street house. It has been much altered. In style it belongs to the early part of the eighteenth century, and would be restored to that appearance.

---

a One has been demolished since 1952.

b Two have been demolished since 1952.

c Eight have been restored since 1952.

d Job Townsend's House has been demolished since 1952. The Captain Peter Simon and the William and Caleb Claggett Houses have been restored.

NOTES

Notes

INTRODUCTION

1. John Russell Bartlett, *Records of the Colony of Rhode Island and Providence Plantations*, III (Providence, 1858), 255.

2. George C. Mason, Jr., "Colonial Architecture," *American Architect and Building News*, X (Boston, August 13, 1881), 71ff. and (August 20, 1881), 83ff.

3. Richard M. Bayles, *History of Newport County, Rhode Island* (New York, 1888), p. 356.

4. Elton M. Manuel, *Merchants and Mansions of Bygone Days* (Newport, 1939), p. 14.

5. Deed abstracts for the Simeon Potter house, filed under Washington Street, Survey Notebooks, Newport Historical Society.

6. See Walnut Street, deed abstracts and notes for the Matthew Calbraith Perry house, Survey Notebooks, Newport Historical Society.

7. Maud Lyman Stevens, "Newport Streets," *Newport Historical Society Bulletin*, no. 67 (Newport, December 1928).

8. Abstracts of deeds and notes are filed under house numbers and names of individual owners, Bridge Street, Survey Notebooks, Newport Historical Society.

9. Thomas R. Hazard, *Recollections of Olden Times* (Newport, 1879), *passim*, gives a full account of Hannah Robinson's life and marriage. He includes a description of the Captain Peter Simon house, p. 51; Manuel, *op. cit.*, pp. 15–16.

10. Abstract of deeds, Caleb and William Claggett houses, Bridge Street, Survey Notebooks, Newport Historical Society.

11. Abstract of deeds for no. 44 Thames Street, Survey Notebooks, Newport Historical Society; *Gentleman's Progress, The Itinerarium of Dr. Alexander Hamilton, 1744*, ed. by Carl Bridenbaugh (Chapel Hill, 1948), p. 102.

12. Manuel, *op. cit.*, p. 17.

13. See Susan Bailey Franklin, "Division Street," *Newport Historical Society Bulletin*, no. 104 (March, 1948), for an account of this street, its houses, and its inhabitants.

14. George Champlin Mason, *Reminiscences of Newport* (Newport, 1884), pp. 330–340; Ruth Thomas, *Catalogue of Retrospective Exhibition of Works of Artists Identified with Newport*, The Art Association (Newport, 1936), p. 12.

15. Mason, *op. cit.*, pp. 390–391.

16. *Diary of Frederick MacKenzie*, I (Cambridge, 1930), 256.

CHAPTER ONE

Early Settlement

1. "Peter Easton's Notes," *Rhode Island Historical Society Collections*, XI, no. 3 (Providence, July, 1918), 78–79.

2. Henry Bull, "Memoir of Rhode Island, 1636–1783." Published in the *Rhode Island Republican*, January 3, 1832 to December 26, 1838 and the *Newport Mercury*, January 14, 1854 to November 23, 1861. In 1888, Charles E. Hammett made a typewritten indexed copy in two volumes, volume one of which is in the Newport Historical Society and volume two in the Rhode Island Historical Society. It is in the form of a chronological calendar. Under date of 1641, Bull records that Easton's house was burned April 4th.

3. William Babcock Weeden, *Early Rhode Island* (New York, 1910), p. 60; William P. Sheffield, *Historical Address, July 4, 1876* (Newport, 1876), Appendix, pp. iv–vii.

4. Bartlett, *Records of the Colony of Rhode Island*, I, 374–380.

5. John Callender, *An Historical Discourse on the Civil and Religious Affairs of the Colony of Rhode Island*, ed. by Romeo Elton (Boston, 1843), pp. 242–243.

6. Carl Bridenbaugh, *Cities in the Wilderness* (New York, 1938), p. 98.

7. *Touro Synagogue*, published by the Society of the Friends of Touro Synagogue, National Historic Shrine, Inc. (Newport, n. d.), pp. 28–33; *Historic Newport*, Newport Chamber of Commerce (1933), pp. 30–31.

8. Weeden, *op. cit.*, pp. 68-69.

9. Bartlett, *Records of the Colony of Rhode Island*, II, 127, report dated 1665; cf. also *Callendar of State Papers, Colonial Series, America and West Indies*, ed. by W. N. Sainsbury (London, 1893), 1675-1676: No. 543, Ap. 29, "An Account taken from Mr. Harris of New England," p. 221. "In Rhode Island the houses are very good especially at Newport, where there are more sheep than any where else in New England. The haven is very commodious, being just upon the sea, whereas that of Boston is 2 or 3 miles within the land, and is large enough for 100 ships; this island is about 12 miles long and 2 broad, and is the garden of New England."

10. Bridenbaugh, *op. cit.*, pp. 23-24.

11. Quoted in full in Bull's "Memoir of Rhode Island," under date of 1680.

12. *The Letter Book of Peleg Sanford 1666-1688*, printed for the Rhode Island Historical Society (Providence, 1928).

13. Howard M. Chapin, *Privateer Ships and Sailors, 1625-1725* (Toulon, France, 1926), pp. 71-76.

14. Bartlett, *op. cit.*, report dated 1678-1706, III, 385.

15. Chapin, *op. cit.*, pp. 69-70, 76-78.

16. Weeden, *Early Rhode Island*, p. 66.

17. *New England Historical and Genealogical Register*, XXXVIII (Boston, 1884), 380.

18. William P. Sheffield, *Historical Address*, Appendix, p. vi.

19. *Rhode Island Historical Magazine*, VI (Newport, July, 1885), Will of Governor Benedict Arnold, 20-38.

20. Dr. Henry E. Turner, *William Coddington in Rhode Island Colonial Affairs*, Rhode Island Historical Tracts, ed. Sidney Rider (Providence, 1877), no. 4, pp. 51-52.

21. *Newport Mercury* (October 17, 1835); *Herald of the Times* (October 15, 1835), p. 2.

22. *Rhode Island Land Evidence, 1648-1696* (Providence, 1921), pp. 54-56.

23. Sheffield, *op. cit.*, Appendix, pp. vi-vii.

24. Benjamin B. Howland, "The Streets of Newport," *Magazine of New England History*, II, no. 2 (Newport, 1891), 77-81.

25. Newport and Middletown Proprietors Records, 1701-1756, copied by G. H. Richardson, Book no. 976, Newport Historical Society, Vault, p. 7.

26. Quoted in Gertrude Selwyn Kimball, *Pictures of Rhode Island in the Past* (Providence, 1900), p. 13.

27. "Memoir of Rhode Island," under date of 1770 (Hammett, II, 271-280).

28. Mason, *Reminiscences of Newport*, p. 27.

29. Howland, *op. cit.*, p. 80; Town Meeting Records (in the Newport Historical Society), I, 138.

30. "Memoir of Rhode Island," under date of 1707 (Hammett, I, 507).

31. *Some Cursory Remarks Made by James Birket in his Voyage to North America, 1750-1751* (Yale University Press, 1916). Excerpts published in the *Rhode Island Historical Society Collections*, XIII, no. 2 (April, 1920), under title of "Rhode Island in 1750," 62-63.

32. *Gentleman's Progress*, ed. Bridenbaugh, p. 101.

CHAPTER TWO

Early Building

1. For a discussion of medieval English tools see C. F. Innocent, *The Development of English Building Construction* (Cambridge, England, 1916), pp. 95ff. See also Henry F. Mercer, "Ancient Carpenter's Tools," published serially in *Old Time New England* (Boston), beginning vol. XV, no. 4, April, 1925, for a study of colonial tools and their uses.

2. N. M. Isham, *Early American Houses* (Boston, 1928), *passim*.

3. Bull, "Memoir of Rhode Island," under date of 1687.

4. *Ibid.*, under date of 1711-1712.

5. *Ibid.*, under date of 1738.

6. Friends' Records, in the Newport Historical Society. For excerpts relating to the building of the Meeting House, see "Friends' Meeting House," filed under Farewell Street, Survey Notebooks, Newport Historical Society.

7. "Rhode Island in 1750," *Rhode Island Historical Society Collections*, XIII, no. 2 (April, 1920), 62.

8. W. S. Godfrey, Jr., "The Newport Puzzle," *Archaeology* (Autumn, 1949), pp. 146-149, and "Newport Tower, II," *Archaeology* (Summer, 1950), pp. 82-86.

9. "Peter Easton's Notes," *Rhode Island Historical Society Collections*, II, 78-79.

10. The original document is owned by William Davis Miller. See P. A. Means, *Newport Tower* (New York, 1942), p. 142, as well as footnotes 8 and 9.

11. *Rhode Island History*, VII, no. 1 (Providence, January, 1948), 1-7.

12. Rex Wailes, "Notes on Some Windmills in New England," *Old Time New England*, XXI (Boston, 1931), 99-128.

13. Elisha S. Arnold, *The Arnold Memorial* (Rutland, Vermont, 1935) pp. 1, 13-28, 52-54.

14. Henry-Russell Hitchcock, *Rhode Island Architecture* (Providence, 1939), p. 15.

15. Joan Marion, Correspondence with the Newport Historical Society, 1948.

16. Isham, *Early Rhode Island Houses* (Providence, 1895), p. 73; Mason, *Reminiscences of Newport*, p. 404.

17. Published in the *Magazine of American History*, III (New York and Chicago, 1877), 541ff.

18. In *Old Time New England*, XXI (1931), 99–128.

19. *Newport Historical Society Bulletin*, no. 21 (January, 1917).

20. Isham, *op. cit.*, p. 56; Henry Bull, IV, "The Bull Family in Newport," *Newport Historical Society Bulletin*, no. 81 (October, 1931), pp. 2–5.

21. "Memoir of Rhode Island," under date of 1727 (Hammett, II, 77).

22. W. L. Watson, *A Short History of Jamestown*, reprint of an article prepared for the Rhode Island Historical Society (Providence, 1933), p. 21.

23. According to a little drawing on an old plat of highways in South Kingstown in 1727, Colonel Allen's house had a similar side chimney. See William Davis Miller, *Early Houses of the King's Province* (Wakefield, 1941), pp. 12–13.

24. John Hutchins Cady, "The Stone Ender — From Sussex to R. I.," *Providence Sunday Journal, The Rhode Islander* (October 9, 1949).

25. J. A. and F. W. Tillinghast, *A Little Journey to the Home of Elder Pardon Tillinghast* (Providence, 1908), p. 6.

26. Mason, *Reminiscences*, pp. 404–405.

27. C. P. Coggeshall, *The Coggeshalls in America* (Boston, 1930), p. 9.

28. George H. Richardson, Manuscript Notes, Book no. 999, Vault, Newport Historical Society, p. 29.

29. See abstract of deed records, Bliss farm, filed under Bliss Road, Survey Notebooks, Newport Historical Society.

30. Isham, *Early Rhode Island Houses*, p. 55.

31. Jonas Bergner, manuscript and portfolio of drawings, Vault, Newport Historical Society, floor plan of the Voax house.

32. See inventory of the Ebenezer Flagg Estate, Town Council Book 13, p. 186. Published in the *Newport Gazette*, I, no. 1 (October, 1947). In the Survey Notebook file under Pitt's Head Tavern, Charles Street, Newport Historical Society.

33. Elizabeth C. Brenton, *A History of Brenton's Neck* (Newport, 1877), p. 7.

34. "Rhode Island in 1750," *Rhode Island Historical Society Collections*, XIII, no. 2 (April, 1920), 64.

35. See abstract of deed records, Newport National Bank, filed under Washington Square, Survey Notebooks, Newport Historical Society.

36. The Reverend Edward Peterson, *History of Rhode Island* (New York, 1853), p. 58.

37. See abstract of deed records, Peleg Sanford house, 2, 4, 6 Broadway, Survey Notebooks, Newport Historical Society.

38. See notes, the Lawton house, Marlborough Street, Survey Notebooks, Newport Historical Society.

39. See notes and deed abstracts, Sueton Grant house, Thames Street, Survey Notebooks, Newport Historical Society; Bergner, Portfolio, Drawings, Newport Historical Society; *Newport Daily News*, October 14, 1898, p. 3.

40. Gould Day Book, no. 1234, Vault, Newport Historical Society, records removal.

41. See abstract of deed records, Walter Clarke house, Elm Street, Survey Notebooks, Newport Historical Society.

42. Isham, *Early Rhode Island Houses*, pp. 58–59.

CHAPTER THREE

Society and Commerce

1. See Charles E. Hammett, *A Contribution to the Bibliography and Literature of Newport, R.I.* (Newport, 1886), p. 81, for all the notations Stiles made on both sides of the map.

2. "Commerce of Rhode Island, 1726–1800," I (1726–1774), *Collections of the Massachusetts Historical Society*, Seventh series, IX (Boston, 1914), prefatory note and *passim*.

3. Bridenbaugh, *Cities in the Wilderness*, p. 337.

4. G. C. Mason, "The United Company of Spermaceti Chandlers, 1761," *Magazine of New England History*, II, no. 2 (April, 1892), 163–169; Weeden, *Early Rhode Island*, p. 329; *Commerce of Rhode Island*, I, Prefatory note and 88–92.

5. Bruce M. Bigelow, unpublished doctoral thesis, Commerce between Rhode Island and the West Indies before the Revolution, John Hay Library, Brown University.

6. Chapin, *Privateer Ships and Sailors*, Chapters I, V, and XI; W. P. Sheffield, *Privateersmen of Newport* (Newport, 1883); W. B. Weeden, *Economic and Social History of New England*, II (Boston and New York, 1890), 601–602.

7. *Commerce of Rhode Island*, I, preface and *passim*; Weeden, *Early Rhode Island*, pp. 187–189; Roderick Terry, "Some Old Papers Relating to the Newport Slave Trade," *Newport Historical Society Bulletin*, no. 62 (July, 1927); I. B. Richmond, *Rhode*

b

Island (Boston and New York, 1905), pp. 112–118.

8. "Memoir of Rhode Island," under date of 1715 (Hammett, II, 3).

9. Bridenbaugh, *Cities in the Wilderness*, pp. 413–414.

10. *Rhode Island Historical Society Collections*, XXVI, no. 1 (January, 1933).

11. Bigelow, *op. cit., passim.*

12. G. C. Mason, *Annals of the Redwood Library* (Newport, 1891), pp. 67–69; "Genealogy of the Redwood Family," *Newport Historical Magazine*, I, no. 1 (Newport, 1880), 7–16.

13. Quoted by Alice Brayton in her lively account of the Redwood gardens, in *Gardens of Colony and State*, I (New York, 1931), 218.

14. From "Solomon Drowne's Journal," *The Newport Historical Magazine*, I, no. 2 (October, 1880), 67–68.

15. "A German Gardener at Newport in 1754," *Rhode Island Historical Society Collections*, XXIII, no. 1 (January, 1930), 10–13.

16. "Genealogy of the Redwood Family," p. 13.

17. *Gardens of Colony and State*, I, 219.

18. Fiske Kimball, "Colonial Amateurs and their Models: Peter Harrison," in two parts in *Architecture*, LIII, no. 6 (June, 1925), 155–160; and LIV, no. 6 (July, 1926), 185–190; see especially 186.

19. Bridenbaugh, *Cities in the Wilderness*, p. 413.

20. Richard LeBaron Bowen, "Godfrey Malbone's Armorial Silver," *Rhode Island History*, IX, no. 1, 37–51 and no. 3, 84–94; Peterson, *History of Rhode Island*, pp. 115–116, 134, 135.

21. Mary E. Powel, "A Few Words about Some Old Buildings in Newport," *Newport Historical Society Bulletin*, no. 55 (October, 1925), p. 19, writes that Peter Harrison is supposed to have designed this house, but Harrison did not arrive in Newport until 1738, ten years after it was built. Isham thought, because of its stylistic similarity to the Synagogue, that Harrison may have designed the Francis Malbone house at Thames and Brewer. This latter house, which was built in about 1760, has sometimes been confused with the Godfrey Malbone house. Perhaps this is why the earlier house has been attributed to Harrison. Both of Malbone's houses (town and country) belonged to an earlier style of building than any of Harrison's known work. If attributed at all, these houses should be attributed to Munday or to workmen of his period.

22. "A Newport Painter's Bill," *Newport Historical Magazine*, III, no. 1 (July, 1882), 56.

23. John Stevens' account book, II (owned by John Howard Benson). Entered under date of December, 1749, "to altering your chimney 4-0-0, to setting your marble chimney piece and laying the hearth 15-0-0."

24. Peterson, *History of Rhode Island*, pp. 134–135.

25. See Fiske Kimball, *Domestic Architecture of the American Colonies and Early Republic* (New York, 1922) for a good discussion of the significance of the Hancock house; also W. K. Watkins, "The Hancock House and its Builder," in *Old Time New England*, XVII, no. 1 (July, 1926), 3–19.

26. See Alice Brayton's interesting account of Godfrey Malbone and her history of Malbone Hall in *Gardens of Colony and State*, I, 208ff.

27. Powel, *op. cit.*, p. 19.

28. Peterson, *op. cit.*, pp. 134–135.

29. Bowen, *op. cit., passim.*

30. *Gentleman's Progress*, p. 103.

31. "Rhode Island in 1750," *Rhode Island Historical Society Collections*, XIII, no. 2, 61.

32. "Memoir of Rhode Island," under date of 1766 (Hammett, II, 240).

33. Published in part in the *Newport Historical Society Bulletin*, no. 85 (October, 1932).

34. Dr. H. E. Turner, "Henry Collins," *Rhode Island Historical Magazine*, V, n. 2 (1884), 81–84.

35. Bridenbaugh, *Cities of the Wilderness*, p. 459.

36. Ernest Flagg, *Founding of New England* (Hartford, 1926), pp. 142–143; see also abstract of deeds and the *Newport Gazette*, XI, no. 1 (October, 1947), pamphlet, filed under Pitt's Head Tavern, Washington Square, Survey Notebooks, Newport Historical Society.

37. Peterson, *op. cit.*, pp. 90–92; Mason, *Annals of the Redwood Library*, pp. 26–27.

38. Sheffield, *Historical Discourse*, appendix, pp. xiv–xv; see also abstracts of records of the Town Council Meetings of 1780 pertaining to the Collins property, on file under Washington Street, Survey Notebooks, Newport Historical Society.

39. W. Updike, *History of the Narragansett Church*, II (Boston, 1907), 78–91 and notes, pp. 315–319 gives an excellent account of Collins' Narragansett house and gardens during Rome's ownership.

40. N. P. Bowler, *The Bowler Genealogy* (Cleveland, 1905), pp. 9, 11–15; M. L. Stevens, *A History of the Vernon House in Newport, Rhode Island* (Newport, 1915), pp. 6–7.

41. W. P. and J. P. Cutler, *Life, Journals and Correspondence of Rev. Manasseh Cutler, L.L.D.*, I (Cincinnati, 1888), 68–69.

42. See "Aquidneck," July 21, 1884, Stanhope Book B, p. 32, Newport Historical Society, for an account of the eagles. George C. Mason wrote under the name of Aquidneck. See *Providence Journal*, June 11, 1884.

43. *Rhode Island Historical Society Collections*, XXIII, no. 4 (October, 1930), 101–117.

44. Bartlett, *Colonial Records*, III, 160; Lee Friedman, "In the Early Days," in *Touro Synagogue*, pp. 28–32.

45. See M. A. Gutstein, *The Story of the Jews in Newport* (New York, 1936), particularly pp. 53–57; also *Touro Synagogue*, p. 10.

46. Bruce M. Bigelow, "Aaron Lopez, Colonial Merchant of Newport," *New England Quarterly*, IV, no. 4 (Portland, Maine, 1931), 757–776.

47. *The Literary Diary of Ezra Stiles*, ed. by F. B. Dexter, III (New York, 1901), 24.

48. "Rhode Island in 1750," *Rhode Island Historical Society Collections*, XIII, no. 2, 62.

49. From Monck Berkeley's Memoirs, quoted in *Early Religious Leaders of Newport* (Newport, 1918) in the paper by Stanley Hughes, "Very Rev. Dean George Berkeley, DD," p. 90

50. "Memoir of Rhode Island," under date of 1729 (Hammett, II, 87–98) gives an interesting account of Berkeley's stay in Newport; see also Hughes, *op. cit.*, pp. 79–96.

51. Peterson, *History of Rhode Island*, pp. 127–130.

52. Letter to the Secretary of the Society for the Propagation of the Gospel in Foreign Parts, published in Hawkins, *Historical Notices of the Missions of the Church of England*, pp. 165–167. Reprinted in Updike, *History of the Narragansett Church*, I, 162.

53. Bridenbaugh, *Cities in the Wilderness*, pp. 419–421.

54. Franklin, "Division Street," p. 31.

55. The Reverend Roderick Terry, "Rev. Dr. Ezra Stiles," in *Early Religious Leaders of Newport*, p. 163.

56. *Ibid.*, p. 174.

57. Mason, *Annals of the Redwood Library* (Newport, 1891), pp. 27–28.

58. Mason, *Annals of Trinity Church* (Newport, 1890), pp. 120–121.

59. J. C. Trent, *Benjamin Waterhouse, 1754–1826* (1946); Sheffield, *Historical Address*, Appendix, p. xiii.

60. Sheffield, *ibid.*, Appendix, p. xiv.

61. Lawrence C. Wroth, *Catalogue of an Exhibition Held in the John Carter Brown Library in Honor of the Walpole Society* (Boston, October 26, 1945), pp. 12–13, 17–18, 41–44.

62. H. M. Chapin, "Ann Franklin, Printer," from the *American Book Collector* (September, 1926).

63. See abstract of deeds, Caleb and William Claggett houses, Bridge Street, Survey Notebooks, Newport Historical Society; Manuel, *Merchants and Mansions of Bygone Days*, pp. 17–18 gives a brief account of William Claggett.

64. H. M. Chapin, "Was Claggett the Clockmaker an Engraver," *Rhode Island Historical Society Collections*, XXII, no. 2 (April, 1929), 41–42; *The Boston Evening Post*, March 3, 1746, extract of a letter from Newport; also December 29, 1746:

We hear from Newport, on Rhode Island, that Mr. William Clagget of that Town, has at last succeeded so far in the Electrical Experiments, as to set Fire to Spirits of Wine, the most satisfactory and difficult of all . . . .

Albert L. Partridge, "William Claggett of Newport, Rhode Island, Clockmaker," in *Old Time New England*, XXVII, no. 3 (January, 1937), 110–115.

65. Ruth Thomas, *Catalogue of the Retrospective Exhibition of the Work of Artists Identified with Newport, passim*.

66. *Ibid.*, p. 11.

67. Lawrence Park, *Gilbert Stuart* (New York, 1926); see also Frank Swan, *The Colony House* (Providence, n.d.), pp. 9–10 and Mason, *Reminiscences*, pp. 289–293 for an account of the two portraits of George Washington that Stuart painted for Newport and Providence.

68. *Retrospective Exhibition*, p. 7 and frontispiece; F. W. Bayley, *Five Colonial Artists* (Boston, 1929), pp. 335–340 and plates.

69. Carl Bridenbaugh, *Peter Harrison, First American Architect* (Chapel Hill, 1949), pp. 73, 78 and footnote 17.

70. H. W. Foote, *Robert Feke* (Cambridge, 1930), *passim* and catalogue of portraits; Bayley, *Five Colonial Artists*, pp. 293–296 and the early self portrait, p. 297.

71. *Literary Diary of Ezra Stiles*, I, 52, 65, 131, and 367; *Retrospective Exhibition*, p. 10.

72. *Retrospective Exhibition*, p. 10.

73. *Ibid.*, p. 15.

74. *Ibid.*

75. Mabel Swan, "The Goddard and Townsend Joiners," *Antiques*, XLIX, no. 4 (April, 1946), 228–231 and no. 5 (May, 1946), 292–295.

76. See the abstracts of deed records for the Goddard and Townsend houses on Washington, Bridge, Third, and Walnut streets, Survey Notebooks, Newport Historical Society.

77. N. M. Isham, "John Goddard and His Work," *Rhode Island School of Design Bulletin*, XV, no. 5 (April, 1927), 14–24; Joseph Downs, "The Furniture of Goddard and Townsend," *Antiques*, LII, no. 6 (December, 1947), 427–431.

78. D. M. Casey, "Rhode Island Silver Smiths," *Rhode Island Historical Society Collections*, LIII, no. 3 (July, 1940), 58–64; also D. M. Casey, "Rhode Island Silversmiths," *Rhode Island School of Design Bulletin*, XXIV, no. 2 (April, 1936), 19–25.

CHAPTER FOUR

Richard Munday's Era

1. G. C. Mason, *Annals of Trinity Church* (Newport, 1890), p. 10.

2. N. M. Isham, *Trinity Church* (Boston, 1936), p. 16.

3. Bergner, Portfolio of drawings. Floor plans of the first and second buildings of the Sabbatarian Meeting House, Newport Historical Society.

4. See abstract of deeds and church records, Sabbatarian Meeting House, Barney Street, Survey Notebooks, Newport Historical Society. Church records show that each spring the windows were removed and stored for the summer; each fall they were replaced for the winter.

5. Abstract of deeds and records, Abraham Redwood house; all information filed under Thames Street town house, Survey Notebooks, Newport Historical Society. Entries in John Stevens' Account books show that he was building extensively for Redwood from 1743 to 1748. Redwood bought the property from Daniel Coggeshall in 1743.

6. The kicked-out roof line suggests that the cornice was added later, but a close study of the framing indicates that the cove is part of the original construction. A house with a cove cornice was shown in Moxon, *Mechanic Exercises*, published in London in 1698.

7. Isham, "History of Architecture," Lectures, Rhode Island School of Design, Class Notes.

8. Abstract of deeds, 56 Farewell Street; Abstract of deeds, George Gibbs house, 9 Chestnut Street, Survey Notebooks, Newport Historical Society.

9. Isham, *Early Rhode Island Houses*; Manuel, *Merchants and Mansions of Bygone Days*, p. 18.

10. Isham, Class lectures.

11. Franklin, "Division Street," *Newport Historical Society Bulletin*, no. 104, p. 15.

12. Charles A. Place, "From Meeting House to Church in New England," in *Old Time New England*, XIII, no. 2, 69ff.; no. 3, 111ff.; no. 4, 149ff., and XIV, no. 1, 4ff. See especially no. 4, 151ff.

13. *Annals of Trinity Church*, p. 43.

14. Isham, *Trinity Church*, pp. 50–52.

15. *Ibid.*, *passim* and p. 93.

16. *Wren Society Publications*, I (Oxford, 1924), and XII (Oxford, 1935), *passim*.

17. Isham, *op. cit.*, p. 84.

18. *Annals of Trinity Church*, p. 51.

19. Notes about Trinity Church, manuscript in the Newport Historical Society.

20. W. King Covell, "The Organs of Trinity Church, Newport, Rhode Island," *Musical Opinion* (London, 1935).

21. M. L. Stevens, "Trinity Church and Some of its Members," *Newport Historical Society Bulletin*, no. 77 (October, 1930).

22. Fiske Kimball, *Colonial Amateurs and their Models: Peter Harrison*; also "Peter Harrision" in *Touro Synagogue*, pp. 14–15.

23. *Annals of Trinity Church*, *passim*.

24. John H. Green, *The Building of the Old Colony House at Newport, Rhode Island* (Newport, 1941).

25. Mrs. R. Sherman Elliot, "The Seventh Day Baptist Meeting House," *Newport Historical Society Bulletin*, no. 73 (January, 1930), gives an excellent account of the history of the Sabbatarian Meeting House.

26. George C. Mason, Jr., "The Sabbatarian Meeting House," in *The Georgian Period*, ed. by G. R. Ware (New York, 1898–1900), part 1, pp. 31–32.

27. Elliot, *op. cit.*

28. Isham, *Trinity Church*, p. 74.

29. C. E. Hammett, Jr., History of the First Congregational Church, manuscript, Vault, Newport Historical Society, p. 52.

30. Records of the Second Congregational Society, p. 1.

31. Hammett, *op. cit.*, pp. 40, 55–56; Bergner, Notes from the records of the First Congregational Church, Vault, Newport Historical Society.

32. S. B. Franklin, *Historical Sketch of the Second Baptist Church, Newport, Rhode Island, 1656–1936* (Newport, 1936), pp. 14–16.

33. "Memoir of Rhode Island," under date of 1738 (Hammett, II, 128).

34. "Rhode Island in 1750," *Rhode Island Historical Society Collections*, XIII, no. 2 (April, 1920), 62.

35. Henry James, "The Sense of Newport," in *The American Scene*.

36. *Gentleman's Progress*, p. 103.

37. N. M. Isham, "Colony House or Old State House, Newport, R.I.," *Bulletin of the Society for the Preservation of New England Antiquities*, VIII, no. 2 (December, 1917). Serial no. 17.

38. Acts and Resolves of the General Assembly, May, 1784, p. 25; see also Isham, "The Colony House," *op. cit.*, for extracts from the Acts and Resolves.

39. Roderick Terry, "History of the Old Colony House At Newport," *Newport Historical Society Bulletin*, no. 63 (October, 1927); *Historic Newport*, Chamber of Commerce (Newport, 1933), pp. 26–28.

40. Greene, *The Building of the Old Colony House*.

41. Published in G. C. Mason, Jr., "Colonial Architecture," in *The American Architect*, X, part 2 (1881), 83, and A. F. Downing, *Early Homes of Rhode Island* (Richmond, Va., 1937), pp. 213–214.

42. Records of the Congregational Society.

43. Hitchcock, *Rhode Island Architecture*, p. 18.

44. Jarvis M. Morse, "The Wanton Family and Rhode Island Loyalism," *Rhode Island Historical Society Collections*, XXXI, no. 2 (April, 1938), 32–44.

45. Dr. H. Turner, "Reminiscences of Newport," published in the *Newport Mercury* (August 5, 1916).

46. G. H. Richardson, Notebook, Vault no. 999, Newport Historical Society.

47. See abstract of deeds, filed under Redwood houses, Thames Street, Survey Notebooks, Newport Historical Society.

48. *Ibid.*

49. Letters and notes concerning the history of this door are filed under 54 Washington Street, Survey Notebooks, Newport Historical Society.

50. Isham, *Trinity Church*, p. 63, and Downing, *Early Homes of Rhode Island*, drawing from an old photograph, p. 156.

51. Notes, Cheeseborough house, Bergner, manuscript and portfolio, vault, Newport Historical Society.

52. Original document in the possession of S. S. Sheffield, Cincinnati, Ohio. Copy filed in Survey Notebooks of miscellaneous papers, Newport Historical Society.

53. Louis Jean Baptiste Sylvestre de Robertnier, Journal of the War in America, 1780–1783, Manuscript in the Rhode Island Historical Society. Typescript translation by Professor Edouard Massey, p. 309 (note).

54. Bergner, Notes, Wanton-Lyman-Hazard, Jeffers, Voax houses, Newport Historical Society. Copies in the Survey Notebooks under streets on which the houses stand.

55. Author, personal observation.

56. Abstract of deeds, 56 Farewell Street, Survey Notebooks, Newport Historical Society.

57. Isham, *Trinity Church*, pp. 66–67.

58. Author, observation. The remaining old clapboards are on the north end of the building on the part added before 1765. See the history of the house in the Appendix.

59. Author, observation.

60. Stevens, *The Vernon House*, pp. 45–46. Letter from Samuel Vernon to his father. The Vernon letters are in Vault A, Newport Historical Society.

61. See copy of deed, Nathaniel Sheffield, Washington Street, Survey Notebooks, Newport Historical Society.

62. See J. A. Gotch, *The Growth of the English House* (London, 1909).

63. Fiske Kimball, *Domestic Architecture of the American Colonies and of the Early Republic* (New York, 1922, 1927).

64. Bergner, notes on the Gidley house, manuscript, Newport Historical Society.

65. Abstract of deeds, Robinson house, Washington Street, Survey Notebooks, Newport Historical Society; Anna Wharton Wood, "The Robinson Family and their Correspondence with the Vicomte and Vicomtesse de Noailles," *Newport Historical Society Bulletin*, no. 42 (October, 1922), p. 6.

66. "Rhode Island in 1750," *op. cit.*, 62.

67. Town Council Book, X, 79, Vault, Newport Historical Society. The item reads "2 bundles of paper to paper a room 20/£ 34s."

68. Acts and Resolves of the General Assembly, May, 1784, p. 25.

69. M. E. Powell, "The Parade," II, manuscript, Newport Historical Society.

70. T. W. Higginson, *Old Port Days* (Boston, New York, 1882), pp. 40–41.

71. The date 1740 has been arrived at by internal evidence. The Colony House had been completed (after 1739), but Long Wharf had not yet been extended, as it was in 1741. Newell made his lithograph copy in 1860.

72. The information about the painting of this room is derived from close study of notes taken in the room itself.

73. From a note in Dr. Vinal's handwriting preserved among the records of the First Congregational Society, Newport Historical Society.

74. Abstract of deed history, Cotton house, filed under Cotton's Court, Survey Notebooks, Newport Historical Society.

75. Abstract of deed history, Christopher Townsend house, filed under Bridge Street, Survey Notebooks, Newport Historical Society.

76. Bergner, filed under Charles Greene house, Bridge Street, Bergner folder file, Newport Historical Society.

77. Abstract of deed history, Job Townsend house, under Bridge Street, Newport Historical Society.

78. In the Newport Historical Society.

79. Abstract of deed history, Solomon Townsend house, under Walnut Street, Survey Notebooks, Newport Historical Society.

80. Abstract, deeds, **Thomas Townsend** house, Third Street, Survey Notebooks, Newport Historical Society.

81. Abstract, deeds, **Caleb Claggett** house, 22 Bridge Street, Survey Notebooks, Newport Historical Society.

CHAPTER FIVE

Peter Harrison

1. Kimball, "Colonial Amateurs and their Models: Peter Harrison," *Architecture* (July–August, 1925).

2. Bull, "Memoir of Rhode Island," under date of 1747 (Hammett, II, 160); also Mason, *Annals of the Redwood Library, passim*. An annotated copy in the Redwood Library corrects errors.

3. *Annals of the Redwood Library*, Appendix B, pp. 488–491.

4. Bridenbaugh, *Peter Harrison, First American Architect*, p. 46.

5. Kimball, "Colonial Amateurs," *op. cit.*, LIII, no. 6 (June, 1926), 155–158.

6. W. W. Watson, *History of Jamestown* (Providence, 1949), pp. 41–62 gives excerpts from the records and a good general history. Joseph Harrison was on the committee and he may have helped with the work or design.

7. *Ibid.*, reprint of the map section showing the Lighthouse; Bridenbaugh, *Peter Harrison*, p. 89.

8. Bridenbaugh, *Peter Harrison*, pp. 90–97 gives an excellent account of Fort George.

9. "Memoir of Rhode Island," under date of 1762 (Hammett, II, 216).

10. Bridenbaugh, *op. cit.*, pp. 106–112.

11. Kimball, op. cit., pp. 158–160.

12. *The Story of the Old City Hall*, Newport Chamber of Commerce, n.d.

13. N. M. Isham, "The Brick Market," Special Number, *Bulletin of the Society for the Preservation of New England Antiquities*, VI, no. 2, Serial no. 13, pp. 2–11 and Appendix, pp. 20–23, "Records Collected by Miss Edith Tilly."

14. L. M. Friedman, "The Newport Synagogue," *Old Time New England*, XXXVI, no. 3 (January, 1946), 49–57.

15. December 5, 1763.

16. *Literary Diary of Ezra Stiles*, I, 6.

17. Andrew Burnaby, *Travels Through the Middle Settlements in North America in the Years 1759 and 1760* (London, 1775), p. 68.

18. Kimball, *op. cit.*, LIV, no. 1 (July, 1926), 185–186; *Touro Synagogue*, pp. 14–15.

19. John Marshall Phillips, "Masterpieces in American Silver," *Antiques*, LV, no. 4 (New York, April, 1949), 285; Frances Hill Bigelow, *Historic Silver of the Colonies and its Makers* (New York, 1917), pp. 427–429.

20. The original letter hangs on the wall of the Synagogue. It is quoted in full in Friedman, "The Newport Synagogue," *op. cit.*, p. 57; also *Touro Synagogue*, p. 24.

21. *Touro Synagogue*, p. 9.

22. *Newport Mercury*, August 23, 1790, gives an account of the arrival of Washington and his party.

23. See Fiske Kimball, *Thomas Jefferson, Architect* (Cambridge, 1916).

24. "Memoir of Rhode Island," under date of 1747 (Hammett, II, 160).

25. Gibbs, *Rules for Drawing* (London, 1738), plate 39, shows the model and details for the portico of the Synagogue and the door of Francis Malbone's house.

26. Mrs. William H. Birckhead, "Recollections of My Uncle Edward King, 1815–1875," *Newport Historical Society Bulletin*, no. 71 (October, 1929), p. 10.

27. Kimball, *op. cit.*, p. 186.

28. *Newport Mercury*, July 1, 1765, "to be sold . . . also handsome garden, fronting Redwood Library near John Tillinghast, with fruit trees and pleasant summer house, Abraham Rivera, dec'd, July 1765." Several other notices mentioned summer houses.

29. Abstract of deeds, William Stevens house, 56 Farewell Street, Survey Notebooks, Newport Historical Society.

30. Abstract of deeds, Robert Stevens house, Thames Street, Survey Notebooks, Newport Historical Society.

31. From drawings and notes made in the house by the author.

32. The original drawing and notes made by Arn Hildreth are owned by George Piltz.

CHAPTER SIX

Newport in the Revolutionary War

1. *Literary Diary of Ezra Stiles*, II, 427.

2. Brayton, in *Gardens of Colony and State*, p. 174.

3. Allan Forbes and Paul Cadman, *France and New England*, written for the State Street Trust Company, I (Boston, 1925), 101.

4. *Literary Diary of Ezra Stiles*, II, 459.

5. *Ibid.*, II, 454.

6. Stone, *Our French Allies* (Providence, 1881), pp. 362–372, quotes Updike in full in his extended account of Washington's visit to Newport; H. W. Preston,

Washington's Visits to Rhode Island, Historical Publication no. 5, State Bureau of Information (Providence, 1932), pp. 1–2, 10–15, 17–18.

7. *Newport Mercury*, March 10, 1781.

8. For an account of De Terney's funeral, see Stone, *Our French Allies*, pp. 347–351.

9. A copy of this billeting list is in the Newport Historical Society. There are several others.

10. *Lettres d'Axel de Ferson à son Père*, ed. by le Compte F. U. Wrangel (Paris, 1929), pp. 3–42.

11. "Letters of Ferson, Aid-de-Camp to Rochambeau, Written to his Father in Sweden, 1780 to 1782," *Magazine of American History*, III (1879), 300–309, 369–376.

12. *Lettres d'Axel de Ferson à son Père*, pp. 72–73.

13. Morris Bishop, "That was Newport," *The New Yorker*, July 20, 1935.

14. *Memoires de M. le Duc de Lauzun*, II (Paris, 1822), 170.

15. "Narrative of Prince de Broglie," translated from the original manuscript by E. W. Balch, in *Magazine of American History*, I (in 4 parts), 376; also quoted in Kimball, *Pictures of Rhode Island in the Past*, p. 101.

16. Journal of Louis, Baron de Closen, manuscript, Library of Congress. These quotations are taken from *France and New England*. The manuscript is now being prepared for publication for the *William and Mary Quarterly*.

17. Major General George Cullum, *Historical Sketch of the Fortifications of Narragansett Bay* (Washington, 1884), p. 16; *France and New England*, II, 61–65.

18. Cullum, *op. cit.*, pp. 19–26.

19. "Narrative of Prince de Broglie," p. 378.

20. Journal of Baron de Closen, quoted in *France and New England*, II, 45.

21. *Memoirs and Recollections of Count Segur* (Boston, 1825), pp. 290–291.

22. "Narrative of Prince de Broglie," p. 376.

23. Anna Wharton Wood, "The Robinson Family and their Correspondence with the Vicomte and Vicomtesse de Noailles," *op. cit.*, pp. 11–35.

24. *Ibid.*, Madame de Noailles' letter is quoted in full on page 26.

25. de Closen, Journal, quoted in *France and New England*, II, 44.

26. *France and New England*, II, 45.

27. *The Journal of Claude Blanchard, 1780–1783*, tr. by William Duane, ed. by Thomas Balch (Albany, 1876), p. 81.

28. de Closen, Journal, quoted in *France and New England*, II, 44.

29. Louis Jean Baptiste Sylvestre de Robertnier, *Journal of the War in America, 1780–1783*, p. 309, note.

30. *Ibid.*, p. 16.

31. *Journal of Claude Blanchard*, p. 79.

32. Brissot de Warville, *New Travels in the United States of America, Performed in 1788*, translated from the French (London, 1792), pp. 144–145; quoted in Kimball, *Pictures of Rhode Island in the Past*, p. 115.

33. François Alexandre Frédéric Duc de La Rochefoucauld-Liancourt, *Travels Through the United States of North America in 1795, 1796 and 1797*, II (London, 1800), 275. Quoted in *Pictures of Rhode Island in the Past*, p. 136.

34. Dr. Waterhouse's original letter, dated Newport, Rhode Island, September 14th, '22 is preserved with the Jefferson Papers in the Department of State. Quoted in full in *The Publications of the Rhode Island Historical Society*, New Series, II, no. 3 (October, 1894), 171–179.

35. B. J. Lossing, *The Pictorial Field Book of the Revolution*, II (New York, 1852), 64.

CHAPTER SEVEN

Building and Commerce

1. R. Grieve, *The Sea Trade and its Development in Rhode Island and Providence Plantations* (Providence, 1902), p. 474.

2. See abstract of deeds, Peter Buliod house, Touro Street, Survey Notebooks, Newport Historical Society. Oliver Hazard Perry bought the house in 1818 and it is still known by his name, although he only lived here part of one year before he was placed in command of the "Java," and sailed for Trinidad, where he died in 1819.

3. See *Mercury* notices throughout September, 1803.

4. Pauline K. Weaver, *The Newport National Bank, 1803–1950* (Newport, 1950), p. 10; see also abstract of deeds filed under Newport Bank, Washington Square, Survey Notebooks, Newport Historical Society.

5. I. B. Richmond, *Rhode Island* (Boston and New York, 1905), p. 264; *Commerce of Rhode Island, 1775–1800*, II, *passim*; Letter Books of Christopher Champlin, 1774–1804, 7 vols.; Letter Books of Gibbs and Channing, 1797–1811, 4 vols. The Letter Books are in the Newport Historical Society; Ship Registers and Enrollments of Newport, Rhode Island, 1790–1939, I, The National Archives Project (Providence, 1938–1941), typescript.

6. M. L. Stevens, *The Vernon House* (Newport, 1915), pp. 46–47.

7. Grieve, *op. cit.*, p. 475.

8. Richmond, *op. cit.*, pp. 259–264.

9. *Ibid.*, p. 264.

10. Kimball, *Domestic Architecture of the Colonies and Early Republic*, pp. 145–261 and figs. 124, 162.

11. See Kimball, *Thomas Jefferson, Architect, passim.*

12. Updike, *History of the Narragansett Church*, I, 405–406.

13. See Alice Brayton in *Gardens of Colony and State*, I, 230–233 for an interesting account of Vaucluse and its gardens; *Bulletin of the Metropolitan Museum of Art*, XXIII, no. 3 (March, 1928), architectural details from Vaucluse, p. 71.

14. Fiske Kimball, *American Architecture* (Indianapolis, 1928); Oliver Larkin, *Art and Life in America* (New York, 1949), p. 79 in "The Jeffersonian Promise" and Chapter 7, "The Adamesques," pp. 83–90.

15. Charles A. Place, *Charles Bulfinch, Architect and Citizen* (Boston, 1925), *passim.*

16. F. T. Howe, "Asher Benjamin," *Antiques*, XL (December, 1941), 364; Hitchcock, *Rhode Island Architecture*, p. 31; Larkin, *Art and Life in America*, p. 84.

17. A. F. Downing, *Early Homes of Rhode Island* (Richmond, Va., 1937), pp. 312–345; Aymar Embury, II, "A Comparative Group of Early American Doorways," 2 parts, *The White Pine Series of Architectural Monographs* (New York, 1921), VII, no. 2 (April, 1921), 2–14, and no. 5 (October, 1921), 2–14, also "Early American Ornamental Cornices," 2 parts, *White Pine Series*, X, nos. 2 and 3 (New York, 1924); Charles O. Cornelius, "Some Early American Doorways," *Bulletin of the Metropolitan Museum of Art*, XXII, no. 10 (New York, October, 1927), 239–247.

18. Mason, *Reminiscences*, p. 27.

19. *Dedication of the Sanctuary, March 24, 1946*, St. Paul's Methodist Church (Newport, 1946).

20. W. C. Bronson, *The History of Brown University* (Providence, 1914).

21. A. C. Sherman, *Newport and the Savings Bank* (Newport, 1944), pp. 9–10.

22. Artillery records. See extracts on file, Clarke Street; see also under 63 John Street, McGregor's own house, for further information about McGregor. Survey Notebooks, Newport Historical Society.

23. M. E. Powel, "The Parade," I, Newport Historical Society.

24. Abstract of deeds for the Rogers house, Touro Street, Survey Notebooks, Newport Historical Society.

25. Abstract of deeds, John Townsend house, Washington Square, Survey Notebooks, Newport Historical Society.

26. *The Newport Daily News*, 1884.

27. Abstract of deeds, Joshua Wilbour house, Touro Street, Survey Notebooks, Newport Historical Society.

28. Abstract of deeds, 118 Mill Street, Survey Notebooks, Newport Historical Society.

29. Published in New York in 1878. Mrs. Gale's manuscript notes are in the Newport Historical Society.

30. Samuel Whitehorne was one of Newport's most successful post-revolutionary merchants and distillers. See Ship Registers and Enrollments in Newport Rhode Island, 1790–1939 for the many ships of which he was owner or part owner, dating from 1795 to 1843.

31. From Christopher Fowler's diary. Excerpts, Fowler House, Mary Street, Survey Notebooks, Newport Historical Society.

32. Abstract of deeds, 78 Church Street, Survey Notebooks, Newport Historical Society.

33. John Street, Survey Notebooks, gives information about dividing the land into lots, cutting through John, Williams, and Levin streets, and the history of the Underwood and Swinburne houses, Newport Historical Society.

34. See abstract of deeds, 399 and 199 Spring Street, 73 Division Street, and Sherman and Hazard houses on Mount Vernon Street, Survey Notebooks, Newport Historical Society.

35. See abstract of deeds, 7 Oak Street, Survey Notebooks, Newport Historical Society.

36. See abstract of deeds, 62 Washington Street, Survey Notebooks, Newport Historical Society.

37. Henry E. Turner, Reminiscences of Newport, 1881, manuscript, Newport Historical Society; *Newport Mercury*, October 20, 1860, also gives an account of this building hiatus.

CHAPTER EIGHT

The Greek Revival

1. Fiske Kimball, *American Architecture*, Chapter 8.

2. Talbot Hamlin, *Greek Revival in America* (London, New York, 1944), Chapters 1, 12, and *passim.*

3. Kimball, *Thomas Jefferson, Architect*; Larkin, *Art and Life in America*, "The Jeffersonian Promise," pp. 79–80.

4. Larkin, *op. cit.*, p. 79 and Chapter 13, "Templed Hills," pp. 154–166.

5. Hamlin, *op. cit.*, pp. 134–135n., 333.

6. Larkin, *op. cit.*, p. 79.

7. M. E. Powel, "The Parade," II, Newport Historical Society.

8. Henry E. Turner, "Newport, 1800–1850," a

paper read before the Unity Club, Newport, R. I. (reprinted from the *Newport Daily News*, 1897), pp. 7–8.

9. Downing, *Early Homes of Rhode Island*, pp. 396, 399–410, 446–447; Hitchcock, *Rhode Island Architecture*, p. 32, 46–47.

10. Records of the Second Baptist Society.

11. *Herald and Rhode Islander*, Thursday, May 14, 1846, *Ocean house. This magnificent Gothic structure, rebuilt upon the site of the one which was destroyed by fire last summer . . . now almost entirely completed . . . reflects great credit upon the Architect (Mr. Warren of Providence) who drafted it . . . the builder Mr. Cris J. Bliven of this place, and the committee. . . .*

12. *Herald of the Times*, January 3, 1850:
A new Hall is to be added to the Bellevue House, in this town, immediately. It will be 85 feet long, by 40 feet wide, two stories high. The lower part is to be occupied as a Dining and Dancing Hall, and the second story for Lodging Rooms — The Hall will be 23 feet high, and the second story 10 feet high. The building will stand within 4 feet of the Bellevue House, and the entrance will be by a covered way. There will be four double windows on either side, with sixteen lights of 15 x 24 inch glass, and four transom lights of 15 x 24 inch glass. There will also be one window on the North end, glass 10 x 15 inches.

The Hall is to have a Panel ceiling, and the walls to be painted in Frescoe. It will make one of the handsomest Halls in the country, and will add very much to the already numerous attractions of that deservedly popular House. It is to be built by John B. Weeden, Esq.

and is to be completed by the first day of June next, Russell Warren, Esq. Architect. It is to be finished in the Elizabethian style, and is to have five ventilators in the ceiling.

13. *The Rhode Island Republican*, Thursday, October 8, 1829: "Our custom house is nearly finished, and is highly creditable to the taste and skill of Mr. Warren, the Architect . . . the building has been erected on such a plan, as to be not merely useful to the government but very ornamental to the town."

14. Zion Church Records, 1834. Russell Warren was paid for a draught of the plan.

15. *Newport Herald*, August 14, 1897. See also Hamlin, *op. cit.*, pp. 331–332 for a discussion of the influence of travel on building.

16. See Bergner notes, Decatur house, Vault, Newport Historical Society, *Daily News*, September 4, 1918, p. 3. Filed under Sheffield house, Survey Notebooks, Newport Historical Society.

17. The *Newport Mercury* of 1849, advertising William Vernon's house, states that the house was planned by Warren and built by Tallman and Bucklin.

18. See material about McGregor filed under 63 John Street, Survey Notebooks, Newport Historical Society.

19. *Herald of the Times*, June 9, 1841 advertises the house of Borden Wood, "but three years old," for sale.

20. See abstracts of records and deeds, Newport Artillery, Clarke Street, Newport Historical Society.

---

a Redwood Library.
b Illustrated in Cady's *The Civic and Architectural Development of Providence*, 1957, p 17.
c Now in The Newport Historical Society.

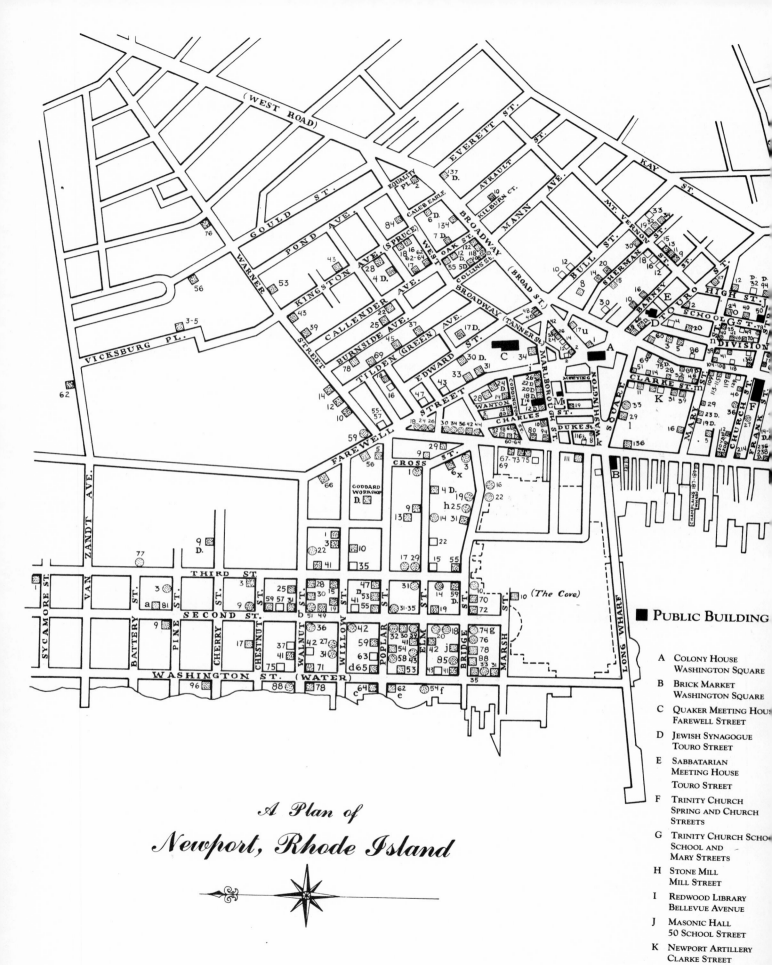

A Plan of
Newport, Rhode Island

■ **PUBLIC BUILDING**

A **COLONY HOUSE**
WASHINGTON SQUARE

B **BRICK MARKET**
WASHINGTON SQUARE

C **QUAKER MEETING HOUS**
FAREWELL STREET

D **JEWISH SYNAGOGUE**
TOURO STREET

E **SABBATARIAN**
MEETING HOUSE
TOURO STREET

F **TRINITY CHURCH**
SPRING AND CHURCH
STREETS

G **TRINITY CHURCH SCHO**
SCHOOL AND
MARY STREETS

H **STONE MILL**
MILL STREET

I **REDWOOD LIBRARY**
BELLEVUE AVENUE

J **MASONIC HALL**
50 SCHOOL STREET

K **NEWPORT ARTILLERY**
CLARKE STREET

BEFORE 1830   □ **GREEK REVIVAL**   ○ **RESTORED SINCE 1952**

D. DESTROYED

a   JOHN AND THOMAS GODDARD HOUSE
    81 SECOND STREET

b   MATTHEW CALBRAITH PERRY CHILDHOOD HOME
    31 WALNUT STREET

c   THOMAS ROBINSON HOUSE
    64 WASHINGTON STREET

d   JOHN DENNIS HOUSE
    65 POPLAR STREET

e   CAPTAIN JOHN WARREN HOUSE
    62 WASHINGTON STREET

f   JONATHAN NICHOLS HOUSE
    54 WASHINGTON STREET

g   CHRISTOPHER TOWNSEND HOUSE
    74 BRIDGE STREET

h   CAPTAIN PETER SIMON HOUSE
    25 BRIDGE STREET

i   WHITE HORSE TAVERN
    26 MARLBOROUGH STREET

j   PITT'S HEAD TAVERN
    BRIDGE STREET

k   NEWPORT NATIONAL BANK
    WASHINGTON SQUARE

l   PETER BULIOD HOUSE
    29 TOURO STREET

m   WILLIAM VERNON HOUSE
    46 CLARKE STREET

n   AUGUSTUS LUCAS HOUSE
    40 DIVISION STREET

o   WILLIAM ELLERY CHANNING
    BIRTHPLACE
    24 SCHOOL STREET

p   JOHN BANISTER TOWN HOUSE
    56 PELHAM STREET

q   GOVERNOR TILLINGHAST HOUSE
    142 MILL STREET

r   CAPTAIN JOHN MAWDSLEY HOUSE
    228 SPRING STREET

s   FRANCIS MALBONE HOUSE
    392 THAMES STREET

t   JOHN BLISS HOUSE (NOT SHOWN)
    BLISS ROAD

u   WANTON-LYMAN-HAZARD HOUSE
    17 BROADWAY

x   THOMAS WALKER HOUSE
    6 CROSS STREET

Supplement: Key to Map

A PARTIAL LIST OF HOUSES BUILT BEFORE 1830

The Preservation Society of Newport County is currently making a comprehensive architectural survey for a Historic Zoning Study which includes the later nineteenth-century buildings and is on file both in the Preservation Society Headquarters and the Newport Historical Society. The following list, based on that in the first edition of the *Architectural Heritage of Newport County*, has been revised and expanded but must still be considered a partial list. So many of the eighteenth-century houses of Newport have been rebuilt into later structures that close inspection of the interiors is often necessary to recognize them. Mrs. Peter Bolhouse and Mrs. Oliver Cushman are responsible for most of the documentary research for this list. Fuller records are on file in a set of Survey Notebooks in the Newport Historical Society.

Houses that have been torn down since the publication of the *Architectural Heritage of Newport* are marked *. More than fifty of the some three hundred and ninety buildings listed here have been lost in the past thirteen years.

Houses that have been restored since 1952 are marked ⊙. About sixty-five buildings have been restored or are now scheduled for restoration. Not all the restored houses will appear on this list since it includes very few structures built after 1830, and Greek Revival and Victorian houses are also being reclaimed as part of a program instituted by private citizens, by *Operation Clapboard* and by the *Oldport Association* to save the smaller Newport houses.

Easton's Point Section. Easton's Point was divided into lots by its Quaker Proprietors in about 1725. Property owners paid an annual quitclaim rental. After the Revolution many houses reverted to the proprietors and were resold.

SYCAMORE STREET

1 Sycamore Street, on the northwest corner of Sycamore and Third streets, is a one-story, gambrel-roofed cottage called "Snug Harbor." It was moved to this site between 1893 and 1907 from the junction of Van Zandt Avenue and Farewell Street where it appears on the Dripp maps as owned by the Sherman family.

PINE STREET

9 Pine Street. This two-story, gable-roofed house with two chimneys stands on the northwest corner of Pine and Second streets on lot #52 of the Second Division of Quaker lands first owned by John Proud. It does not appear on Stiles' map but is shown on the Blascowitz map of 1777. The house belonged to John Dockray before the Revolution. Thomas Sweet bought it early in the nineteenth century and it was still in the Sweet family at the end of the century.

⊙ *3 Pine Street,* a gambrel-roofed, one-story house set end to the street and known as the Robert Dunham house, was moved to its present location by Agatha Mayer in 1853 from Cherry Street between Second and Washington streets where it appears on 'Blascowitz' map of 1777. In 1770 the Proprietors of Easton's Point sold the Cherry Street lot (#39 of the Second Division) to Robert Dunham, cooper. Five years later he sold lot and house to William Carter, mariner. Jonathan Stoddard came into possession of the property before 1792, the year he sold it to Ezekiel Pearce and it has changed hands frequently since then. Agatha Mayer bought it in 1853, the year she moved it to the Pine Street site. It is now being restored.

CHERRY STREET

* *9 Cherry Street.* This one-story, gambrel-roofed house on the northwest corner of Cherry Street and Guerney Court was moved from Washington and Willow streets in 1870. Stiles does not show a house at the original site but it appears on Blascowitz' map of 1777. Quaker records show that it was owned by Jonathan Easton in the 1770's. Josiah Southwick owned it in 1796 and Job Austin, by whose name it is known, in 1798. See Pl. 7.

CHESTNUT STREET

17 Chestnut Street, is a two-story, gable-roofed house with an off-center chimney. The house was moved to this site between 1850 and 1859, and its early history is unknown. It has been altered.

9 Chestnut Street, a two-story, gable-roofed house on the northeast corner of Second and Chestnut streets, is shown on Stiles' map. Abraham Borden bought the land (lots #59 and #60 of the Second Division of Easton Point lands) in 1729. In 1755 George Gibbs bequeathed house and lot to his wife, and it is thought he built the house about 1734. In 1785 George Gibbs, Jr., sold the property to James Wallace. Stephen and Thomas Goddard, cabinetmakers, bought it in 1795. The house has retained its original fireplaces, mantels, paneling, and staircase. It has been restored by its present owner, George Weaver.

3 Chestnut Street, a two-story gable-roofed half-a-house on the northwest corner of Chestnut and Third streets, is shown on Stiles' map. In 1773 Lemuel Wyatt, distiller, sold lots #75 and #76 of the Second Division with the house to Hyam (name illegible) and Simon Levy. It has been in the Defray family since 1869.

WALNUT STREET

This street was at first the only road to the Point.

41 Walnut Street, a one-story gambrel-roofed house, appears on this site for the first time in 1859. Dripp's map of 1850 shows that Thomas Stevens, who owned the land in 1850, had a house on the corner of Washington and Walnut streets. On Dripp's map of 1859 no house is shown at the corner, but one appears on the eastern border of Steven's lot where #41 is now located. He may have moved the corner house to this site. The property remained in Thomas Stevens' family until late in the nineteenth century, and the present large Victorian house now located on the corner was standing before 1873.

⊙ *36 Walnut Street*, a one-story, gambrel-roofed house standing on lot #146 on the southwest corner of Walnut and Second streets, is not shown on Stiles' map, but was built soon after 1760. Joseph Belcher, a pewterer, owned it in 1770 and it is shown on Blascowitz' map of 1777. Edward Watson, cordwainer (shoemaker), bought it after the Revolution, and it remained in the Watson family until 1907. Arthur Leslie Greene, who bought it in 1937, remodeled it considerably. It is now owned by John Benson.

31 Walnut Street, a broad, two-story, gambrel-roofed house with a central entry, was the childhood home of Matthew Calbraith Perry, and perhaps his birthplace. (One account in the Newport Historical Society records that he was born in the Melville House, demolished, on Franklin Street, then known as King Street.) This house appears on Stiles' map, and in 1761 Henry Knowles deeded the lot (#147) with the house to Thomas

Rodman. In 1800 it was given to Christopher Perry by his father-in-law. Stephen Southwick bought it in 1835. *Operation Clapboard* recently negotiated the purchase of the house, and it is to be restored for the Preservation Society of Newport County by Mr. and Mrs. David Van Pelt.

Southeast corner of Walnut and Second streets. See 51 Second Street.

30 Walnut Street is known as the Captain James Townsend House. It was moved by George W. Carr from its original site on lot #104, the northeast corner of Willow and Washington streets, where it is shown on Stiles' map. Edith Cory owned it before 1770, and Katherine Bristoe, just before the Revolution. In 1795 Edmund Townsend bought it, and in 1809 he sold it to James Townsend.

28 Walnut Street. This two-story, gable-roofed half-a-house on lot #152, the southwest corner of Third Street, is shown on Stiles' map. It has a wide overhanging cornice. Sarah Rumereil owned it before the Revolution, but the next record found is dated 1824, when Clarke Burdick bought it from Robert Cranston, Sheriff. George Carr bought it in 1843, and still owned it in 1880.

25 Walnut Street. William Goff owned this lot on the northwest corner of Walnut and Third streets (#153), in 1725, but the house is not shown on Stiles' map. William and Joseph Wanton paid the Quaker rental on it in the 1770's and it appears on Blascowitz' map. Thomas Peckham bought house and lot in 1801. Peckham's heirs sold it to George Hazard in 1881.

⊙ *22 Walnut Street.* This two-story, gable-roofed half-a-house, known as the Davenport House, has an early stairway and woodwork. It appears on Stiles' map, and the lot, #127, was first owned by John Gidley in about 1725. The house was probably built before 1740 and G. H. Richardson says that Nicholas Easton III lived there. Walter Challoner owned it in 1769, and by 1794 it belonged to William Tilley.

WILLOW STREET

⊙ *31 Willow Street* is a two-story, gable-roofed house standing on lot #105, and appears on Stiles' map. It was owned by Thomas Weaver before the Revolution. Charles Brownell, who bought it in 1838, sold it to William Young in 1883.

⊙ *27 Willow Street*, a gable-roofed, two-story house known as the John Carr House, has a pedimented doorway and bull's-eye glass in the over-door transom window. Joshua Peckham owned it (lot #106) before the Revolution. John Grimes, who bought it from Peckham, sold it to Peter Mumford in 1783. A house is shown in this location on Stiles' map.

Southwest corner of Second and Willow streets. See 42 Second Street.

19 Willow Street is a two-story, gable-roofed house. William Lightfoot owned the lot (#110)

in 1771, and sold it to Samuel Hull in 1773, but neither Stiles nor Blascowitz shows a house on this site. Charles Brownell owned the property in the latter part of the nineteenth century.

15 Willow Street, the Grinnell House, on lot #119 on the northwest corner of Willow and Third streets, is a gambrel-roofed, one-story cottage. Thomas Earnsby owned the lot in 1769, but Blascowitz' map does not show a house on the site. The house was probably built by George Earl, who bought the lot from the Proprietors of Easton's Point in 1795. He sold the property to Sarah Weaver in 1827, and James Grinnell acquired it in 1876.

10 Willow Street, a gambrel-roofed, two-story half-a-house standing on lot #136 is shown on Stiles' map, and was owned by John Rogers in 1769. In 1812, the heirs of John and William Caswell sold it to William Caswell, and it was still in his family in 1883. The house has early woodwork and the overdoor transom is filled with bull's-eye glass.

3 Willow Street, a two-story, gable-roofed house set side to the street, stands on lot #128 of the Second Division of Quaker Lands. Stiles shows a house in this location. The property belonged to Samuel Rhodes before the Revolution, and was later known as the Spencer lot. By 1850 it belonged to Pitts-Southwick, whose family still owned it in 1907.

1 Willow Street, known as the Stacy house, is an eighteenth-century, two-story, gable-roofed house set end to the street and remodeled. George Harrington moved the house to this site between 1850 and 1855. He sold it to William Stacy in 1856, and it was still in the Stacy family in 1921. Its early history is not known.

POPLAR STREET

65 Poplar Street, now St. John's Rectory, is best known as the Dennis House. It is a big two-story, gambrel-roofed "mansion house" with a central chimney and entry. It appears on Stiles' map, and was built about 1740 or 1750, probably by William Grafton, sailmaker, who bought lot #69, located on the northeast corner of Washington and Poplar streets in 1739. John Dennis owned it in 1770 and Thomas Dennis in 1797. It has a stairway with twisted balusters and the paneling in the dining room is like that in the south parlor of the Wanton-Lyman-Hazard House. The house originally stood on the sidewalk's edge but Benjamin Smith, whose family owned the house from 1852 to 1922, had it moved back, added an ell, and installed the western pediment from the Jonathan Nichols House over a new Washington Street door. Interior alterations made at the same time by Charles Follen McKim included changing the location of the stairway from its position in front of the central chimney, and making a back living room of the original kitchen. In 1927 the Nichols House pediment was

placed on the Poplar Street entrance of the Dennis House, under the supervision of Norman Isham. The foliage scrolls are copies. See Pls. 98, 102, 192.

59 Poplar Street, a long one-story, gambrel-roofed house set end to the street known as the Crandall House, is shown on Stiles' map. It stands on lot #73, and Quaker records show that it was owned by David Huntington before the Revolution. Thomas Chadwick, who sold it to Alexander Jack in 1823, bought it from Thomas Forrester's estate in 1796. The Crandall family bought it in 1860 and sold it in 1940. See Pl. 99.

⊙ *58 Poplar Street* is a one-story, gambrel-roofed house. Stiles' map shows a shop in this location in 1758, and according to a note in Dr. Hunter's *Account Book* dated 1776 the "widow Dyer" owned the property then. It remained in the Dyer family until 1864 when Thomas Dyer sold the house, which he had inherited from his mother, Martha Dyer, to Caleb Carr. It is still in the Carr family.

54 Poplar Street appears on Stiles' map as a shop. John Chadwick owned it in 1770, and in 1800 Jonathan Chadwick sold it to Benjamin Marble, shipwright. It has been thrown together with No. 56 Poplar Street, and considerably altered.

Southwest corner of Poplar and Second streets. See 32 Second Street.

Southeast corner of Poplar and Second streets. See 31 and 35 Second Street.

55 Poplar Street, on the northeast corner of Second, lot #114, is shown on Stiles' map. It belonged to Caleb Peckham in 1769, and to Thomas Forrester in 1771. The next record is dated 1850, when David Braman sold it to Solomon Braman. John Case bought it in 1869.

* *53 Poplar Street* also belonged to Caleb Peckham in 1769.

47 Poplar Street, a two-story, gable-roofed house with a large central chimney, stands on the northwest corner of Poplar and Third streets on lot #115 of the Quaker Lands owned by William Lawton before the Revolution. Stiles shows a two-story house on this site in 1758, and it also appears on Blascowitz' map. William Wilson owned the property in 1850, and it was still in the Wilson family in 1907.

5 Poplar Street, a two-story, gable-roofed end-chimney house set side to the street, stands just east of Cross Street on land owned by Sanford (first name illegible) before the Revolution. Stiles shows a two-story one-chimney house in this location. The property was owned by David Braman in 1850, and the Braman family still owned it in 1907.

SMITH'S COURT

* *Smith's Court*, John and Thomas Goddard's workshop, moved from the northwest corner of Washington and Willow streets in about 1870. Originally it was a one-story, gambrel-roofed

building, but the front has been changed. In very poor repair. See Pl. 7.

ELM STREET

⊙ *43 Elm Street* is known as the Barker House. David Huntington bought it from the proprietors of Easton's Point in 1787. It appears on Stiles' map, and deeds indicate that it is the house on lot #39 that Nathaniel Sheffield divided with his son James in 1719. Quaker records show that it belonged to Sarah Tucker before the Revolution. The house is very long, has a gable-roof and a wide early overhanging cornice. It originally faced Elm Street, but in the nineteenth century it was turned end to the street, and a porch was added.

42 Elm Street. The Phillips House. This gambrel-roofed half-a-house was moved from lot #18 on the southeast corner of Washington and Poplar streets, where it appears on Stiles' map. John Warren owned it in 1770. The Marine Society bought it in 1800, and Samuel Phillips, mariner, in 1806. It has a wide overhanging cornice and a doorway with a segmental pediment, one of the few left in Newport.

41 Elm Street, a two-story, gable-roofed half-a-house, located on lot #57 of the Quaker lands, is shown on Stiles' map. It was owned by John Simpson in 1769, and by Richard Simpson in 1785. In 1839, George Tilley sold the Richard Simpson estate to Thomas Sharpe, and it remained in the Sharpe family until the end of the century.

⊙ *39 Elm Street,* on the northwest corner of Elm and Second streets, is not shown on Stiles' map but appears on the Blascowitz map of 1777. John Simpson sold part of this lot (#57) "with buildings" to Henry Freeborn in 1802. The gable-roofed two-story house was rebuilt during the Greek Revival period.

⊙ *31 Elm Street,* a two-story, gambrel-roofed house standing on the northwest corner of Elm and Third streets, was built after Stiles made his map, but it is shown on the Blascowitz map. Quaker records show that Samuel Nichols owned the property (lot #157 of the Second Division) in 1771, and John Scott bought it in 1800. George Cornell acquired the house in 1833, and the Cornell family sold it to Whitman Peckham in 1875. It is now being restored.

⊙ *29 Elm Street,* a two-story, gable-roofed half-a-house with a wide overhanging boxed cornice and Greek Revival detail located on the northeast corner of Third and Elm streets, appears on Stiles' map, and belonged to Samuel Nichols in 1771. James Tanner owned it in 1775. Gideon Spooner bought it in 1835, and it is still known as the Spooner House. It is now being restored.

⊙ *14 Elm Street* was moved from about 84 Bridge Street in the mid-nineteenth century. According to Oliver Read's list, Captain Weaver lived there in 1810. It is a two-story, gable-roofed house with a fanlight door.

13 Elm Street, rear, a two-story, gable-roofed house with lintel block window caps and some early Greek Revival detail, was built after Blascowitz made his map. It was moved back from the Elm Street front between 1883 and 1893.

9 Elm Street, a steeply pitched, two-story, gable-roofed house, was the home of John Stevens, stonemason, whose shop is still in operation on Thames Street. It is shown on Stiles' map, and was built in the first quarter of the eighteenth century. Stevens bought the land of Gideon Cornell in 1709. His widow sold the house to Charles Davenport in 1782. William Friend bought it in 1805, and it remained in the Friend family for more than a hundred years.

* *4 Elm Street,* a two-story gambrel-roofed house of very early type, was moved from old #70 Thames Street in 1853 by Isaac Gould. It was inherited from the Clarke family by Samuel Vernon, and tradition says that it was Walter Clarke's house, built before 1700. The deeds verify this claim. See Chapter One.

⊙ *1 Elm Street,* a large two-story gambrel-roofed house with a big central chimney and set side to the street, is shown on Stiles' map. It came into the possession of the Spooner family before 1800, and is still known as the Spooner House.

BRIDGE STREET

⊙ *3 Bridge Street,* on the northwest corner of Bridge and Cross streets, is a two-story gable-roofed house with two chimneys and a central entry. It appears on Stiles' map and Joseph Stevens sold it to William and James Burroughs in 1761. G. H. Richardson says that George Lyndon (Penny Post, 1850) lived there. It is now known as the George Burdick House. It is being restored.

⊙ *16 Bridge Street.* William Claggett, the clockmaker, bought this land from John Rhodes before 1725. His widow, Rebecca, sold the house and lot to John Lyon of Rehobeth in 1750, and Stiles' map shows a house here. In 1822, George Norman, housewright, bought it from Benjamin Hall, and it is still known as the Norman House. It is a two-story gable-roofed house, but it has been much altered, and the old central chimney has been torn out. It is being restored. See Pl. 9.

* *19 Bridge Street,* a two-story, gable-roofed house, is known as the Jonathan Rogers House. In 1747, John Rogers bequeathed it to his son Jonathan. It is shown on Stiles' map. In 1809, the estate of Mary Rogers, widow, was sold to Abiel Lawton in whose family it remained until 1871. It is in poor repair.

⊙ *22 Bridge Street,* Caleb Claggett's house, is a two-story, gambrel-roofed house with a central chimney and a brick-end wall. In 1725 William Claggett gave his father Caleb, a baker, this land with the understanding that Caleb was to build a house, bakehouse, and wharf within twenty-five years. In 1750, George Gardner sold the property to Wing Spooner and Rufus Church, house carpenters. A house is shown here on Stiles' map. Caleb Tripp, by whose name it is still known, bought it in 1818, and it remained in the Tripp family until 1901. It has been restored. See Pls. 9, 46.

⊙ — *Bridge Street*, formerly No. 29 Bridge Street. This one-story, gambrel-roofed house has been moved twice. It now stands on the site of No. 19 Bridge Street, and replaces the Jonathan Rogers House, described above and recently demolished. Originally it stood on the sidewalk line of Bridge Street just west of No. 25 (the Peter Simon House), where it is shown on Stiles' map. It was moved back when the Freeborn House (now No. 31) was moved to Bridge Street. James Gardner, goldsmith, owned it in the last part of the eighteenth century. In 1796, his heirs sold it to Robert Dunham, a chairmaker, who sold it to Robert Dunham, a baker. It remained in the Dunham family until 1871. It has been restored.

⊙ *25 Bridge Street.* The Captain Peter Simon House, where Peter Simon, Jr., brought his bride, Hannah Robinson. A house was standing on this lot in 1727, when the estate of Edward Thurston, mariner, was sold to Peleg Carr. Carr's heirs indentured the house to Peter Simon in 1736, and he owned it in 1766. Joshua Hammond bought the house after the Revolution, and it remained in the Hammond family until 1900. The early house was evidently enlarged by Peter Simon. It is now a two-story, square, hip-roofed building with two interior chimneys and a central entry. The stairway has twisted balusters and ramped rails, and the parlors have paneling dating from several periods, some of it as early as 1730. The doorway formerly had a pineapple-crowned pediment. The present doorway dates about 1800, and came from Bristol. It has been restored. See Introduction and Chapter Four.

31 Bridge Street, a two-story, gable-roofed house, was moved here from Walnut Street (lot #137) by Thomas Southwick Freeborn in 1884. Quaker records show that Stephen Ayrault owned it in 1790, and Josiah Southwick owned it after 1796. See Pl. 9.

55 Bridge Street, a two-story, gambrel-roofed house located on part of lot #87 on the northeast corner of Bridge and Third streets, is shown on Stiles' map. Thomas Townsend, innholder, bought the house in 1795. A list compiled by George C. Mason from information given him, probably by the early historian Thomas Hornsby, records that William Gardner owned it before the Revolution.

* *59 Bridge Street.* The home of Job Townsend I and II, built about 1730. See Chapter Four and Pl. 96.

62 Bridge Street. See 10 Third Street.

70 Bridge Street. This tiny two-story, central-chimney, gable-roofed house of two-room ground plan is shown on Stiles' map, and Mary Nichols owned it in 1771. John Townsend, cabinetmaker, bought it from Kendall Nichols' estate before 1792. Avis Knowles bought it in 1810, and William Barker in 1835. It has been enlarged across the back. See Pl. 8.

72 Bridge Street, on the southeast corner of Second and Bridge streets, is the site of John Townsend's workshop. The shop, originally a large gambrel-roofed building, has been built into the mansard structure now standing here. See Pl. 8.

⊙ *74 Bridge Street*, an early two-story, gable-on-hip-roofed house with a large central chimney, is located on the southwest corner of Bridge and Second streets, and was known for many years as the Charles Greene house. It was built by Christopher Townsend, cabinetmaker who specialized in maple ship furniture, soon after he bought the land in 1725. He also built the shop adjoining the house on the west, and both house and shop are shown on Stiles' map. Townsend bequeathed the property to his son Christopher, a watchmaker. The house was enlarged across the back later in the eighteenth century. According to the French billeting list, De Lombard, Corps de Marine, was quartered with Christopher Townsend. The house is now being restored. See Chapter Four and the ground plan on Pl. 95, also Pls. 8 and 96.

78 Bridge Street, built on lot #52, is known as the Isaac Lawton or Freeborn House. It is shown on Stiles' map, and in 1785 James Milward, shipwright, owned it. In 1795 he deeded it to Meriam Allen and Ann and Esther Milward. James Lawton, a cordwainer (leatherworker), bought it in 1815. It is in poor repair.

— *Bridge Street.* Pitts' Head Tavern, built about 1726 and enlarged in 1744, originally stood on Washington Square, then was moved to 5 Charles Street, and in 1965 was moved again to this site on Bridge Street west of Second. See Appendix A and Pls. 1, 43–45, 122.

85 Bridge Street is the ell of the George Topham House. It was moved from the northeast corner of Washington and Chestnut streets in 1930, where William Cranston was listed as owner in 1770, and Joseph Tillinghast in 1774. See 41 Washington Street.

88 Bridge Street, known as the Jonathan James House, is shown on Stiles' map. It was owned by Isaac Dayton in 1772, who deeded it with part of the 26th and 27th lots to his grandson, Benedict Dayton, in 1797. Benedict sold it to Jonathan James in 1850. It is a two-story gambrel-roofed building set with end to the street.

MARSH STREET

10 Marsh Street, on the southwest corner of Marsh and Second streets, is a one-story, gambrel-roofed cottage. It was moved to this site from the southwest side of Washington and Marsh streets, and its early history is not known.

WASHINGTON STREET

31 Washington Street (also 37 Marsh Street)

is a big gambrel-roofed building known as the Simeon Potter House. It appears on Stiles' map, and was built before 1749 by Jacob Duhane. The first free public school was established here in 1795. It was run by Joseph Finch. Much of the interior woodwork is still intact. See Introduction and Pl. 8.

⊙ *33 Washington Street.* G. H. Richardson records that this two-story, gambrel-roofed house was built after 1815 by Edward Gladding. See Pl. 8.

⊙ *35 Washington Street,* a two-story, gable-roofed house, standing on part of lot #27, is known as the Nancy Murphy House. Stiles' map shows a two-story house here, and Quaker records show that it belonged to Isaac Dayton before 1769. George Munro owned it in 1793, and Nathaniel Lyndon bought it from Thomas Dennis in 1806. See Pl. 8.

41 Washington Street, on the northwest corner of Washington and Bridge streets, is known as the George Topham House. It was moved from the northeast corner of Washington and Chestnut streets in 1930, where it belonged to William Cranston in 1770 and Joseph Tillinghast in 1774. It is best known as "The Faisneau," a popular nineteenth-century boardinghouse. It is a two-story gable-roofed house, now a good deal changed. The front door and some of the mantelpieces have been removed.

53 Washington Street, the big gambrel-roofed house with a central fanlight doorway is known as the Minturn House. It is shown on Stiles' map, and Quaker records show that it was owned by James Potter before the Revolution. Abraham Riviera owned it by 1794. He sold it to Thomas Handy in 1799, who sold it to Simon Newton in 1801. The Minturn family owned it from 1836 to 1855, and Sarah Kendall bought it in 1881. She moved the house from its position next the sidewalk to its present location set back and turned end to the street. She also made some interior changes.

⊙ *54 Washington Street.* Nichols-Wanton-Hunter House. See Chapter Four, Appendix A, pp. 441 ff. and Pls. 7, 88–94.

62 Washington Street, The Captain John Warren House, now owned by Mrs. John Howard Benson, is a large two-story, gambrel-roofed house with a central fanlight door, double steps, and wrought-iron railings. It has some excellent interior paneling and a stairway with delicately scaled turned balusters and drops. In 1736, Benjamin Hazard sold his lot, #17, to Charles Dyer who sold house, wharf, and warehouses to Joseph Willson in 1749. Stiles' map shows a two-story house with one chimney on the site.

By 1774 Captain John Warren owned the property, and he may have enlarged the original one-chimney house to a central hall house with two interior chimneys. When Ebenezer Trevett advertised it for sale in 1844, he described it as "the Mansion house on Washington Street, next north of Hon. William Hunters and south of Job Wilbour's boarding house (the Robinson House). . . . built by Capt. Warren for his own use of the best materials, white oak frame with a large and deep cellar paved and with a large cellar store room." The fireplace paneling and stairway details agree with this date. However, the construction of the huge former kitchen fireplace in the northwest room, with its oven in the old-fashioned place in the back wall, would seem to belong to the earlier house built by Charles Dyer about 1736.

In 1786, Warren sold the property to Walter Easton, who was probably responsible for the installation of the fanlight door. Ebenezer Trevett bought it in 1822. During his ownership, Gilbert Stuart's widow and family lived here, and Stuart's artist daughter Jane had her painting studio in the house. Here she painted the portrait of her neighbor, Tom Hunter, that now hangs in the Newport Historical Society. Trevett sold the house to Maraduke Cope in 1851. It has been in the John Howard Benson family since 1942.

Like the Robinson House just north, this fine house has fortunately been little changed, and some of its present furniture was made by Thomas Goddard and John Townsend.

This building has been confused with Henry Collins' town house, built on lot #16 next south. The latter house was taken over for bankruptcy by George Rome, agent for Hayley and Hawkins, confiscated at the time of the Revolutionary War, and torn down for fuel by order of the Town Council Meeting of February 4, 1780. See Pls. 7, 125.

64 Washington Street. The Thomas Robinson House. See Appendix A and Pls. 7, 80.

69 Washington Street. St. John's Rectory. See 65 Poplar Street.

71 Washington Street, on the southeast corner of Walnut Street, is known as the Pitts-Southwick House. It is shown on Stiles' map, and was built about that time, probably by Stephen Tripp who, according to Quaker records, owned it in 1769. Joseph Southwick owned it after 1799, and sold it to Pitts-Southwick in 1824. Solomon Southwick, the colonial printer, lived here. Edwin Angell remodeled it completely in the late nineteenth century.

78 Washington Street was built by Captain William Finch, commander of a Rhode Island privateer during the Revolutionary War. In 1770, Stephen Tripp sold the land to Finch, who was listed as a house joiner, and the house is shown on Blascowitz' map of 1777. Captain Thomas Brownell, Commodore Perry's sailing master at the Battle of Lake Erie, bought the house in 1850, and in 1865 sold it to Murray Shipley. It is a two-story gambrel-roofed house set with end to the street, and has been almost unchanged from the time it was built. See Pl. 124.

⊙ *88 Washington Street.* The John Tripp

House, a one-story, gambrel-roofed house with a partly exposed end chimney of brick and stone, was built about 1725. This important little house originally stood back from Manton Avenue in Providence, and was saved from demolition when it was moved to Washington Street in 1965 where it will be restored. It has two rooms on the main floor, a beehive oven that appears on the exterior wall of the chimney, and an early combination of sheathing and overmantel paneling in the keeping room. See Downing, *Early Homes of Rhode Island*, pp. 88–93.

96 Washington Street was moved from the southeast corner of Washington and Chestnut streets, where it appears on Stiles' map. Quaker records show that it belonged to George Irish in 1769, and Ann Potter in 1797. Jabez Gardner bought it in 1801. Originally a two-story gambrel-roofed house, it was very much altered by Miss Anna Paul, who owned it in the 1850's.

SECOND STREET

18 Second Street, a two-story, gable-roofed half-a-house with a late cornice treatment, stands on part of lot #55 of the First Division of Quaker Lands, one of three lots (#53, 54, 55) John Brown sold to Joseph Boss in 1794. In 1824, Elliott Boss inherited all three lots together with the dwelling house mentioned in the deed from John Brown (on lot #53, and now demolished) and other buildings. Samuel Smith acquired the same property in 1837, and probably built this house soon afterward (judged by its architectural character). Anne Randall, one of the heirs of Samuel Smith, inherited the house in 1898. It is now being restored.

19 Second Street. Lot #81, on which this two-story, gambrel-roofed house stands, is part of the entire block between Second, Third, Elm, and Bridge streets formerly owned by the Townsend family. Christopher Townsend owned lot #81 in 1769, and in 1773 he bequeathed it to his son John, together with the house that stood on lot #82 (now gone). John Townsend evidently built this house soon afterward because it is shown on Blascowitz' map of 1777.

20 Second Street, also a two-story, gable-roofed half-a-house, stands like No. 18 on part of lot #55 of the First Division, and has the same history except that, when the estate of Samuel Smith was divided, this property was allotted to Mary Wilson. The boxed cornices and other details suggest that the house may have been standing in 1824 when Elliott Boss inherited. It is being restored.

30 Second Street is known as the Michael Moulton House. It is a one-story, gambrel-roofed cottage, and was moved here in 1870 from the southeast corner of Washington and Elm streets. It is not shown on Stiles' map, but Quaker records show that Joseph Boss owned it in 1771, and Blascowitz shows a house on this site in 1777. It stood on the north part of the Boss property on Bridge

Street, and was owned by the family for many years.

⊙ *31 and 35 Second Street* stands on lot #77, on the southeast corner of Poplar Street. This picturesque, gambrel-roofed house with its old ell and nearby shop is not shown on Stiles' map, but the whole group was probably built soon after 1760, and appears on Blascowitz' map. John Frye owned it in 1770, and in 1781, when the Frye estate was settled, it was purchased by William Douglass. He sold the property to Alexander Barker in 1827, who sold it to Henry Barker in 1848. It is still known by that name.

32 Second Street, located on lot #60 of the First Division of Quaker lands on the southwest corner of Poplar and Second streets, and known as the Fowler House, is a two-story, gable-roofed half-a-house with a wide overhanging boxed cornice. This lot was owned by Joseph Gardner in 1725, and the house may have been built soon afterward. It appears on Stiles' map. In 1761, when it was sold to William Taggart in order to pay debts due John Tillinghast, it was known as the homestead estate of Henry Taggart. Benjamin Weaver owned it in 1798, and George Fowler before 1850. It was still in the Fowler family in 1921. See Pl. 84.

Northeast corner of Poplar and Second streets. See 55 Poplar Street.

⊙ *42 Second Street*, a two-story, gable-roofed house located on the southwest corner of Willow and Second streets, stands on lot #76 purchased by James and Sarah Davis from the Proprietors of Easton's Point in 1731. They probably built the house soon afterward. It is shown on Stiles' map, and by 1773 belonged to Thomas White. In that year his widow, Sarah, paid the quitclaim rent to the Proprietors. She sold the house to Jonathan Hull in 1804, and Hull's widow, also named Sarah, sold it to Martha Almy in 1851. Joseph Sharpe bought it in 1862. It is now being restored.

49 Second Street is a two-story, gable-roofed house with two interior chimneys set end to the street. It stands on lot #145 owned by James Brown before the Revolution, and a house is shown here on Stiles' map, but the present house was probably either built or rebuilt about 1810. It belonged to Stephen Burdick before 1829, and to George Comstock in the latter part of the nineteenth century.

⊙ *51 Second Street* is on the southeast corner of Walnut streets. This two-story, gambrel-roofed house stands on lot #146 of the Second Division of Quaker Lands, and was bought by Solomon Townsend in 1725. It was probably built soon afterward, and appears on Stiles' map. Thomas Rogers owned it in 1770, and in 1781 he gave it to his son John. It is now known as the Hamilton House. See Chapter Four.

⊙ *59 Second Street*, on the southeast corner of Chestnut and Second streets, is a two-story, gable-roofed house with Greek Revival detail. It stands on lot #150, and was sold by the Proprietors of Easton's Point first to Edward Thurston. Isaac and Mary Gifford acquired it before 1743, the year they sold lots #149 and 150 to John Pont, a baker, and William Claggett, Jr. In 1758, Stiles shows a one-story house here, and Thomas Claggett owned the property in 1771. It reverted to the Proprietors after the Revolution, and in 1799 John Faxon sold it to Giles Slocum. It belonged to Clarke Weaver in 1850, and was still in the Weaver family in 1907. Clarke Weaver may have rebuilt the one-story house shown by Stiles into the present structure. It is now being restored.

81 Second Street, once the home of the cabinetmakers, John and Thomas Goddard, is a gambrel-roofed, two-story house with an unusual curved stairway. It originally stood at the corner of Willow and Washington streets, where it is shown on Stiles' map. It was moved together with his workshop and the house just north when Milton Sanford built "Ednavilla," now the W. King Covell House. It has been acquired for restoration. See Pl. 7.

THIRD STREET

This street was called the road to Dyer's farm on Stiles' map.

⊙ *10 Third Street,* a two-story, gable-roofed house, stands on part of lot #95 on the southwest corner of Bridge and Third streets. Abigail Nichols Oatley, daughter of Kendall Nichols, inherited it from her grandfather John Pain. She sold it to Alexander Jack in 1790, who sold it to Josiah Greenman in 1810. Since Stiles' map shows a one-story house here, this one was either rebuilt or built anew, probably after the Revolution. It is now being restored.

Northeast corner of Bridge and Third streets. See 55 Bridge Street.

⊙ *14 Third Street.* This gambrel-roofed, two-story house has the date 1767 painted on one of the attic beams. In 1764, Job Townsend gave the lot of land to his son Thomas, a cabinetmaker. Thomas sold the house and lot to William Borden in 1784. It was bought by Phillip Caswell in 1854, and is called the Caswell House. See Chapter Four. See also No. 19 Second Street for note about Townsend ownership of the block this house is in.

16 Third Street. See 31 Elm Street.

Northeast corner of Third and Elm streets. See 29 Elm Street.

⊙ *17 Third Street,* a two-story, gable-roofed house, built on lot #97, is known as the Manuel House. It appears on Stiles' map, and was owned by Jane Rouse in 1769. Francis Anderson bought it from the Quaker Proprietors in 1801, and sold it to Richard Williams in 1832. Samuel Manuel bought it in 1836.

38 Third Street. See 15 Willow Street.

41 Third Street, a two-story, gambrel-roofed house, is shown on Stiles' map. It stands on lot #122 of the Second Division, first owned by Isaac Borden. Benjamin Dunham, peruke maker,

who owned it before the Revolution, sold it to Benjamin Dunham Weeden in 1812. George Washington Carr bought it in 1820, and it is still in the Carr family. G. H. Richardson records that it is one of the oldest houses on the Point.

⊙ *77 Third Street* is a mid-eighteenth-century, gambrel-roofed, two-story house. William Holt, who lived on Washington Street in the late nineteenth century, records that it originally stood on the east side of Washington Street, and belonged to the Southwick family. Matthias Petzka moved it to its present location. It has been restored since 1952.

CROSS STREET

⊙ *6 Cross Street* is a very important early-eighteenth-century house. It stands on land Nathaniel Coddington owned in 1706, and records show that Thomas Walker and his son John, tanners, had acquired the property sometime before 1713.

In 1721, Thomas Walker sold a "Dwelling House, Tan Falls, and all other buildings" to Captain Edmund Thurston. The square two-story house with a wide overhanging cornice and roof hipped on one end and gabled on the other is built with the heavy framing common at this early date. The great pilastered brick chimney, in the center of the house, has three large fireplaces on each floor. Those on the main floor are constructed with the rounded side walls and cove above the chimney beam like those found in such early houses as the Wanton-Lyman-Hazard House, the White Horse Tavern, and the now demolished Micah Spencer House.

Peleg Carr bought the house and other appurtenances in 1727, and when he sold it to Nicholas Carr in 1733, the deed mentioned the "Bark House" (for the tannery). Nicholas Carr bequeathed the property to his children in 1760.

A colorful chapter for the house began in 1773 when Abigail Stoneman opened her coffee-house here at the sign of the "King's Arms." The following year Christopher Maidenbrough, "late of St. Christopher, West Indies," bought it from John Farruit, mariner. Maidenbrough sold it to Samuel Barker in 1796, and it is still known as the Barker House. It has recently been purchased for restoration through the interest engendered by *Operation Clapboard.*

9 Cross Street, a two-story, gable-roofed half-a-house, known as the Boss House, is shown on Stiles' map. Sometime in the 1740's William Stevens, stonecutter, sold lot and house to Abner Coffin of Nantucket, who sold the property to Barzilla Baley in 1748. William Sanford bought it in 1751. It changed hands a number of times until Daniel Boss acquired it in 1907. It is still in the Boss family.

Streets between Warner and West Broadway. Many houses have been moved into this area from other parts of Newport, and their history is often unknown.

WARNER STREET

10 Warner Street is a one-story, gambrel-roofed house. In 1770 Timothy Balch sold the lot of land to Deacon Joseph Pike, who built the house. In 1811 his heirs sold the property to Thomas Aylesworth, by whose name it is still known.

12 Warner Street is a two-story, gable-roofed house with an early overhanging end gable. It is set end to the street, and stands on land owned by Timothy Balch in 1770. It is not shown on Blascowitz' map of 1777, but was probably built soon afterward. Benjamin Tew owned the property in 1835, and it was in Thomas Tew's name in 1866. It belonged to Peter Knowe in 1885, and to Lucinda Scott in 1931.

14 Warner Street, a two-story, gable-roofed house set end to the street, stands on land owned by Benjamin Stevens in 1850. It is not shown on Blascowitz' map, and was probably built about 1800.

39 Warner Street, a one-story, gambrel-roofed cottage now considerably altered, is known as the Lake House. When James Taylor, mason, sold this lot to Jonathan Lake in 1800, the house was mentioned, and it remained in the Lake family until after 1870. It is not shown on Blascowitz' map.

43 Warner, on the southeast corner of Kingston and Warner streets, is a one-story, gambrel-roofed house. Blascowitz shows a house here, but the first record found is dated 1836 when Nathaniel Rodman, a colored man, bequeathed it to his wife.

53 Warner Street, a square, hip-roofed house with an early dentil cornice, was moved to this site between 1893 and 1907. Its early history is unknown.

76 Warner Street, a two-story, gable-roofed house on the southwest corner of Warner Street and Hall Avenue, was moved to this location between 1859 and 1876. George Richardson, in his notebooks in the Newport Historical Society, records that it is the David Gould House, and was moved from the corner of Cranston and Broadway.

GOULD STREET

56 Gould Street, (formerly #48 Gould Street), is a very old two-story, narrow gambrel-roofed house set end to the street. It was moved to this site between 1859 and 1876. Its early history is not known.

KINGSTON STREET (FORMERLY SPRUCE)

This street is shown on Blascowitz' map laid out as a gardened street with some twenty houses located on or near it. All but one of these houses have disappeared, and the old houses now found here were moved from elsewhere.

16 Kingston Street is a two-story, gable-roofed house. It was moved to this site between 1893 and 1907, and its early history is unknown.

18 Kingston Street, another early two-story, gable-roofed house. It was moved here between 1907 and 1921, and its early history is unknown.

28 Kingston Street is a one-story, gambrel-roofed house. It is shown on the nineteenth-century maps, and appears on Blascowitz' map of 1777, but its history has not been traced.

43 Kingston Street. This building is half of a very fine mid-eighteenth-century, gable-on-hip-roofed, two-story house with Palladian windows set in two handsome dormers. It was moved to this site between 1876 and 1883 by Thomas Preese, and served until recently as the African Methodist Episcopal Church. The house is supposed to have come from Middletown. The other part of the house was moved at the same time, and now stands at

VICKSBURG PLACE

3–5 Vicksburg Place. Each half has retained one of the dormers.

CALLENDER AVENUE

Callender Avenue was opened between 1850 and 1859.

17 Callender Avenue is a large two-story, gambrel-roofed house now in poor repair. It was moved to this site between 1893 and 1907.

22 Calender Avenue is an early two-story, gable-roofed house, now much altered. It is shown on Dripp's map of 1859 for the first time in this location.

PEARL STREET

* *4 Pearl Street* is a one-story brick house. Thomas Pitman, tanner, bought the lot in Newtown, as this section was called, in 1798. He bequeathed the "brick house" and lot to his daughter, Abby P. Coleman, in 1842. Two years later she sold it to George B. Hazard, teamster. The house was probably built about 1800. It has sheathed staircase walls; otherwise it is very plain.

BURNSIDE AVENUE

Burnside Avenue was opened between 1859 and 1876.

78 Burnside Avenue. The history of this early two-story, gable-roofed house has not been successfully traced, but the wide overhanging cornice and narrow windows indicate that it was built in the first quarter of the eighteenth century. It was moved to this site sometime between 1859 and 1876.

TILDEN AVENUE (FORMERLY GREEN LANE)

37 Tilden Avenue is a two-story, gable-roofed house with early-nineteenth-century and Greek Revival detail. It is shown on Dripp's map of 1850.

45 Tilden Avenue is a two-story, gable-roofed half-a-house with late-eighteenth-century detail. It appears on Dripp's 1850 map, and is now in good condition.

69 Tilden Avenue is a one-story, gambrel-roofed cottage with two hip-roofed dormers. It is shown on Dripp's 1850 map.

WHITE STREET

18 White Street is a two-story, gable-roofed,

late-eighteenth-century house with a central chimney and an attractive fanlight door. It is shown on Dripp's 1850 map in this location. A note in the Historical Society records that it is the Texeira house, and that it was moved here from Washington Square.

EDWARD STREET

* *17 Edward Street.* This gambrel-roofed, two-story house was moved here from the northwest corner of Washington Square and Thames Street by Edward Goffe. It is half of the house that stood on land Francis Brinley sold to Job Lawton, ropemaker, in 1721, but the next record known is dated 1799 when Patience Durfee sold the property to Israel Ambrose. Stephen Northam bought it in 1834. The part that remained on Thames Street was torn down in 1950. In poor repair. See Pls. 14 and 128.

* *30 Edward Street.* This early gambrel-roofed, two-story half-a-house originally stood on Touro Street on land now occupied by the Perry House. In 1728 Clarke Rodman, physician, sold the land and "all buildings" to Isaac Anthony, goldsmith. In 1732 Josiah Lyndon, later Deputy Governor, bought the house and lot. On his death he left his property to the First Baptist Church to be used as a parsonage. A note in the Gould Day Book records that the house was moved in 1864.

62 Van Zandt Avenue is a two-story, broad, gable-roofed house with two interior chimneys and an early type of cornice. It was moved to this site between 1907 and 1921, and its early history is not known.

On *Brandt Street* stands a very old, one-story, narrow, gambrel-roofed house. It was moved here between 1893 and 1907.

North of Washington Square.

THAMES STREET

⊙ *18 Thames Street* is a two-story, gable-roofed house with framed construction heavy enough to indicate a very early eighteenth-century date. It is shown on Stiles' map, but at the present time the first record known is dated 1774 when Merriam Johnson, widow, offered the house for sale. In 1788 she sold it to David Braman, caulker, and it has been in the Braman family until recently acquired for restoration. See Pl. 10.

⊙ *24 Thames Street*, a two-story, gable-roofed half-a-house set side to the street, stands on land owned by the Braman family for more than a hundred and fifty years, but this particular house was moved to its present location between 1859 and 1876. Its earlier history is not known, although its construction suggests a late-eighteenth-century date. It has been restored. See Pl. 10.

⊙ *26 Thames Street*, a two-story, gable-roofed half-a-house with a large chimney, stands on the northeast corner of Sanford Street on part of John Sanford's original estate acquired by David Braman in 1806. Stiles shows a house here, but George Mason, who made a list of early Newport

houses in 1849, records that the house on this site, then occupied by Ezekiel Burroughs, was pulled down by the British during their occupation of Newport. When David Braman, Sr., sold the property to his son, David, a cordwainer (shoemaker), in 1813, it was described as a lot, but the heavy construction, the large chimney, and some of the details suggest that part of the building may have survived and been built into the house David, Jr., put up soon after he bought the land. The house has been restored. See Pl. 10.

29 Thames Street. John Stevens' Shop. The first John Stevens set up his stonemason's shop in Newport in 1705, and it has been in continuous operation since that time. The third John Stevens bought this lot from Israel Woodward sometime after 1757. John Howard Benson, sculptor, bought the shop in 1927, restored it, and his family still runs it under the original name. The Stevens family were masons, marble workers, painters, glaziers, surveyors, and map makers, and their shop was passed down in the family, generation after generation. Three of the shop account books, dating from 1705 to 1750, and one dating after 1780 are owned by the Benson family. See Pl. 11.

⊙ *30 Thames Street.* The John Stevens House. This house was in the Stevens family of stonecutters for over two centuries. A plat in the Newport Historical Society shows that John Stevens owned the land in 1745, and G. H. Richardson says he built the southern part in 1709 and the northern in 1750. Stiles' map shows a two-story house with one chimney here in 1758, indicating that the house was enlarged after that date. It is a long two-story, gable-roofed building with a wide overhanging cornice. It has recently been restored. See Pl. 10.

⊙ *34 Thames Street* is also a Stevens house. John Stevens owned the land, part of the above plat, in 1745, and the house is shown on Stiles' map. Phillip Stevens, painter and glazier, bought it in 1816, and in 1876 the Stevens heirs sold it to George Popple. Amon Parmenter, by whose name the house is known, bought it in 1891. It is a two-story, gable-roofed house with a pedimented doorway. It has recently been restored. See Pl. 10.

⊙ *36 Thames Street* is a two-story, gambrel-roofed house set end to the street. According to the plat mentioned above, Richard Roas owned the land in 1745. In 1760 Roas sold the lot with a "messuage" to James Keith, merchant. In 1791 William Cole bought the house, and in 1803 John Williams bought it. James and William Stevens, who acquired it in 1812, sold it to William Covell, boatbuilder, in 1829. It remained in the Covell family until Ade Bethune bought it in 1940. It is shown on Stiles' map. It has recently been restored. See Pl. 10.

42 Thames Street, a long two-story, broad, gambrel-roofed house, is shown on Stiles' map. The above-mentioned plat shows that James Nicoll owned the land in 1745. In 1759 he sold house and lot to James Keith. This is the Dr. Keith that Alexander Hamilton mentioned in his *Itinerarium*. After Keith's death in 1781, the house was sold together with his house next north, to William Cole. John Williams bought it in 1795, and William Brownell, tinplate worker, in 1838. It remained in the Brownell family until it was sold to Ann Sullivan in 1898. See Pl. 10.

⊙ *44 Thames Street* is a picturesque, square, gable-on-hip-roofed house with a big central chimney. The property belonged to Job Bennett in 1721, and the house was probably built about that time. The stairway, with its heavy turned balusters, boarded sheathing and closed string course, agrees with this early date, as does the huge kitchen fireplace. Bennett built a one-story, gambrel-roofed house adjoining No. 44 on the south which was used for many years as a shop. Both buildings are shown on Stiles' map. Later they came into the possession of the Stevens family. The shop was torn down at the end of the nineteenth century. The house is being restored.

⊙ *52 Thames Street*. The Jeremiah Lawton House, a two-story, gable-roofed house shown on Stiles' map, was built about 1740. In 1714 Jonathan Lawton, shopkeeper, bought a "garden spot of land" from John Hammett, scrivener. In 1744, Jonathan Lawton, house carpenter, bought the lot with a "messuage" from Jeremiah Lawton. The property remained in the Lawton family until Thomas and Joseph Weaver, hatters, bought it in 1816. Miss Caroline Stevens, the great-granddaughter of Thomas Weaver, was still living in the house in 1952. It has been restored.

58 Thames Street, a square two-story house now covered with a mansard roof, belonged, before the Revolution, to the Captain William Read who gave the Liberty Tree lot at the junction of Farewell and Thames streets to the town. His son John inherited the property, and William Lovie owned it in 1850. The interior detail and the stairway resemble those in the Stevens house at 59 Farewell Street. It is not shown on Stiles' map.

60–64 Thames Street, the second house north of Coddington Street, is a two-story, gable-roofed house set side to the street. It stands on the site of Eleazer Trevett's house and joiner's shop. Trevett's house was taken down by the British, and when he sold the property to Henry Marchant in 1785, only the shop was mentioned in the deed. In 1796, Marchant gave the lot and shop to his son William, who built the present house before 1800.

67–69 Thames Street. This gable-on-hip-roofed house with its big central chimney is shown on Stiles' map. In 1785, Henry Peckham sold to Elizabeth Irish the house and lot designated as his inheritance from Thomas, Ebenezer Richardson's son. In 1798, McIntosh Alexander, mariner, bought the property, and in 1829 his widow sold the "Red

house in the Main Street" to William Slocum, who kept it until 1872. It now serves as a tailor's shop.

73 Thames Street, known as the Jonathan Almy House, is a gable-roofed, two-story building with a fanlight doorway. In 1733, Thomas Richardson bought some of John Coddington's land. In 1801, when the heirs of Ebenezer Richardson sold this lot to Jonathan Heath, no house was mentioned, but it was there by 1824. G. H. Richardson says it was moved there, which accords with the early architectural style of the house. Heath's widow sold the house to Jonathan Almy in 1836. His heirs sold it to Henry Young in 1872.

75 Thames Street. This steeply pitched, gable-roofed building is known as the Betsey Coddington House. It is shown on Stiles' map, and may have been built by Nathaniel Coddington, who gave John Coddington the land "with buildings" in 1721. The doorway, with its cushion frieze and heavy fanlight, suggests, however, a date of about 1735 or 1740. In 1822, Betsey Coddington sold the house to James Hart, rigger, who sold it to Edward Jones in 1894.

Northeast corner of Coddington and Thames streets. —The Reverend Daniel Wightman House. See 2 Coddington Street.

80 Thames Street, on the southeast corner of Coddington and Thames streets. This two-story, gambrel-roofed house with central chimney and doorway is shown on Stiles' map, and was probably built by Captain Ebenezer Vose before 1744. In 1732, John Coddington owned the land here, but the plat made when he sold his own house in 1744 shows that Captain Vose then owned this piece along the south side of Coddington Street. The property remained in the Vose family until Joseph Sherman bought it in 1837. He sold it to Thomas Lawton in 1892. The house has been raised, and is now occupied by the Newport Paint and Furniture Company.

94 Thames Street. John Coddington's Mansion House. See Marlborough Street.

111 Thames Street. This building, now the Blue Moon Tavern, stands on land acquired by Jonathan Thurston in 1721, and owned later in the eighteenth century by Christopher Champlin. A photograph taken about 1870 shows that it was originally a very handsome square gable-on-hip-roofed house with a roof balustrade. A similar house, owned first by Christopher Almy and then by Walter Chaloner, stood just north. The two houses were built about the same time, but Almy's house is shown on Stiles' map and this house, #111, is not. It was probably built about 1760. See Pl. 14 for the early appearance of these houses.

FAREWELL STREET

This street was laid out before 1654.

The Quaker Meeting House near the corner of Marlborough Street. See Chapter One and Pl. 21.

* *24 Farewell Street*, a two-story, gable-roofed half-a-house, is shown on Stiles' map. In

1725 Nathan Townsend, carrier, sold the lot with a dwelling house to William Hall. The property remained in the Hall family until 1856 when John Beattie bought it. It is known as the Mather House.

28 *Farewell Street*, a two-story, gable-roofed building set back from Farewell Street, stands on land Richard Clarke gave his daughter, Martha G. Pitman, in 1743. She gave the property to the Second Congregational Church in 1765. Stiles shows a shop here. This house was probably rebuilt either from Stiles' shop or from a barn. William Freeborn owned the property in 1850 and 1876, and M. E. Austin owned it in 1907.

31 *Farewell Street*, known as the Shaw House, is a two-story, gable-roofed house with a central chimney and fanlight doorway. Samuel Easton bought the lot of land from the Friends in 1708 but the next known record is dated 1789, when Benjamin Grafton, sailmaker, and Edward Muffy, blacksmith, sold the house, inherited from Easton, to John Hadwen. William Shaw bought it in 1805, and it remained in his family until 1894. The present house was probably built (or enlarged) by William Shaw.

33 *Farewell Street* is known as the George Lawton House. Jackson's map of 1853 shows a schoolhouse here as early as 1711–1712. In 1787, Clarke Rodman lived there and in 1818, the Society of Friends sold "The schoolhouse lot and house" to Elijah Sherman. The present house has an attractive fanlight doorway. Most of the detail is post-Revolutionary, and the house was probably rebuilt by Sherman. It was later owned by George Lawton. See Pl. 12.

56 *Farewell Street*, known as the Taggart House, is a two-story, gambrel-roofed house set with end to the street. It appears on Stiles' map, and its construction indicates that it was built about 1720. It was in the possession of Michael Burn before 1750, when it was taken over by Joseph Warren. Job Almy owned it in 1770 and it may have been his house "newly painted blue" advertised in the *Mercury* in 1760.

⊙ 59 *Farewell Street*. This large gambrel-roofed building was built as a double house by William and Joseph Cozzens, hatmakers, before 1770. Paul Cartwright bought it in 1787. Later owners were William Langley, John Northham, and William Stevens, by whose name it is known. See Chapter Four and Pl. 125.

66 *Farewell Street*. This two-gambrel-roofed house, built before the Revolution, originally stood on Long Wharf. It was moved here between 1839 when Edward Jones, blacksmith, bought the lot, and 1850 when he sold house and lot to Alfred Martin, but its early history is not known.

CHARLES STREET

5 *Charles Street*. Pitt's Head Tavern. Now moved to Bridge Street south of Second Street.—See Appendix A and Pls. 1, 43–45, 122, 128.

19 *Charles Street*. This two-story, gambrel-roofed half-a-house was the home of Lieutenant Etienne Decatur, French Navy, the grandfather of the hero of the War of 1812, Commodore Stephen Decatur. It originally stood at the head of Washington Square to the right of the Colony House. In 1714 John Taylor owned this land, and the house, shown on Stiles' map, was probably built during the first quarter of the century. Taylor still owned it in 1763. In 1783 Robert Brayton bought it. In 1823 Sarah Gardiner gave it to her sister, the wife of Levi Gale. In 1833 the Gales moved it to Charles Feke's garden lot in Charles Street to make room for their new Greek Revival house, now moved to Touro Street.

Southeast corner of North Baptist and Charles streets. A two-story, gable-roofed house with a big central chimney, known as the Denman house. It is not shown by Blascowitz, but was probably built soon afterward.—Greek Revival exterior detail has been added.

MARLBOROUGH STREET

⊙ 26 *Marlborough Street*. Whitehorse Tavern. See Appendix A and Pl. 37.

* 22 *Marlborough Street*, a two-story, gable-roofed building was erected just before the Revolution as a cabinetmaking shop by Walter Nichols, son of Jonathan, Jr. Walter Nichols and his son Joshua were known for their mahogany cases for tall clocks. William Nichols, silversmith, had his shop here later. See Pl. 37.

* 18 and 20 *Marlborough Street*. Weston Clarke House. See Appendix A.

* 16 *Marlborough Street*. St. Paul's Methodist Church. See Chapter Seven and Pl. 129.

12 *Marlborough Street*, the Solomon Townsend House, is a gambrel-roofed, two-story building with a big central chimney and central entry. It now serves as the parish house of St. Paul's Church. In 1725, Weston Clarke sold the land to Nathan Townsend, carrier. The house was standing by 1749, when Solomon Townsend is listed as the owner. Samuel Fowler bought it in 1781. See Pl. 129.

10 *Marlborough Street* was built soon after 1800 when James Perry and B. Wightman sold the land to Benjamin Pearce, cordwainer. See Pl. 13.

John Coddington's Mansion House, on the northeast corner of Marlborough and Thames streets, was built about 1730. In 1723 Nathaniel Coddington gave the Old Governor William Coddington House of 1641 together with the land between Marlborough, Thames, Coddington, and Charles streets to his son John. The new house was built before John's death in 1732, but in 1737 John Stevens made a shell-hooded doorway for it. Martin Howard, Sr., bought it in 1744. His son, Martin Howard, Jr., who lived in the Wanton-Lyman-Hazard House, left Newport after the Stamp Act riot, but his granddaughter lived in the Marlborough Street house, and the property remained in her family until 1855. The shell doorway has vanished, and the house has been much altered, but it must once have resembled Daniel Ayrault's house, built by Richard Munday in 1739. See Pl. 13 and P. 62.

The Newport Jail. A note on Henry Jackson's map of 1853, written by Henry Taggart, jailer, records that the present brick building was built about 1772, under the supervision of George Lawton and Oliver Ring Warner. It was enlarged about 1800. The earlier jail, built on the same site in 1680, was moved and has since been demolished. Altered in 1965. See Chapter Seven and Pl. 128.

CODDINGTON STREET

2 Coddington Street. The Reverend Daniel Wightman House. See Appendix A.

6 Coddington Street. The William Hookey House. See Appendix A.

* *8 Coddington Street.* This central-chimney, gable-roofed house has seventeenth-century construction, with chamfered summer beams, but the earliest record yet found is dated 1750 in a list of "estates of those that have left the colony or don't live in the Government liable for debt," when it belonged to Zebulon Spinney, and was sold to Jonathan Sheldon, mariner. In 1787 Perry Weaver, hatter, bought it, and it remained in the Weaver family until 1882. It has been altered.

12 Coddington Street, a two-story, gable-roofed house, is shown on Stiles's map, and stands on land owned by Gideon Wanton before 1730. The steep pitch of the roof and the early stairway indicate that part of Gideon's house is incorporated into the present building. After Gideon Wanton's death, the property was owned by Christopher Fowler who sold it to Perry Weaver in 1815. Joseph Freeborn owned it in 1850, and it was still in the Freeborn family in 1907.

14 Coddington Street, a two-story, gable-roofed house with an early cornice, stands on land Samuel Warkman sold to John Coleman in 1717. Captain John Draper bought the property in 1721, and in 1750 his heirs sold it, with no house mentioned, to Benjamin Sherburne, whose mansion house just east on the corner of Coddington and Farewell streets was later taken down by the British. Stiles shows a shop on this piece in 1758, and when Sherburne sold it to Samuel Nichols in 1774, a building was included. The shop was probably converted into the present house about this time. William Manchester acquired it in 1811, and it was still in his family after 1850. George Burroughs owned it in 1876.

BROADWAY

Broadway was called, in early deeds, the Broad Street leading out of town to Portsmouth. Stiles' map shows it filled with houses to Equality Place. The ones that remain are now in poor condition, and their lower floors have been converted into shops. Those least altered are included in this list.

1 Broadway. Pardon Clarke bought this property from John and Martha James, who had inherited it in 1751 from Dr. William Arnold. The house does not appear on Stiles' map, but it was built before 1783 when Clarke sold house and lot to Parker Hall of Middletown. Andrew Winslow, blacksmith, bought the corner half of it in 1809, and his heirs released it to Sarah Sherman in 1845. Winslow set up his hay scales here. The house is in poor condition.

2, 4, 6 Broadway is a mid-nineteenth century house, but according to G. H. Richardson, it is built over what is probably part of Governor Peleg Sanford's house. Sir Edmund Andros is supposed to have hidden here. Sanford's daughter Bridget married Job Almy. The earliest deed found is one dated 1723 when Jeremiah Wilcox sold the house formerly belonging to Thomas Mallet to Job Almy. It remained in the Almy family until 1827. It is now known as the Shaw estate, or Lalli's. See Chapter One.

17 Broadway, the Wanton-Lyman-Hazard House, was probably built by Stephen Mumford just before 1700. See Appendix A and Pls. 29–37, 101.

22–24 Broadway, a two-story, gable-roofed house with a wide overhanging cornice, is shown on Stiles' map. In 1783 Nicholas Easton and John Manchester bought this lot with two dwelling houses on it from William and Mary Davis. It was the property John Davis owned in 1729. Isaac Manchester sold it, still with two dwelling houses, to James Perry in 1797. Alexander McGregor bought it in 1859, and Cyrus Peckham in 1874. The lower floor is used for shops.

26, 28, 30½ Broadway is a two-story, gambrel-roofed house built next 22–24. Although Stiles shows a house here, G. H. Richardson, records that, according to a plate in the chimney, Edward Stanhope, baker, built this house in 1792. Stanhope had bought the lot with buildings from James Davis in 1790. The lower floor is used for shops. Bragg, the counterfeiter, is supposed to have hidden his money in the cellar of this house.

46 Broadway, on the northwest corner of Branch, is a narrow two-story, gambrel-roofed house with end to Broadway. Stiles shows a one-story house here, and George Richardson says that Edward Simmons, who owned the property in 1784, built this house just before the Revolution. His heirs sold it to Samuel Oxx in 1836. It belonged to Peleg Bryer for many years.

48–52 Broadway, a broad gable-roofed building now in poor repair, was owned by Samuel Cranston and David Holloway before 1806. In that year they sold it to Moses and William Thurston who sold it to Benjamin Wilbur in 1832. Stiles shows a shop here.

* *108 Broadway,* on the northwest corner of Collins Street, is a two-story, gable-roofed house. Samuel Collins owned land here in 1726, and the property remained in the family until John Avery Collins sold house and lot to Joseph Allen in 1797.

Stiles shows a two-story house here, but 1726 is too early for this house. It was probably built after 1750.

116–118 Broadway, just south of 122, is a two-story, gable-roofed house. It appears on Stiles' map and in 1763 John Heath, cordwainer, sold this lot with a house on it to Benoni Peckham, barber and peruke maker. It was still in the Peckham family in 1850. The lower floor is used for shops.

120-122 Broadway, on the southeast corner of Oak Street, is a two-story, gable-roofed house shown on Stiles' map. It belonged to Benjamin Holt in 1763, and remained in the Holt family until Cornelius Wilbour bought it in 1829. He sold it to James Shaw Blacksmith, in 1856. The lower floor is used for a market.

134 Broadway, a two-story, gable-roofed house, now the Newport Furniture Store, stands on property Caleb Earl owned before 1800. In 1801 Matthew R. Johnston sold the lot "excepting the small house not conveyed by this instrument" to David Williams, clockmaker. Williams probably built his own house, known as his homestead estate, soon afterward. He sold it to James Chase in 1825, and the house was subsequently owned by Richard Randolph, Nathaniel Holt, Susan Hubbard, and others.

* *137 Broadway*, a two-story, gable-roofed house with a central chimney, was the estate of Felix Peckham. Robert Chase owned it in 1790 and his heirs sold it to Augustus Peckham in 1831. It was moved to the south corner of Everett Street when Calvert Street where it originally stood was cut through.

Broadway at Mile Corner. "The Bird's Nest" is an eighteenth-century, two-story, gable-roofed farmhouse with an older ell, added Greek Revival detail, and a Gothic Revival porch. Dr. Rowland Hazard, who named it, bought it from Charles Collins in 1845. When Job Almy sold it to William Almy in 1796, he mentioned "an old dwelling house," and called it the old Tripp place. William Tripp owned it before the Revolution, and may have built the house. In *This Is My Newport*, Maud Howe Elliot tells of the formation of the "Town and Country Club" at "The Bird's Nest" in 1871.

Broadway at Miantomoni Avenue. Elmhyrst, William Vernon's House, 1834. Russell Warren, architect. See Chapter Four and Pl. 151.

WEST BROADWAY (FORMERLY TANNER STREET)

In the sketch map Henry Bull made in 1852 of the central part of Newport as it looked in 1641 he shows "the Broad Street" extending from Broadway to West Broadway. Mumford's map shows two separate streets in 1712. See maps opposite pp. 14 and 15. Because of the tan pits and tanyards in this vicinity West Broadway was known as Tanner Street for many years. It is so called on the Dripp maps of 1850 and 1859 and on the Atlas of 1876. Stiles shows only two houses on the street, but more than twenty-five separate buildings are shown on Blascowitz' map made about twenty years later. Most of the older houses have been demolished, and the histories of the few remaining buildings have not been traced. Among the remaining buildings, the following should be mentioned:

62–64 West Broadway, on the northeast corner of West Broadway and Callender Avenue is a two-story, gable-roofed half-a-house. It is an eighteenth-century type and appears on Dripp's 1850 map.

84 West Broadway, located between Kingston and Pond, is another two-story, gable-roofed half-a-house. It is also shown on Dripp's 1850 map.

55 West Broadway, on the southwest corner of Oak Street, is a two-story, gable-roofed half-a-house of eighteenth-century type. It is now raised for shop space below.

EQUALITY PLACE

2 Equality Place. The Israel Lake House has been much rebuilt and has lost its handsome enclosed fanlight doorway since 1952. It appears on Stiles' map. It was the home of William Douglass before the Revolution. In 1824 Douglass, listed as a trader, sold it to Israel Lake, trader, and it was still in the Lake family in 1883.

CALEB EARLE STREET

* *6 Caleb Earle Street* is a two-story, gable-roofed house with a fanlight doorway. William Webb, trader, sold the lot to John and Charles Cannon, chaisemakers, in 1810. In 1815 they mortgaged their land with dwelling house to John Lawton. James Easton bought it in 1829, and sold it to Robert and Thomas Franklin, bakers, in 1831. It was still in their family in 1883.

OAK STREET (FORMERLY HOLT'S LANE)

* *7 Oak Street*, known as the Billy Smith House, a square hip-roofed house with delicate nineteenth-century detail, originally stood at the corner of Oak and Broadway. William Smith, carpenter, bought the land with buildings for fifty-one dollars in 1827. He built his new house soon afterward, and still owned it in 1870. See Chapter Seven and Pl. 144.

* *12 Oak Street* is a two-story, gable-roofed house, now in poor repair. Isaac Burdick sold the lot to Thomas Peabody in 1810. Peabody built his new house soon afterward, and in 1850 his heirs sold it to John Pearson.

KILBOURN COURT

* *10 Kilbourn Court* is an early nineteenth-century double house with a good flatheaded Doric entrance. It was moved to this location after 1883, but its history has not been traced.

WASHINGTON SQUARE

The north side of the Square was originally called Queen Street. In the eighteenth century there was a short street in front of the Colony House, the southern side of which was called Ann Street (now part of Tuoro). The town schoolhouse stood on the side facing Queen Street. Three of the buildings here burned down in 1770, and the rest were torn down later to make the present open square. See Stiles' map, opp. p. 29.

The Colony House. See Chapter Four and Pls. 1, 5, 47, 63–70.

8 Washington Square, the Newport National Bank, is a two-story, gambrel-roofed building with central doorway and pedimented dormer windows. In 1722 John Gardner bought land with a house on it from John Rathburn. Gardner probably enlarged the original house, and Stiles shows it as a two-story building with two chimneys in 1758. George Gardner inherited the house in 1763, and Abraham Rodrigues Riviera bought it in 1793. In 1804, it became the home of the newly opened Newport Bank, and still serves in that capacity. It was restored in 1950. See Chapter Seven and Pl. 87.

The Brick Market. See Chapter Five and Pls. 6, 106, 107, 128.

TOURO STREET

(See above, for section formerly called Ann Street.) Early deeds show that the part above Spring Street was known as Griffin Street.

29 Touro Street, now the headquarters of the Salvation Army, and much changed, is a large three-story, hip-roofed house. It was built some years before 1757, when Peter Buliod gave to Lewis Buliod the "large new house fronting Ann Street." Moses Levy owned it in 1760, and devised it to Moses Seixas in 1792. In 1795, when the new Rhode Island Bank was opened with Seixas as cashier, the house became the Bank building. The French billeting list places Marechal De Beville, the billeting officer, and his aide-de-camp, De Beville, with Moses Levi. Oliver Hazard Perry bought the house in 1818, and it remained in the Perry family until 1865. The Salvation Army bought the house in 1914. See Chapters Five and Seven and Pls. 116, 128.

⊙ *33 Touro Street,* a three-story, hip-roofed house, was built about 1790 by Joseph Rogers, merchant. Rogers' heirs sold it to the Reverend Thomas Dunn in 1823, and St. Joseph's Church acquired it in 1887. The building was handsomely restored in 1961 in memory of Charles Patterson Van Pelt by Dr. and Mrs. David Van Pelt, and now serves as the Headquarters for the Society and for the Newport Chamber of Commerce. See Chapter Seven and Pl. 139.

Zion Episcopal Church. See Chapter Eight and Pl. 147.

51 Touro Street. See Appendix B.

* *66 Touro Street* is a gambrel-roofed, two-story house, now much changed. It was built after Stiles made his map, and the first record yet found is dated 1783 when Jacob Barney, Jr., discharged his mortgage against the house. James Easton, mariner, bought it in 1817 and it remained in the Easton family until 1870. It stands on Jonathan

Barney's garden lot whose house stands next west.

Touro Synagogue. See Chapter Five and Pls. 108–110.

4 Division Street (facing Touro). The Levi Gale House was built by Russell Warren in 1835. It was moved from Washington Square, and now serves as the Jewish Community Center. See Chapter Eight and Pls. 148, 149.

The Sabbatarian Meeting House, now incorporated in the Newport Historical Society. See Chapter Four and Pls. 56–60.

Southwest corner of Touro and School streets. See 2 School Street.

117 Touro Street, a two-story, gambrel-roofed building now much changed, is known as the Fludder House. A deed dated 1716 shows that this lot "with a new house" was then in the possession of John Chadwick. It appears on Stiles' map, and part of the house bears evidence of very early construction. It was owned by Trinity Church in 1777, and served as the Rectory for many years. The Reverend Salmon Wheaton lived there.

See Lloyd Robson's account "115 Touro St. Was Trinity Glebe House" in the Newport *Daily News* for June 12, 1965, on file in the Newport Historical Society.

BARNEY STREET

10 Barney Street, known as the Nicholas Hazard House, is a two-story, gable-roofed building with a central fanlight doorway. In 1797 James Perry, mariner, bought land "together with the stables thereon" from Isaac Manchester. Although the house is mentioned for the first time when Benjamin Gray bought the property in 1816, James Perry probably built soon after he acquired the land in 1797. Nicholas Hazard owned it from 1835 to 1916.

16 Barney Street, known as the John Tennant House, is a two-story, gable-roofed building set on a high basement. It was built by Jonathan Green soon after he bought the lot from John Earl in 1804. William Rider, who bought house and lot in 1817, sold it to John Tennant in 1842. The steps and doorway have been altered.

SHERMAN STREET

Sherman Street was opened after 1800.

8 Sherman Street, a narrow one-story, gambrel-roofed cottage, was the home of Holmes Weaver, Newport cabinetmaker who worked in the early part of the nineteenth century. Mr. Rutherford, a descendant of Holmes Weaver, has reported that, according to the Sherman family records, this house was moved here from a site near the Bull family mansion formerly located at Spring and Sherman streets. It may also have served as the Widow Phillips' school, described as being so many yards from Henry Bull's house in Spring Street.

14 Sherman Street is a two-story, gable-roofed house, built about 1800. Robert Sherman, who bought the land in 1797, sold it with a dwelling house to Henry Bull in 1821. Robert Coggeshall bought it in 1845, and it still belongs to the Coggeshall family.

15 Sherman Street stands on the land Robert Sherman bought in 1797. The house was built by 1817, and Albert Irish bought it from Andrew Winslow in 1853.

20 Sherman Street, known as the Isaac Sherman Homestead, is a two-story, gable-roofed house with two interior chimneys and a fanlight doorway. Robert Sherman bought the land (which included the old Bull House on Spring Street) in 1797. In 1811 he sold this lot to Isaac Sherman who built the house soon afterward. It remained in the Sherman family until 1905.

30 Sherman Street, known as the Duncan Hazard House, is a two-story, gable-roofed house with a fanlight doorway. It was built between 1809 when Caleb Green sold the lot of land to Paul Bailey, carpenter, and 1816 when Bailey sold house and lot to John Allen. The Allen family kept the property until 1870. General Gates' sister once lived here.

32 Sherman Street. Caleb Green sold this lot to William Stanhope in 1809. His heirs sold house and lot to John Stanhope in 1836. The two-story, gable-roofed house has been made into apartments.

34 Sherman Street is a one-story, gambrel-roofed house. In 1811 Asa Gates sold the land to Henry G. Place, who built the house. In 1858 his heirs sold it to George S. Sherman. It has been in the Sherman family since then.

MOUNT VERNON STREET

9 Mount Vernon Street is the old part of the Townsend Hotel, which stood originally on the northwest corner of Pelham and Thames streets where it appears on Stiles' map. It was built about 1750.

11 Mount Vernon Street, built by John Tilley, was standing in 1809. It was originally a two-story, gable-roofed house, but has been altered.

13 Mount Vernon Street was built by John Tilley's brother William, soon after he bought the land in 1809. The two houses originally looked alike, and this one has been little changed.

19 Mount Vernon Street is a two-story, gable-roofed, early nineteenth-century building with a roundheaded second-story landing window. In 1809 Caleb Green sold the lot to Benjamin Chace, who built the house. Mary Fish bought it in 1830, and Edward Fish sold it to George Mumford in 1850. The house has an unusual and attractive second-story, round-headed window over the central doorway.

There are several excellent Greek Revival houses on Mt. Vernon Street.

HIGH STREET

12 High Street, known as the William Littlefield House, is a two-story, gable-roofed house with a fanlight doorway and excellent interior woodwork of post-Revolutionary date. The house itself may be earlier, since deeds show that Caleb Arnold bought a house here from Sarah Clarke sometime before 1775. Sion Arnold, his son, sold the house to Benjamin Marshall in 1801, and it changed hands several times until Mr. William Littlefield bought it in 1831. He gave it to the Newport City Hospital in 1882, and Dr. Edwin Robinson bought it in 1913. Sion Arnold was probably responsible for rebuilding the house and installing the delicately detailed mantelpieces designed in the early Federal style. See Chapter Seven and Pl. 135.

CORNÉ STREET

2 Corné Street. Michele Felice Corné's house. Corné bought the land and a stable from Silas Gardner in 1822. Tradition says he converted the stable into this two-story, gable-roofed house with a central fanlight doorway soon afterward, but he may have built a new house. He decorated the walls of the southwest chamber with seascapes and views of sailing vessels which have since been removed. See Introduction and Pl. 17.

SCHOOL STREET

2 School Street, known as the Mawdsley or Turner House, is a gable-roofed house, now much altered. It is shown on Stiles' map, and was the home of Charles Bardin before 1778. In 1803 his granddaughter, Mary Mawdsley, a widow, came into possession of the property. She married Captain Joseph Smith, known for his beautiful gardens, who, according to Dr. Henry Turner, brought the first cuttings of the Napoleon willow to Newport. Dr. Turner bought the house in 1847.

24 School Street, now the Children's Home, was the birthplace of William Ellery Channing. In 1712, Walter Clarke sold the lot to Joseph Borden and Stiles' map shows a house on the site in 1758, but the next record is dated 1782 when Walter Channing bought the house, then part of the confiscated property of Joseph Durfee. The door and roof have been altered, but the interior woodwork, especially the staircase, is similar to that of the Mawdsley house at No. 228 Spring Street, and suggests a date of about 1750.

25 School Street, Trinity Church School House, southwest corner of School and Mary, was built in 1799 on land given in the first years of the eighteenth century by Walter Clarke and financed by the Nathaniel Kay Foundation of 1741. The building now serves as the Shiloh Baptist Church.

40 School Street, recently the home of the Aquidneck Industries and now made into apartments, is known as the Finch, Caleb Green, or Governor Collins House. A drawing in the deed books shows that originally it was a two-story, gable-roofed house with a central flatheaded doorway. James Sisson, innholder, owned the land in 1738, and Stiles shows a two-story house here in 1758. The Sisson heirs sold house and lot to John Crooker in 1781. Caleb Green bought it in 1796, and sold it to Governor Charles Collins in 1823. Benjamin Finch bought it in 1843. Governor Collins built the third story to use as a ballroom, and the front portico was added some years later. The staircase is especially fine. It, as well as some of the other woodwork, is similar to that in the Channing house next north, and is part of James Sisson's house.

50 School Street. The Masonic Hall. The Reverend Andrew Burnaby, visiting Newport in 1760, reported that he saw the foundations and plans drawn by Mr. Harrison for "a very pretty building" for a Mason's Hall. This building evidently never progressed beyond the foundations, although in 1761 the Committee voted to give Captain Peter Harrison twenty-five tickets in the Masonic Hall lottery for his trouble in drawing the plans. The hall was still not built when Blascowitz made his map, but a tablet on the present greatly enlarged building (composed of two buildings with gable ends set to the street tied together by a recessed entry section) records that at least part of it was dedicated in 1803.

DIVISION STREET

Division Street is an old street. It was known at first as the Back Street, later as High.

3 Division Street, known as the Tanner House, is a narrow gable-roofed house with wide overhanging cornice and heavy structural beams. It may have been built by Samuel Rhodes soon after he bought the land in 1713. Tillinghast bought the house in 1727, and kept it until about 1783. See Susan Braley Franklin, Division Street, Newport Historical Society Bulletin no. 104, pp. 9 and 10.

4 Division Street. See the Levi Gale House. Touro Street.

5 Division Street is also a small gable-roofed house with an overhanging cornice. It stands on land Elisha Gibbs bought soon after 1727 and kept until 1796. It was probably built about 1745, when he married Lydia Peckham. See Franklin, pp. 11 and 12.

20 Division Street, known as the Slocum House, is another narrow gable-roofed house with a very wide overhanging cornice. Daniel Carr, who bought the land in 1723, probably built the house soon afterward. When Sayles Carr sold the property in 1762, the house was built, and Stiles shows a house on this site in 1758. See Franklin, pp. 6 and 7.

39 Division Street, the Underwood House, is a two-story, gambrel-roofed building with a pedimented doorway and some good interior woodwork. Nassau Hastie, barber, who bought the lot in 1760, sold lot and house to John Hart in 1768. Nicholas Underwood bought it in 1810. See Franklin, p. 28.

⊙ *40 Division Street,* the Augustus Lucas or Augustus Johnston House. It was probably built about 1721 and enlarged about 1745 or 1750. See Appendix A and Franklin, pp. 14 to 20.

41 Division Street was owned by Nassau Hastie before he bought the adjoining lot north. His widow sold the house to Henry Tew in 1783. It has been enlarged and changed. See Franklin, pp. 28 and 29.

42 Division Street, known as the Ailman House, was standing in 1748, the year George Buckmaster bought it from John Jepson. It has been enlarged. See Franklin, pp. 22 and 23.

46 Division Street, known as the Hopkins House, is a two-story, gambrel-roofed house with end to the street. It was built sometime between 1750 and 1772. The Reverend Hopkins, hero of Harriet Beecher Stowe's *The Minister's Wooing,* lived here, as did Isaac Touro. See Franklin, pp. 23 and 24 and Pl. 99.

73 Division Street, a two-story, gable-roofed house with a fan pedimented doorway, was built by Edward Hammett in 1811. It was restored in 1950. See Franklin, pp. 37 and 38 and Pl. 137.

77 Division Street, a two-story, gable-roofed house, was bought by Edward Hammett, housewright, from Norton Wilbour in 1811. It has been much changed.

80 Division Street, a square hip-roofed house, was probably built between 1750 and 1760 on land Benjamin Ellery had given to his son Christopher. It has good early interior woodwork, but the house has been somewhat altered. See Franklin, p. 35.

83 Division Street was owned by John Mowatt in 1818. It has been altered.

92 Division Street, a square gable-on-hip-roofed house, with excellent early nineteenth-century detail, stands on the site of William Ellery's house, burnt in the Revolution. James Pitman bought the land in 1828, and sold house and lot to David Holloway in 1836. G. H. Richardson notes that the house was moved here. The style, which should date the house about 1810, bears this out.

MARY STREET
(FORMERLY MARY LANE OR NEW LANE)

29 Mary Street, a two-story, gambrel-roofed house with a fanlight door and some excellent early nineteenth-century mantels, was built by Christopher Fowler in 1801. See Chapter Seven and Pl. 134.

* *23 Mary Street,* a two-story, gable-roofed house, has been altered, and the fanlight door, shown here among the measured drawings, is now gone. Samuel Hudson, who bought the land from Jacob Smith in 1800, built the house soon afterward. He sold it to Simon Newton in 1833, whose heirs still owned it in 1883. Now a parking lot. See Pl. 143.

* *19 Mary Street* was built by William Price soon after he bought the land from Jacob Smith in 1800. It was still in the Price family in 1883. It has been much altered. Now a parking lot.

16 Mary Street, a narrow two-story, gable-roofed, early-eighteenth-century house set with end to the street, has a wide overhanging cornice.

It stands on land originally part of the estate of John Cranston. Cranston's granddaughter sold the property, including two houses, to Charles Feke in 1791. John Cranston's seventeenth-century stone castle, which Feke soon tore down, was one of them. This house has been altered.

CLARKE STREET
(See Appendix B and Pl. 62.)

SPRING STREET

Laid out by 1642. Known at first as the Back Street or the Way Leading to the Neck.

30 Spring Street, the First Baptist Church, was built in 1846 and rebuilt in 1949. It stands on the site of the meetinghouse built in 1738, and is the fourth building for the church. The first was at Green End. The second, built in 1707, stood on Tanner Street.

58 Spring Street, on the northeast corner of Spring and Touro streets, now Tubley's Spa, is a broad gambrel-roofed house built with a very heavy frame, including summer beams, all closed in. Benjamin Barney sold the house and lot to Jacob Barney in 1730. Ezra Stiles' map shows a two-story house here in 1758. The old staircase and mantels have been removed, and the house has been raised.

60 Spring Street, on the southeast corner of Spring and Touro streets, is a gable-on-hip-roofed house known as the Joseph Tweedy House. In 1709 Walter Clarke sold the land to Elizabeth Newby, who in 1720 left land and house to her daughter, Sarah Rider. It remained in the Rider family until 1784. Stiles' map shows a two-story house here. Colonel de Buzelot, Chief of Brigade, Regiment d'Auxonne, was quartered here during the French stay in Newport in the Revolution. See Introduction.

69 Spring Street, William Redwood's house, is shown on Stiles' map. In 1778 Abraham Redwood bequeathed the house "I bought of my brother William Redwood" to his daughter Mehitable Ellery. It is a two-story, gable-roofed house with a brick end and a fanlight doorway added about 1800.

* *75 Spring Street* is a gable-roofed, two-story house. In 1773 Ebenezer Davenport, cordwainer, sold it to Ebenezer Burrill, silversmith, who owned it until 1800. It is not shown on Stiles' map, but E. Burrill is listed as owning the house in the British list of 1777.

* *89 Spring Street,* an old two-story, gambrel-roofed half-a-house, is shown on Stiles' map, but the earliest deed yet found is dated 1817, when Moses Norman sold the house to Freelove Casey.

104-108 Spring Street, a two-story, gable-roofed half-a-house on the southeast corner of Spring and Mary streets, was mentioned in a deed dated 1797 when the heirs of Abigail Cahoone sold their right in the dwelling house to Aaron Dyre. Stiles shows a two-story house here, and the British list shows that the Widow Cahoone and eight other occupants were living here in 1777. Cornelius Wilbour, who bought the property at a mortgage sale in 1827, sold it to Jacob Lake in 1845. Howard E. Read owned it in 1883, and it remained in Read ownership until 1912.

109-111 Spring Street, on the southwest corner of Spring and Mary streets, where Jonathan Otis, Newport goldsmith lived, is a very old, long, two-story, gable-roofed house, one room deep and built with a brick end. In 1705 Walter Clarke sold the land to John Odlin, who is supposed to have built the house. Stiles' map shows it, and the British list gives Jonathan Otis as owner in 1777. Otis sold it to Clarke Rodman in 1788. See Lloyd Robson's story, "Rodman House Quaker School Master's" in the Newport *Daily News,* June 19, 1965, on file in the Newport Historical Society.

115 Spring Street is a gable-roofed, two-story house. In 1725 John Edy sold a house on this site to Benjamin Wilson. According to the British list, it was owned by the Widow Bridges in 1777. Robert Bridges sold it "in ruinous condition" to Joseph Mumford, tinplate worker, in 1786, who probably rebuilt it.

119 Spring Street, known as the Samuel Barker House, is a two-story, gambrel-roofed house with brick ends and a central fanlight doorway. Stiles shows a house here, and part of it goes back to 1714 when James Brown, joiner, sold a house to Daniel Pearce, "bunner." Jonathan Thurston bought it in 1720. According to the British list, his widow was living here in 1777. Joseph Thurston owned it in 1786, and Susannah Thurston sold it to Samuel Barker in 1829. It was still in the Barker family in 1907.

134-136 Spring Street, located on the northeast corner of Spring and Church streets, and known as the Borden House, is a two-story, gambrel-roofed house with two chimneys and an ell at the rear which is part of an older building. Stiles shows a house here, and James Pitman inherited it from his father in 1762. In 1785 James, Jr., sold the estate to William Burroughs who sold it to John Ailman in 1845. Ailman's heirs sold to Arthur Mumford in 1872, and it was owned by Patrick Murphy in 1920.

Trinity Church, between Church and Frank streets, Richard Munday, architect, 1726. See Chapter Four.

⊙ *166 Spring Street,* the Norton Wilbour House located on the northeast corner of Spring and Mill streets, was owned by Silas Huddy in 1815. It is a two-story, gambrel-roofed half-a-house of pre-Revolutionary date. It is not shown on Stiles' map, but the British list of Newport occupants shows that Morton Huddy lived there in 1777. Silas Huddy's heirs sold the property to Norton Wilbour in 1823, and it remained in the Wilbour family until 1914. Now being restored.

* *167 Spring Street* on the southwest corner of Mill Street is an early two-story, gable-roofed

house. In 1773, Ann Brewer, who had inherited the house from her father, Thomas Brewer, in 1749, sold it to Lemuel Finley, and the British list gives John Hull as owner in 1777. Hull sold it to Robert Brattle who sold it to Simon Davis in 1792. Elizabeth Burlingham bought it in 1820, and it has been in the Burlingham family since that time. James Fenimore Cooper supposedly wrote *The Red Rover* in this house.

175 Spring Street, a two-story, gambrel-roofed building set end to the street, is not shown on Stiles' map, but was built and in the possession of Samuel Bours, merchant, in 1777. In 1805 it belonged to his son John Bours, who bequeathed it in 1813 to Frances Loring, his daughter. Mrs. John Bours was Hannah Babcock, daughter of Dr. Joshua Babcock of Westerly. Blackburn painted her portrait, and Copley painted that of John Bours. Both are in the Worcester Museum of Art. John Bours, an important merchant, owned the shop on Thames Street "The Golden Eagle." The wooden eagle, one of a pair formerly from the gateposts of Metcalf Bowler's Portsmouth house, which served for many years as Bour's shop sign, is now in the Newport Historical Society.

181 Spring Street, a one-story, two-room, gambrel-roofed cottage, was built by Jonathan Gibbs, housewright, before 1777, when, according to the British list, James Brattle and four others were occupying the house. Gibbs sold it to William Martin in 1782, and John Bours bought it in 1813. He gave it and the big house just north to his daughter Frances Loring.

185 Spring Street is a two-story, gable-roofed house with some added Greek Revival detail. According to a notice of sale published in the Newport *Mercury*, this house was built in 1774 by Jonathan Gibbs. Gibbs sold the house to Lydia Sanford in 1783, who bequeathed it to Simon Fleet in 1797. In 1809 Fleet sold it to John Ferguson, tobacconist, and Isaac Sherman bought the property in 1836. Charles Crandall, who owned it later, sold it in 1915.

189 Spring Street, the Daniel Vaughn House. See 50 Pelham Street.

199 Spring Street, known as the Cremin House, is a two-story, gable-roofed house with a handsome fanlight door and sandstone steps. It stands on part of Thomas Banister's land, confiscated during the Revolution. In 1785 this piece was granted to John Kerber for twenty years. He probably built the house soon afterward. See Pl. 138.

204 Spring Street, a square two-story house on the northeast corner of Spring Street and Bowen Court, is known as the Tobin House. It stands on land Francis Brinley sold Nathaniel Coggeshall in 1810, and was built by Stephen Bowen soon after he acquired the property in 1825. It remained in the Bowen family until 1892 when the heirs sold it to Dudley Newton, the architect who built

many nineteenth-century summer houses. Originally the house was set back from Spring Street in a gardened lot, but it has been moved forward, and now has a mansard roof with a high mansarded center turret. It has retained its handsome fanlight doorway.

205 Spring Street, a two-story, gable-roofed house on the northwest corner of Spring and Green streets, was altered during the Greek Revival period. It is not shown on Stiles' map, but Benjamin Howland owned it before the Revolution, and the British list shows him here in 1777. It was still in the Howland family in 1891.

209 Spring Street, southwest corner of Green Street, was Robert Brattle's house before the Revolution, and according to the British list he was living there in 1777. He sold it to Robert Champlin in 1784. It is a two-story, gambrel-roofed house with Greek Revival detail added later. It is not shown on Stiles' map, but was built soon afterward.

216 Spring Street, the Joseph Cottrell House located on the northeast corner of Spring and Prospect Hill streets, is a handsome two-story Greek Revival house with flat siding and an unusual curved corner bay finished with open curved and columniated porches at the first- and second-story levels. It was built about 1843 on the site of a house Christopher Bliven sold to Joseph Cottrell in that year, and it was in the Cottrell family until after 1893.

219 Spring Street, on the northwest corner of Spring and Franklin streets, was originally a square hip-roofed house. It is not shown on Stiles' map but, according to the British list, was owned in 1777 by Lyn Martin. Martin's property was confiscated during the Revolution, and in 1784 Joseph Clarke, General Treasurer, sold it to Daniel Gardner, mariner. Nathan Hazard bought it from the estate of Benjamin Wanton Gardner in 1811. It has an excellent fanlight doorway. The monitor roof was added later.

228 Spring Street. The Mawdsley House. See Chapter Five and Appendix A. *The Jireh Bull House* and the Mawdsley-Gardner-Watson-Pitman House and Pls. 38, 117–120, 142.

229 Spring Street (also 45 Franklin Street), known as the Pitman House, is a two-story, gambrel-roofed half-a-house set end to Spring Street. It stands on land Benjamin Bull, cordwainer, sold to William James, shipwright, in 1711. Samuel Gibbs James mortgaged lot and house to Richard Phillips in 1772. John Pitman bought it from Phillips in 1794. The main doorway has been put on the ell of the Mawdsley House.

238–240 Spring Street, a two-story, gable-roofed house with an interesting carpenter detail meander cornice and an old store below, stands on land owned by Joshua Rathbone in 1781, and described as a garden lot in 1802. The Rathbone heirs sold this lot to Robinson Potter in 1814, and

John Pitman acquired it in 1816. He probably built the house soon afterward. It was described as his dwelling house in his will dated 1862. His heirs sold it to Stephen Hammett in 1872, and it was still in the Hammett name in 1907.

244 Spring Street, on the northeast corner of Levin Street, is a long two-story, gable-roofed house with a big central chimney and added Greek Revival detail. Maps show that it was enlarged between 1859 and 1876. Like 238–240, it stands on land owned by Joshua Rathbone in 1781. Blascowitz shows a building here in 1777, but the first mention of a house yet found in deed records is dated 1801 when Benjamin Rathbone sold to Ann Rathbone his right to the messuage and estate of Joshua Rathbone bounded northerly on a street (John Street) southerly on Mushroom Lane (Levin Street) and westerly on the Back Street (Spring Street.) A house and a store were mentioned in deeds of 1802 when the other heirs sold their rights to Ann Rathbone. In 1811 the heirs of Joshua Rathbone sold the piece with the store and the house on the Levin Street corner to John Bailey, distiller. John Bailey sold the property to Hannah Gorton in 1865, and she sold to Margaret Goggin after 1893.

* *266 Spring Street* is a small gambrel-roofed building with end to the street, now in ruinous condition. It was owned for many years by the Greene family, and used as a store. It has been torn down to make a parking lot for St. Mary's Catholic Church.

265 Spring Street, on the southwest corner of Gidley Street, is a two-story gable-roofed house with a narrow boxed cornice set end to Spring Street. It was owned by Stephen Deblois in 1787. David King bought it from John Deblois in 1824, and sold it to Jonathan Record in 1827. It is still known as the Record House.

268 Spring Street, northeast corner of Golden Hill Street, is a narrow two-story, gable-roofed house. It was built about 1740 by Samuel Greene, one of the carpenters who signed the contract for Redwood Library. Fleet Greene lived here, and it is known as the William Greene house. It has now been torn down for a parking lot for St. Mary's Catholic Church.

271–273 Spring Street, on the northwest corner of Ann Street, is known as the William Austin House. It is a big two-story gambrel-roofed house set end to Spring Street with a lower two-story, gambrel-roofed ell attached at the right. Stiles shows a shop on the site of the ell, and Blascowitz shows buildings on both sites, but when Abigail Wilkinson sold the land to Gaspar Castoff in 1787, no buildings were mentioned. The house was probably built about this time, and by 1824 John Castoff owned it. Eliza Austin inherited it, and it was still in the Austin family in 1907.

283 Spring Street, on the northwest corner of Brewer Street, is a two-story, gambrel-roofed

house. It stands on land Stephen Wanton divided into lots before the Revolution. Elisha Shearman owned this lot in 1775, and Blascowitz shows a building here. It remained in the Shearman family until 1841 when John Shearman's heirs sold his estate to John Northam. Joseph Northam sold it to Peter Lee in 1864, and it is still known as the Lee House.

329 Spring Street has been much altered, but it is very old, and is shown on Stiles' map. James Honeyman, Jr., is said to have lived there. James Easton sold house and lot to James Easton, Jr., in 1769. The dining room was originally painted in a pattern consisting of red and white diamonds above the chair rail, and red and white vertical stripes below.

352 Spring Street, owned in the mid-nineteenth century by Isaiah Crooker, was built in 1803 by Samuel Durfee. It is a two-story gable-roofed house with two interior chimneys, an attractive fanlight doorway, and a lightly scaled dentil cornice.

465 Spring Street. This handsome square stone two-story mansion with characteristic Federal detail and monitor roof on the northwest corner of Spring Street and Lee Avenue was once owned by Henry James. According to a note by George Richardson in his book #999 in the Newport Historical Society, it was built in 1834 by Robert P. Lee, and it resembles some of the New Bedford stone mansions built about this same date. The house stands on a large tract of land between Thames and Spring streets that Nicholas Easton sold to William Lee, Jr., in 1786. Samuel Lee bought the piece this house is on in 1814 and sold it to another William Lee in 1815. Robert P. Lee bought it at a sheriff's sale in 1831 and built the house soon afterward. William Breese, who bought the property in 1852, sold it to Henry James in 1866. A letter from Mary Rotch Hunter, in the Hunter Papers now in the Newport Historical Society, to her husband, Charles Hunter, describing a trip to Providence on the boat *R. C. Gibbs*, gives the following account:

"Mr. James was on the boat, he told me he had purchased Captain Breeze's stone cottage in Spring Street just below Emanuel church. House and furniture for $6,000— . . . he did not intend to live in Newport . . . when Alfred Smith met him accidently in the street and persuaded him just to look at this house." James soon sold the house to James Paul, and General I. V. Palmer owned it in 1876. John A. Griswold, who bought it from Paul, sold to Patrick O'Neill, and it is still in the O'Neill name.

Streets South of Washington Square.

CHURCH STREET

214 Thames Street and 5, 7, 9, 11 Church Street stand on the site of James Honeyman's house, built before 1706. Honeyman's heirs sold the house to Simeon Martin in 1768. These buildings are late-eighteenth-century, probably built by Martin. T. Mumford Seabury bought the property in 1864, and it is still known by his name. See Lloyd Robson's account of the house, "Martin House Was Built by Importer," in the Newport *Daily News,* July 10, 1965, on file in the Newport Historical Society.

* 12 *Church Street,* a two-story, gambrel-roofed house, standing on part of James Honeyman's land, is shown on Stiles' map. Thomas Ayres owned it in 1772 and Jethro Briggs, in 1809. In 1853 Mary Irish sold it to John Eldred, and it was designated then as part of the Jethro Briggs estate. Now a parking lot.

⊙ 27 *Church Street* was built by Joseph Wood soon after 1810 when he bought land from Simeon Martin which had originally belonged to James Honeyman. It is a gable-roofed, two-story house with two interior chimneys and a very fine fanlight doorway. See Chapter Seven and Pls. 140–141.

⊙ 36 *Church Street* is a two-story, gambrel-roofed house with a Dutch kicked-out roof line, unique in Newport, and a wide overhanging cornice. Erastus Pease bought the land from heirs of James Honeyman in 1785, and although some of the detail of the house seems earlier, he evidently built the house about this time. The interior woodwork is intact. See Pl. 100.

46 *Church Street* is a two-story gambrel-roofed house. William Allen bought the land from the Reverend George Bisset, one of James Honeyman's heirs in 1788, and built the house soon afterward. Captain Thomas White bought it from Allen in 1797, and his heirs still owned it in 1918.

Trinity Church. See Chapter Four and Pls. 4, 47–56.

70 *Church Street,* a Greek Revival house, stands on the site of the ministerial house where the Reverend Mr. Nathaniel Clapp lived. It was built by John Vars soon after he bought the land in 1833. He sold it to Benjamin Tisdale, the silversmith, in 1846.

⊙ 78 *Church Street,* on the northwest corner of Church and School streets, is a two-story, gable-roofed house with central doorway, rusticated window caps, and early-nineteenth-century interior detail. The first house on this site was torn down during the Revolution, and Caleb Greene sold the lot to Thomas Goddard in 1798. The house had been built by 1801, when Ebenezer Shearman bought the property. See Pl. 136.

* 94 *Church Street,* on the northeast corner of Church and High streets, known as the Irey House, is a two-story, gambrel-roofed house. It is now much changed, but it still retains some bolection paneling. John Allison, peruke maker, bought the lot in 1752, and the house was built by 1758 as shown by Stiles' map. Allison's heirs sold it to Mary Clarke, who sold it to Samuel Vernon in 1783. It remained in the Vernon family until

1879. It has now been demolished for the Viking Motor Hotel parking lot.

CHURCH COURT

1 *Church Court,* a one-story, gambrel-roofed cottage with a big central chimney, is known as the home of Sarah Osborne. It was moved to this location.

MILL STREET

It was called Carr's Lane in the seventeenth century.

* 26 *Mill Street,* the old Clarke house, now the Nason Cottage and much changed, is shown on Stiles' map. The French list shows that Lieutenant Colonel de Bressoles was quartered "with Joseph Clarke, 195 Mill Street" in 1781. After 1800 it was the home of Audley Clarke, President of the Bank of Rhode Island, who was responsible, according to Jonas Bergner, for the fanlight door. It was originally a two-story, gambrel-roofed building. See Pl. 135.

47 *Mill Street,* the Joseph Beattie House, is a two-story, gambrel-roofed house. It appears on Stiles' map, and was owned by the heirs of Joseph Beattie in 1773. By 1807 it was in the possession of Samuel Carr, and was still in the Carr family in 1937.

62 *Mill Street,* a two-story, gable-roofed house, was built in 1807. It was owned by Joshua Sayer, baker, in 1810, came into the possession of William Guild, and still belonged to the Guild family in 1900. It has now been covered with tarpaper brick.

⊙ 70 *Mill Street,* on the northwest corner of Mill and Division streets, known as the Billy Bottomore House, is a two-story, gable-roofed house, built soon after the Revolution, but the earliest record yet found is dated 1818, when James Chappell sold it to Joshua Sayer. Abby Chappell inherited the house, and on her marriage to Billy Bottomore, confectioner and Michele Felice Corné's servant, they lived here. The house, now owned by Ralph Wilcox Taylor, is being restored.

76 *Mill Street,* on the northeast corner of Mill and Division streets. See 92 Division Street.

83 *Mill Street.* The First Congregational Church, Cotton Palmer, architect, 1735. See Chapter Four and Pl. 61.

104 *Mill Street* is a brick two-story, gambrel-roofed house set end to the street. Stiles' map shows a house on this site in 1759, and a deed dated 1758 gives Benjamin Reynolds of Jamestown, ferryman, as an even earlier owner. Samuel Mumford, cordwainer, owned it in 1784. In 1797 Robert Brattle bought it, and in 1800 he sold it to William Ellery. The Mumford family acquired it again in 1821. Charles Hammett bought it in 1867. According to an account in the *Mercury* of June 16, 1860, George Mason completely restored and rebuilt the interiors in 1858–1860. It is one of the very few colonial brick houses built in Newport.

118 *Mill Street,* known as the Henderson or

Paul House, is a three-story, hip-roofed brick house. G. H. Richardson records that it was built by Robert Lawton soon after he acquired the land in 1809, and the style accords with a date in the first decade of the century. James Tanner, however, owned and lived in a house on this site as early as 1777. He sold it to Samuel Gardner in 1807, who sold it to George Lawton. Lawton may have rebuilt the earlier house. The entry porch was added later, and Miss M. E. Powell records that George C. Mason remolded the interiors in 1860, but she may have confused this house with 104 Mill Street. See Pl. 133.

142 Mill Street. The Governor John Tillinghast House, a handsome, square, three-story, gable-on-hip-roofed house, is shown on Stiles' map, and was built about 1758. Tillinghast's heirs sold it to Archibald Crary in 1792, and George Gibbs bought it in 1803. It remained in the Gibbs family until 1874 and was subsequently owned by Luther Bateman and Frederick Tuckerman. The house has been much enlarged, the original doorway with its segmental-headed pediment has been replaced by an entry porch, and most of the interior paneling has been elaborated, but the beautiful staircase with its twisted balusters and ramped rails is unchanged. Baron Von Steuben and Kosciusko visited here during the Revolutionary War, and General Nathanael Greene was quartered here. See Introduction.

TOURO PARK
The Stone Mill. See Chapter Two and Pls. 3, 22, 61.

PELHAM STREET
Pelham Street was cut through from Thames to Spring in 1741. Upper Pelham was opened before the Revolution, but is not shown on Stiles' map. Lower Pelham was first called Banister's Lane.

32 Pelham Street, a two-story, gambrel-roofed building, now much changed, is supposed to have been built by Nathaniel Langley in the first half of the eighteenth century. It is illustrated in Edwin Whitefield's *Homes of Our Forefathers* as the Dr. David King House, and dated 1710. It originally had a front doorway with a high broken scroll pediment belonging to the period of about 1740. It stands on land John Banister was dividing into lots in 1741 and is shown on Stiles' map of 1759. Deeds show that Charles Handy owned it, together with a spermaceti factory just west, before 1781. William Handy, his son, sold it to David King in 1810, and the property remained in the King family until the latter part of the nineteenth century. This once beautiful house is in poor repair and has been much altered. See Pls. 15, 84.

35 Pelham Street, now "The Lennox," was originally a two-story, gable-roofed house with a central fanlight doorway. It was built by Jonathan Bowen soon after 1804, when he bought the land, #16 of the John Banister lots. He sold the house to George Bowen in 1829, and it remained in the family until 1881. The roof has been changed to a mansard, but the fanlight door remains.

36 Pelham Street, now "The Pelham," is shown on Stiles' map. G. H. Richardson says that this house was built in 1744 by John Gidley, and was later owned by Captain Rodman Gardner. Deeds show that James Honeyman owned it before the Revolution. John Honeyman inherited the house in 1778, and the French list places Prevôt de Ronchamp with John Honeyman, 153 Pelham. Daniel Mason bought it in 1784. The house has been much enlarged. See Pl. 15.

43 Pelham Street is a one-story, gambrel-roofed house known as "The Little Old Woman in Gray" house, because of the poem of that title written by Governor Charles C. van Zandt. According to a deed dated 1803, Lucina Langley built the house on land bought in 1771. It was used by the British as a guardhouse from 1777 to 1779. The house remained in the Langley family until Elizabeth Langley, supposedly the heroine of van Zandt's poem, died in 1899. See Pl. 18.

44–46 Pelham Street, stands on land confiscated from Thomas Banister in 1781 and bought by Daniel Vaughan, victualler, from the General Treasurer in 1785. It was still a lot in 1795, but deeds show that the house was standing in 1813. Originally a two-story, gambrel-roofed building, the front has been raised to make three stories, and this part has been covered with a gable roof. See Pl. 15.

50 Pelham Street, a much altered house on the northwest corner of Spring and Pelham streets, stands on Thomas Banister's land "confiscated to the use of the state" in 1781. Ezra Stiles shows a shop on this spot in 1758 but, according to the list of Newport houses made by the British, Daniel Vaughn, victualler, and two others were living here in a house of six rooms in 1777. The house has since been owned by James Stevens, Job Peckham, and Benjamin Bateman, among others. It was altered in the Greek Revival period and again in the Victorian period when the roof was changed, but some of the eighteenth century interiors have survived.

56 Pelham Street. John Banister's town "house on the hill." See Appendix A and Pl. 97.

70 Pelham Street, known as the Van Zandt House, a Greek Revival house built by John Ladd for Augustus Littlefield in 1836. See Chapter Eight and Pls. 14, 97, 150.

Pelham Street has several other excellent Greek Revival houses.

GREEN STREET
* *12 Green Street,* a two-story, gambrel-roofed house, is shown on Stiles' map, but the earliest record yet found is dated 1784, when John Weeden sold the house to John Andrews. In 1793 Andrews sold it to Joseph Gardner. Rufus Kingsley bought it in 1829, and when Peleg Sherman

bought it in 1873, it was designated as the Kingsley estate.

27–29 Green Street, a long, two-story, gable-roofed, double house on the south side of Green Street, was built between 1763 and 1777 by James Cahoone and Stephen Yates, painters, whose names appear frequently in eighteenth-century Newport building records. The house stands on land owned by Peter Coggeshall in 1748, purchased by James Nixon from Daniel Coggeshall and Peter Bours, and sold by Nixon in two separate parcels to James Cahoone and Samuel Yates in 1763. The house was evidently built jointly soon after the purchase of the land, because Blascowitz shows a long double building in this location, but the first mention of a building occurs in 1805 when Nathan Hammett sold Yates' half, with dwelling house, to Benjamin Love and William Greene. Cahoone sold his part, with dwelling house, to Mary Sayer in 1815, and each half had separate owners until Thomas Lynch acquired the whole property in 1874. He hold it to George Williams in 1898, and it has changed hands several times since then.

* *40 Green Street* is a two-story, gable-roofed half-a-house of early-eighteenth-century type. In 1796 Joseph Howland's heirs deeded this house to Henry Howland, and it was still in the Howland family in 1883.

PROSPECT HILL STREET

Prospect Hill Street is an old road, one of the few early ways cut from Thames Street over the hill. It is shown on Stiles' map well filled with houses in 1758. The houses were built on lots laid out by John Chapman, who divided his plat about 1750.

40 Prospect Hill Street, the Boss House, is a two-story, gable-roofed house with a fanlight door, now partially obscured by a porch. In 1807 Sarah Martineau sold lot #2 of the Prospect Hill lands to Solomon and Benjamin Weaver, hatters, who built the house. Thomas Boss bought it in 1878.

94 Prospect Hill Street is a very old gambrel-roofed house with end set to the street, and early narrow heavy sash windows. It was built between 1751, when John Chapman sold lot #7 of his divided land to Peter Treby, sailmaker, and 1755, when Treby mortgaged the house and lot to Samuel Carr, ferryman. It is shown as a two-story house on Stiles' map. According to the British list, the widow Treby was living here in 1777, but Benjamin Church took up the mortgage, and the house remained in the Church family until Benjamin Carr bought it in 1837. It was still in the Carr family in 1911.

108 Prospect Hill Street, a gambrel-roofed house with end to the street, is now owned by Arthur Washburn. The house is marked on Stiles' map, and is part of Latham Thurston's estate, but the earliest mention found to date is in a deed dated 1798 which gives Robert Brattle as owner at that time. Latham Thurston's estate was sold to William Thurston, hatter and dyer, in 1826. George Vaughan bought it in 1839, and William Sisson in 1874. He sold to Lucinda Washburn in 1895. This is an important house. Now covered with clapboards on the sides and shingled on the ends, it was originally finished with rusticated siding like that of the Vernon House on Clarke Street. Some of the rusticated finish may still be seen in an exterior cellarway, and its old sanded and painted surface has fortunately been preserved in this protected spot. The color is a good strong gray mixed with sand filled with black particles. The house thus furnishes excellent documentary evidence of an authentic eighteenth-century painted and sanded surface.

122 Prospect Hill Street. This two-story, gambrel-roofed house built with end to the street was owned by Metcalf Bowler in 1760. It appears on Stiles' map, and according to the British list, Charles Wickham owned it in 1777. He sold it to James Burdick in 1781. It remained in the Burdick family until Sewell Merrill bought it in 1872. It is still in the Merrill family.

128–130 Prospect Hill Street, is a big double two-story, gambrel-roofed house. In 1752 Samuel Buroughs sold to Anthony Shaw lot #9 of the land laid out by John Chapman. The house is shown on Stiles' map, and was advertised for sale in the *Mercury* in 1760. The British list shows that John Thurston and Anthony Shaw were owners in 1777. In 1795 Anna Shaw sold her half (the east) to Abraham Read, hatter. In 1853 Joseph Weaver bought the whole house. Henry de Blois bought it in 1900.

* *136 Prospect Hill Street*, a gable-roofed building with a good doorway and mid-eighteenth-century construction, is known as the Stedman house. It was in the possession of Samuel Henshaw in 1770, the widow Henshaw in 1777, and owned by John Henshaw in 1803. Stephen Stedman bought it in 1845.

* *146 Prospect Hill Street* is a big gable-roofed house with narrow early sash windows and a big central chimney. Its history has only been traced to Elisha Coggeshall's will of 1805, when he divided the house among his children, but the house was built long before the Revolutionary War, and deeds of 1794 and 1798 show that Charles Wickham owned the property then. The British list placed Robert Crooke there in 1777. The Coggeshall family owned the property until 1870.

152 Prospect Hill Street is a one-story, gambrel-roofed house. Dripp's map of 1859 does not show a house here, but G. H. Richardson says that this is the little Harkness cottage. It originally stood on the east side of Thames Street near the north corner of Pelham, and was moved to the site near the Harkness Mill on Old Beach Road. From there it was moved to Prospect Hill Street.

FRANKLIN STREET (FORMERLY LEWIS OR KING)

* *10–12 Franklin Street*, a two-story, gam-

brel-roofed house, has a very wide overhanging cornice. In 1800 it was designated as the Nathaniel Langley estate, and was still in the Langley family in 1883. It has been raised and is in poor repair.

20 Franklin Street is shown on Stiles' map, and G. H. Richardson says that it was built by John Gidley just before his death in 1744. Captain John Jepson, who owned it before the Revolution, bequeathed it to his grandson Robert Wheatley Hicks in 1787. Henry Cranston bought it in 1811, and it remained in his family until 1874. It is a two-story, gambrel-roofed house with a central entry, now altered. The lower floor has been made into shops, and the house is in poor repair. See Lloyd Robson's account, "The Gidley House Became the Holly Tree," in the Newport *Daily News*, May 2, 1965, filed in the Newport Historical Society.

29 Franklin Street, a two-story, gable-roofed house with Victorian detail added, has been very much rebuilt, but it also appears on Stiles' map. In 1745 Timothy Peckham sold the land to Benjamin Norton. Norton probably built the house, but the next record found is dated 1796, when John Tillinghast, cabinetmaker, bought it from Caleb Greene, William Tillinghast, and Charles Russell. Elizabeth Banister bought it in 1811, and it remained in her family until George Monroe bought it in 1842. He sold it to John Martin in 1895.

30 Franklin Street, a large gambrel-roofed house set end to the street and much rebuilt, was put up sometime between 1790 and 1810. In 1790 Henry Stevenson sold William Davis land he had bought of the heirs of John Chapman. In 1792 Davis sold to John McWhorter of Taunton; John Baker bought the property in 1799 and in 1810 when he sold it to Henry Clannen, a sailmaker, the house was mentioned. Thomas Townsend, of Syracuse, William Townsend, and Joseph Bradford were later owners.

33-35 Franklin Street is a much altered two-story, gable-roofed house. It appears on Stiles' map, and in 1766 Joshua Saunders bequeathed to his daughter, Freelove Remson, "my dwelling house in King's Street, I bought of Timothy Peckham." Freelove Remson gave it to Daniel Rogers in 1786. It was later owned by Alexander Swazey, Nathan Chafee, and Mary Atkinson.

32-34-36-38 Franklin Street. This two-story, gambrel-roofed house with corner quoins stands on land Caleb Godfrey inherited from his mother Abigail Chapman Godfrey in the early eighteenth century, but it was not built until after the Revolution. In 1786 Godfrey sold lot and house to Henry Stevenson. Robinson Potter bought it later. It originally stood on the Prospect Hill side of the lot. It has been moved forward, the lower floor made into shops, and the fanlight doorway is now in the Historical Society. It is known as the Dean House.

43-45 Franklin Street is a gambrel-roofed, two-story house with a fanlight door. It is almost joined to the Pitman house on the southwest corner of Spring and Franklin streets, and stands on land Benjamin Bull sold to Timothy Peckham before 1711. Deeds show that it belonged to John Easton before 1785, and was owned by Samuel Lawton and his family later. Ellen Neil owned it in 1876.

Southwest corner of Spring and Franklin streets. See 229 Spring Street.

JOHN STREET

This street was opened between 1758 and 1775. Most of the land was being divided into lots by William Handy about 1800.

17 John Street. This two-story gambrel-roofed house with a very large central chimney stands on one of the lots laid out by Godsgift and Ozias Pitkin, originally part of Benedict Arnold's land. In 1789 William B. Arnold and Sanford Arnold sold the land to Samuel Yeates, a painter. The house, probably built soon afterward, was standing in 1805 when James Yeates, who had inherited it, sold it to his brother Samuel.

29 John Street is a two-story, gable-roofed house with a fanlight doorway and a big central chimney. In 1760 Joseph Vickery, a chairmaker, bought the lot from Francis Skinner. He probably built the house before the Revolution, but the first definite date is 1818 when his heirs sold house and lot to Thomas Spooner, also a chairmaker. Spooner had already bought Vickery's chairmaking shop next east (now gone).

41 John Street, known as the Lake House, is a two-story, gable-roofed building with two interior chimneys. It was probably built by Thomas Hudson, housewright, about 1808, when he mortgaged the property to Samuel Hudson. Thomas Spooner was granted title to house and lot in 1848. John Lake bought it in 1889.

⊙ *46 John Street.* The Martin House, on the northeast corner of John and Martin streets. Robert Brattle, boatbuilder, sold house and lot to George Martin in 1773. It remained in the Martin family until 1917. It is a two-story, gable-roofed house with a central chimney, but a projecting two-story gabled entry has been added. The house has recently been restored.

47 John Street, known as the Ross House, is a gambrel-roofed building with a big central chimney and a pedimented doorway. In 1803 Richard Hazard sold Constant Tabor part of lot #22 of the land divided by William Handy. Tabor probably built the house soon afterward. On his death he bequeathed it to the Six Principles Baptist Church who sold it to Mahlon van Horne in 1894. Samuel Ross bought it in 1904.

See Lloyd Robson's "Tabor House Was Negro Official's Home," Newport *Daily News*, June 8, 1965, on file in the Newport Historical Society.

63 John Street, a square Greek Revival house,

was built by Alexander McGregor, stonemason, soon after he bought the land from Richard Hazard in 1835. Abbie McGregor sold house and lot to John Fontaine in 1911. See Chapter Eight and Lloyd Robson, "McGregor, Home of Worker in Stone," Newport *Daily News,* June 26, 1965, on file in the Newport Historical Society.

66 John Street, known as the Underwood House, is a two-story, gable-roofed building with a fanlight doorway. In 1801 John Tompkins bought lots #2 and #3 from William Handy. He built the house soon afterward and lived there until his death. In 1857 Charles Underwood bought it. See Pl. 137.

⊙ *80 John Street,* known as the Swinburne House, is a two-story, gable-roofed building with a fanlight doorway and early-nineteenth-century interior woodwork. In 1807 John Thurston sold lot #3 of William and Abigail Handy's land to Isaac Peckham, blockmaker. He probably built the house soon afterward. Henry Vernon bought it from the Peckham heirs in 1863, and sold it to George Swinburne in 1867. See Chapter Seven and Pl. 136.

**101 John Street.* This two-story, gambrel-roofed house was probably built by Robert Seattle soon after he bought the land from William and Abigail Handy in 1801. His heirs sold house and lot to John and William Spooner in 1864. Simon Koschny bought it in 1898. It is now used for shops.

⊙ *115 John Street,* is a plain two-story, gambrel-roofed building with end to the street. It was probably built about 1810. In 1807 Benjamin Fairbanks sold Robert Seattle lots 12, 13, and 14 of William Handy's land. In 1810 Seattle sold part of this land to Samuel Dexter, blacksmith. The house was standing when Robinson Potter sold the property to Perry Sherman in 1832. It has been restored since 1952.

There are a number of attractive Greek Revival houses on John Street.

MARTIN STREET
See *46 John Street.*

LEVIN STREET
Levin Street, cut through from Spring to Thomas after Stiles made his map in 1758, is shown well filled with houses on Blascowitz' map of 1777.

10 Levin Street stands on land Robert Brattle sold to James Westgate in 1770, and a house was standing on the property by 1801 when Westgate sold it to Joseph Rogers. Rogers' heirs sold to Abigail Castoff in 1833, and in 1851 James Weeden bought it from the Castoff heirs. It was still in the Weeden family in 1921. The original house was much rebuilt in the Victorian period.

12 Levin Street, a two-story, gable-roofed house with Greek Revival detail, stands on land that belonged to Benoni Mumford in 1770. When this lot was sold by James Cummings to Joseph

Martin in 1784 no house was included. The property was inherited by the Mumford family, and house and lot were sold for Richard Mumford at a mortgage sale in 1842. James Fitten took up the mortgage in 1851, and in 1894 Charles Frasch sold the property, inherited from Rosanna Wiggenhauser, to Bridget Maguin.

18 Levin Street, a small two-story, gable-roofed house with a large central chimney and an attractive simple type of Greek Revival doorway, stands on land Othniel Tripp bought of John Chapman before 1783. Blascowitz shows a house here, and when Tripp sold the lot to Mary Fowler in 1791, he mentioned the "dwelling house standing thereon." The Fowlers sold the house to Samuel Albro in 1808, and William Borden bought it in 1810. He sold it to James Smith in 1830, who may have added the Greek Revival detail. It was later owned by Clarke Sanford, W. J. Holt, and others.

30 Levin Street, a small two-story, gable-roofed house set side to the street, was acquired by John and William Ronayne in 1854 and was still in the Ronayne family in 1921. It is shown on Blascowitz' map, and its history goes back to 1769 when John La Selles sold the lot and house to Woodman Billings. Billings sold the same lot and house to John and James Henderson in 1816, and they sold to Albert Watson in 1837. The Ronaynes bought the property from Watson.

32 Levin Street, the Charles Dring House, is a two-story, gable-roofed central chimney house. Thomas Dring bought it from Nathan Hammett's heirs in 1821, and it was still in the Dring family in 1921. Nathan Hammett had bought the land from John and Elizabeth Chapman before the Revolution and after 1750, when the Chapmans were first dividing their property into lots.

33 Levin Street. The Tompkins House is a small two-story, gable-roofed, central chimney house with a fanlight door. The land belonged to Benjamin Hammett in 1785, who probably built the house. Nathan Hammett bought house and lot in 1819. Samuel Hill, who bought it from John V. Hammett, sold it to John Tompkins in 1844.

57 Levin Street is a one-story, gambrel-roofed house. It was built by Edward Willis soon after 1807 when he bought the land from Jonathan Chadwick. Mary Willis sold house and lot to George B. Hazard in 1862.

59 Levin Street, a two-story, gable-roofed house, with an attractive fanlight doorway, located on the southwest corner of Levin and Thomas streets, was built by Alexander Jack, Jr., cordwainer, after he bought the lot from John Rodman in 1811. It still belonged to Jack's heirs in 1881.

WILLIAM STREET
* *23 William Street,* a one-story gambrel-roofed cottage, was built by Nathan Hammett, Jr., soon after 1808 when Nathan, Sr., gave his

two sons adjoining lots. It was being restored in 1952, but it has since been demolished for a parking lot for St. Mary's Roman Catholic Church.

27 William Street is like 23 William. It was built by Nathan's brother Edward. The Hammetts, father and both sons, were house carpenters.

36 William Street, a gambrel-roofed, one-story house was built after 1790 when Benjamin Hammett bought the lot from John Chapman's heirs. John Tompkins bought it when he bought his house at 33 Levin Street.

37 William Street, a gable-roofed, two-story house, belonged to Samuel Wilson before 1864. In 1815 Benjamin Hammett sold the lot to Samuel Hicks, who built the house soon afterward.

51 William Street, southeast corner of William and Thomas streets. See 26 Thomas Street.

Northwest corner of William and Thomas streets. See 23 Thomas Street.

Northeast corner of William and Thomas streets. See 24 Thomas Street.

68 William Street, the Popple House, is a two-story, gable-roofed house with a central chimney and a long lean-to. It looks early but was evidently built after 1804 when Samuel Green sold the lot to John Davis, colored man. Abner Hathaway, housewright, sold house and lot to Timothy Peckham in 1824. George Popple bought it in 1835, and it was still in the Popple family in 1892. It is now in poor condition.

GOLDEN HILL STREET

Originally named for the Goulding family who had property near here, the name was corrupted to Golden Hill.

* *22 Golden Hill Street*, is a two-story, gable-roofed building with a central chimney and a fanlight doorway. In 1771 Nathaniel Gladding bought lot #15 of the land laid out by John Chapman from Nathaniel Smith, barber. Blascowitz shows a house here in 1777, but the house mentioned in the deed when Gladding sold the property to Joseph Hayward, shipwright, in 1796 was on the eastern half of this lot. In 1810, when Hayward sold the west half to Jonathan Record, housewright, only land was mentioned. Record built the house soon after he bought the lot and it is still called the Record property. The house has recently been demolished for a parking lot.

26 Golden Hill Street. This two-story, gable-roofed house stands on the east half of the lot described above that Nathaniel Smith sold to Nathaniel Gladding in 1771. The earliest deeds are lost, but Blascowitz shows a house here, and it was standing in 1796 when Gladding sold the entire lot, with dwelling house, to Joseph Hayward. The Record family acquired the property after 1810, and it belonged to Catherine Record in 1840.

30 Golden Hill Street stands on lot #20 of the lands laid out by John Chapman. A house is shown here on the Blascowitz map of 1777, and

in 1783 William Giles, merchant, sold the lot with a house on it to John Wilbour. Eleazer Read owned it in 1825, and his heirs sold it to Charles Williams who sold it to David Ronayne in 1873.

34 Golden Hill Street stands on land owned by David Fairbanks before 1783. A house is shown here on the Blascowitz map, and deeds show that this two-story, gable-roofed house was standing in 1783. In 1825 Benjamin Fairbanks sold it to James Easton, "mariner alias rigger," and it was still in the Easton family in 1883. It has a fanlight doorway, but is in poor repair.

THOMAS STREET

23 Thomas Street, a long two-story, gable-roofed house on the northwest corner of Thomas and William streets, stands on land William Handy inherited from his father, Charles Handy, and laid out in lots about 1800. He sold this lot to Peter Kaighn in 1801. It changed hands several times, and was still an unimproved lot in 1809 when Elizabeth Lincoln sold it to John Mein. The house was probably built about this time. It was in the possession of Isaac Rice before 1855 when he gave a mortgage deed to Henry O. Remington, and the house is still in the Rice family.

24 Thomas Street, a two-story, gable-roofed house on the northeast corner of Thomas and William streets, stands on the lot Samuel Greene bought of William Handy in 1801. In 1804 Green sold the lot to John Davis, who probably built the house soon afterward. His widow sold house and lot to David Holloway in 1843, and he transferred title to Robert Carr in the same year. John Hynes, who bought it from Benjamin Burton in 1872, sold to Edwin Smith in 1882 and it was still owned by Smith in 1907.

26 Thomas Street, a two-story, gable-roofed half-a-house with an attractive fanlight doorway on the southeast corner of William and Thomas streets, is known as the Cremin House. It was built by Stephen Greene soon after 1801 when he bought the lot from William Handy. His heirs quitclaimed their shares in the property to William Greene from 1827 to 1829, and Greene sold it to Edward King in 1851. Thomas Crimmin bought it from King in 1861, and it remained in the Cremin family until 1951.

31 Thomas Street, a two-story, gable-roofed house set on a high basement on the southwest corner of Thomas and Golden Hill streets, stands on a lot Stephen Greene sold Alexander Jack in 1810 who probably built the house soon afterward. William Fludder acquired it about 1842 and sold it to Mary Eggleston in 1853. Peter Peterson, who bought it from Mary Eggleston's heir, William McGee, in 1888, still owned it in 1921.

CANNON STREET

23-25 Cannon Street is a long two-story, gable-roofed, double house with two interior chimneys and some added Greek Revival detail. It was probably built soon after 1784 by Billings Coggeshall, cooper, who bought the land and a barn or stable (all other buildings excepted) from Timothy Ingraham, hairdresser. Coggeshall's heirs sold the lot and buildings to Charles E. Hammett, grocer, in 1830, and in 1839 Hammett sold to John L. Barber, carpenter. John B. Durfee inherited the property, and it was still in the Durfee family in 1907.

FAIR STREET

18 *Fair Street* is a two-story, gable-roofed house with a fanlight doorway. It was built by John Langley soon after he bought the land from Jacob Smith in 1807.

* 32 *Fair Street*, a gable-on-hip-roofed house, was built by Thomas Wickham between 1758 and 1772. It is almost unchanged. See Chapter Four and Pl. 121.

* 42 *Fair Street*, known today as the Dawley House, belonged to Charles Wickham in 1785. It is shown on Stiles' map, probably a new house then. It originally resembled the Thomas Wickham house just west of it, but has been altered.

GIDLEY STREET

27 *Gidley Street* is a two-story, gable-roofed house with two interior chimneys and a glazed fanlight doorway, built about 1800. It has been moved to this location.

ANN STREET

28 *Ann Street* is a small two-story, end-chimney house with a steep gable roof and a wide overhanging cornice. It may have been moved here since, when Jonathan Wallen sold the lot to George B. Hazard in 1808, no house was mentioned. David King bought house and lot in 1819, and sold it to William Austin in 1869.

BREWER STREET

Brewer Street was called "Stillhouse Lane" in early deeds.

25 *Brewer Street* is a two-story house with a gambrel roof of a high early-eighteenth-century form. Early deeds show that Benjamin Mason owned it before the Revolution. In 1785 his heirs deeded the property "in Still-house Lane" to Daniel Mason, and James Tuell owned it before 1730. It was still in the Tuell Family in 1883. It now has a Greek Revival door.

30 *Brewer Street* is a two-story, gambrel-roofed house set with end to the street. In 1796 Nathan Gardner owned it, and Richard Hazard bought it "with the brewery" in 1797. In 1835 Hazard gave it to his daughter, and in 1873 she sold it to Alfred Wickes Hill.

DENNISON STREET

Dennison Street appears in the Newport Directory for the first time in 1840.

12 *Dennison Street*, a little gambrel-roofed, one-story cottage with a central chimney, was built by William Mansfield between 1836 and 1837. It stands on a lot Samuel Whitehorne sold to Joshua Langley in 1824. Horatio Tracy bought the lot in 1831 and sold it to William Mansfield in 1836. When Mansfield sold to Clarke Burdick a year later the house had been built.

16 *Dennison Street*, a two-story, gable-roofed half-a-house, has a tight three-run stairway and horizontal boarding in the stair hall. It has the same early history as No. 12, being the east half of the lot Samuel Whitehorne sold Langley. Tracy still owned the lot in 1836, and in 1846 when it was in the possession of George Clarke, the house had been built.

YOUNG STREET

* 21 *Young Street*, a two-story, gable-roofed house with two interior chimneys and a central fanlight doorway, was built about 1810, probably by Benjamin James. In 1832 Mary Ann James sold it to Susan Bliven. John Carney bought it in 1887.

* 36 *Young Street* is a gable-on-hip-roofed house like the Wickham houses on Fair Street. It was probably built between 1758 and 1770, but the earliest record yet found is dated 1825, when it was turned over to Robinson Potter. It was then designated as part of the property confiscated from the loyalist Robert Robinson during the Revolutionary War.

HOWARD STREET

29 *Howard Street*, known as the Isaac Crooker House, was once a very fine gable-on-hip-roofed house. It was built about 1760, and belonged to the loyalist Edward Cole, who served as recruiting officer for His Majesty's Army during the British occupation of Newport. Benjamin Howard bought it before the Revolution, and sold it to Stephen Deblois. Henry Moore, who bought the house in 1818, gave it to his widowed daughter-in-law Harriet Moore in 1820. Harriet Moore later married Captain Isaac Crooker, Captain of the *Audley Clarke* on her voyage from Newport to California in the gold rush of 1849. The Reverend Francis Vinton, who married Commodore Perry's daughter, also lived in this house. The front has been disfigured by a bay.

Note: Extension Street and South Baptist Street were cut through to Spring Street between 1840 and 1850. They were built up rapidly and are shown on the 1850 maps well filled with little houses. Some buildings on both streets seem earlier, and may have been moved in.

POPE STREET

Pope Street is an old street, and is shown on Blascowitz' map with three houses on it. Several houses still standing have early characteristics. No. 18, a two-story, gambrel-roofed house, and No. 21, a two-story, gable-roofed house, are located approximately where Blascowitz shows buildings. Their history has not been traced.

THAMES STREET (SOUTH OF WASHINGTON SQUARE)

The Brick Market, Peter Harrison, 1761. See Chapter Five and Pls. 6, 106–107.

131 *Thames Street*, known as the Erastus Allen House, is a two-story, gambrel-roofed house set

with end to the street. It now serves as a restaurant. It is shown on Stiles' map, and was owned by Isaac Gould in 1760. *Mercury* advertisements indicate that James Brooks first established the Pitts' Head Tavern in this house. Robert Lawton owned it in 1773, and Samuel Watson in 1800. See Lloyd Robson, "Allen Building, House of Glass" Newport *Daily News*, May 1, 1965, on file in the Newport Historical Society.

130 Thames Street, an old two-story, hip-roofed house with a wide overhanging cornice, now much altered, has survived almost concealed by surrounding stores. It is shown on Stiles' map, and George Mason lists it as belonging to Nicholas Tillinghast, apothecary, before the Revolution. Afterward it belonged to Edward Lawton.

No other old houses remain in this block between Washington Square and Mary Street, but on the east side, back of the present line of the street, stood Jeremy Clarke's house (the Sueton Grant House) and John Cranston's Stone Castle. The Jahleel Brenton house stood south of Mary Street, on the same wide line.

187–189 Thames Street. Champlin's Wharf on the west side on Thames Street, a little south of Mary Street. Part of Christopher Champlin's property, consisting of a two-story, gable-roofed building on the Thames Street front and a one-story, gambrel-roofed ell with a brick end, still remains on the south side of the old Champlin's Wharf. The interior has an old stairway, fireplaces, overmantels, doors, and floors. Two picturesque gambrel-roofed wharf buildings have also survived.

COTTON'S COURT

5 Cotton's Court. The Cotton House. This square gable-on-hip-roofed house is shown on Stiles' map. Nathaniel Coggeshall gave it to his daughter, Ruth Champlin, in 1764. Dr. Charles Cotton bought it in 1817, and it is still in the Cotton family. The interiors have been remodeled. It is the only house left on the old wide Thames Street line.

* *204 and 208 Thames Street*, just south of Cotton's court, are now altered almost beyond recognition. Originally gambrel-roofed buildings, set with end to the street, they were built in 1785 by George Champlin. No. 204 has been demolished since 1952.

214 Thames Street, on the southwest corner of Church and Thames streets, known as Seabury's Store, stands on the site of James Honeyman's house built before 1706. See Church Street.

* *236–238 Thames Street*, now the Star Clothing Company, is shown on Stiles' map. It stands on the northeast corner of Mill Street on Caleb Carr's land, and was built in front of Caleb Carr's original seventeenth-century house (which stood on the old line of Thames Street). John Carr leased this corner piece to Alexander Mason in 1707 with the stipulation that Mason was to build a two-story house 42 × 34 feet in size. The new house

was built by 1715, and reverted to the Carr family some years later. This steep gable-roofed house may be the shell of Mason's house, but it is in poor repair, and no interior detail remains.

* *240 Thames Street*, a two-story, gambrel-roofed house on the southeast corner of Mill Street, also appears on Stiles' map. Paul Mumford, dealer in dry goods, owned it before the Revolutionary War. The building has been demolished.

243–245 Thames Street, opposite Mill Street on the southwest corner of Thames Street and Market Square, formerly James H. Drury, Grocers, Inc., and now Gray's Typewriter Company, appears on Stiles' map. It is a two-story, gambrel-roofed house, and originally had a plaster-cove cornice (now boarded in). In 1677 this property belonged to Pardon Tillinghast and to Charles Tillinghast's heirs in 1740. The house itself was probably built about 1710 or 1720. The next record is dated 1772 when John and Judith Freebody owned it. John Norris bought it in 1793, and Benjamin Reynolds was in possession in 1800. According to the French billeting list, De Chabannes and Brintaneau, aides-de-camp of Baron de Viomesnil were quartered here, with "John Freebody at 150 Thames Street." See Lloyd Robson's account of the House, "The Tillinghast House Was Once Confiscated," published in the Newport *Daily News*, May 8, 1965, and on file in the Newport Historical Society.

246 Thames Street, a two-story, gable-roofed building, the second house south of Mill Street on the east side, is shown on Stiles' map. It stands on land owned by Penelope Pelham in 1741, and according to George Richardson's notes in the Newport Historical Society, was occupied by Silas Dean before 1800. E. C. Blaine owned the property in 1876, and it was still in the Blaine family in 1907.

* *254 Thames Street.* The Rhode Island Union Bank Building, Asher Benjamin, 1818. See Chapter Seven. Benedict Arnold's house, built in 1654 and described in Chapter One, stood just at the back of this building, set on the old wide line of Thames Street. See Pl. 145.

261 Thames Street. The Robert Stevens House. Peter Harrison's wife inherited this property from her father, Edward Pelham, who inherited it from Benedict Arnold. The double house was probably built just after the Revolution. See Chapter Five and Pl. 127.

BOWEN'S WHARF

Bowen's Wharf. (The old Robert Steven's Wharf) now the George Bowen Fuel Company, formerly the Stevens' Ship Chandler's Shop. See Chapter Five and Pls. 125, 126.

* *274–276 Thames Street*, known as Dr. Mason's house, stands on the north corner of Mason's Court. This historic and once beautiful gable-on-hip-roofed house was built in the first half of the eighteenth century, probably by Robert

Stoddard. Christopher Champlin owned it before the Revolutionary War, and Dr. Benjamin Mason bought it in 1785 at the time of his marriage to Champlin's daughter Margaret, who danced with General Washington in 1781. Years later, Oliver Hazard Perry was married to Dr. Mason's daughter in the drawing room. The main rooms were once paneled, and the stairs had twisted balusters, but the building has been much altered and now serves as Murphy's Grocery Store. A handsome fanlighted doorway was removed as late as 1947, and the exterior has been stuccoed.

279 Thames Street, on the west side of the street a little south of Pelham Street, is a two-story, gambrel-roofed house set with end to the street. Its history has been traced back to 1784 when Joseph Clarke, General Treasurer in charge of city property, sold Sherman Clark's house, which stood on part of Thomas Banister's confiscated property, to Aaron Sheffield. It was the post office in 1813. Joshua Sayer bought it later, and in 1887 Simeon Davis acquired it. See Lloyd Robson, "Sherman Clark House Was the Post Office" in the Newport *Daily News,* May 15, 1965, on file in the Newport Historical Society.

281–283 Thames Street, on the northwest corner of Thames and Old Sayer's Wharf nearly opposite Green Street, is a two-story, gambrel-roofed building set end to the street. In 1781 Peleg Brown, mariner, sold this property to Charles Handy, merchant, it being "the same lot and house my grandfather Captain John Brown purchased of the Widow Wickham and gave . . . to my deceased father, Jeremiah Brown." It was later owned by Silas Dean, who built the wharf where he carried on an extensive business. Joshua Sayer owned it by 1850, and it was still in his family in 1876.

285 Thames Street, a two-story, gambrel-roofed building set side to the street on the south side of old Sayer's Wharf opposite Green Street, was built by Clark Cook soon after the Revolutionary War, according to George Mason's list. It has been stuccoed over, and the lower story is now covered with wood boarding. Formerly El Commodore Restaurant, it is now Dorian's Tavern. See Lloyd Robson's account published in the Newport *Daily News* for May 22, 1965, titled "Clark Cook House—A United Family," on file in the Newport Historical Society.

315–317 Thames Street, a much altered, square, two-story, hip-roofed house on the west side of Thames Street between Franklin and Cannon streets, stands on the old Honeyman Wharf, later the estate of Jonathan Langley. Colonel Sherbourne owned it before 1800. According to George Richardson's notes in the Newport Historical Society, a slave pen formerly stood on the site of this building.

324–340 Thames Street, on the northeast corner of Cannon Street, is the site of Godfrey Malbone's town house. See Chapter Three and Pl. 74.

337 Thames Street, the Perry Mill, a long, two-story, stone mill building on the west side of Thames Street between Cannon and Fair streets, was built by Alexander McGregor in 1835. It was one of four mills built along Thames Street in the 1830's and 1840's. It now is used for the General Electric Company Monowatt Department.

343–345 Thames Street, the Redwood Building, on the west side of Thames Street opposite Fair Street, stands on the site of Abraham Redwood's Thames Street house. Redwood's house was moved west on the wharf between 1876 and 1883, and was later torn down. Photographs on file in the Newport Historical Society show it after it was moved. See Chapter Three and Pls. 72, 73.

* *353 Thames Street,* a two-story, gable-roofed building with two interior chimneys and rusticated window caps is one of the two buildings put up after 1800 on Abraham Redwood's property just south of his town house. Nathan Hammett, who built the house, devised it to his son Nathan in 1808.

381–383 Thames Street, on the west side of Thames Street opposite Brewer Street, is a two-story, gable-on-hip-roofed house with hip-roofed dormer windows and pre-Revolutionary detail. Its history has been traced to 1796 when John Martin of Providence sold Ebenezer Woodward the property that Josiah Brown had owned before the Revolutionary War. William Robinson bought it in 1799, and sold it to Archibald Crary a year later. Silas Cottrell bought it in 1837.

392 Thames Street. The Francis Malbone House. See Appendix A and Pl. 111.

405–411 Thames Street on the northwest corner of Brown and Howard's Wharf opposite Dennison Street, a row of two-story Greek Revival buildings with a long clerestory, is mentioned here because of its similarity to the double row of workers' houses formerly at Richmond and Thames streets, and now demolished. The buildings were owned by John D. Williams in 1850, and were probably built ten or fifteen years earlier.

410 Thames Street, on the northeast corner of Dennison Street is a two-story, gable-on-hip-roofed house. It was owned by James Carpenter, a descendant of Thomas Willett, first English mayor of New York City, who received his appointment from Colonel Nichols in 1665, and by the Carpenter-Howland families in the nineteenth century. Old photographs show that it originally had a doorway with a broken scroll pediment on the Dennison Street side. This has since been removed. Avis Howland, author of *Rhode Island Tales,* lived in the house for many years.

414 Thames Street. The Samuel Whitehorne House, 1804. See Chapter Seven and Pl. 133.

424 Thames Street, on the northeast corner of Thames and Young streets, is a two-story, gable-roofed house with an overhanging end gable of an early form. Blascowitz shows a house on this site, but George Mason records that the present house was built after the Revolution by John Price, and George Richardson notes that the Price family still occupied the building in 1892. Tax records show that it was owned by Elisha Atkins in 1840, and J. Berkinshaw had title to the property by 1876. It was still in the Burkinshaw family in 1907.

428–430 Thames Street, on the southeast corner of Thames and Young streets, known as the John Whitehorne House, is a two-story, hip-roofed house with a pedimented doorway and some interior paneling of various periods. The house belonged to Henry Hunter before the Revolution. He also owned a distillery, and both house and distillery became the property of John Whitehorne.

* *437 Thames Street* is a gable-roofed house set with end to the street. It has pre-Revolutionary exterior and interior detail, but its history is not known. It was moved to this location.

451–459 Thames Street, south of West Howard Street, is part of the old Newport Steam Mill, later known as the Acquidneck Mill. A handsome two-story stone building, it was built in 1831 and served as a mill until 1883. It now forms the rear part of the Newport Electric Company.

481–483 Thames Street, on the southwest corner of West Extension Street, is an old two-story, gambrel-roofed building set end to the street, with an ell that extends down West Extension Street. Blascowitz shows a building in this location, and the property has been traced to the Overing family who owned land here before the Revolution. In 1804 Henry Overing sold this lot and house to Thomas Voax who sold it to Captain Charles Devens in 1809. Clarke Burdick acquired it from Devens in 1827, sold it to Benjamin Seattle in 1831 and bought it again in 1854. It was still part of the Burdick estate at the end of the nineteenth century.

505–507 Thames Street, the second building north of Coddington's Wharf, is a two-story, gable-roofed house with two interior chimneys and eighteenth-century detail. It was owned by Nathan Hammett before 1850.

* *Thames at Richmond Street*. A double row of workers' houses for the Coddington Mill built about 1836 in the Greek Revival style. In very poor repair.

600 Thames Street, located on the southeast corner of McAllister Street, was moved to this site between 1859 and 1876, and its early history is unknown. It is a handsome eighteenth-century, three-story, hip-roofed house similar to others dated about 1750.

8 Lee Street, a two-story, gambrel-roofed half-a-house with a big off-center chimney and an old three-run staircase set in a small entry in front of the chimney, was moved to this site between 1859 and 1876. It stands on part of the property Nicholas Easton sold to William Lee, Jr., in 1786, and may be the house shown on Thames Street between Lee and Holland streets on the 1850 and 1859 maps. This latter house stood on property that belonged to Mary and Abby Lee in 1850, but it is not mentioned either by George Mason or George Richardson in their lists of early Thames Street inhabitants.

23 Batchelder Street, a long one-story, gambrel-roofed house with an early staircase and good interior detail, was moved to this site between 1859 and 1876 when it was owned by Bridget Brennan. Its early history is unknown except that it was called "the old farmhouse." It has been attractively restored, and is now owned by Edith Bozyan.

43 Wellington Street, a two-story, gable-roofed house, was moved to this location after 1921. It has been much altered, but the steep pitch of the gable roof indicates an early-eighteenth-century date. Its history is unknown.

20 Houston Avenue is a picturesque, two-room, central-hall, one-story house covered with a steeply pitched gambrel roof that overhangs at the cornice line. It was moved to this location, and its early history is not known.

61 Roseneath Avenue is a two-story, gable-roofed house with eighteenth-century characteristics. It was moved to this site between 1893 and 1907, and its early history is unknown.

INDEX

Index

Illustrations, including plate numbers, are italicized